AGRICULTURAL DEVELOPMENT IN CHINA AND AFRICA

This systematic comparative study of agricultural development in China and Africa provides a unique basis for African countries and international organizations seeking to understand agricultural development in China, and for China to understand agricultural development on the African continent. It compares the similarities and discrepancies in conditions, processes and outcomes between China and Africa from the perspectives of investment, science and technology, policies and international development aid. Based on this it explores which experiences and lessons from China's agriculture development can be shared with African countries in order to contribute to the sustainable improvement and transformation of African agriculture. It does not claim that China has all of the answers, but while recognizing the diversity within both China and Africa, concludes that much can be gained from such a comparison.

Li Xiaoyun is the Dean of the College of Humanities and Development Studies at China Agricultural University, and the Vice President of China Rural Sociology Association. He is also Executive member of the China Rural Economics Association, a scientific advisor to the State Council leading Group for Poverty Reduction and Development and member of the Advisory Group for the UK ESRC and DFID joint program in China. He is the director of the China-OECD Development Assistance Committee Study Group.

Qi Gubo is a professor and rural development researcher at the College of Humanities and Development Studies at China Agricultural University. She is also the coordinator of the Farmer-Centred Research Network in China, an informal academic group focusing on participatory technology and management research.

Tang Lixia is a lecturer at the College of Humanities and Development Studies at China Agricultural University, and has been involved in numerous development related projects funded by international organizations. Her main fields of specialization are poverty reduction and rural development, and natural resource management.

Zhao Lixia is a PhD candidate majoring in Rural Development and Management, having received her Master degree in Sociology from the College of Humanities and Development Studies at China Agricultural University in 2006. She worked in the Centre of Sustainable Forest Development of Chinese Academy of Forestry as research assistant for 2 years.

Jin Leshan is Professor of Economics with the College of Humanities and Development Studies, China Agricultural University, and also works as researcher and consultant for many development projects. His main specializations are environmental and development economics, water use in agriculture and rural development, and socio-economic and livelihood analysis of natural resources management.

Guo Zhanfeng is a lecturer at the College of Humanities, Northwest Agriculture and Forestry University. He got his PhD in rural development and management at China Agricultural University and had worked for ActionAid International China as project coordinator for two years.

Wu Jin is Associate Professor at the College of Humanities and Development Studies at China Agricultural University. Her main fields of research are agricultural development in Africa and international development Aid. She has conducted field work in Nigeria and Tanzania.

AGRICULTURAL DEVELOPMENT IN CHINA AND AFRICA

A Comparative Analysis

Li Xiaoyun, Qi Gubo, Tang Lixia,
Zhao Lixia, Jin Leshan,
Guo Zhanfeng and Wu Jin

Routledge
Taylor & Francis Group

LONDON AND NEW YORK

First published 2012
by Routledge
2 Park Square, Milton Park, Abingdon, Oxon OX14 4RN

Simultaneously published in the USA and Canada
by Routledge
711 Third Avenue, New York, NY 10017

First issued in paperback 2017

Routledge is an imprint of the Taylor & Francis Group, an informa business

British Library Cataloguing in Publication Data
A catalogue record for this book is available from the British Library

Library of Congress Cataloging in Publication Data
Agricultural development in China and Africa : a comparative analysis / by
Li Xiaoyun . . . [et al.].
    p. cm.
  Includes bibliographical references and index.
  Agriculture–Economic aspects–China. 2. Agriculture--Economic
aspects–Africa. 3. Rural development–China. 4. Rural development–Africa.
5. Agriculture and state–China. 6. Agriculture and state–Africa. I. Li, Xiaoyun.
  HD2097.A375 2012
  338.10951–dc23   2011045018

ISBN 13: 978–1–138–09722–3 (pbk)
ISBN 13: 978–1–84971–388–7 (hbk)

Typeset in Bembo
by Swales & Willis Ltd, Exeter, Devon

CONTENTS

LIST OF FIGURES AND TABLES

Figures

Tables

FOREWORD

Richard Carey
Former Organisation for Economic Co-operation and Development (OECD)
Director for Development Cooperation, and Founding Co-Chair of the
China–OECD Development Assistance Committee Study Group

This book tells two still largely unknown stories about agricultural development in the last 30 years – in China and in Africa – and interweaves them in a tapestry backgrounded with the grander sweep of history, geography and demography, illuminating some of the most pressing development debates of our times. Uniquely, these stories are constructed by Chinese researchers, using the perspective of China's recent experience to look at the performance of agriculture in these two huge arenas of contemporary development.

That China is now a giant factory to the world is an everyday reality to billions across the globe, visible in what they buy at the supermarket and electronics store and even in town and village markets in developing countries. However, few people, even among the academic and business communities, are aware that a Chinese agricultural revolution beginning in 1978 was the foundation for that larger development process that has transformed the Chinese and global economies. This book shows how, starting from a grass roots-initiated reform of land tenure arrangements which was scaled up to become the Household Responsibility System, the Chinese authorities provided incentives and policies to stimulate the emergence of family farm-based agricultural modernization as a primary focus of China's economic development strategy. Productivity rose dynamically and agriculture diversified, satisfying China's rapidly growing food needs, generating an economic surplus and allowing a massive move of labour off the farm into rural enterprises and, famously, into the manufacturing centres of the eastern seaboard. The creation of a major agricultural and research extension system, with new human and institutional capacities and drawing on the agricultural know-how of donor countries, was of fundamental importance.

Meanwhile, with a few exceptions, African agriculture received declining policy attention and investment effort in the 1980s and 1990s, from both governments and donors. Growing demand for grain by urban populations was met by imports. Only in the early years of this century did an African policy framework emerge in the form of the Comprehensive African Agricultural Development Programme to generate agricultural growth across the continent, with cross-border supply chains and expanded science and technological support for farmers, backed by a ministerial commitment to make agriculture a major public investment priority and a new effort to coordinate and disseminate African agricultural research. It was even more recently that traditional donors made a high-level commitment to multiply the aid effort to support this African-led movement. This book makes a major contribution to the deepening understanding of what is required to realize Africa's great potential to meet the food needs of its own people, and to engage competitively in global supply chains for food and for traditional and new agricultural exports.

Despite the great differences in context, the Chinese experience shows that what matters essentially for an agricultural 'miracle' is the attention and priority of political leaders, the construction of a dynamic, benign interaction between farmers, the state and the market, the emergence of a large community of researchers and tertiary institutions that work closely with farmers and enterprises and external actors to form a permanent agricultural innovation system, and massive investment by farmers, public authorities and agro-enterprises in rural infrastructure.

The authors of the book do not hesitate to point up the costs and mistakes emerging in the Chinese experience – rural welfare problems that were unaddressed for too long and the persistence of significant absolute poverty in rural areas; environmental degradation and pollution from the high input–high output carbon-intensive model that now has to be repaired at great cost, and the implications of retreating from that model; and unclear land rights that have been exploited by urban interests to the cost of farm householders and contributing to the emergence of a highly unequal society. These are lessons that the authors believe African policy-makers can learn from, ensuring that their own strategies and land policies do not create parallel problems.

The book ends with a vision: that China can bring its experience and capacities into a wider development effort on African agriculture, alongside other countries with funding and knowledge. Working within the new African policy frameworks, processes and institutions, these joint efforts could create a win-win partnership to transform African agriculture, focused on food production in a modern knowledge-based, small farm-centred agricultural system. With such a joint strategic endeavour, African farmers could respond to the rapid growth of Africa's food demand, reflecting the changing food needs of fast-expanding urban populations, thus making food production a growth centre in a dynamic region of successfully integrated economies, also with the capacity to supply international markets in a world that needs the realization of Africa's agricultural potential.

ACKNOWLEDGEMENTS

This book is based on research supported by the Swiss Agency for Development and Cooperation. We would like to thank Dr Walter Meyer, counsellor, and Dr Christoph I. Lang, First Secretary, from the Embassy of Switzerland, for their guidance and support in the whole period of research. The Foreign Economic Cooperation Center, Ministry of Agriculture of the People's Republic of China provided valuable information and technical support. We thank all of them for their precious input.

Thanks are also given to the experts for their hard work and thoughtful advices in internal review: Professor Jiang Zhongjin from Nanjing University, Professor Yao Guimei from Chinese Academy of Social Sciences, Professor He Xiurong from China Agricultural University, Mr Cao Zhongming from the Ministry of Foreign Affairs, Mr Zheng Wei from the Ministry of Commerce, Mr Lu Xiaoping, Mr Tang Shengyao, Mr Yang Yi and Mr Zhu Zidong from the Ministry of Agriculture, Mr Wu Zhong, Mr Huang Chengwei, Mr Wang Xiaolin and Mr Zhang Huidong from International Poverty Reduction Center in China. James Keeley from the Institute for International Environment and Development contributed a lot to the research and writing of this book, and his experiences on African studies enlightened us with much insightful thinking. We extend special thanks to Mr Richard Carey from the Organisation for Economic Co-operation and Development (OECD) for his comments, critical review and constructive suggestions and revisions on the draft of this book. We appreciate four anonymous Earthscan reviewers for their specific suggestions, and would like to thank Professor Tony Fuller for his careful and patient review to polish the book.

A group of people helped us a lot in our field work in Africa, including:
Mr Stephen Tembo from RuralNet, a non-governmental organization (NGO) in Zambia, other staff members in RuralNet, particularly Mr Kanyanta Musonda, Ms

Janet Tembo, Ms Janet Mulilo, Mr Mabwibwi Chirwa, who joined in the whole process of field survey in Zambia; all the villagers in Museke Village and Kanshisa Village in Chongwe District; the Makombiro Farm and its manager, Ms Makombiro; Mr Charles Simulunda, Director of Chongwe District Agricultural and Cooperatives Ministry, Mr John Lungu, Vice-Director, Mr Chanda Bwalya, who was responsible for data collection and Ms Loveness, Camp Extensionist. Mr Wang You, counsellor at Commercial Centre in China Embassy, Mr Jiang Jian at China-Jiangsu Prospect Co. Ltd, Mr Si Su at Sunlight Co. Ltd, Mr Hong at Sino-Zambian Farm Co. Ltd, Mrs Liu at Liu Chang Ming Farm Co. Ltd and Ms Li Li at China Agricultural Development Co. Ltd; staff members working in those farms and companies who are from either Zambia or China, and the villagers and farms near to them.

Mr Iddi Simba, Mr Rashid Malima, Mr Mhando, Mr Ali and Miss Safi from PRIDE Tanzania, an NGO in Tanzania; Representative Mr Liu Yulin, and Mr Song Bo from the Economic and Commercial Representation of the PRC in Tanzania; Mr Guan Shanyuan, Managing Director, Mr Hao Jianguo, Mr Wang Lusheng and Mrs Wang, Mr Wang Linshan, Mr Hu Jing, Mr Lu Hao and Mr Maqsood at China State Farms Agribusiness (G) Corp. Tanzania Ltd; village head Mr Hamisi Mwakanyekela and all the villagers in Pea Pea Village, Kilosa District.

Professor Reginald W. Fannoh from the Information Division at the Ministry of Agriculture, Liberia; Professor C. Morlee Mends-Colf, Dean of the Agroforestry College at Liberian University; Professor F. Wolie from Booker Washington Institute, Liberia; Mr Jimmy Glayeneh and Mr Emmaanuel D. Freeman, who are extensionists working in Bong State; village head Mr Moses Dennis and villagers in Durtuta Village.

Thanks are given to China Agricultural University students Mr John Alexander Nuetah, PhD candidate for his help in fieldwork in Liberia, Mr Gabriel Corsetti, MSc candidate and Mr Makundi Julius and Ms Rabina Rasaily, PhD candidates for their work on translating and proofreading this report.

Thanks are given to the publication contribution from the Special Specialty Construction Programme sponsored by the Ministry of Education in China and the Beijing Municipality Education Commission, through China Agricultural University.

Last but not least, thanks to the Earthscan editors for their professional guidance on copy-editing and book design, with special appreciation to its senior commissioning editor, Tim Hardwick.

The opinions expressed in this book do not necessarily represent the viewpoints of the Chinese government, the Swiss Agency for Development and Cooperation or the organizations for which the research team work.

LIST OF ABBREVIATIONS

AGRA	Alliance for a Green Revolution in Africa
AQUASTAT	Food and Agriculture Organization (FAO) Information System on Water and Agriculture
ARENET	Agriculture Research and Extension Network (Uganda)
ASARECA	Association for Strengthening Agricultural Research in Eastern and Central Africa
AusAID	Australian Agency for International Development
CAADP	Comprehensive Africa Agriculture Development Programme
CGIAR	Consultative Group on International Agricultural Research
COMESA	Common Market for Eastern and Southern Africa
CORAF/WECARD	West and Central African Council For Agricultural Research and Development
ECA	United Nations Economic Commission for Africa
FOCAC	Forum on China–Africa Cooperation
FAO	Food and Agriculture Organization
FARA	Forum for African Agricultural Research
FDI	Foreign Direct Investment
GDP	Gross Domestic Product
GMO	Genetically Modified Organism
HIV	Human Immunodeficiency Virus
IMF	International Monetary Fund
ISNAR	International Service for National Agricultural Research
NAADS	National Agriculture Advisory Services (Uganda)
NEPAD	New Partnership for Africa's Development
NERICA	New Rice for Africa

NGO	Non-governmental Organization
ODA	Official development assistance
OECD	Organisation for Economic Co-operation and Development
REPOA	Research on Poverty Alleviation
SADC	Southern African Development Community
SADC/FANR	Southern African Development Community's Food, Agriculture and Natural Resource Directorate
SIDO	Small Industries Development Organization (Tanzania)
SPAAR	Special Program for African Agricultural Research
UN	United Nations
UNDP	United Nations Development Programme
UNEP	United Nations Environment Programme
WFP	World Food Programme
WTO	World Trade Organization

INTRODUCTION

This book builds on research that was carried out by a team from the College of Humanities and Development Studies, China Agricultural University, with the support of the Swiss Agency for Development and Cooperation. The study compares agricultural development between China and Sub-Saharan Africa, and reflects on the origins of agriculture in China and on the Africa continent, paying special attention to agricultural development since the mid-twentieth century, when the People's Republic of China (PRC) was founded and African countries began to obtain independence. The comparison covers:

1   performance and achievements within the agricultural sector;
2   the origins and historical changes in agriculture;
3   strategies and policies related to agricultural development;
4   natural conditions for agricultural production;
5   production inputs to agriculture;
6   agricultural science and technology;
7   small farmers' agriculture production; and
8   learning from outside and external support for agricultural development in China and Africa.

Background and Objectives

Poverty Remains a Persistent Headache for Africa

The agricultural sector in Africa has failed to effectively contribute to poverty alleviation. Today, 80 per cent of the poor in Africa live in rural areas (Sahn *et al.*, 1997; World Bank, 2000) and nearly 90 per cent are engaged in agricultural production (World Bank, 2000). Through the New Partnership for Africa's Development

(NEPAD), African governments have set an ambitious annual agricultural growth target of 6 per cent, which is without doubt a huge challenge for most African countries (Cleaver *et al.*, 1994). Although the agricultural growth rate for Africa has reached 5 per cent since the new millennium, actual agricultural productivity is still very low, with grain productivity even less than half of the world's average level. In most African countries food self-sufficiency is less than 50 per cent, and food security remains a severe issue for much of Sub-Saharan Africa. Since 2007, rising food prices have negatively impacted on food supply in Africa, resulting in a 24 million increase in the population affected by hunger in Sub-Saharan Africa. Of the 16 countries with above 15 per cent incidence of hunger, 15 are in Africa (World Bank, 2008). According to the United Nations Food and Agriculture Organization (FAO, 2009a), 26 per cent of the total number of 1.02 billion hungry people in the world live in Africa, south of the Sahara.

As one of the pillars of African development, agriculture has important meanings for growth and poverty reduction in terms of employment and food security. Only by achieving sustainable agricultural development can the battle against poverty be given real substance (Gabre-Madhin and Haggblade, 2004). Without adequate income, employment and affordable food provided by agriculture, it is impossible to either eradicate deep-rooted poverty in Africa or achieve the Millennium Development Goals.

Failure of Development Assistance

Development research and development (R&D) assistance targeting African agriculture has failed to promote the stable and sustainable development of African food and farming systems. Since the 1960s, agricultural development strategies in Africa have evolved through several distinct phases, and these can be linked to fluctuations in overall levels of agricultural production. During this period, African countries and the international community have been committed to finding answers to problems of stagnation and exploring ways to achieve stable and sustainable agricultural development in Africa. However, to date these research endeavours and the following intervention measures have not only failed to realize their original intentions, but have often caused new problems repeatedly. Since the 1960s, development interventions have been influenced by paradigms associated with the World Bank and the Consultative Group for International Agricultural Research (CGIAR). These have emphasized farm-level productivity economics and linear input–output focused interventions aimed at raising agricultural productivity. Such approaches have worked in many parts of the world, but largely ignored complex conditions such as the social, political and institutional factors which ultimately affect input efficiency in Africa. This kind of economic analysis does not easily include other broader patterns and longer term trends which impinge on input choices and output scenarios (Scoones *et al.*, 2005). When African countries have been unable to ensure stable inputs, they have stepped into a technology trap rather than an effective 'Green Revolution'. Other research analyses this technology plight from social and cultural perspectives, arguing that modes of cultivation or market selection is not the result of single-product economic formulae, rather an outcome of contestation and negotiations between, for example, husbands and wives, wives and parents and children (Guyer and Peters, 1987). Unfortunately, because of a lack of effective alternatives, technology-led interventions are still considered as the core strategy for resolving agricultural problems in Africa. Even today, the idea of 'new Green Revolution' in Africa emanates from a technological mindset. From the 1980s to the 1990s, the Washington Consensus encouraged popular liberalization in many African countries, resulting in a widespread implementation of agricultural reforms across Africa based on market mechanisms. However, a market dilemma emerged, in that liberal reform is more beneficial for producers who are well connected with effective markets, and have products to sell for good prices. Concomitantly, households without access to market resources have been unable to benefit from reform processes. Take fertilizer input as an example: households with an annual income of USD200 are hard-pressed to afford fertilizer at USD60 per sack. The market dilemma caused by liberalization and marketization has produced a policy dilemma: that without government support for agricultural research, agricultural products from the majority of individuals and households have stagnated during the reform process, and only a minority of people have benefited.

Explanations and predictions about agricultural development pathways in Africa continue to generate controversy. After experiencing several large-scale political and economic reforms, African countries have faced recurring policy dilemmas. The agricultural sector has failed to contribute to food security and support people's livelihoods and well-being. In turn, failure in this sector has exacerbated social and political crises.

Agriculture in Africa Has Stagnated while China Has Experienced Significant Improvements in Agricultural Productivity

In China, the agricultural sector has been a propeller for poverty reduction. Chinese experiences are drawing attention from African analysts and the international donor community. What lessons can China's experiences in agricultural development offer for the African continent?

Agricultural development in China has been highly successful, both in terms of improving farmers' livelihoods and tackling the problem of food security. Since the 1970s, China has reached and exceeded the food security standard set by the FAO, magically feeding more than 20 per cent of the world population with about 9 per cent of the world's arable land. Meanwhile, the food self-sufficiency rates in many African countries remain below 50 per cent, with imports of corn and wheat accounting for 45 per cent and 80 per cent of total consumption, respectively. Having overcome technology, market and policy dilemmas, China's agriculture has realized stable and sustainable development, constantly contributing to poverty reduction and social development. The population under the USD1.25 line in China decreased to 208 million in 2005 from 835 million in 1981, and poverty incidence in rural areas has dropped to 26.11 per cent from 94.08 per cent (2005PPP; Purchasing Power Parity).[1] Farmers' living standards have improved dramatically, and rural services have developed comprehensively.

China and Africa have a long history of cooperation in agriculture. In the 1950s, China began to send agricultural experts to many newly independent African countries. Since the new millennium, Sino-Africa cooperation has entered a new phase. On 9 November 2009, the Chinese premier Wen Jiabao announced eight measures in his speech entitled 'Comprehensively Boosting the New-type Sino-African Strategic Partnership'. The fifth measure proposed is to strengthen agricultural cooperation further by increasing agricultural technology demonstration centres built by China in Africa to 20, sending 50 agricultural technology teams and training 2,000 agricultural technology personnel for Africa in order to strengthen its capacity to ensure food security (Wen, 2009). The Chinese government has already made Africa's food security problem a priority within its assistance programme for Africa.

China's rapid agricultural development has drawn attention from the international community, including African countries that have been suffering from food security problems for a long time. International development organizations and African countries are all actively beginning to understand China's experiences and to explore whether and how to share them.

Value of Comparative Study

Comparative study can help both Africa and China understand the differences in agricultural development between them, and contribute to effective mutual learning about agricultural development.

Many African countries are becoming increasingly interested in learning from China's experiences in achieving effective agricultural development, and the Chinese government and academic community are willing to share their experiences and lessons with Africa. China has made agriculture one of its development assistance priorities. Therefore, a systematic comparative study on agricultural development in China and Africa will provide a useful basis for African countries and international organizations to understand agricultural development in China, and for China to understand Africa's agricultural development.

The present study aims to highlight the experiences and lessons that China has provided and in particular, to analyse why Africa has not yet been able to emulate the trajectory of China's agricultural development. The study compares the similarities and discrepancies in conditions, processes and outcomes between China and Africa from the perspectives of investment, science and technology, policies and external support. Based on this, it explores which experiences and lessons from China's agriculture development can be shared with African countries in order to contribute to the transformation of African agriculture.

Research Framework and Method

It is difficult to carry out a strict comparison between China as one country and Africa consisting of 53 states:[2] this holds true whether examining the historical, sociocultural, economic or political aspects of development. Furthermore, agriculture in the broadest sense covers crop planting, animal husbandry, agroforestry, agricultural machinery and many other activities, but the research that forms the basis for this book mainly focuses on crop-based agriculture, looking in particular at food crops. Therefore, it is limited to data analysis on food production generally, notwithstanding the heterogeneous agro-ecological zones either in Chinese regions or African countries. This research is not a strict comparative study, but more of an illustration and exploration. Africa's agricultural development problems are reviewed mainly from the Chinese perspective, based on our own understanding of agricultural development paths, rather than reviewing the issue from a western-centred perspective as to why China can achieve rapid development in agriculture, but Africa cannot. Therefore, it is hard to avoid partiality and bias in the viewpoints and conclusions that are drawn out.

Starting from a comparative analysis of agriculture achievements, this research makes a thorough analysis of the primary causes for the differences. The analysis is carried out by referring to the analytical framework of major factors involved in agricultural development such as natural resources, human resources, capital resources, technological advances and system innovation from both macro and micro-level viewpoints. From the macro perspective, the research is based on secondary data such as published reports by the FAO and other literature regarding Chinese and African agricultural development. From the micro perspective, field studies were conducted in Liberia, Tanzania and Zambia. In each country, a village was selected to conduct surveys, and participatory interviews were carried out to provide supplementary data. This approach, along with 30 household surveys using questionnaires, key informant interviews, semi-structured interviews and group discussions with nearby medium-scale farmers, elders in the communities, village heads and agricultural extentionists, form the sources for first-hand data. These three cases do not represent the situation in Africa, but we expect them to offer insights at the micro level for a comparison of agricultural development between China and African countries.

Another important data source is secondhand materials such as agricultural development strategy papers, relevant policy papers and grey literature from organizations engaged in agricultural development collected in the country in order to understand overall agricultural development visions and goals, the position and strategy of agricultural development at the national level and current implementation of agricultural policies.

In order to visualize the extent of assistance and investment in the agricultural development sector in China, data were combined from interviews with information derived from local residents with different professions and backgrounds, farm staff funded by the Chinese government and marginal households. In addition, comparative analysis was made between Chinese villages with similar agricultural production structures and villages from the three field countries in Sub-Saharan Africa.

Contents

This book presents the results of a comparative analysis from different perspectives, based on normative understandings, and covers the following.

- Similarities and differences in the history of agricultural development in China and Africa and links with modern agricultural development.
- Differences in agricultural development achievements in both China and Africa since China's reform and opening up and during the Structural Adjustment Programme era in Africa.
- Natural conditions, production inputs, science and technology and systemic influences on agricultural development in China and Africa.
- In the history of agricultural development, changes to processes and approaches in China and African countries receiving external assistance; the concrete external assistances that they have received; the processes in which, and reasons why, these external assistances were deployed, handled and internalized.
- At the micro-level, to explain how small farmer households have been organized and operated as units for agricultural production.
- Whether the various accomplishments by China and Africa in the arena of agricultural production can be mutually replicable or provide guidance for the process of agricultural development.

Findings

The main findings in this book are as follows. Outstanding lessons learned from China's agricultural development include the importance of effective interaction between government, market and households based on efficient allocation of resources. Government-formulated agricultural development strategies and policies address concerns of economic growth and food security, and continuously provide large volumes of financial input based on a clear public financing regime. The market is opening up and infrastructure for production, storage and trading has been improved. A considerable number of agribusinesses have been developed, which have significant capacity. Markets for agricultural products have improved with greater levels of integration. Rural households have long been doing intensive farming. Intensive labour inputs guarantee a high yield level and enable the implementation of rural water facility construction programmes. With support and signals from the government and market, China's rural households have successfully entered the market and have access to production materials and other inputs. Comprehensive production capacity of China's agriculture is high, and one of the main achievements of its agricultural development: rural households have made a great contribution to this.

In contrast, Africa's government, market and households often have not worked in a coordinated fashion. On the one hand, African agriculture has either been in the trap of high dependence on the state or the market: not one African country has had a political regime with the capacity to mobilize financial and human resources in the way that China has. Longstanding dependence on foreign aid has undermined African countries' political commitment and financial management capacity, although governance capacity is given great importance. On the other hand, in history, African smallholder farmers for the most part have had no tradition of household-based intensive farming, although there are several exceptional cases such as the highland areas in eastern Africa and Dongo Commune in Mali. The role of smallholder farmers is beyond the vision of the state, and smallholders often have been rejected by the market. Based on this assessment, this research concludes that African states should strengthen their capacity to formulate and implement agricultural strategies and policies, reasonably using markets for resource allocation and reform small-farming systems in order to realize food self-sufficiency. For the Chinese government and international development organizations, Chinese lessons on agricultural development are worthy of dissemination in Africa through foreign aid mechanisms. Local policy processes in Africa should be supported. It is important to transfer technologies to smallholder farmers in order to improve food security and alleviate poverty at the household level.

This book is organized as follows. Chapter 1 highlights the status quo of agricultural development in China and Africa, and analyses the agricultural achievements that China and Africa have made from the late 1970s to the early 1980s, especially their contributions to national economy, export earnings for foreign exchange, food security and employment.

Chapter 2 provides insights into the historical background of agricultural development in China and Africa, its characteristics and achievements, agricultural civilization and analysis of ongoing trends and drawbacks during the evolutionary process of the agricultural civilization.

Chapter 3 compares the differences in agricultural policies in China and Africa from the perspectives of strategy orientation, concrete content and implementation measures, and mainly explains how different effects are generated when the same or similar policy instruments and measures are applied in different situations in China and Africa.

Chapter 4 compares agricultural production conditions in China and Africa including natural conditions and agricultural disasters, and discusses the differences between China and Africa in their capacity to allocate resources through regional coordination under diversified agricultural production conditions.

Chapter 5 compares the differences between China and Africa in agricultural production inputs such as financial support, labour and investment in agricultural production elements, especially fertilizer, applying technologies for intensification in agricultural production, causes and impacts, and provides corresponding solutions based on realities in Africa from Chinese experience.

TABLE 0.1 Major Approaches in Comparative Study on Sino–African Agricultural Development

Content	Investigation and Analytical Approach	Data Source
Macro level: analysis of agricultural achievements and key factors influencing agricultural development	1. Literature review 2. Secondhand data analysis 3. Field investigation: • Field investigation in Africa • Interviews with key people in villages, agricultural departments and medium-scale farmers • Household questionnaire: 30 households/village/country • Related agricultural policy documents and secondhand data • Field investigation data in China	• Periodicals, books and reports • FAO database • Open statistical data of different countries • One village in each of the three countries • Policy documents related to agricultural development in the three countries • Village in China which has a similar production structure to those interviewed in Africa
Micro level: analysis of forms of agricultural organization	1. Literature review 2. Field investigation • Field investigation in Africa • Interviews with key people in villages, agricultural departments and medium-scale farmers • Household questionnaire: 30 households/village/country • Related agricultural policy documents and secondhand data • Questionnaire to urban residents concerning evaluation of the effects of China's assistance to Africa • Interview with staff in farms funded by China and peripheral households • Field investigation data in China	• Related papers and reports on micro organization of China's agricultural development • One village in Liberia, Tanzania and Zambia • Policy documents related to agricultural development in the three countries • Village in China which has similar production structure to those interviewed in Africa

Chapter 6 gives a detailed comparison and analysis of the development of agricultural science and technology in China and Africa, development strategies, policy measures, agricultural science research capacity, extension mechanisms and examines the reasons for variations between China and Africa.

Chapter 7 is a unique feature of this research, namely a comparative analysis of the organization and operation of agricultural production in China and Africa at the small farmer household level by examining the similarities and differences between small households in terms of agricultural resource allocation, access to and utilization of agricultural information, technologies, other inputs and access to markets and credit. It also analyses the influence of agricultural policies towards small farmers in both China and field sites in Africa.

Chapter 8 reviews and analyses the agricultural supports that China and Africa have acquired and how these have been used, with a focus on analysing China's agricultural assistance to Africa since the 1950s and the potential for economic cooperation and technology transfer in agriculture between China and Africa.

Finally, the Conclusion summarizes the major research findings and offers policy recommendations.

1

AGRICULTURAL DEVELOPMENT IN CHINA AND AFRICA

An Overview

China and African countries started their own reforms and structural adjustments in the late 1970s and early 1980s. This chapter will compare agricultural development in China and on the African continent since then, with special attention to the performance of the agricultural sector.

Over the last 30 years, 'sound policies and advanced technologies' (Deng, 1982: 22) have boosted agricultural development in China. With only 10 per cent of global farmland and one-quarter of the global average for water resources per capita, China has successfully fed its huge population, more than one-fifth of humanity (J. Huang, 2008). Although agricultural gross domestic product (GDP) in Africa is also growing, agricultural production in Africa cannot yet meet the food demands of African people; grain self-sufficiency in many African countries has decreased to below 50 per cent. Corn is the only crop where there is a high level of self-sufficiency, although 5 per cent of its consumption still comes from imports; 45 per cent of the wheat and 80 per cent of the rice consumed in African countries also has to be imported. As shown in statistical data, 21 out of 53 African countries need grain aid (Li and Shi, 2008). In 2005, the gross output of cereals in the African continent reached 88 million tonnes with a deficit of 24 million tonnes, and imports or food aid accounting for around 21.7 per cent of Africa's gross demand for cereals. Food crises occurred in 24 countries (FAO/GIEWS, 2005). Despite this, according to World Bank (2008) research, African nations, especially those in Sub-Saharan Africa, are traditional agricultural nations where agriculture is the engine of national economic growth, contributing on average 32 per cent of GDP. Agriculture is still the pillar of African countries' growth: the agriculture sector feeds 70 per cent of the total population, provides 60 per cent of employment, contributes 70 per cent of the rural population's income and counts for 20 per cent of GDP and export income (Economic Commission for Africa (ECA), 2008).

China is a typical country in transition, characterized by an economy where agriculture no longer directly contributes a substantial part of the country's economic growth and accounts for a relatively low percentage of GDP.[1] As pointed out by the World Bank (2008), global agricultural development has derived from progress in science and technology, market reforms and increasing investment in agriculture over the past several decades. Science and technology progress plays a major role in enhancing agricultural productivity and supplying affordable foods to a large group of consumers, especially in Asian countries such as China.

Achievements of Agricultural Development in China and Africa

Data show that agricultural production has seen strong overall growth in China and Africa since the 1980s. In 1979 to 1981 Africa's agricultural GDP was USD49 billion on average; this figure almost doubled to USD96 billion in 2004. During the same period China's agricultural GDP increased from USD69 billion to USD205, nearly a threefold increase. As illustrated in Figure 1.1, the growth rate of China's agricultural GDP was much higher than that in Africa's before 2000, but its growth rate has been almost the same since 2000, which suggests that African countries have regained agricultural development momentum since 2000.

In terms of China's and Africa's shares of global agricultural GDP (Figure 1.2), China has had an increasing share since 1979, up from 9.5 per cent to 16.71 per cent in 2004, but Africa's shares in global agricultural GDP have been increasing slowly in the past nearly 30 years, from 7.42 per cent to 9.1 per cent.

In terms of agricultural GDP per capita for the rural population, China's agricultural GDP per capita has increased significantly over the past 30 years, but Africa's agricultural GDP per capita has remained almost unchanged (Figure 1.3). During the period from 1979 to 1981 the agricultural GDP per capita of China's rural population decreased below that of Africa and was only 42 per cent of the latter, suggesting that the agricultural productivity of China's rural labour force was

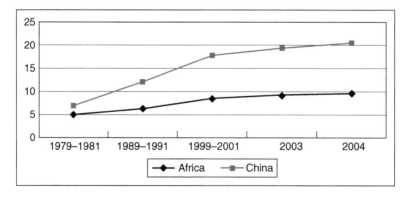

Figure 1.1 Agricultural GDP Growth of China and Africa (Unit: USD10 billion)

Source: FAOSTAT

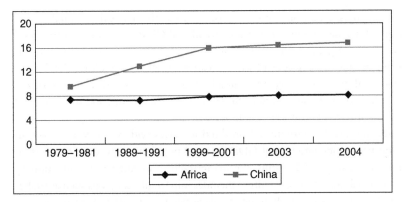

Figure 1.2 Share of Global Agricultural GDP (Unit: %)

Source: FAOSTAT

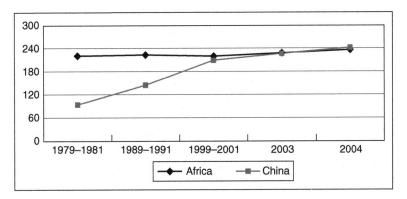

Figure 1.3 Comparison of Agricultural GDP Per Capita in China and Africa (Unit: USD)

Source: FAOSTAT

lower than that of Africa. The agricultural GDP per capita of China's rural population only exceeded that of Africa in 2004, suggesting that, in sharp contrast with the rapid development of China's agricultural labour productivity, Africa's agricultural growth was relatively slow. Of course, population growth partly explains the change in GDP per capita. In the last 30 years, both the populations in China and Africa have been booming, but because GDP in China has been increasing faster than in Africa, so the growth rates of GDP per capita also have been changing.

Although per-capita agricultural GDP growth rates have shown different features in China and Africa over the past 30 years, it is worth stressing that the difference between the absolute value of China's and Africa's agricultural GDP has been insignificant since 1999, and the growth rate of Africa even exceeded that of China for a long period of time before 1999. The main reasons for this situation include, first, differences in the composition of agricultural GDP between China and Africa, with exports of agricultural crops and cash crops with high value-added always occupying a large percentage of Africa's agricultural GDP. According to the Food and Agriculture Organization of the United Nations (FAO), agricultural exports account for around 20 per cent of the African continent's agricultural GDP over this period, with the percentage remaining high. China's agriculture has prioritized self-sufficiency in food consumption, therefore the total amount and percentage of exports is comparatively low (see Table 1.1).

Second, the level of agricultural production varies widely across countries in Africa, and per-capita agricultural GDP for rural populations in some countries is very high: for example, Mauritius, whose agriculture includes the confectionery industry, and Gabon, whose agriculture includes important cash crops such as rubber (see Table 1.2). The reason for high per-capita agricultural GDP in African countries is that many countries have substantial cash crop export sectors or advanced animal husbandry industries. However, even the four countries mentioned above cannot achieve grain self-sufficiency and have to import it; furthermore, Algeria remains one of the top 10 grain importers in the world. The per-capita agricultural GDP of the rural population in some countries has stood at a low level for a long time, and in countries such as Ethiopia, Kenya, Zambia and Mozambique it has fallen below USD100 in recent years.

Data for the production of all agricultural crops show that China's output of key foodstuffs such as cereals, meat, vegetables and fruit far exceeds that of the African continent. In 2004 for example, the total output of China's cereals reached 413 million tonnes, while that of Africa was only 126 million tonnes; the total output of meat in China reached 74 million tonnes, whereas that of Africa was 11.6 million tonnes; China's total vegetable, fruit and melon output reached 507 million tonnes, whereas that of Africa was 114 million tonnes. China's total output of cereals, meat and vegetables, fruit and melons was 3.27 times, 6.42 times and 4.44 times that of Africa, respectively. In terms of shares in global output of agricultural crops, China plays an important role and produces 18.2 per cent of the world's cereals, 28.57 per

TABLE 1.1 Comparison of China's and Africa's Export Value (Unit: USD1 million)

		1979–1981	1989–1991	1999–2001	2003	2004
Africa	Export value of agriculture	12,538	12,298	15,076	18,731	20,729
	Percentage in agricultural GDP (%)	25.15%	19.54%	17.82%	20.49%	21.52%
China	Export value of agriculture	5,041	14,527	16,648	20,460	20,827
	Percentage in agricultural GDP (%)	7.30%	12.05%	9.34%	10.61%	10.16%

Source: FAOSTAT

TABLE 1.2 Top 10 and Bottom 10 African Countries by Agricultural GDP Per Capita

	Countries	1980	1990	2000	2004	2009
Top countries by agricultural GDP per capita	South Africa	931.80	1032.15	1388.53	1524.43	1933.04
	Mauritius	488.02	945.94	1243.58	1531.13	1694.26
	Nigeria	189.84	313.55	518.43	609.68	719.19
	Côte d'Ivoire	387.99	402.79	506.48	496.69	565.12
	Swaziland	500.19	529.90	451.47	514.90	550.60
	Gabon	301.10	340.38	430.85	451.24	516.93
	Cape Verde	124.19	198.23	274.00	296.54	401.90
	Ghana	190.39	175.82	299.60	342.73	399.02
	Benin	180.23	238.83	366.77	404.10	358.97
Bottom countries by agricultural GDP per capita	Seychelles	98.98	80.53	96.50	73.63	48.79
	Eritrea	n/a	n/a	49.27	40.00	49.45
	Equatorial Guinea	116.15	107.84	82.14	69.97	61.76
	Democratic Republic of the Congo	130.46	136.91	89.48	79.38	72.32
	Comoros	86.85	80.64	79.81	77.46	76.20
	Djibouti	67.62	86.04	62.54	65.32	79.84
	Mozambique	89.77	78.00	85.01	91.47	89.35
	Burundi	139.28	135.40	103.53	107.32	94.01
	Lesotho	146.60	139.20	126.55	116.14	98.44
	Ethiopia	n/a	n/a	82.43	93.50	104.55

Source: FAOSTAT

cent of the world's meats and 36.62 per cent of the world's melons, fruit and vegetables, while African shares in global output for all major crops are rather low (see Table 1.3).

China's output of the three main grain crops, wheat, rice and maize, exceeds African levels. For example, in 2007 China's output of maize, rice and wheat was 3.18 times, 5.49 times and 5.78 times higher than African output, respectively. However, African output of sorghum and barley was higher than that of China. Among the cash crops, China's output of seed cotton, tea and groundnut exceeded that of Africa, but its coffee output was much lower than that of Africa. It should be noted that Africa's cocoa output was large and kept increasing rapidly. In addition, as indicated by the output of different crops, China's agricultural production structure differed from that of Africa as grain crops hold an indisputably dominant position, while many African countries prefer the planting of cash crops, especially coffee and cocoa (Figure 1.4).

TABLE 1.3 Production of Main Agricultural Crops in China and Africa (Unit: 1,000 tonnes)

			1979–1981	1989–1991	1999–2001	2003	2004
Africa	Cereals	Output	65,091	91,307	112,016	128,489	126,228
		Global share	4.14	4.8	5.37	6.16	5.56
	Meat	Output	5935	7842	10653	11357	11572
		Global share	4.36	4.37	4.54	4.48	4.45
	Vegetables, fruit and melons	Output	59602	79195	104540	112091	114001
		Global share	9.46	9.74	8.66	8.33	8.24
China	Cereals	Output	286488	390171	420308	376123	413166
		Global share	18.21	20.49	20.16	18.03	18.2
	Meat	Output	14526	30644	62833	71155	74306
		Global share	10.66	17.06	26.77	28.05	28.57
	Vegetables, fruit and melons	Output	67497	150228	387916	488694	506634
		Global share	10.72	18.48	32.12	36.33	36.62

Source: FAOSTAT

Comparison of China and Africa's Agricultural Production Capacity

Analysis of productivity indicators for principal agricultural crops shows that China's production capacity has expanded significantly over the past 30 years, with productivity in agricultural crops all increasing year by year; however Africa's productivity indicators for most crops saw little change in 30 years (Figure 1.4).

More specifically, productivity growth data show that China's productivity levels for major agricultural crops doubled during the period from 1978 to 2007, and wheat under the category of grain crops registered the biggest growth in 2007 with production 2.49 times 1978 levels and per unit yield of cash crops such as coffee, seed cotton, tea and groundnut expanding at an even quicker pace. Among the main African agricultural crops, only wheat, tea and cocoa recorded clear output growth, and the growth in per unit yield of other agricultural crops was insignificant as compared with 1978 (Figure 1.5). However, the increase in Africa's agricultural production capacity was rather limited. This also suggests that over the past 30 years, the difference in land productivity is the main form of expression for the divergence in performance of China and Africa in agricultural development (Table 1.4).

Therefore, it is clear that the production capacity of China's agriculture was much higher than that of Africa in terms of land productivity, while China's per-unit yield of other key agricultural crops (excluding tea) was more than twice that of Africa.

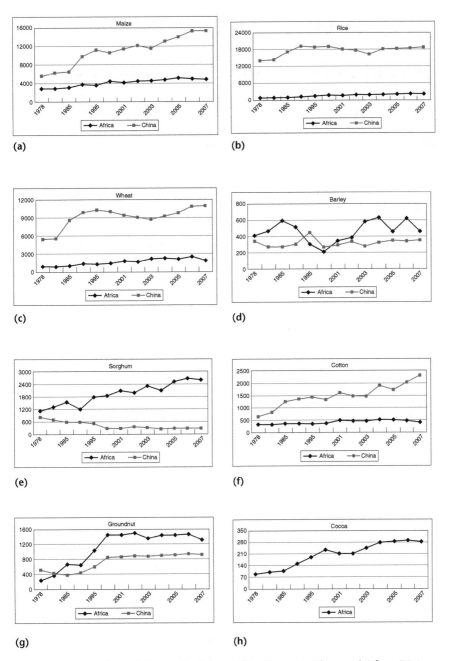

Figure 1.4 Comparison of Output for Selected Key Crops in China and Africa (Unit: 10,000 tonnes)

Source: FAOSTAT

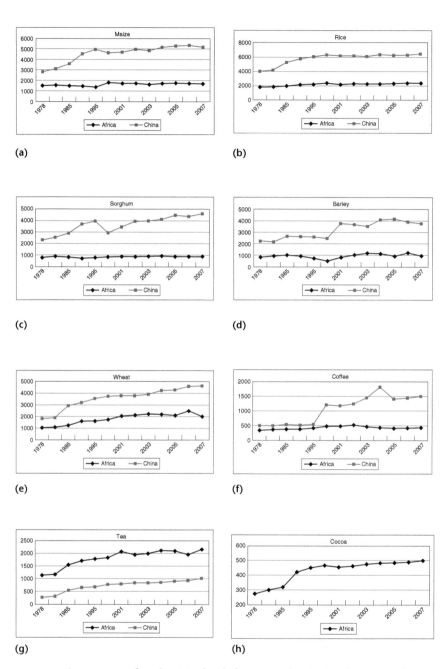

Figure 1.5 Comparison of productivity levels for principal agricultural crops in China and Africa (Unit: kg/ha)

Source: FAOSTAT

TABLE 1.4 Growth in Productivity of Main Agricultural Crops in China and Africa, 1978–2007

	Maize	Rice	Wheat	Barley	Sorghum	Coffee	Seed cotton	Tea	Peanut
China	1.83	1.6	2.49	1.67	1.96	2.99	3.14	3.7	2.11
Africa	1.1	1.3	1.9	1.14	1.10	1.27	1.24	1.9	1.2

Source: FAOSTAT

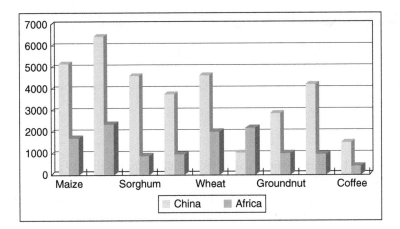

Figure 1.6 Comparison of Per Unit Yields for Principal Agricultural Crops in China and Africa (Unit: kg/ha)

Source: FAOSTAT

Chinese agricultural production capacity is obviously higher than Africa (Figure 1.6). In this regard, the key to Africa's agricultural development is promoting production capacity and increasing productivity levels.

Contribution of Agriculture to Economic Development in China and Africa

Agricultural development has made a remarkable contribution to the economies of both China and African countries (Figure 1.7). In 1980, the percentage of GDP from value-added agriculture for China and Africa was similar. During the period from 1979 to 1981 agriculture accounted for 29 per cent of China's GDP and 25 per cent of Africa's GDP. Agriculture as a percentage of China's GDP declined following economic reform, and was 10.77 per cent by 2004; however, Africa saw a mild rise in the percentage of GDP coming from agriculture, and the overall figure is still more than 25 per cent.

For most African countries, agriculture holds a paramount position in the national economy and is the primary source of national income. According to the FAO, in

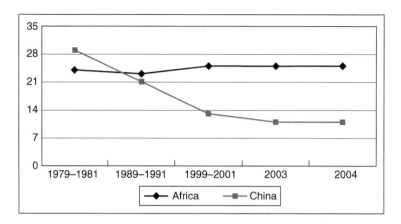

Figure 1.7 Contribution of Agriculture to Total GDP in China and Africa (Unit: %)
Source: FAOSTAT

2004 there were 11 countries whose agriculture accounted for less than 10 per cent of GDP, 12 countries whose agriculture accounted for 10 to 20 per cent of GDP, seven countries whose agriculture accounted for 20 to 30 per cent of GDP, nine countries accounting for 30 to 40 per cent, six countries accounting for 40 to 50 per cent and five countries accounting for more than 50 per cent (Table 1.5). In Liberia agriculture took the biggest share of GDP, hitting some 77 per cent in 2004.

The contribution of agriculture to economic development is shown through its provision of capital and labour to other industries in addition to its direct contribution to GDP. Before reform began in 1978, China adopted a strategy of 'agriculture as the foundation, industry as the pillar' of the economy. In the process of centrally planned industrialization, agriculture provided initial capital through 'price scissors' for industrialization (i.e. a higher price for industrial products but a lower price for agricultural products). In the early years of the People's Republic of China (PRC), 40 per cent of national financial revenue came from agriculture. According to incomplete statistics, Chinese farmers contributed CNY600 billion (around USD100 billion) for industrialization through the effect of price scissors from 1953 to 1983. In the command-and-plan regime, the costs of rural labour were kept low or even at zero to produce a capital surplus. Rural labour still provides important inputs to the construction of rural infrastructure, even after the reform: annual inputs of rural labour were 7.22 billion workdays during 1989–2000. Since the 1980s and particularly the 1990s, the agricultural sector and farmers have provided initial capital for industrialization through 'land scissors', by which the value of land is captured by the urban and industrial sector. Moreover, since 1984 migrant farmers have become the main labour force in cities. Farmer-workers migrating from rural to urban areas have accounted for 52.6 per cent of the labour force in urban industry. They account for 68.2 per cent in the manufacturing

TABLE 1.5 Percentage of Agriculture in African Countries' GDP in 2004

	Below 10%	10%–19.9%	20%–29.9%	30%–39.9%	40%–49.9%	Above 50%
Number	11	12	7	9	6	5
Country	South Africa	Zambia	Sierra Leone	Sao Tome and Principe	Niger	Central African Republic
	Sudan	Zimbabwe	Rwanda	Nigeria	Mali	Chad
	Seychelles	Eritrea	Comorin	Mozambique	Malawi	Guinea Bissau
	Mauritius	Swaziland	Cameroon	Madagascar	Ghana	Liberia
	Libya	Senegal	Burundi	Gambia	Burkina Faso	Democratic Republic of the Congo
	Equatorial Guinea	Morocco	Ethiopia	Guinea	Benin	
	Congo	Mauretania		Côte d'Ivoire	Tanzania	
	Botswana	Cape Verde			Togo	
	Angola	Algeria			Uganda	
	Gabon					

Source: FAOSTAT

industry, and 79.8 per cent in the building industry. It is estimated that each migrant farmer produces CNY23,000 (around USD3,382) of GDP, which gives a figure of CNY3.3 trillion (around USD21.1 billion) from all 145 million migrant farmers (Xu, 2009). The remittance returning to the home of the migrant farmers totalled CNY0.97 trillion in 2009 (Household Survey Office, NBSC, 2011).

In contrast, African agriculture has contributed little to industrialization. Agricultural policies focus on production rather than on farmers: they present incentives to farmers but at the same time have suppressed prices and encouraged monopolies. Profits were retained within semi-state-owned enterprises (Crees, 2000). Over-investment in mechanization, especially tractors, has taken place. The measures promoting African agricultural development have promoted mechanization to some extent, but agricultural processing industries have not been properly set up. Once, some African countries tapped agriculture to provide initial capital for industrialization, leading to a net capital outflow from agriculture and, paradoxically, underdevelopment of both agriculture and industry. One of the main reasons is that Africa countries have lacked labour as a substitute for scarce capital.

In Tanzania, for example, 'we do not have either the necessary finances or the technical know-how', according to Nyerere (1967), so the country changed its industrialization strategy, attaching much importance to rural development while taking industrial development as its foundation. In the long-term plan (1975–1995), the strategic goal for industry was to set up independent and natural resource-based industries so as to meet domestic needs. It promoted the development of small-scale industry by setting up the Small Industry Development Organization (SIDO). The goal of industry was to meet 'basic needs', and to fulfil 'economic self sufficiency'. Agriculture in turn was marginalized in national budget allocations. There were not enough financial inputs for agriculture in Tanzania. The *Ujamaa* movement led by the state did not create a similar institutional context to China, where rural labour was mobilized for large-scale construction of agricultural infrastructure (such as irrigation facilities). Collectivization in Tanzania gathered people together for cultural education and rural production. Farms were divided into 'public farms' and 'private farms', and people cared only about their own privately-held farms. One of the reasons leading to the failure of *Ujamaa* collectivization was that the government forced farmers to grow tobacco and offered very low purchasing prices.

After structural adjustment and liberal reform, control over smallholder farmers was weakened further; grain crop production capacity has not improved, foreign aid and food aid became a substitute for national financial capacity, and migrant farmers did not contribute as much to the economy as they did in China. Agriculture contributed little to other sectors of the economy, excluding export-oriented crops and biofuel crop production dominated by foreign countries.

Contribution of Agriculture to Import and Export Trade in China and Africa

In developing countries, agriculture not only makes important contributions to the national economy but also plays an important role in import and export trade. This is especially the case in African countries, and the reason they adhere to agricultural production structures by focusing on the planting of cash crops is precisely because agricultural trade is so important as a source of foreign exchange generation. Some African countries rely heavily on the export of single cash crops to obtain the foreign exchange needed for their development. According to relevant data, the gross output value of Africa's agriculture was much below that of China's, but the gap between the export of China's agricultural products and that of Africa was not so wide. As illustrated in Table 1.6, the gross output value of Africa's agriculture has increased only modestly over the past 30 years, but the growth rate of Africa's agricultural exports has been almost the same as that of China since 1990. However, when looking at total global levels for agricultural exports, the agricultural exports of China and Africa are relatively small, although these two regions are both devoted to agricultural development.

In addition, agricultural imports to China and Africa are significant. It can be seen that agricultural imports to China and Africa have maintained high growth rates over the past two decades, and have accounted for 5 to 6 per cent of the world's total agricultural imports over these years. However, the percentage of agricultural imports within China's total imports has decreased significantly since 1989, and is now only around 4 per cent, but the percentage of agricultural imports in Africa's total imports actually has been rising, illustrating the high dependence of Africa's agriculture on exports (Table 1.7).

As shown by China's and Africa's agricultural import and export values, the agricultural situation in China is more independent and accounts for only a small percentage of import and export value. In addition, China boasts a highly self-regulating agriculture and a strong supply capability. By contrast, Africa's agriculture is more dependent on exports, so that the sales and supply of agricultural products

TABLE 1.6 Comparison of Agricultural Exports from China and Africa

		1979–1981	1989–1991	1999–2001	2003	2004
Total agricultural exports (USD1 million)	Africa	12,538	12,298	15,076	18,731	20,729
	China	5,041	14,527	16,648	20,460	20,827
Global share (%)	Africa	5.59	3.85	3.64	3.58	3.43
	China	2.25	4.55	4.02	3.91	3.45
Shares in total exports of the region (%)	Africa	44.94	36.15	26.67	26.69	24.76
	China	8.89	6.65	2.98	2.53	2.02

Source: FAOSTAT

TABLE 1.7 Comparison of Agricultural Imports to China and Africa

		1979–1981	1989–1991	1999–2001	2003	2004
Total agricultural	Africa	16,662	18,904	24,583	28,797	34,057
imports (USD1 million)	China	10,612	17,254	23,544	31,886	41,688
Global share (%)	Africa	6.81	5.47	5.60	5.23	5.37
	China	4.34	5.00	5.36	5.80	6.57
Shares in total imports	Africa	19.37	21.10	20.32	20.88	22.49
of the region (%)	China	17.86	8.55	4.44	4.12	4.15

Source: FAOSTAT

are deeply influenced by the international market. This is also an important indication of the economic dependence of African countries.

According to FAO statistics (2005/06), there are eight African countries whose agricultural exports account for more than 50 per cent of their total exports, and among these countries, agricultural exports account for 90 per cent of total exports in Guinea Bissau and 81 per cent in Malawi. There are nine African countries whose agricultural exports account for 30 to 50 per cent of their total exports, including Ethiopia, Burundi and Tanzania. There are 19 African countries whose agricultural exports account for less than 10 per cent of their total exports, and most of these countries are mineral exporters (Table 1.8): for example, Nigeria and Angola are oil exporters and South Africa is a major producer of diamonds and copper. Although China's agricultural exports differ little from the African continent in terms of value, the percentage of agricultural exports within China's total exports is relatively low, totaling 2.02 per cent in 2004.

TABLE 1.8 Percentage of Agricultural Exports in Africa's Total Exports (2004)

	Number	Country
Below 10%	19	Algeria, Angola, Equatorial Guinea, Congo, Guinea, South Africa, Cape Verde, Lesotho, Mauritania, Democratic Republic of the Congo, Central Africa, Morocco, Nigeria, Sierra Leone, Seychelles, Swaziland, Libya, Eritrea, Gabon
10%–29.9%	14	Zambia, Sudan, Sao Tome and Principe, Senegal, Niger, Namibia, Mozambique, Zimbabwe, Mauritius, Madagascar, Liberia, Cameroon, Djibouti, Egypt
30%–49.9%	9	Ethiopia, Burundi, Côte d'Ivoire, Kenya, Mali, Togo, Rwanda, Tanzania, Uganda
Above 50%	8	Chad, Malawi, Komodo, Ghana, Guinea Bissau, Gambia, Burkina Faso, Benin

Source: FAOSTAT

BOX 1.1 COCOA PRODUCTION IN CÔTE D'IVOIRE

Côte d'Ivoire is one African country with satisfactory agricultural development where agriculture plays an important role in the national economy. It is the most important cocoa producer in the world, exporting 947,900 tonnes in 2004 which accounted for one-third of the world's total cocoa exports; Côte d'Ivoire's cocoa exports amounted to USD1.5 billion or 48.50 per cent of its total export value.

The value of Africa's agricultural exports is relatively high, but there is also a huge demand for imported agricultural products because of the prevalence of single cropping systems. Therefore, the import value of most African countries exceeds the export value, which makes them net importers of agricultural products. Agricultural export value exceeds import value in only 12 African countries: Côte d'Ivoire, Kenya, Madagascar, Malawi, Mali, Chad, Togo, Zimbabwe, South Africa, Tanzania, Uganda and Zambia, while agricultural export value falls short of import value in the remaining 40 countries in Africa. The agricultural trade deficit of Africa reached USD13 billion in 2004.

Africa is the main exporter of tropical cash crops in the world, with two-thirds of agricultural exports deriving from six key cash crops: cocoa, coffee, cotton, sugar, tobacco and tea. Exports of cocoa and coffee alone accounted for more than 50 per cent of Africa's total agricultural exports in the mid-1990s. However, the percentage of Africa's tropical cash crop exports in the global total has plummeted in the face of competition from other regions (Table 1.9). For example, the percentage for cocoa dropped from 76.4 per cent in 1970 to 64.8 per cent in 1989, groundnuts from 77.8 per cent to 12.1 per cent, coffee from 30.8 per cent to 21.1 per cent, and rubber from 7 per cent to 6.9 per cent. In 2008, the export proportion of several crops has been decreasing continually with, for example, coffee dropping to 10 per cent, and palm kernel to 16.1 per cent. The gap between Latin American countries and Africa in the production and export of coffee and cocoa has declined. However, Tanzania is still the second largest sisal production area in the world.

Contribution of Agriculture to Employment in China and Africa

As expounded by Lipton (2001), no other sector has such huge potential as agriculture for the creation of employment opportunities and alleviation of poverty. Data show that agriculture is a main sector of the economy for labour absorption in both China and Africa. In 2004 the rural population accounted for 64 per cent of the total in China, and 54 per cent in Africa (Table 1.10). In terms of the numbers of people engaged in agricultural economic activities, the proportion was 64 per cent in China and 62 per cent in Africa. From this it can be seen that agriculture is

TABLE 1.9 Change in the Exports of Africa's Main Cash Crops

	1970		1980		1989		2008	
	Export Volume (1000 t)	% in the World (%)	Export Volume (1000 t)	% in the World (%)	Export Volume (1000 t)	% in the World (%)	Export Volume (1000 t)	% in the World
Coffee	1010.4	30.8	894.8	23.9	1014.7	21.1	639.6	10.0
Cocoa	867.7	76.4	758.7	71.3	1234.5	64.8	1819.8	66.7
Peanut	764.6	77.8	158.3	21.8	110.3	12.1	–	–
Sisal	372.3	63.7	109.4	49.5	50.0	31.9	17.9	39.6
Tea	109.3	14.5	181.8	18.5	258.8	21.5	551.6	29.1
Rubber	200.8	7.0	137.7	4.1	302.1	6.9	390.8	6.0
Palm kernel	381.8	83.3	140.0	69.8	86.0	83.1	4.9	16.1

Source: FAOSTAT

TABLE 1.10 Comparison of the Agricultural Population in China and Africa

		1979–1981	1989–1991	1999–2001	2003	2004
China	Agricultural population	742,341	833,139	853,602	851,028	849,417
	Total population	1,004,204	1,160,914	1,282,320	1,311,709	1,320,892
	% of agricultural population in total	73.92%	71.77%	66.57%	64.88%	64.31%
	Economically active population in agriculture	407,728	491,230	510,816	510,573	510,010
	% in total economically active population	74%	72%	67%	65%	64%
Africa	Agricultural population	277,359	331,457	433,898	450,828	456,282
	Total population	424,186	560,974	775,808	829,063	847,133
	% of agricultural population in total	65.39%	59.09%	55.93%	54.38%	53.86%
	Economically active population in agriculture	121,029	144,447	193,201	202,203	205,148
	% in total Economically active population	71%	67%	64%	63%	62%

Source: FAOSTAT

a key sector for employment in both China and Africa. However, agriculture's contribution to employment has been decreasing in both China and Africa.

Contribution of Agriculture to Food Security in China and Africa

As illustrated in Figure 1.8, Africa's per-capita grain production remained around 150kg and has changed little within 25 years. China's per-capita grain production had reached 285kg in the late 1970s and early 1980s, and then exceeded 300kg in other periods, except in 2003 when it decreased to 286kg. In 2007 China's total grain output reached 501.5 million tonnes and per-capita grain production reached 379.6kg, enough to meet the consumption levels of the current population. As measured by FAO's food security standards,[2] China's grain output totalled 501.5 million tonnes in 2007, net cereal exports were 7.96 million tonnes and net soybean imports were just under 31 million tonnes, while the self-sufficiency ratio for grains (including soybean) exceeded 95 per cent, meaning that per-capita grain production would be 400kg when divided by a population of 1.3 billion. The stock consumption ratio at the end of 2006 stood around 35 per cent and was estimated to be 40 to 45 per cent at the end of 2007.

At the same time, Africa's cereals output approximated 143 million tonnes in 2007 including 20.8 million tonnes of wheat, 100.5 million tonnes of brown rice and 21.6 million tonnes of rice. Africa's population had reached 963.68 million in 2007, and per-capita grain production was 148.4kg. The grains that Africa imports or receives from aid amount to 22.67 million tonnes every year, which accounts for 20 per cent of total demand: within this figure, grain aid totals 2.42 million tonnes. Now, the grain self-sufficiency ratio is lower than 50 per cent in many African countries. Maize production can meet most local demand, and imports account for only 5 per cent of Africa's total consumption. For wheat, 45 per cent, and for rice, 80 per cent of total consumption needs to be imported.

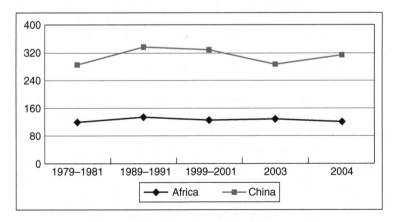

Figure 1.8 Per-capita Grain Production for China and Africa (Unit: kg)

Source: FAOSTAT

Many African countries allocate the most fertile land and the largest proportion of water conservancy facilities, capital funds, labour, chemical fertilizers and pesticides to the development of cash crops, but fail to recognize the importance of planting food crops. Grain production has been sluggish for a long time, and grain shortage has become an increasingly serious problem in Africa. Africa's per-capita grain production was 176kg in 1970, decreased to 146kg in 1979 and was less than 125kg in 1983. Although this figure increased again on entering the twenty-first century, it is still lower than in the 1970s: for example, 141kg in 2005. The grain self-sufficiency ratio remained at 96 per cent between 1962 and 1964, declined to 83 per cent during the period from 1972 to 1974, and further to 76 per cent in 1983. The grain self-sufficiency ratio kept decreasing while grain imports increased continuously as Africa's grain imports recorded an average annual growth rate of 11.1 per cent during the 1971–1980 period, with net grain imports standing at no more than 2 million tonnes in the mid-1960s, increasing to 12 million tonnes in 1978. Africa has already become the region of the world most vulnerable to experiencing famine (Lu, 2000). The modest progress observed in Sub-Saharan Africa from 1995–1997 and 2001–2003 has not been enough to decrease undernourishment in many populations, which remains at high levels (FAO, 2006). According to FAO (2011), the number of undernourished people in Sub-Saharan Africa stood at 201.2 million in 2005–2007, which accounts for 28 per cent of the total population in Sub-Saharan Africa; this ratio changed to 30 per cent in 2010. This is still much higher than the average percentage of 13 per cent in the world, and much higher than the average of 16 per cent in developing countries. Countries in protracted crisis are characterized by long-lasting or recurring crises and often limited or little capacity to respond, exacerbating food insecurity problems in those countries. Agricultural and rural-based livelihoods are critical to the groups most affected by protracted crises. Agriculture accounts for one-third of GDP in countries in protracted crisis, and two-thirds of their employment, yet agriculture accounts for only 4 per cent of humanitarian official development assistance (ODA) received by countries in protracted crisis and 3 per cent of development ODA. According to data in 1996–2010, out of 22 countries in protracted crisis, there were 17 in Sub-Saharan Africa.

FAO statistics reveal that African agriculture is utterly inadequate in terms of food production, as shown by the doubling of Africa's cereal imports during the period from 1974 to 1987, reaching USD1 billion (Diouf, 1989), and accounting for 33 per cent of total agricultural imports over the same period. China's cereal imports also accounted for a high percentage, reaching 34 per cent of total agricultural imports from 1979 to 1981, higher than that of Africa. The percentage of cereal imports in China's total agricultural imports had dropped to 8.68 per cent in 2004, yet the percentage in Africa remains at a high level of 25.63 per cent (Table 1.11).

In terms of the change in exports, the percentage of cereal exports in China's total agricultural exports has teetered up and down, reflecting the production cycle of cereals in China. However, the percentage of cereal exports in Africa's total agricultural exports has remained low all the time. This supports the argument that

TABLE 1.11 Comparison of China and Africa's Cereal Imports and Exports

		1979– 1981	1989– 1991	1999– 2001	2003	2004
Percentage of cereals in	Africa	32.95	30.88	28.72	27.46	25.63
total agricultural imports	China	34.15	19.98	6.91	5.19	8.68
	World	17	11	9	8	8
Percentage of cereals in	Africa	3.14	2.87	2.52	2.61	3.26
total agricultural exports	China	8.44	5.62	8.15	13.01	4.01
	World	17	11	9	8	8

Source: FAOSTAT

Africa is the biggest cereal importer and the smallest cereal exporter in the world.

According to the FAO, 24 million people in Sub-Saharan Africa fell into hunger in 2007 due to soaring food prices. Among the 16 countries with hunger incidence at more than 15 per cent, 15 countries are in Africa, making them much more vulnerable. China's agricultural production has grown rapidly and stably from the mid-1970s, and the reason for such growth is already well identified and recognized by many scholars. The average annual growth rate of China's agricultural GDP has reached 4.4 per cent while annual outputs of oil crops, fruit, meat and aquatic products all maintain average growth rates of more than 8 per cent. China's annual grain output has increased from 300 million tonnes to 500 million tonnes, representing an historic turnaround for the main agricultural crops from a position of longstanding short supply to an overall positive balance. China's per-capita grain possession has expanded year after year, rising from 317kg per person in 1980 to 378kg per person in 2006, such that China has basically addressed grain supply self-sufficiency and food security for its population.

Contribution of Agriculture to Poverty Alleviation in China and Africa

Agricultural development is especially important for poverty alleviation. The GDP growth resulting from agricultural development is twice more than that from non-agricultural sectors (World Bank, 2008). Since 1978, China has made great progress in poverty alleviation: the total Chinese population in poverty has decreased from 630 million in 1981 to 128 million in 2004, based on a World Bank standard of consumption of USD1.08 a day ppp. The corresponding rate of poverty incidence has decreased from 63.7 per cent to 9.9 per cent. The main lesson learned from China's poverty reduction experience is that the Chinese economy is growing quickly and central policies are pro-poor. Agriculture is decreasing as a percentage of GDP in the Chinese economy, but agricultural GDP has been growing at about 10 per cent per annum since 1996 and even at a rate of 30 per cent in some years. At the same time, the percentage of the population in poverty has decreased rapidly.

World Bank (2000) research shows that poverty incidence is linked to the proportion of agriculture in the economy. The population in poverty decreases slowly in the provinces, where the agricultural share in GDP decreases quickly. Initial linear regression indicates that a 1 per cent decrease in agriculture's share in GDP will lead to a 1.9 per cent decrease in the rate of reduction of population in poverty, given an unchanged GDP growth rate (World Bank, 2000). In China, agriculture's contribution to poverty alleviation is 3.5 times more than that of other sectors (World Bank, 2008), since most people work in the agricultural sector.

In recent decades, the African population in poverty has increased from 168 million in 1981 to 298 million in 2004 based on the standard consumption of USD1.08 a day at 1993 ppp (Chen *et al.*, 2007). African poverty incidence has not changed, and has stood at about 42 per cent for decades: it remains outstanding and is the biggest obstacle to fulfilling the Millennium Development Goals. Much research exists on why Africa cannot meet its goal of poverty alleviation: the reasons listed include insufficient economic growth, unstable political systems and weak policy implementation capacity, high dependence on foreign aid and constraints resulting from traditional cultural influences.

However, it should not be overlooked that agriculture has contributed to poverty alleviation, providing basic food to smallholder farmers; nonetheless, agricultural development has been slow. Most African countries have a cash-crop oriented agriculture: the goal of agriculture is to export for foreign exchange, not for domestic consumption. The reason for this dates back to colonial times before state independence, when colonial powers planted coffee, peanuts and other cash crops for export to the world market. Grain crops were increasingly not grown, leading to the present agricultural structure. After state independence, a strategy of industrialization dominated, along with an aspiration to change the colonial agricultural structure. African countries used exports of cash crops to earn foreign exchange to fund industrialization. The best land and infrastructure are used to grow cash crops and this agricultural structure, created in colonial times, persists to the present day. The insufficient growth and market-oriented structure of agriculture have weakened the contribution of agriculture to poverty alleviation in Africa. 'Agriculture [has] failed to promote development effectively', as the World Bank (2008) puts it.

Conclusion

Over the past 30 years, both China and Africa have taken active measures to develop agriculture, sharing many similarities in agricultural development trajectories. For example, agricultural production plays a foundational role in national economies, and agriculture has created employment opportunities for a majority of people in both China and Africa. However, China and Africa also show remarkable differences in agricultural development due to historical and present conditions particular to their respective regions. First, China has displayed a positive tendency towards rapid development in agriculture over the past 30 years, and its growth rate of agricultural GDP and per-capita GDP is impressive, while most African countries have failed to maintain strong impetus after their independence. In the early 1970s, the growth rate of per-capita GDP of Africa's rural population was near zero, and in the 1980s and the early 1990s Africa even encountered stagnation. However, aggressive growth in the past decade has changed this unfavourable trend (World Bank, 2008).

Second, agricultural development makes contributions to national economies in different ways in China and Africa. The top priority of agriculture in China is grain security, and a direct result of agricultural development is a high grain self-sufficiency ratio so that the food supply to its large population is now basically guaranteed. Most African countries deem the role of agriculture to be primarily a source of foreign exchange, and therefore Africa's agricultural development relies more on the production of export-oriented cash crops. The grain self-sufficiency ratio is very low, which leads to more urgent food security vulnerabilities and a wider gap between grain demand and supply, so Africa has to import grain from the international market or receive food aid to meet domestic demand.

Third, significant agricultural development in China has resulted from increasing productivity, whereas the same thing has not happened in Africa. Fast-growing populations in Africa compromise the benefits from productivity improvements. In this sense it can be concluded that China has made more remarkable achievements in agricultural development when compared to Africa. Similarly, China's current agricultural development is also much better than Africa's. This notable situation in China is mainly attributed to diverse positive factors such as natural conditions, agricultural inputs, technology and development policies. This rapid and steady agricultural growth is not only a major accomplishment for China, but also a source of national pride within the nation's development experience.

While China has experienced rapid agricultural development, accelerated urbanization and industrialization damage to natural resources and the environment have impeded prospects for further agricultural development, with its attendant benefits. As for African countries, current agricultural development has been impeded, although significant potential to contribute to development exists. China's experiences in agricultural development may provide some insights for Africa to unleash the potential of agriculture to the utmost. The following chapters of this book will consider the different agricultural strategies and policies, natural conditions, agricultural inputs, agricultural technologies, organization and operation at the household level, as well as external support for agricultural development in China and Africa, and make suggestions for Africa's agricultural development.

2

AGRICULTURAL DEVELOPMENT IN CHINA AND AFRICA IN HISTORICAL PERSPECTIVE

In order to understand the current performance of agricultural development in different countries, it is necessary to trace back to historical factors. China and Africa are both cradles of the world's agricultural civilization. China emerged 4,000 years ago at the far eastern end of the Eurasian continent as a unique and autonomous society established on the basis of agriculture rather than commerce and was ruled by landlords and bureaucrats rather than merchants and politicians (Stavrianos, 1999). China's ancient and modern rulers placed importance on agriculture while restraining commerce. After 1949 China began to emphasize industrialization and modernization; nevertheless, agriculture still played a leading role in the development strategy of the nation. Similarly, development in Africa has always been underpinned by agriculture, from the early fifteenth century when Africa maintained a self-sufficient economy, to the middle of the twentieth century. However, agricultural development in Africa has displayed different characteristics at different historical stages. Agriculture is the pillar of development in most African countries, except for those relying primarily on mineral resources.

In this chapter the history of agricultural development can be divided into three stages for comparing China and Africa:

1   the early history of Chinese and African agriculture;
2   a development stage of Chinese and African agriculture up to national independence; and
3   a stage of agricultural adjustment in the early days of independence.

A comparison of performance and results between China's agricultural development following reform and opening in 1978 and Africa's agricultural development following structural adjustment has been discussed specifically in the former chapter.

Origin of Chinese and African Agriculture

There are three main centres of agriculture in the world: the West Asian region, the East Asia region and the Central American region. The East Asian region (Li, 1991) includes four geographical belts from the north to the south. These are:

- the north China belt covering the Yellow River reaching to the southern part of north-east China;
- the south China belt spreading from the Qinling Mountains in the west and covering most parts south of the Yangtze River in the east;
- the South Asia belt; and
- the South Sea Islands belt.

Africa was not recognized as one of the centres of origin of world agriculture until the 1960s and 1970s. The American scholar George Murdock, in his famous work *Africa: Its Peoples and Their Culture History* (1959), argued from his research on the origins of agriculture in West Africa that African agriculture had an independent origin and development path and that this fact had been long neglected, regardless of the existence of various domesticated crops in Sub-Saharan Africa. We can say that Sub-Saharan Africa is one of the four agricultural centres which have played an important role in human history (Li, 1991). This viewpoint was shared by David Niemeijer (1996), who paid attention to the high flexibility and adaptability of African agriculture 10,000 years ago. Africa's crop planting and animal husbandry activities were similar to those in East and South Europe during the sixth and seventh centuries BC. The US National Academy of Sciences published several volumes of *Lost Crops of Africa* in 1996 (National Research Council, 1996), which show that Africa is the centre of origin for numerous crops including African rice, coffee, sorghum, pearl millet and cowpea (Stavrianos, 1999). The argument that China and Africa are both centres of origin for world agriculture has been convincingly supported by many discoveries from agricultural archaeologists.

Major Crops Originating in Central Africa

According to Murdock's (1959) research on the origins of agricultural crops all over the world, the African continent, East Asia (China in particular), South-West Asia and America are primary centres of origin for major crops used in the world today. Six independent centres of crop origin are nominated by Gepts (2001):

- Meso-America (Southern Mexico and Northern Central America) for maize, phaseolus beans, sweet potato and tomato;
- the Andes of South America for potato, cassava (manioc) and pineapple;
- South-West Asia for wheat, barley, pea and lentils;
- the Sahel region and Ethiopian highlands of Africa for sorghum, coffee, melon and watermelon;

- China for Asian rice, soybean, adzuki bean, orange, apricot, peach and tea; and
- South-East Asia for cucumber, banana and plantain.

Chinese agricultural historians have conducted investigations into the main crops originating in China. As shown by studies from agricultural archaeologists, approximately 250 out of 600 major plant crops across the globe originated from Africa (Li, 1991), around 136 originated from China. Of the four major cereal crops in the world today, rice and certain types of wheat and millet originated from China and Africa (Table 2.1).

Time of Origin of Chinese and African Agriculture

As mentioned previously, both China and the African continent are cradles of the world's agricultural civilization, with the Hemudu Clan starting cultivation of rice in early 7000 BC, which made China the first country in the world to plant rice. Almost at the same time, communities in the central Sahel embarked upon primitive farming (Lu, 2000). According to relevant historical studies, Egypt was the earliest origin of Africa's agricultural civilization, commencing the cultivation of barley in early 18000–12000 BC (Kong, 1986), millet from 6100–4850 BC and wheat from around 3600 BC. Stavrianos wrote in his masterpiece *A Global History: From Prehistory to the 21st Century* (1999) that African agriculture was established in the upper reaches of the River Niger about 5000 BC and along the reaches of the River Nile around 4000 BC. However, China, as noted previously, started artificial cultivation of rice about 7000 BC and planted wheat and millet around 5000 BC (Table 2.2).

Distinct Characteristics of Multiple Centres of Origin of Chinese and African Agriculture

In discussing the characteristics of the origins of agriculture in Africa, Louis Putterman (2006) clearly states a multi-centre theory, i.e. that there were six centres of agriculture origin on the African continent including semi-arid West Africa, West Africa, the Ethiopian highlands, the Bantu farming area, Egypt and Madagascar. Madagascar is a centre of exchange for African and South-East Asian agriculture (Table 2.3).

Research by Wang and Chen (1995) on the origin of China's agriculture shows that China enjoys a wide geographical territory, favourable climate, adequate rainfall, fertile soil, abundant animal and plant resources, and has many (at least eight) centres of origin for agriculture (Table 2.4).

It can be seen from the centres of origin for agriculture in China and Africa that the origin of agriculture was to support the development of animal husbandry rather than meet demand for food. The reason for this is that agriculture in China and Africa first appeared in the places with animal husbandry activities as well as dryland areas. Putterman (2006) argues that the domestication of animals in Africa occurred several thousand years earlier than the cultivation of crops, and that farming in Africa was motivated by the search for exploitable resources for survival in drylands.

TABLE 2.1 Main Crops Originated in China and Africa

Category	Africa		China	
	Crops	Place of Origin	Crops	Place of Origin
Cereal	African rice	Middle reaches of River Niger, Senegal and Gambia	Rice	Hunan
	Sorghum	West Africa, Nile-Ethiopia and East Africa	Sorghum	Gansu
	Pearl millet	West Africa	Millet	Hebei
	Teff	Ethiopia	Wheat	Gansu
	Eragrostis pilosa	Ethiopia	Barley	Gansu
			Broomcorn millet	Gansu
Beans	Cowpea, groundnut		Soybean	Heilongjiang
Tubers	Kafir potato	Sudan		
	Coleus dioscoreaceae	West Africa	Taro	
	Fruitless banana (enset)	Ethiopia		
Melon and fruit	Abelmosk		Celery Cabbage	Shaanxi
	Pumpkin, morel	West Africa	Mustard	Shaanxi
	Gourd, albizia	Sudan	Rape	Gansu
Beverage crops and herbs	Kola	West Africa	Tea	n/a
	Coffee	Ethiopia		
Oil crops	Palm oil	Equatorial Africa	Rape	Gansu
	Caster, sesame	East Africa, Ethiopia	Sesame	Zhejiang
Textile crops	Cotton	Sudan	Hemp	Xinjiang
			Ramie	Zhejiang, Jiangsu

Source: Li (1991), Wang and Chen (1995)

TABLE 2.2 Summary – Time of the Earliest Cultivation of Main Crops in China and Africa

	Rice	Wheat	Millet
China	10,000 BC	5000 BC	5000 BC
Africa	–	3600 BC	6100–4850 BC

The origins of agriculture in China and Africa have had deep and long-lasting effects on its development. Sorghum and millet used to be the most important crops in African agriculture and still remain significant today; in the same way, rice and wheat were the most important crops in the centres of origin of Chinese agriculture and remain main major food crops in China today. For example, in 2007 the harvested area for sorghum and millet in Africa reached 29.5 million hectares and 21 million hectares respectively, accounting for 29 per cent of the total harvest area and 48 per cent of the total grain harvest area. The harvest area for rice and wheat on the Chinese mainland reached 29 million hectares and 24 million hectares respectively, accounting for 32 per cent of the total harvest area and 61 per cent of the total grain harvest area. This kind of cropping structure also meant that agricultural development in China and Africa took on different features in the 1970s and 1980s. The 'Green Revolution', which focused on innovations in wheat and rice, resulted in the rapid development of Chinese agriculture, but bypassed Africa (Baum and Lejeune, 1986).

Agriculture Development in China and Africa before Independence

Following the early period of agricultural civilization, both China and Africa experienced a transition from a primitive agricultural state centring on hunter-

TABLE 2.3 Centres of Origin of Agriculture in Africa

Centre	Territorial Scope	Main Crops	Time
Semi-arid West Africa	Senegal, Gambia, Guinea Bissau, Mauritania, Western Sahara, Mali, Burkina Faso, Niger	Sorghum, pearl millet	3,500–4,000 years ago
West Africa	Guinea, Sierra Leone, Liberia, Côte d'Ivoire, Ghana, Togo, Benin, Nigeria	Pearl millet	4,000 years ago
Ethiopian highlands	Ethiopia, Eritrea, Djibouti, Uganda, Kenya, Somalia	Wheat, barley, sorghum, pearl millet	3,500–4000 years ago
Bantu farming area	Democratic Republic of the Congo, Rwanda, Burundi, Tanzania, Malawi, Mozambique, Botswana, South Africa, Zambia, Zimbabwe, Swaziland, Lesotho, Cameroon, Equatorial Guinea, Congo, Gabon, Angola, Namibia, Central Africa	Millet	3,000 years ago
Egypt	Egypt, Sudan, Libya, Tunisia, Algeria, Morocco	Barley, emmer wheat, flax, millet	7,200 years ago

Source: Putterman (2006)

TABLE 2.4 Centres of Origin of Agriculture in China

Centre	Territorial Scope	Main Crops	Time
Farming and animal husbandry in south-west China	Yunnan, Guizhou, Sichuan, Tibet	Rice, taro, potatoes	7,000 years ago
Dry farming and animal husbandry in north-west China	Xinjiang, Gansu, Qinghai, Ningxia	Broomcorn millet, rape, wheat	9,000 years ago
Dry farming and animal husbandry in the central plain	Shanxi, Shaanxi, Henan, Hebei	Broomcorn millet, foxtail millet, sorghum, paddy, mustard	7,000 years ago
Dry farming and animal husbandry in north-east China	Liaoning, Heilongjiang, Jilin	Grain millet	7,000 years ago
Farming and animal husbandry in Yellow River and the Huai River area	Shandong, Anhui, Jiangsu	Rice, grain millet, foxtail millet	7,000 years ago
Farming and animal husbandry in the middle reaches of the Yangtze River	Hunan, Hubei	Rice	5,000 years ago
Farming and animal husbandry in the Yangtze River Delta	Jiangsu, Zhejiang and others	Rice	7,000 years ago
Courtyard farming and animal husbandry along the reaches of the Pearl River	Guangdong, Guangxi, Taiwan	Tuber crops	5,000 years ago

Source: Wang and Chen (1995)

gathering to domestication and cultivation linked to the development of agricultural production. Agricultural production systems with particular geographical characteristics gradually appeared in both China and on the African continent.

Based on geographical conditions and crop planting traditions, agricultural production in Africa can be divided into four areas:

1   Mediterranean coastal agricultural areas in North Africa – focusing on planting cereals and beans;
2   an inland agricultural area in West Africa – based on planting cereals and tubers;
3   highland agriculture in East Africa – focusing on cereals and fruitless bananas (*enset*) and
4   the agricultural area south of the equator – centred on planting tuberous crops.

As shown by the geographical distribution of agricultural production, agricultural development in Africa was based on the utilization of available resources, and from this diversification and adaptability were achieved. Agricultural production in Africa remained relatively advanced until the middle of the fifteenth century, when western colonialists arrived. At that time African society was based on a highly localized economy with a high-degree of self-sufficiency (Bates and Lofchie, 1980). Other research also suggests that different natural and climatic conditions in different ecological areas in Africa were the reasons behind the different agricultural activities taken up in these areas. This geographic disparity helps explain patterns of agricultural trade development across the African continent between clans and tribes and within the region until the 1980s.

With the dissemination and evolution of agriculture, three types of agricultural economy emerged in mainland China: millet-based agriculture along the reaches of the Yellow River, millet and rice-based agriculture centring on the Yellow River and the Huai River region, and rice-planting agriculture in the Yangtze River watershed. Chinese farming civilization also began to take shape in this period, including dry farming focused on planting millet in the northern Yellow River watershed, and irrigated farming focused on planting rice on the southern reaches of the Yangtze River (Yin and Xu, 2004).

As shown already, the African continent was a centre of origin for agriculture and did not lag behind other countries in terms of its spread (Table 2.5). Africa was also the first continent to experience slavery (there was considerable slavery by Arab traders in Congo and East Africa before the Europeans arrived). During the first century when European colonialists arrived in Africa, their first destination was the Atlantic coast. At this time some African regions along the Mediterranean Sea, Red Sea and the Indian Ocean had already entered into the development stage of feudal society, but slavery societies still existed around the Senegal River, River Niger, River Congo, Zambezi River Valley and the Great Lakes region.

Furthermore, the people in equatorial tropical forests, south of the Zambezi River, on the edge of the Sahara Desert and the Kalahari Desert and in the eastern part of the Great Rift Valley in eastern Africa still lived in primitive hunter-gatherer societies or as nomads and in agro-pastoralist societies (Ai and Lu, 1995). The effect of this unbalanced agricultural development has been illustrated in Stavrianos' (1999) research: his map entitled the *Regions of the Cultures in the World to 1500* shows that despite substantial economic, political and social progress in Africa, most areas of the African continent were still locked in forms of what he labels 'primitive agricultural production'. China, meanwhile, had entered into more sophisticated forms of agricultural production. Overall, the development of African agriculture was not as fast as that of Chinese agriculture.

The expansion of Europe from the sixteenth century onwards had deep and ever-lasting impacts on African agriculture and the whole African continent. Stavrianos (1999) marks 1500 as the threshold of a new era of development in Africa. Africa had achieved considerable economic, social and political progress up to 1500, but other parts of the world overtook it after this period. The reason for this rupture was partly because Africa's internal development, including agricultural development, was severely distorted as it was parcelled out among external powers (especially after the

TABLE 2.5 Development of Agriculture in the African Region

Main Region	Water Basin	Main Countries	Main Crops	Main Crops before Colonization
Mediterranean North–African coast	Nile River region	From Egypt to Morocco, including parts of the Sahara	Cereals, beans	Rice, wheat, barley, beans, flax
Inland area in West Africa	River Niger, Senegal River, Gambia River	From the edge of Sahara Desert in the north, reaching the Atlantic in the west and extending to the Gulf of Guinea in the south	Cereals, tubers, oil crops	Sorghum, millet, cotton, rice, cassava
East African Highlands		Ethiopia, Eritrea, Kenya	Cereals, fruitless banana	Wheat, barley, beans, cotton, sesame, groundnut
South of the Equator	Great Lakes Region	Zambia, Tanzania, South Africa, Cameroon	Tuberous crops	Maize, potatoes, banana, taro, sugarcane

Source: Li (1991), Lu (2000)

end of nineteenth century). This damage has three major facets. First, there was a vast loss of agricultural labour in Africa because of the slave trade. According to research by Burghardt Dubois (1896), Africa lost 75 million people as a result of slave trafficking to America, and another 25 million people were sold as slaves to Asian countries, making a total of 100 million people lost to the slave trade. This figure is equivalent to the total population of the African continent in 1800. According to reports submitted to expert meetings under the auspices of the United Nations Educational, Scientific and Cultural Organization (UNESCO), Africa lost a vast population of 210 million to the slave trade between the fifteenth and nineteenth centuries (Lu, 2000). The decrease in population and labour meant that farmland was underutilized or unused, resulting in an immediate loss in agricultural production. Frequent riots and turbulence in Africa, leading to social unrest and rural decline, became inevitable. Agricultural production almost came to a standstill.

Second, monoculture farming was introduced into Africa by western powers, replacing its traditional agricultural crops with export-oriented cash crops. This meant that the development of African agriculture was totally distorted and dominated by the planting of cash crops. This irrational development shattered the diversified and agro-ecologically, well-adapted agricultural production system that had been in existence for several thousand years on the African continent. Monoculture planting took hold in the cotton production area in Egypt and around the Nile River in Sudan; in the cocoa, oil palm, coffee and rubber production areas on the West African coast; in the groundnut and cotton production areas within the African inland region; in the clove and sisal production areas on the East African coast and neighbouring islands; in the tea, cotton and coffee production areas of African inland regions; and in the tobacco and sugarcane production areas of southern Africa. The rapid penetration of cash crops soon made Africa a major producer and exporter and by the 1950s, cotton yield in Africa accounted for around 12 per cent of world market share. For palm oil the share was 80 per cent, cocoa 75 per cent, groundnut 30 per cent, tea 40 to 50 per cent and sisal 65 per cent. In contrast with these significant shares in global cash crop markets, Africa contributed an extremely low percentage of the global grain output in the same period: its wheat output occupied less than 4 per cent of the global total, and corn output less than 7 per cent. Food shortages were very pressing on the African continent prior to the period of decolonization.

Third, there was a deep and everlasting impact arising from the expropriation of land by western migrants who earmarked relatively fertile lands on the continent for their own possession. Land acts were adopted mainly by western colonial countries and the area of land cultivated by African people was gradually reduced; the land that did remain was often of poor quality. Even if the Africans kept fertile lands in their own hands, they usually did not have the ability to maintain sufficient input. Large-scale commercial farms owned by new arrivals to the continent coexisted with African smallholders, and this situation persists in many parts of Africa today. In Zambia for example, there are around 3,000 modern farms, of which almost none are run by local people. Most small farms operated by Zambian people cover only a few hectares.[1]

However, it is worth stressing that the plantation system adopted by western colonialists in Africa promoted the dissemination of new crops and agricultural technology to a certain extent including corn, the second largest crop in Africa by planting area, and cassava from South America, introduced by Portuguese colonialists in the seventeenth century, which shares a large planting area in Africa; in addition there is cocoa, a crop holding an important position in Africa's economic growth, which was introduced by the French in the same period. New crops introduced from South America and North America included corn, cassava, sweet potato, pepper, pineapple and tobacco. These expanded rapidly after being introduced into Africa by the Portuguese (Stavrianos, 1999), and are now all major food crops in Africa.

In contrast with the sluggish and interrupted development of agricultural civilization in Africa, agricultural development has been continuous throughout Chinese history. Chinese society has witnessed the change of several dozen dynasties, and agricultural production has been affected by wars and conflicts; however, these impacts have been temporary and China remains one of the oldest uninterrupted civilizations (Stavrianos, 1999) thanks to geographical isolation and its consistently large population. First, the pro-agricultural policies adopted by every dynasty supported the continuity of agricultural development in China. Its total farmland area expanded by 5.6 million hectares in the middle and late Warring States Period (c. 475–221 BC), to 13.5 million hectares in the Tang Dynasty (AD 618–907), to 54 million hectares in the early Qing Dynasty (AD 1636–1911), and to 81.2 million hectares at the beginning of the twentieth century, almost equivalent to the total farmland area of modern China (Table 2.6). Second, grain crops had absolute predominance as a percentage of the total cropping area. Third, the productivity of grain production increased from 1620kg per hectare at the beginning of historical records to 2752.5kg per hectare in the early Qing Dynasty, which only mildly decreased after the Opium Wars broke out in 1840 (Wu, 1988). Fourth, the quality of grains and yields remained stable with some modest fluctuations. Finally, high per-capita grain production meant that China was basically self-sufficient.

Although the per-unit area yield of grain has been on the rise in China, it has not kept pace with soaring demand. China has continuously witnessed rapid increases in its population. In the Ming and Qing Dynasties (from the eighteenth century onwards), the tax system of converting labour service into land tax thoroughly put an end to the system of poll tax, a tax levied based on the population which had been practised for more than 1,000 years. The result was that the population nearly doubled, and this meant that reclaiming more arable land was the only way to meet demand for grain. At that time, the Qing Government encouraged land reclamation, resulting in rapid growth in agricultural acreage. According to relevant studies, agricultural acreage in the Qing Dynasty was largely equivalent to that in the early days of the People's Republic of China (PRC), around 0.14 billion hectares of arable land in 1840 and 1949 (Zhou, 2001). While land reclamation has helped ensure food security (Table 2.7), it has inevitably damaged forests, grassland and wetlands, posing a potential threat to the sustainable

TABLE 2.6 History of China's Agricultural Development

Dynasty and Year	Farmland Area (10,000 ha)	Grain Land Area (10,000 ha)	Population (100 million)	Land Productivity (kg/ha)	Raw Grain Per Capita (kg)	Unprocessed Food Grain Production Rate (%)	Per-capita Grain Consumption (kg)
Middle and Late Warring States Period (341–221 BC)	600	564	0.2	1,620	460.5	61.1	284
End of Western Han Dynasty (141 BC–AD 23	1,587	1,493	0.595	1,980	496.5	60.13	298.5
Tang Dynasty (618–907)	1,593	1,353	0.6	2,505	565	52.96	299
End of Northern Song Dynasty (1119–1127)	3,300	2,800	1.25	2,340	524	52.2	273.5
Late Ming Dynasty (early Wanli) 1572–1644)	3,180	2,800	1.25	2,595	561.5	56	314
Early Qing Dynasty (middle Qianlong) (1644–1757)	6,333	5,400	2.71	2752.5	546.5	55.7	304.5
1914–1918	9,533	8,120	4.3	1,845	348	76	264.5
1931–1936	9,800	8,333	5.2	1972.5	315.5	70	239.5

Source: Wu (1988)

TABLE 2.7 Land Reclamation in the Recent History of China

Year	1661	1685	1724	1753	1763	1812
Area: 10,000ha	549.36	607.84	683.99	708	741.45	791.53

development of Chinese agriculture. At present, although the Chinese government has set 120 million hectares of arable land as a red line, indicating the minimum area that must be conserved, China remains confronted with the enormous challenge of keeping agricultural acreage at a suitable level, given annual losses in available arable land due to the spread of urban areas as well as other factors such as land degradation. In contrast, arable land on the African continent has been far from well developed, largely because it has been free from such population pressure. This has created favourable conditions for agricultural development. In some African countries the utilization rate of arable land available for development is very low: for example, only about 10 per cent in Sierra Leone.

In summary, China and Africa are both centres of origin for world agriculture and have long histories of farming civilizations; however, they are different in that China established a united multi-ethnic country as early as 221 BC. Farming civilization developed organically despite frequent changes of dynasty. The longstanding agricultural production system and basic cropping system are still in use today, and remain the backbone of China's smallholder economy. The situation was different in Africa, as no united country came into being and traditional farming civilization was interrupted deeply by the invasion of western colonialism, such that agricultural development in Africa was oriented towards meeting the demands of western countries. Even after the nations' independence, neo-colonialism still presented the characteristics of racism, national chauvinism and hypocrisy (Martin, 1985). The former colonists continued to impose their interests on African states, although not necessarily intentionally. At the same time Africa's cropping structure, cropping system and land distribution were damaged to a certain extent, and the planting of cash crops came to play an important role in agricultural production and the foundation of the economy in many African countries. Most of these crops were rain-fed and could fully utilize the sunlight and rainfall in Africa, however, this hindered the development of irrigation. Meanwhile, China's traditional agriculture centred on the planting of wheat and rice. Intensive production of these crops increased demand for agricultural water and soil fertility inputs, which in turn led to the development of irrigation and utilization of on-farm organic material as key components of China's agricultural technology development.

Chinese and African Agriculture after Independence

All African countries gained national independence after the end of the Second World War (Table 2.8). The PRC was also founded in 1949. This initiated a period of relative political stability and ushered in a new stage of agricultural development.

TABLE 2.8 Evolution of Independence of Some African Countries

African Country	Independent from	Year	African Country	Independent from	Year
Sudan	UK and Egypt	1956	Gabon	France	1960
Morocco	France	1956	Mauritania	France	1960
Tunisia	France	1956	Sierra Leone	UK	1961
Ghana	UK	1957	Algeria	France	1962
Republic of Congo	Belgium	1958	Burundi	Belgium	1962
Somalia	Italy	1960	Rwanda	Belgium	1962
Nigeria	UK	1960	Uganda	UK	1962
Cameroon	France	1960	Kenya	UK	1963
Mali	France	1960	Malawi	UK	1964
Senegal	France	1960	Zambia	UK	1964
Madagascar	France	1960	Gambia	UK	1965
Togo	France	1960	Maldives	UK	1965
Niger	France	1960	Botswana	UK	1966
Democratic Republic of the Congo	Belgium	1960	Mauritius	UK	1968
Central Africa	France	1960	Mozambique	Portugal	1975
Chad	France	1960			

Source: Li *et al.* (2009)
Note: Egypt, Ethiopia and Liberia, which were nominally independent before the Second World War, are not included

China and some African countries took similar measures to promote agricultural development in the early days of independence, including land reform (many African countries echoed China's post-1949 experiences), agricultural cooperatives (Tanzania), communal agriculture (Mozambique) and so forth. These measures boosted the recovery and development of agricultural production. This was especially the case in Africa, where the fastest development in agriculture was seen during the period from independence to the mid-1970s.

Prior to the founding of the PRC, China had a landholding system dominated by a small landlord class and a strata of rich peasants. Most rural families had no land of their own and had to rent it from landlords or become farm labourers. The new government carried out land revolution all over the country, seizing lands from landlords and distributing them to poor peasants and farm labourers. This transformed rural power relations and the structure of agricultural production. By 1952 landless peasants had almost disappeared in China. Land reform enhanced agricultural productivity substantially and using a 1949 baseline, China's grain output increased by 17 per cent in 1950, 28 per cent in 1951, and 45 per cent in 1952, with an average annual growth rate of 15 per cent. The output of other agricultural crops in 1952 also exceeded those of the peak year before liberation.

At the initial period of their independence, African countries had different land ownership systems and therefore selected different approaches to land reform (Table 2.9). In the countries dominated by feudal land tenure systems where colonial plantations existed, the governments put land previously possessed by landlords into state ownership by means of nationalization without compensation, and divided land among landless rural people (or those with limited land). In Ethiopia farmers had to pay a price for land, which could be made in instalments. In countries where colonial plantations prevailed alongside tribal land ownership, or where most lands were possessed by small farmers and tribal chiefs alongside a colonial plantation economy, land reform was implemented principally through the establishment of a land tenure system, where customary tenure coexists alongside individual title – as in Kenya, for example (Gu, 1999).

China also launched an agricultural cooperative movement after land reform because a considerable number of peasants who had recently obtained lands were still poorly equipped with production equipment, and individual rural households remained unable to undertake farming on their own. Furthermore, forms of agricultural cooperative evolved from mutual aid teams to elementary cooperatives, to advanced cooperatives and then to people's communes. The agricultural co-operative movement in its early days produced positive impacts on China's agricultural production, with Gross Output Value of Agriculture index showing a constant upward trend during the period from 1952 to 1958. Using a 100 baseline for 1952, the Gross Agricultural Output Value index reached 127.8 in 1958 with a rise of 27.8 per cent from the base period, and consumption of grain per capita also increasing from 288kg in 1952 to 306kg in 1958 (Department of Planning of Ministry of Agriculture, 1949–1986). From an overall perspective it can be seen that China's agricultural production expanded sluggishly during the 1957–1978 period.

TABLE 2.9 Land Reforms in China and Some African Countries

Land Ownership before Reform	Country	Major Contents of Reform
Landlord-based system	China	Confiscating the lands previously owned by landlords and distributing them to rural landless and small farmers for free
Landlord-based system	Egypt, Tunisia, Algeria, Ethiopia	Confiscating and redeeming land, with a specified amount allotted to landlords and distributing the rest to rural landless and small farmers who had to pay in instalments
Owned by western migrants	Kenya, South Africa, Zimbabwe	Confiscating and redeeming land and distributing to rural landless and small farmers who had to pay relevant expenses
Tribal ownership	Guinea, Togo, Chad, Zambia, Cameroon, Tanzania, Uganda	Placing land into state ownership and distributing it to be cultivated by rural landless and small farmers

Source: Lu (2000)

The Gross Agricultural Output Value index and total grain output both increased in that period mainly due to the adoption of biotechnologies and mechanical technologies in agriculture, and the construction of water conservancy facilities on farmlands. According to statistics, the use of chemical fertilizers increased from 373,000 tonnes in 1957 to 8.84 million tonnes in 1978, and deployment of tractors increased from 14,674 units to almost 2 million units (Table 2.10). In addition, remarkable achievements were made in the construction of farmland water conservancy, as the area of effectively irrigated land increased from 27 million hectares to nearly 45 million hectares during the same period. Following the growing usage of chemical fertilizers, some high-yielding varieties of rice and wheat were widely adopted. According to the Ministry of Agriculture, in 1979 the uptake of improved varieties of rice, wheat, cotton and groundnut accounted for 80 per cent, 85 per cent, 75 per cent and 70 per cent of total cultivation areas, respectively.

The commune movement also contributed to a serious agricultural crisis lasting from 1959 to 1961 (caused by the 'Great Leap Forward' movement and serious natural disasters). Compared to 1958, the Gross Output Value of Agriculture index dropped by 33.7 per cent in 1961. Grain output was 200 million tonnes in 1958, down to 170 million tonnes in 1959 and dropped further to 148 million tonnes in 1961. Grain consumption per capita plummeted from 303kg in 1958 to 253kg in 1959, and 224kg in 1961.

Egypt was the first African country to engage in the agricultural cooperative movement, followed by Tunisia, Algeria and Morocco. Sub-Saharan African countries such as Ghana, Senegal, Tanzania, Guinea, Botswana, Mozambique,

TABLE 2.10 Agricultural Production during the Early Years of the PRC

Year	1957	1962	1965	1970	1975	1978	1980
Total area of crop cultivation (1,000 ha)	157,244	140,229	143,291	143,487	149,545	150,104	146,380
Gross Agricultural Output Value Index (1952 = 100)	124.8	101.6	132.9	163.6	179.4	191.3	203.6
Grain output (1 million tonnes)	19,505	15,441	19,453	23,996	28,452	30,447	32,056
Per-unit grain yield (kg/ha)	1,240	1,101	1,358	1,672	1,903	2,028	2,190
Fertilizer (10,000 tonnes)	37.3	63	194.2			884	
Tractor (unit)	14,674	55,857	75,564			1,930,538	
Area of effectively irrigated land (1,000 ha)	27,339	30,545				44,965	

Source: Rural–Social Economic Survey Team, National Bureau of Statistics of China, period 1949–2004

Democratic Republic of the Congo, Republic of Congo, Madagascar, Benin, Togo and Ethiopia also experimented with forms of agricultural cooperative after 1960. The clearest example was in Tanzania, which followed a collectivist policy known as *Ujamaa* (Ibhawoh, 2003). During this period, African countries increased agricultural investment and adjusted the structure of agricultural production with agricultural cooperatives as the instrument. Governments also created many initiatives such as providing seeds, pesticides and chemical fertilizers at favourable prices or for free to improve the effectiveness of land utilization, reclaim new farmland and encourage water conservancy facilities, so that the area of tillable fields increased from 154 million hectares in 1962 to 170 million hectares in 1980, with the area of irrigated fields increasing from 7 million hectares to 9 million hectares. The implementation of such pro-agriculture policies and measures resulted in the clear growth of agricultural production on the African continent in the 1960s, with the average annual growth rate reaching 2.7 per cent. Grain output also increased remarkably, thanks to the development of agricultural crop cultivation, which went up from 50 million tonnes at the beginning of the 1960s to 71 million tonnes in 1980, such that grain self-sufficiency was raised. According to the United Nations Food and Agriculture Organization (FAO), the grain self-sufficiency rate was 96 per cent during the 1962–1964 period, and 83 per cent during the 1972–1974 period.

BOX 2.1 ADJUSTMENT OF AGRICULTURAL PRODUCTION STRUCTURE IN AFRICAN COUNTRIES

Egypt

- total cotton planting area was 523,000 ha in 1980, down 31.6 per cent as against 1952
- rice planting area was 408,000 ha, up 72 per cent against 1952.

Côte d'Ivoire

- rice output was only 160,000 tonnes in 1960 and increased to 508,000 in 1980.

Tanzania

- sisal planting area was 451,000 hectares in the middle 1960s and reached 148,000 hectares in the late 1970s.

Source: Lu (2000)

TABLE 2.11 Africa's Agricultural Development during the Agricultural Cooperative Period

	1962	1965	1969–1971	1975	1978	1980
Tillable field (1,000 ha)	154,158	158,051	163,032	166,396	169,524	170,275
Irrigable area (1,000 ha)	7,384	7,770	8,434	8,943	9,117	9315.1
Tractor (10,000 sets)	33.13				42.80	
Gross Agricultural Output Value index	100				115	
Grain output (10,000 tonnes)	50.47 million tonnes on average		61.55 million tonnes on average			7,083
Chemical fertilizer application						313.07

Sources: FAOSTAT, Lu (2000)

African agriculture attained many achievements during this period as most peasants acquired lands of their own; cropping structures and agricultural production tended to become more diversified; and the adoption of new technologies and mechanization increased Africa's grain self-sufficiency ratio (Table 2.11). However, Africa's serious dependence on the export of cash crops did not change at all (Table 2.12). The agricultural development initiated and guided by the government stimulated farmers' enthusiasm for farming in the early days of independence; however, African countries failed to give support for sustainable agricultural development and shifted their focus to industry and other sectors. Agriculture was unable to offer a solid foundation for the development of industry and other sectors which, in turn, restricted the further development of agriculture. The severe drought in the mid-1970s was a heavy blow to Africa's economy, and to agricultural production in particular. Consequently, Africa's agriculture registered a growth rate of only 1.3 per cent from 1970 to 1977, which was less than one-half of 2.8 per cent, the average growth rate of all developing countries in the world (Zhuang, 1982).

In summary, African countries all made agriculture a development priority in order to revitalize their economies. A package of measures to realize the rapid development of agriculture were put in place to achieve the following:

- change land ownership from colonial ownership and state-owned land tenure to state ownership, redistributing and privatizing land;
- steer agricultural production through state power, with certain measures similar to the agricultural cooperative movement in China;
- government funding for infrastructure construction, agricultural subsidies and agricultural investments, resettlement for the purpose of promoting agricultural

TABLE 2.12 Africa's Shares in Global Market for Principle Crops, 1978

	Percentage of the World's Total Output	Percentage of the World's Exports
Sisal	47.1	46.7
Cotton	8.6	12.2
Peanut	27.4	37.6
Palm oil	33.4	–
Cashew	54.1	–
Sesame	26.7	47.5
Coffee	23.8	27.2
Cocoa	60.3	72.3
Tea	10.7	19.7
Cereals	4.49	Imports: 12 million tonnes

Source: Lu (2000)

development and rural development, and operation of state-owned farms through the confiscation of colonial plantations and construction of foreign-aided projects, so that the government could control the production of important cash crops and export crops; and

- boost the progress of agricultural science and technology with two foci – the cropping system and cultivation technologies aimed at improving grain self-sufficiency, and processing technology aimed at increasing export income.

Progress in science and technology in these two aspects facilitated the cultivation and dissemination of new crop varieties. However, this positive development trend was not maintained, and in the mid-1970s Africa's agricultural development began to stagnate at the same time as agriculture in other parts of the world stepped up a gear. Conditions worsened in the early 1980s. Meanwhile, although China's agricultural development had been dampened by the premature collective production system, it still retained a strong impetus on rapid development through government capital investment and wide application of Green Revolution technologies. The land reform carried out in 1978, which centred on the Household Responsibility System, further contributed to the stable and rapid development of China's agricultural production.

The Impact of Historical Factors on Current Agricultural Development in China and Africa

Analysis of the history of Chinese and African agricultural development reveals that the biggest difference between the development paths for Chinese and African agriculture was that Africa experienced external interventions that were profoundly disruptive. African economies became heavily reliant on the production of export-oriented cash crops alongside cropping systems based on drought-resistant local crops such as sorghum and millet, for which high-yielding cultivars had not been identified. However, China's agricultural civilization was not subject to the kind of disruptions that distorted African agricultural development. China was able to establish a complete agricultural production system which proved to be highly effective at increasing land productivity through applications of labour and technology. This had far-reaching significance for China's modern agricultural development.

China and Africa inherited different assets from their own histories of agricultural development. Although Africa boasted an advanced traditional agriculture, it suffered interruptions to agricultural development by the slave trade and western colonial domination. By 1914 the continent had been changed by Europe in many ways:

> [T]he traditional self-sufficient economy of the African people was destroyed and they no longer worked just for the sake of feeding themselves and their families. African people were increasingly involved in the global monetary economy and also came under the influence of global economic trends. This meant that there were dual impacts on Africa, on the one hand plunging the African people into the monetary economy of the new century and on the other hand keeping them under the control of white men, no matter where they were. (Stavrianos, 1999)

Central government and local officials in many African countries have a long tradition, stemming from colonial experience, with the latter methods of governance and little experience or knowledge of the former (Rondinelli *et al.*, 1989). This being the case, Africa's economic development was highly dependent: many African countries relied heavily on cash-crop planting and a management approach to exporting.

By contrast, the agricultural production system in China has not suffered from any interruptions or breakages akin to those in Africa (Table 2.13). From the inauguration of the Qin Dynasty in 221 BC to the termination of the Qing Dynasty in 1911, farm production based on feudal relations of production was the foundation of social and economic development. Due to separate land ownership and limited farmland resources, the development strategy of Chinese agriculture was designed to advance land productivity, especially cereal and fibre production, through fully cultivating land potential and increasing productivity unremittingly.

In China, specific measures such as rotation, fertilizer application and irrigation (where possible) for soil improvement and soil fertility maintenance were widely adopted by smallholders, so a consistent farming system comprising continuous cropping, multiple cropping, intercropping and relay intercropping was realized (Yin and Xu, 2004). These characteristics still influence China's modern agricultural development and can be understood as essential features of China's rapid agricultural development. It has been argued that the important reason underlying China's remarkable achievements in agriculture is its advanced agricultural science and technology knowledge system (Yin and Xu, 2004). This includes crop breeding,

TABLE 2.13 Comparison of Agricultural Development History in China and Africa

Stage	Africa	China
Origins of agricultural civilization	The origin of agriculture with many centres of agriculture appearing and a cropping structure dominated by sorghum and millet	The origin of agriculture with many centres of agriculture appearing and a cropping structure dominated by rice and wheat
Farming society before the sixteenth century	Agriculture developed rapidly with many agricultural development regions and basic agricultural structures established	Agriculture developed rapidly with many agricultural development regions and basic agricultural structures established
Sixteenth century– mid-twentieth century	Traditional agriculture was damaged, cash crops developed rapidly and gradually became the central pillar of many African economies	Agricultural production developed in a steady fashion, the mode of agricultural production remaining almost unchanged and focusing on the production of cereal crops, despite the predation of wars and disasters
1950–1975	Agricultural production recovered to a certain extent and was kept at a high level of development	Agricultural production began to expand, but the momentum of rapid development was dampened by some restrictive policies
1975–1985	Agricultural production came to a standstill, with sluggish agricultural growth and food security becoming an ever-pressing issue	China's agriculture stepped into a boom stage jointly driven by Green Revolution technologies and institutional innovation
1985–the present	Africa's political and economic situation changed for the better and agricultural development came back on track as development speed reached the level of the early years after independence, but food security remained a pressing issue	Agricultural development followed a stable upward trend and grain production remained the priority, promoted through macroeconomic policies

Source: Lu (2000)

land utilization, cropping system management, development of agricultural implements, appropriate fertilizer applications as well as agricultural science and technology dissemination. China has made significant advances in these areas throughout history, and all of them still play an important role in its agricultural development.

The Chinese began crop breeding at the time that crops began to be domesticated. The two main types of rice grown in China, indica rice and japonica rice, were both grown more than 6,000 years ago. During the Warring States Period, China had already formulated seed selection standards for the main cereal crops, and the single-spike selection method was adopted in the Han Dynasty (Table 2.14). So far, China has more than 40,000 rice varieties and more than 15,000 millet varieties, and still follows the tradition of selecting and breeding high-yield varieties. China was also the first country to successfully develop hybrid rice (J. Huang, 2008).

The second major achievement of Chinese agricultural development has been the improvement of land productivity through the development of intensive agriculture and measures such as land reclamation, water conservation facility construction, multiple cropping and improvements in field management (Table 2.15). As noted by the American economist D. H. Perkins (1969), the improved method of cultivation adopted by the Chinese during the period from the fourteenth century to the nineteenth century contributed significantly to increases in productivity. According to the American agronomist N. E. Borlaug (1979), Chinese people have completed one of the most important innovations in the world, namely: the 'dissemination of double-harvest and triple-harvest per year cultivation technologies'.

TABLE 2.14 History of Crop Breeding in Ancient China

Time	Main Measures
Over 6,000 years ago	Two different kinds of rice already being planted: indica rice and japonica rice
Zhou Dynasty (1046–256 BC)	Before the planting of crops, the seeds were selected grain by grain – only those with a bright colour and plump shape would pass the test
Warring States Period (c. 475–221 BC)	The Timing chapter (*Shen Shi*) of Lu's Spring and Autumn Annals (*Lu Shi Chun Qiu*) set out seed selection standards for six grain crops as standing grain: foxtail millet, grain millet, rice, hemp, beans and wheat
Han Dynasty (202 BC–AD 220)	The quality-based seed selection and seed reserve were documented. The *Book of Fansheng* (*Fan Sheng Zhi Shu*) recorded the single-spike selection method
Sixth century	*Important Arts for the People's Welfare* (*Qi Min Yao Shu*) gave a summary of fine-variety breeding technology similar to today's seedbed. The 'Seed Harvesting and Sowing' (*Shou Zhong*) chapter set out that foxtail millet, grain millet, broomcorn and sorghum should be harvested in a selective manner, and that spikes with good colour and shape should be reserved as seeds for next year's planting
Early Qing Dynasty (1644–1911)	The single-plant or single-spike selection method prevailed in sorting the fine varieties to be planted

Source: Yin and Xu (2004)

TABLE 2.15 Overview of Intensive Agriculture in Ancient China

Category	Agricultural Technology	Time Commenced
Expanding tillable field	Terraced land Land reclaimed from lakes Sandy land Improved saline alkali land Stony land	First century Han Dynasty (202 BC–AD 220) Tang Dynasty (618–907) n/a Ming and Qing Dynasties (1368–1644; 1644–1911)
Raising the multiple cropping index	Crop rotation Multiple-cropping system consisting of continuous cropping and crop rotation; the crop rotation of rice, wheat and beans with three harvests in two years along the reaches of the Yellow River, and crop rotation of rice and wheat with two harvests in one year along the reaches of the Yangtze River Two crops a year and three crops a year of rice Rapid development of intercropping and relay intercropping	Zhou Dynasty (1046–256 BC) Warring States Period (c. 475–221 BC) Song Dynasty (960–1279) Ming and Qing Dynasties
Fertilizing	Application of manure to crops and storage of moist farmyard dung; production of barnyard manure Placing manure on land and adoption of household manure and manure-spreading methods for soil improvement and fertilizer application, based on actual soil conditions Foot-treading compost production: methods to test that the manure is fully decomposed before being applied to crops. The methods of applying base fertilizer and additional fertilizer also recorded in detail Application of fertilizer should be in accordance with both crop and season The fertilizer shall be applied at the right season, on the right soil and to the right crops	Shang Dynasty (1600–1046 BC) Warring States Period Sixth century Twelfth century Eighteenth century
Constructing farmland water conservation	12 Canals of Zhang River in Hebei Dujiangyan Dam in Sichuan Zhengguo Canal on the Guanzhong Plain Pond irrigation works Pond-side enclosed land system	Warring States Period Third century BC Third century BC Warring States Period Tang Dynasty

TABLE 2.15 Continued

Category	Agricultural Technology	Time Commenced
	Seawall works	Five Dynasty and Ten Kingdoms Period (AD 907–960)
	Well irrigation	Over 4,000 years ago
Improving agricultural implements	Water intake facilities and machines: waterwheel	Eastern Han Dynasty (AD 25–220), Three Kingdoms Period (AD 220–280)
	Land tillage and levelling: iron plough	Western Han Dynasty (202 BC–AD 9)
	Seed sowing: animal-drawn seed plough	Western Han Dynasty
	Cultivation and weeding: iron hoe	Warring States Period
	Harvesting: sickle	Warring States Period

Source: Yin and Xu (2004)

In addition to improvements in the agricultural technology system, the dynasties throughout history all attached great importance to agricultural development, and their adherence to the development strategy of 'build the country through agriculture' produced positive impacts on China's agricultural development. When any dynasty in Chinese history was established, the rulers all carried out reforms of agricultural management and adopted compensatory measures so that agricultural production could recover from the destruction associated with the change in political power. China valued highly the dissemination of agricultural technology, even in ancient times (encouraging farming and sericulture). An emphasis on agricultural demonstration contributed to widespread dissemination of agricultural technologies (Table 2.16).

Ancient China's agricultural practices had positive impacts on modern China's agricultural development. Ancient China also made great advances in the documentation of agricultural technologies: there were a large number of agricultural books in the period; as many as 542 are listed in *A Bibliography of Chinese Agricultural Books*, 643 in *A Bibliography of Ancient Chinese Agricultural Books*, 243 in *Textual Research on Ancient Chinese Agricultural Books* and around 600 agricultural books and items listed in the citation index attached (Yin and Xu, 2004). All these texts played an important role in the development of agricultural technology (Table 2.17).

The development of agriculture in modern China has benefited from successful experiences throughout history (Liu, 2001). A diversified structure of agricultural production emerged which included the farming areas and grassland areas north and south of the Great Wall, dry farming and rain-fed farming south and north of the Huai River as well as transitional areas of grassland and crop fields from the east to the west (Li, 1993). This laid a solid foundation for today's agricultural development strategy, which seeks to improve land productivity through the Household Responsibility System.

TABLE 2.16 Ancient China's Agricultural Technology Dissemination System

Time	Measures
Zhou Dynasty (1046–256 BC)	Training of agricultural officials; establishment of a land ownership system; construction of farmland water conservation; classification of soil types and development of techniques for ploughing, sowing, planting and harvesting
Warring States Period (c. 475–221 BC)	Pre-Qin scholars, as recorded in agricultural books, all gave suggestions to policymakers on making agricultural production a priority and advocated farming and sericulture
Eastern Han Dynasty (AD 25–220) Western Han Dynasty (202 BC–AD 9)	The Imperial Decree of Agricultural Promotion (*Quan Nong Zhao*) was issued and demanded that farming and sericulture be important indicators of the performance of government officials at different levels
Tang Dynasty (618–907)	The central government had one agricultural promotion minister and two vice-ministers. The vice governors of province, prefecture and county were held responsible for advocating farming and sericulture, which also reached the village level, with every 100 households grouped in one community and one community chief (village junior officer) appointed for the allocation of farming and sericulture tasks to each household
Song Dynasty (960–1279)	The 'Essay on Agricultural Promotion' (*Quan Nong Wen*) was composed to advocate farming and sericulture. In some ways this is like today's publications on agricultural technology. It differed from other agricultural books in that it paid more attention to local farming conditions and was more compactly worded and shorter in size
Yuan Dynasty (1271–1368)	*Summary of Farming and Sericulture* (*Nong Sang Ji Yao*) was compiled and circulated nationwide
Ming and Qing Dynasties (1368–1644; 1644–1911)	Many unofficial agricultural technology promoters existed
1903	Zhang Zhidong formulated the Regulations of Schools (*Xue Tang Zhang Cheng*). After this period, China set up modern agricultural schools, experimental farms and other agricultural dissemination methods and organizations

Source: Yin and Xu (2004)

TABLE 2.17 Important Ancient Chinese Agricultural Literature Still in Existence

Time	Name of Book	Major Contents
Second century BC	The chapters 'Farming Commencement' (*Shang Nong*), 'Land Cultivation' (*Ren Di*), Soil 'Identification' (*Bian Tu*) and 'Timing' (*Shen Shi*) in Lu's *Springand Autumn Annals* (*Lu Shi Chun Qiu*)	Agricultural policies and experiences of agricultural production in pre-Qin times
Sixth century AD	*Important Arts for the Peoples Welfare* (*Qi Min Yao Shu*)	Dryland agricultural technology in north China
Seventh–ninth centuries	*Classics of Ploughs and Ploughshares* (*Lei Si Jing*)	Special topic on agricultural implements with an elaborate and correct description on the structure and function of every part of farming ploughs
Wu Zetian Period (690–705)	*The Agricultural Book for Common People* (*Zhao Ren Ben Ye*)	Dissemination of agricultural technology
End of Tang Dynasty–Five Dynasties (907–960)	*Essential Farm Activities in All Four Seasons* (*Si Shi Zuan Yao*)	Compiled and edited on a monthly basis with two items related to agriculture, including cropping and animal husbandry
1149	*Chen Fu's Book on Agriculture* (*Chen Fu Nong Shu*)	Discussion on the planting of rice and wheat and sericulture
Yuan Dynasty (1271–1368)	*Summary of Farming and Sericulture* (*Nong Sang Ji Yao*) *Agricultural Book* (*Nong Shu*)	A nationwide agricultural book with technical instructions Composed from the summary of dryland farming in the reaches of the Yellow River and rain-fed farming in Jiangnan
Seventeenth century	*Complete Treatise on Agricultural Administration* (*Nong Zheng Quan Shu*)	Discussion of the whole country's agricultural production with a focus on political measures to secure agricultural production, farmers' livelihood security, three basic agricultural policies of land reclamation, support for the armed forces, farmland water conservancy construction and famine preparation and relief
Eighteenth century	*A General Study on Issue: Almanac of Farming Activities* (*Shou Shi Tong Kao*)	An old-school agricultural book with relatively comprehensive contents

TABLE 2.17 Continued

Time	Name of Book	Major Contents
Eighteenth–nineteenth centuries	The chapter 'Rice Cultivation for Agricultural Promotion in Jiangnan' (*Jiang Nan Cui Geng Ke Dao Pian*) in *A Bibliography on Rainfed Farming* (*Ze Nong Yao Lu*), *Record of Facts on Agriculture* (*Nong Yan Zhu Shi*), *Farming Proverbs and Ballads in Mashou* (*Ma Shou Nong Yan*) and *Comprehensive Records of Customs at Bin* (*Bin Feng Guang Yi*)	Written in accordance with the demands and characteristics of local region

Source: Yin and Xu (2004)

Conclusion

It can be concluded from historical investigation that China and Africa are two of four centres of origin for world agriculture. Agriculture has always been of vital importance in the development of China and Africa.

First, there are several significant differences between the development paths taken in Chinese and African agriculture. These are that agricultural development in China has been relatively consistent without any destructive ruptures of agricultural civilization (several political movements have changed traditional practices in rural China, but has never turned the whole small farmer-based agricultural system upside down), whereas Africa's agricultural tradition was broken down and some agricultural production structures destroyed with colonization. After the independence of African countries, the governments carried out a package of measures to promote agricultural development. However, success was temporary and by the mid-1970s agricultural development in Africa had deteriorated again, due to the frequent occurrence of natural disasters and a heavy dependence on external forces. Another agricultural crisis occurred in the mid-1980s when other parts of the world embraced a surge of agricultural development linked to the Green Revolution. Despite the institutional restrictions on agricultural development, such as agricultural collectivization and the agricultural cooperative movement in the 1960s and 1970s, China remained involved in the Green Revolution through the adoption of new crop varieties and increased application of chemical fertilizer and pesticides. This meant that while the growth rate of agricultural development decreased somewhat, it still remained high. Institutional innovations since 1980 have given a new impetus to China's agricultural development, and this has been well sustained to date. African countries took a favourable turn for agricultural development after 1985, with supportive policies adopted by the international community and domestic governments, but political unrest at the beginning of the 1990s caused huge losses in agricultural production. By the late 1990s agricultural development in African countries had got back on track, but there were still many difficulties arising from historical legacies, institutional arrangements, government capacity and the international context. Some encouraging signs have been shown in Africa's agricultural development in the past few years: according to the FAO (2007b), the average growth rate of Africa's agriculture was 5 per cent in 2007, with that of North African countries reaching 7 per cent.

Second, China and Africa have inherited different agricultural assets as legacies of their own histories. In China, agriculture production always has been based on food crop planting, and the food crop varieties planted in China were the same as those promoted in the modern Green Revolution. Meanwhile, to date it has been nearly impossible for local varieties of key African food crops, or cash crops introduced by colonial powers, to benefit from the modern Green Revolution.

Third, modern agriculture in China and Africa has a historical basis, but in the case of China, traditional agricultural civilization offered a highly adaptable agricultural production system and structure and cultivation methods. China's agricultural development focused on increasing land productivity by intensive land and technology inputs instead of capital inputs. This continues to be well-suited to the realities of modern China, and is also the foundation of smallholder agriculture in most of the countryside. Traditional agricultural civilization in Africa was interrupted by the incursions of European countries. The agricultural production structure was altered by colonialism such that the traditional small farmer economy, focused on cereal planting, could no longer meet the requirements of food security on the African continent. At the same time, capital-intensive plantation operations focusing on the production of cash crops could not create effective employment opportunities. This situation still shapes the development of African agriculture.

Fourth, land reclamation always has been an important way for the Chinese to develop agriculture. While large-scale land reclamation starting in the seventeenth century has provided food security to an expanding population effectively, inevitably it has occupied a variety of land including forests, grassland and wetlands and, in the process, posed a serious challenge to sustainable agricultural development. Worse still, arable land utilization in China has reached saturation point. Therefore, it is a great challenge for China to ensure effective and ample arable land for its future agricultural development amid accelerated urbanization and industrialization. In Africa, most countries have not fully utilized their arable land, and the proportion of cultivated to cultivatable land is relatively low – even less than 50 per cent in some countries. This means that there is enormous potential for agricultural development in many countries.

3

COMPARISON OF STRATEGIES AND POLICIES FOR THE DEVELOPMENT OF AGRICULTURE IN CHINA AND AFRICA

Alongside historical heritage, agricultural strategies and policies can be considered to be one of the important factors contributing to China's significant achievements in agriculture development. 'China's agriculture relies both on policies and technologies' (Deng, 1982: 22). This chapter will compare the strategies and policies for the development of agriculture in China and Africa. These strategies include strategic considerations, specific policies and implementation measures.

Strategic Considerations of Agriculture Policies: China

Agriculture has been the foundation of the state and basis for development throughout the history of China. Attention to the agricultural development and protection of agricultural production in China have been deep-rooted national concerns for a long time. Agricultural development was also the basis for industrialization in China after 1949. Agriculture was the foundation that guaranteed the preferential development of heavy industries, military capacity and subsequently light industry. However, periods of excessive politicization at times caused agricultural policies to deviate from real conditions and development goals. The gap between policies and real conditions distorted the objectives of agricultural production instead of encouraging real productivity improvements, causing imbalances in the internal structure of agriculture and damage to agricultural education. One consequence of this was that market reforms in China originated from rural areas.

At the end of 1978, 18 households in Xiaogang village, Fengyang County in Anhui Province secretly signed the Agricultural Products Contract, making it clear that after deducting enough for the country and the collective, surplus production would be kept by the farmers themselves. China's reforms began from this point. This innovation starting from the bottom-up has become the basic principle for the country in improving its governing efficiency, and has evolved into a reform with a market orientation guided by the government. The next five No. 1 Documents (the first document issued by the central government every year to highlight the focus of its annual mission) defined clear directions for countrywide reforms.[1] In this century, Chinese agriculture has maintained a good development momentum. The percentage of agricultural gross domestic product (GDP) in gross national product (GNP) has been decreasing, while its gross amount is continuously increasing. With gross grain output steadily increasing, the foundational role of agriculture remains unchanged. In addition, agricultural fiscal expenditure is increasing. In accordance with the general development goal in this phase, which is to build a harmonious society reflecting the socio-economic vision of Chinese leader Hu Jintao's signature ideology of the Scientific Development Concept, the focus of the agricultural development strategy has shifted from an exclusive emphasis on increasing grain production to promotion of a more multifaceted agriculture.

Seven No. 1 documents were issued consecutively from 2004 to 2010 (Box 3.1).

BOX 3.1 THE NO. 1 DOCUMENTS IN THE NEW MILLENNIUM

1982 – defined 'fixing production quotas on an individual household basis' and the 'work contracted to households' system to form a socialist economy; both to be encouraged across China.

1983 – specified the institutional reform of the commune.

1984 – emphasized the development of rural commodity production.

1985 – cancelled the unified and fixed state purchase system for agricultural and other products which had been implemented for more than 30 years.

1986 – reaffirmed the direction of rural reforms.

1987 – publication ceased for 17 years.

2004 – addressed the problem of increasing farmer income by the promotion of three subsidy policies.

2005 – addressed problems of improving general agricultural production capabilities.

2006 – addressed problems occurring during the construction of the New Socialist Countryside.

2007 – dealt with modern agricultural development problems.

2008 – dealt with strengthening agricultural infrastructure.

2009 – dealt with how to sustainably increase farmer income and secure national food security, with a series of policies enacted focusing on stabilizing grain output, increasing income, strengthening infrastructure and supporting livelihoods.

2010 – called for greater efforts to coordinate development between urban and rural areas, stressing that the agriculture sector will see a sustained increase in the volume of inputs and a steady rise in the proportion of the country's overall fiscal spending.

In Africa, the oil crisis and rising fuel costs and deterioration of trade conditions meant that agricultural production began to decline in most countries from the late 1970s. The new changes to world trade patterns brought about by the conclusion of the Cold War in the 1980s weakened Africa's position as a material exporting country. In addition, political conflict, climate impact and severe agricultural crises swept across Africa and shocked the world in the 1980s. Facing this situation, African countries and the international community carried out a series of measures to promote the revival of agriculture in Africa. During this period, most African countries experienced a complete shift in their development paradigm. They began to initiate structural adjustment[2] plans promoted by the World Bank and International Monetary Fund (IMF) with an emphasis on reducing the role of government and expanding market forces. Because African countries had their own political economies and agendas for the future of Africa, it was difficult to avoid conflict with the guidelines of donors and development agencies.

Taking the foundation role of agriculture as an example, the realization of grain self-sufficiency as a primary policy target would dramatically reduce grain exports and promote domestic grain production and consumption. This was brought forward for the first time in the Lagos Plan of Action in 1980. This plan also stressed that 'agricultural sectors must provide necessary inputs for processing industries and markets for domestic products from industrial sectors', and suggested that 'over the period 1980 to 1985 the objective should be to bring about immediate improvement in the food situation and to lay the foundations for the achievement of self sufficiency in cereals and in livestock and fish products' (Organization of African Unity, 1980: 8). However, the World Bank's Berg Report (1981) stressed export-oriented development strategies, arguing that export crops should be developed as a priority. The African Priority Programme for Economic Recovery (1986–1990), being adopted by the Assembly of Heads of State and Government of the Organization of African Unity in 1985, lay considerable emphasis on the agricultural sector, which would amount to 44.8 per cent of the total cost of implementing the Programme. In 1989, the African Resolution for Replacing Structural Adjustment Plans was formulated to achieve the following reforms in agriculture:

1   in terms of fund allocation and policy setting, the emphasis should be on grains and increasing agricultural production and employment opportunities, taking into account efficiency and equity;
2   establishing sustainable strategic grain reserves to guarantee and stabilize minimum food prices;
3   implementing policies such as selective subsidies and price control policies to ensure commodity supply for maintaining social stability;
4   ensuring infrastructure and production investment;
5   gradually establishing and strengthening all kinds of agriculture support systems such as the grain production credit system and agricultural services system.

In 1986 the United Nations Food and Agriculture Organization (FAO) brought forward specific reform measures covering four aspects of African agriculture in the next 25 years:

1   placing agriculture in a more highly prioritized position and carrying out internal reforms of the national economy;
2   improving factors that limited the development of agriculture;
3   implementing natural resource protection strategies; and
4   improving the external economic environment.

Structural adjustment was promoted across Africa, but the results were not encouraging (Box 3.2). Naiman and Watkins (1999), among others, pointed out that 'countries in Africa subject to ESAF programs have actually seen their per capita incomes decline'. From 1980 to 1992, average annual growth of GNP per capita in Sub-Saharan Africa was −0.8 per cent (World Bank, 1994). For Sub-Saharan Africa, debt rose as a share of GDP from 58 per cent in 1988 to 70 per cent in 1996 (Naiman and Watkins, 1999). The undesirable outcomes of reforms triggered the need for social and political reforms in Africa, and the appropriate role of the state became central to the debate. African countries initiated democratization processes which were characterized by multiparty systems and parliamentary democracy, especially after the issuance of the World Bank report: *Sub-Sahara Africa: From Crisis to Sustainable Growth* (1989).

BOX 3.2 STRUCTURAL ADJUSTMENT IN AFRICAN COUNTRIES

Tanzania

Tanzania featured the *Ujamaa* movement following the socialist path. Through the *Ujamaa* Village Bill 1975, all private enterprises in rural areas were confiscated. Structural adjustment policy reforms began in the 1980s with the National Economy Security Plan in 1981. Tanzania initiated a Structural Adjustment Plan that lasted three years from 1983, hoping to reach the economic output level of that before the crisis in 1978. In 1984, the Human Resources Development Act was passed to encourage youth employment in non-agricultural sectors as a way to control the rising rate of unemployment. Subsequently, the Economic Recovery Programme, held jointly with the IMF in 1986, and the Economic and Social Action Plan further promoted market reforms. Since the mid-1990s, government policy reforms began to concentrate more on poverty reduction strategy plans, with a national investment strategy issued in 1990. Moreover, the National Land Policy issued in 1995, the Agriculture and Livestock Breeding Policy issued in 1997 and the Law on Plant Protection 1997 were focused on attracting and increasing investment, improving system capacity building and strengthening the influence of the private sector.

Senegal

Senegal had experienced severe grain shortage problems caused by the value of agricultural output decreasing in the 1980s. Due to the long-implemented semi-industrialization development strategy and a tradition in the agricultural sector of concentrating on economic crops and neglecting grain production, Senegal suffered from unprecedented famine and hunger, which triggered a series of economic reforms starting with the agricultural sector. A new agricultural policy was announced in 1984 and implemented in 1985. The Senegalese President, Jacques Diouf, believed that agriculture should be the foundation of the national economy and that 'no real independence' could be achieved without being self-sufficient in agriculture (quoted in Xiang, 1987).

Malawi

Malawi has been following principles to develop its economy based on agriculture since 1964. President Hastings Banda concentrated on building the country's infrastructure and increasing agricultural productivity, arguing: 'We have no minerals. The soil is our goldmine.' To strengthen leadership in the agricultural sector, President Banda also served as the agricultural minister after assuming the office of president. Under his leadership, Malawi not only strengthened self-sufficiency in agriculture, but also had a net gain from foreign currency. This period was labelled the 'Malawi Miracle' and gained considerable attention (Wang, 1988).

Côte d'Ivoire

Côte d'Ivoire enacted three-year agricultural development plans for 1989–1990 in 1987 and a long-range plan, aiming to achieve a 4 per cent annual average increase in its gross agricultural production and grain self-sufficiency (particularly for rice). This was intended to make Côte d'Ivoire a granary for West Africa, with grain exported to neighbouring countries. Therefore, the existing export structure, which was heavily dependent on cocoa and coffee, was adjusted to promote the export of grain and new economic crops.

Considering the results of market reform, some researchers (Jayne *et al.*, 2002) suggested that this premise was incorrect. They do not think that some countries implemented reform in the 1990s in reality; furthermore, they think that the most difficult part of improving agricultural markets is not necessarily the technical aspect of identifying appropriate institutional and infrastructure investments to overcome market failure; rather, it is developing the incentives for governments to deliver such investments after being identified. The governments in most countries did not provide market supportive investment when it was needed, so government support is an essential condition during privatization reform, which can be further proved by China's government supporting input and the food market after 1978, and the case of Malawi after 2005.

Compared with China, Africa is still facing severe food security issues, even in the new millennium. Now, agricultural development strategies for Africa are beginning to deal with the conditions that restrict the development of agriculture, food security being the priority. The agricultural sector's functions have been expanded to social fields such as poverty reduction. In the meantime, agricultural development issues are considered in broader international political and economic schemes (Box 3.3).

BOX 3.3 AGRICULTURAL STRATEGIES IN AFRICA SINCE THE NEW MILLENNIUM

Serving as the general strategic blueprint for Africa's economic development, the New Partnership for Africa's Development (NEPAD) programme emphasizes the importance of agricultural development, which is known as the 'engine for economic growth of Africa'. NEPAD identifies four pillars for Africa's agricultural development:

1 land and water management;
2 rural infrastructure and trade-related capacities for improved market access;
3 increasing food supply and reducing hunger; and
4 agricultural research, technology dissemination and adoption.

By 2015, the agricultural development goal of Africa should include the following strategies:

- attain food security (in terms of both availability and affordability and ensuring access of the poor to adequate food and nutrition);
- improve agricultural productivity to attain an average annual growth rate of 6 per cent, with particular attention to small-scale farmers and especially focusing on women;
- have dynamic agricultural markets among nations and between regions;
- have integrated farmers into the market economy, including better access to markets, with Africa to become a net exporter of agricultural products;
- achieve more equitable distribution of wealth;
- be a strategic player in agricultural science and technology development; and
- practise environmentally sound production methods, and have a culture of sustainable management of the natural resource base (including biological resources for food and agriculture) to avoid their degradation.

Donors are also taking action, represented by the World Bank and IMF. According to the World Bank (2008), it is important to make agricultural development work for poverty reduction and growth in transforming countries, especially for Sub-Saharan African states. After the series of economic reforms driven by donors and Sub-Saharan African countries themselves, it is even more important to enable the voice of small farmers to be heard in the processes of democratization, privatization, marketization and decentralization.

Agricultural strategy reforms in Africa over the last ten years have been increasingly based on the premise that both external pressures and domestic policy mistakes have contributed to poor agricultural development records. Therefore, new strategies should focus on both external and internal factors (Shu, 2005). Nevertheless, key reforms in the 1980s and in the new millennium have been driven largely by external forces. External donors have ignored the key factors that determine agricultural investment and growth, such as domestic policy, export orientation, rural infrastructure and local governance. In the main, African countries have not been successful when transferring policies from state and semi-state agricultural development projects to the private sector (World Bank Independent Evaluation Group, 2011).

It can be seen that reforms in China since 2003 have continued and deepened the reforms begun in the 1980s. These reforms contained a variety of measures beneficial to farmers, and include current incentives for industry to support agriculture. While emphasizing food security and maintaining 1.8 billion mu (equivalent to 0.12 billion hectares) of arable land, reforms have expanded to other aspects of agricultural production. The focus of recent large-scale agricultural projects initiated in China has been the transformation of traditional production, storage and research and development (R&D) projects to integrate social development projects which are part of the New Rural Construction policy. Discussions on issues of agriculture, farmers and rural areas ('*San Nong*') have switched from the 'Two Leaps'[3] of the Mao Zedong era to 'Two Transfers' (2008). Two Transfers requires household operations to shift to the application of advanced technologies and capital, leading to more intensive production. Farmer cooperatives are also encouraged, along with the creation of a diverse and multi-tiered agricultural service system. It should be pointed out that the formulation of agricultural strategies in China is endogenous and involves constant iterations between central levels of government and the grass roots. This process is supported by the administrative structure, which guarantees institutional support and human resource inputs.

In comparison, some African countries (such as Malawi) have adopted similar measures to those of China and yielded agricultural production increase. High maize production was attributed to subsidised fertilizer which was sold to farmers at MWK950 (about USD6.50) per 50kg bag in 2007; in 2004 the price was around MWK4,000 [about USD27] per 50kg bag (Humanitarian News and Analysis, 2008; Juma, 2011). African governments were unable to intervene or regulate liberalized markets on the basis of either efficiency or justice. The majority of countries were still highly dependent on foreign aid, with donors often encouraging a key role for non-governmental organizations (NGOs) in aid delivery. Abugre (nd) notes that partnership is at the centre of the so-called new agenda for development assistance: central to this new agenda is a framework where civil society organizations (including, but not restricted to, non-governmental organizations) are expected to work in partnership with participatory and accountable governments as the only means of ensuring and sustaining participatory, equitable and sustainable development (Hearn, 2001). Governments have tried to promote the development of agriculture through supportive policies such as macroeconomic reform, trade liberalization, taxation reform and appropriate land policies (Crees, 2000). However, the effects of such measures on activity in rural areas have been limited, especially for small farmers. Summarizing agricultural development in Africa in the last century, Delgado (1995) notes that the socialist planning models of the 1950s have given way to market liberalization strategies (Figure 3.1). Furthermore, the equation between growth and development as objectives in the 1960s has shifted to more general policy concern with the fate of the poor. However, governments have lacked the policy tools to address poverty issues arising from the new growth paradigms being adopted. This meant that it was not possible to stop an agricultural crisis from happening in Africa (Yao, 2002).

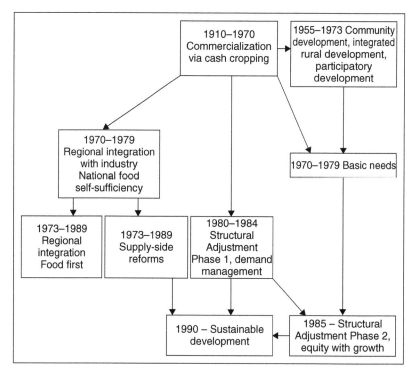

Figure 3.1 Dominant Paradigms for Agricultural Development in Africa

Source: Delgado (1995)

Reforms undertaken in Africa have been inadequate to fully address the challenges of development. Policymakers are unable to create incentives for farmers within adequate supportive frameworks. Compared with the situation more than 20 years ago, not only has Africa not achieved substantial economic growth, but some stagnation and even regression is evident, and Africa's peripheral position in the global economy remains unchanged (Box 3.4).

BOX 3.4 ADJUSTMENTS IN AGRICULTURAL STRATEGIES IN AFRICAN COUNTRIES SINCE THE NEW MILLENNIUM

Liberia

In Liberia, a draft of the Food and Agricultural Policy Strategy (developed within the broader context of the Poverty Reduction Strategy) was announced in 2008, to:

- identify strategic options and sources of poverty-reducing growth for the agricultural sector between then and 2015;
- develop existing and new strategic analysis and knowledge support systems to facilitate mutual review, dialogue and evidence-based planning and implementation of agricultural sector policies and strategies; and
- improve food security through capacity-building and investment to enhance productivity.

Malawi

In 2005, Malawi's agricultural sector employed 78 per cent of the labour force, more than half of whom operated below the subsistence level. Maize is Malawi's principal crop and source of nutrition, but for decades low rainfall, nutrient-depleted soil, inadequate investment, failed privatization policies and deficient technology have led to low productivity and high prices. The 2005 season yielded just over half of the maize required domestically, leaving 5 million Malawians in need of food aid. The president, Bingu wa Mutharika, declared food insecurity his personal priority and set out to achieve self-sufficiency and reduce poverty. The president took charge of the Ministry of Agriculture and Nutrition and initiated a systematic analysis of the problem and potential solutions. After a rigorous assessment, the government designed a programme to import improved seeds and fertilizer for distribution to farmers at subsidized prices through coupons. This ambitious programme required considerable financial, political and public support. The president engaged in debate and consultation with Malawi's parliament, private sector and civil society, while countering criticism from influential institutions. With support increasing and the ranks of the hungry swelling, the president devoted approximately USD50 million in discretionary funds and some international sources to forge ahead with the programme (Juma, 2011). Extraction of surplus through market channels which perpetuated poverty within the subsistence economy was the order of the day (United Nations Capital Development Fund (UNCDF), 2008).

Tanzania

The goals of Tanzania's Agricultural Sector Development Strategy in 2001 were to achieve modernization, commercialization and high-efficiency production in the agricultural sector by 2025. Natural resources were to be sustainably utilized to make the agricultural sector an effective foundation for cross-sectoral development. The goals of the Agricultural Sectors Development Projects in 2006 were to ensure that farmers could attain and utilize better agricultural knowledge, technologies, market and infrastructure to improve productivity, profitability and income. In addition, reform of policies and regulations to promote private investment has been important. In the National Strategy for Growth and Poverty Reduction for Tanzania, the operational goals for agriculture were to:

- increase grain output to 12 million tonnes by 2010 from 9 million tonnes in 2004;
- maintain at least four months' strategic grain reserve;
- increase the agricultural growth rate to 7 per cent by 2010 from 5 per cent in 2003;
- increase irrigation facilities;
- expand the area under irrigation, improve water utilization efficiency and encourage application of low-cost technologies; and
- provide more training on the safe utilization and storage of agricultural chemicals along with the application of pest management, ecological agriculture technologies and traditional knowledge.

Zambia

As indicated in the National Agricultural Policy (2004–2015), the overall objective of Zambia's agricultural policy is to promote the sustainable and competitive development of the agricultural sector to ensure national and household food security and maximize the agriculture sector's contribution to GDP. Specific goals include the following:

- provide sufficient basic food at competitive prices through production and post-harvest management for the whole year in order to ensure national and household food security;
- contribute to the sustainable development of industries by providing raw materials derived from agriculture;
- promote agricultural exports in order to increase the agricultural sector's contribution to the national balance of trade;
- improve agricultural productivity and increase income and employment by promoting agricultural production; and
- ensure that current agricultural resources are maintained and improved.

In the meantime, the administrative organizational structure of the agriculture sector is under adjustment. The National Decentralization Policy in 2004 decentralized national agriculture extension services to local authorities from the National Agriculture and Cooperation Department.

Uganda

In February 2005 the Ugandan government passed the budget for the 2005–2006 fiscal year, covering mid-term planning for rural development. The following measures were brought forward to develop agriculture:

- increase agricultural consultancy services and the range of subjects covered (expand to 37 regions from 29);
- strengthen agriculture research and implement a nationwide agricultural research system;
- strengthen the extermination of disease and insect pests for crops and livestock;
- improve management services and quality of supervision of crops, livestock and fisheries;
- restore and develop key infrastructure, with a focus on restoring the irrigation system, fisheries construction, dam construction and quarantine station construction;
- study food storage systems;
- establish and implement an agricultural statistics system; and
- guarantee provision of agricultural investment and technologies accessible to farmers.

Key Areas of Agricultural Policy

China and Africa are different in many respects, but several policy objectives for agriculture have been very similar. However, detailed implementation measures and instruments have been quite different. Yao (2008) argues that the centralization of state power in China's administrative system is able to reduce the cost of reform by avoiding prolonged debates about the change associated with democratic political systems. Following independence, many African states have spent a majority of their time involved in scrambling for power (Wade, 2008). Importantly, frequent regime changes associated with external and donor pressure for democratization have led to a lack of continuity in policy implementation.

Agricultural Land System

The quality and quantities of land in Africa and China are totally different, and this has led to the evolution of different land utilization patterns and land management institutions. In China, land is a scarce resource. Dynastic rulers all used land reform as a major strategy for consolidation of their regimes, and land distribution was always an issue in peasant uprisings. In Africa, with plentiful land and extensive agricultural production systems, there has never been an urgent need to establish or improve land surveys, land registration and land management systems as in ancient China.

Since the People's Republic of China (PRC) was founded in 1949, there have been three land reforms to establish socialist public ownership: the first is the Household Responsibility System and the Classification Management System (based on different utilization purposes). By the end of 1983, about 98 per cent of basic accounting units were contracted to households, and the household contracted land area accounted for 97 per cent of total arable land. This model guaranteed households' independent land management rights based on collective ownership and allocation of access to rural land. The core of the All-Round Responsibility System established in 1978 was to end the principle of free and unlimited usage of land to one of limited usage of land with compensation. This reform broke the singular administrative allocation system and established a new system for land allocation based on the market. In order to stabilize land contract relations and protect farmers' long-term cultivation rights, a second reform announced in the Measurements of Policies on Agricultural and Rural Economic Development by the Community Party of China and State Council on 5 November 1993 was enacted, which allowed for the renewal of land contracts and guaranteed the usage of land for 30 years. The third reform started from 2008, which confirmed full land ownership for the farmers' household including rights of use, and transfer of land use rights and operation. Current policy has established a limited land market.

Land and labour are the most important inputs for agricultural production in China, the unique feature being the registration system, which entitles rural residents to a rural land allocation. Although this residency system, which in the past has prevented people classified as rural from moving to cities, is subject to constant reform and change, rural residency remains the basis of land allocation in the countryside.

Scarce land resources and a relative labour surplus are the basic determinants of China's land tenure and registration system. During the early years of the PRC privatization was not an effective strategy, given the scattered nature of agricultural operations: in order to achieve economies of scale, collective forms of land owner-ship made more sense. The cooperative movement organized rural labour to produce a surplus from agricultural production to contribute to industrial accumu-lation. However, the separation of ownership and use rights put limits on the extent of economic benefits enjoyed by smallholders. Rural labour was tied to the land through the registration system, and smallholders could only improve land produc-tivity through labour input because they were unable to finance additional technical input. This approach accelerated the recovery and development of agriculture in the 1950s and 1960s. However, incentives for farm households to invest in production were limited. The current Household Responsibility System addresses this problem of incentives, by giving land use rights to farmers.

Compared to China, Africa has not had such an urgent need to advance land productivity. After independence, African countries set up new land policies, but these reforms and subsequent adjustments and redistribution have not fundamentally altered traditional land ownership patterns in many places. Land ownership systems in Africa are more complicated than China due to factors such as tribalism and colonial history. Havnevik *et al.* (2007) illustrates how Africa has been characterized by a range of farming systems with multiple forms of tenure, including private landholding with freehold title deeds, communal public lands under customary tenure, and state-held land, where the state retains legal ownership but with various forms of household tenure based on either leaseholds or permit systems – all under-pinned by complex legal and administrative systems.

Usually, the state bureaucracy plays a significant role in rural land administration, with traditional leaders being provided with limited responsibilities over land management and people in areas where usufruct rights to the land are still practised. The World Bank (2007) revealed that in many African countries, most of the lands are legally state-owned, which means that land ownership rights of those cultivating land are not secure and may only be valid for a limited period. Bruce *et al.* (1994) observed that the majority of land in Africa was still controlled by village chiefs, although farmers have ownership rather than use rights. Market liberalization and democratization polices have not affected the traditional land management system. Land titling processes are slow and difficult. Traditional tenure systems are coming under stress in many countries, as pressure on resources grows – especially where the value of the resource is increasing rapidly and where there is migration in response to population pressure, environmental degradation or conflict (Box 3.5).

BOX 3.5 LAND SYSTEMS IN AFRICAN COUNTRIES

Almost all African countries claim that their land reforms are designed to promote poverty reduction, equity, employment and improved systems of land ownership.

South Africa

The goals of land reform in South Africa are 'to reduce population density in the former homeland areas, to create employment opportunities for the rural population, to improve nutrition and to increase income'.

Zimbabwe

In Zimbabwe the goal is 'to alleviate the poverty of rural families and agricultural labourers and to achieve domestic food self-sufficiency'.

Ethiopia

The aim of land redistribution in northern Ethiopia is to ensure that everyone owns land, but there is a tension with economic efficiency, given the small size of farm plots (Havnevik *et al.*, 2007). Sometimes these land goals are not well integrated into general development strategies, therefore land redistribution is not linked with provision of infrastructure, services and other investments to jointly improve land productivity and build sustainable livelihoods for rural families.

Guinea Bissau

There is a lack of land policies and regulations in Guinea Bissau, and land is almost entirely privately owned, however land-users do not pay land-holding taxes to the government. The Guinean government is now taking measures to strengthen the management of territorial resources, and is planning to reclaim land nationwide to be allocated for proper development and usage by the state.

Zambia

Land ownership in Zambia is subject to customary tenure and formal property ownership. Under customary rules, chiefs are responsible for land allocation through village headmen. Chiefs can apply for transition of state land according to traditional methods first, and formal land ownership confirmation procedures are conducted later. In the formal land ownership system, regional or municipal authorities must announce land ownership to the public, and the successful applicants receive a map of the land and a land qualification certificate: the president then approves the land ownership application and grant the applicants a land ownership certificate (source: field investigation).

Liberia

There are neither appropriate land utilization plans nor mechanisms in Liberia, nor descriptions of the location and usage of each area of land (source: field investigation).

Due to unstable land ownership arrangements and conflicts, 'landless farmers' also exist in Africa. Currently, about one-fifth of the fallow land in the world is in Africa.[4] However, population densities in some areas of Africa are very high and the populations supported are near feasible limits, given current agricultural technologies and soil fertility status. The difference between China and Africa is that land losses in China are linked with processes of modernization and urbanization, but in Africa loss of land is linked mostly to unclear land ownership, lack of protection of land rights, and processes of land concentration reflecting unequal power between different actors. Although small farmers can use each acre of land more equally and effectively, large farmers or businesses are more likely to benefit from preferential policies from the government. Hence, small-scale farmers in many settings are often highly vulnerable to loss of land. An increasing number of farmers are losing their lands in countries such as South Africa, Zimbabwe, Kenya, Côte d'Ivoire, Burundi and Namibia.[5] Food insecurity can drive small-scale farmers to expand the agricultural frontier into forest and other fragile areas associated with limited rainfall and degraded soil. While small-scale farmers are barely making a living on small land areas, large households and foreign investors can create higher economic value that does not even require them to utilize their land fully. For example, rural areas in Rwanda are extremely crowded and farmers have to cultivate sloping fields without proper technologies to conserve soil and water (Havnevik et al., 2007). African governments hope to diversify agricultural production by encouraging private enterprise and foreign investors, but they do not have the political will to challenge large commercial land-holders. With large-scale households being provided with more support and protection, small-scale farmer demands on land redistribution have been neglected; meanwhile, customary land ownership arrangements have become less secure.

Land ownership issues have been problematic in many African countries since at least the colonial period. In countries such as South Africa, Namibia, Malawi, Kenya and Zimbabwe, land ownership conflicts and disparities originating from colonial times are severe, contributing to rural poverty and political unrest. From 1994 to 1995, the tense situation in northern Ghana linked to land finally led to racial conflict; the same situation happened in the Lake Tana region of Kenya in 2001. Land issues contributed to the civil war and genocide in Rwanda. Côte d'Ivoire and Zimbabwe have also witnessed riots and land conflicts (Havnevik *et al.*, 2007). In Africa, land struggles are not only limited to farmers, but also to those who do not own land, including agricultural labourers, unemployed miners, industrial and urban workers and even middle-income people and rich farmers.

Land ownership, allocation, utilization and management have a direct impact on agricultural development in Africa (Box 3.6). With land often subject to competing claims which can result in conflict, agricultural productivity in many areas has remained at a low level. Land certification and ownership determination processes have triggered land disputes which impact negatively on land productivity. For example, in Uganda lands that are subject to dispute are one-third less productive than those without dispute (World Bank, 2007).

BOX 3.6 THE NEW LAND LAW AND SMALL FARM LIVELIHOODS IN MOZAMBIQUE

The majority of people in Mozambique live in rural areas and are reliant on farming for their livelihoods. Land is perhaps the most important resource available to the poor. The Land Law was passed in 1997 to ensure that Mozambique's people are able to use land fairly and securely. However, several years later the law is still not well known in many rural communities. This has led to unfair deals and conflict between tenants and landowners. The Department for International Development (DFID) supports a project – the Community Lands Initiative – which aims to ensure wide implementation of land law. Under the 1997 law, land in Mozambique is still owned by the state and cannot be bought or sold; however, the law does recognize the rights of people and communities to use the land and sell assets on it (source: DFID website).

Mozambique's recent Poverty Reduction Strategy Paper (PARPA 2005–2009) establishes targets for the sustainable and equitable management of natural resources including land, with the explicit aim of improving the livelihoods of the rural poor.

Land tenure reform in China and African countries is also related to marketization, liberalization and poverty reduction for disadvantaged groups. China has alleviated lower labour productivity by land reform, paying attention to both equity and efficiency. Some African countries are moving faster than China in terms of land transformation and investment. This is consistent with unbalanced economic development patterns and dependence on foreign aid and investment. In China, 'arable land for farming' and 'farmers use farming land' are principles that have been guaranteed through land reform. This made farmer use rights stable and encouraged farmers to invest in farmland or transform land appropriately. Certainly, China and African countries are still facing some issues in relation to land reform, especially the separation of land ownership and use rights, as well as 'land grabbing' or land deals.

Differences in land tenure between China and African countries are based on different resource profiles or factor endowments. Due to scarce land resources, China has implemented land reform based on equity, which improved land productivity and ensured food security (see Chapter 1). However, labour productivity in China is much lower than in many African countries. A new round of land tenure reform in China has made land a real production factor that can go into the market, while the stable land contracting relationship over the long term has stimulated per-capita agricultural GDP growth (see Figure 1.3). Relatively abundant land resources in Africa ensure higher land productivity with low use rates, so there are not the same pressures or incentives for African countries to fully solve land tenure problems.

Agricultural Taxation Policy

Taxation policy always has been deeply embedded in land policies throughout Chinese history. The integrated land tenure system and land-based residency system were used as a taxation base. In African history, there were also some kinds of taxation policy based on land holding by tribes, but they were more like tributes in ancient China: namely, a payment given to a feudal overlord instead of a sophisticated, well-established tax assessment and collection system. African countries never built up a high centralized taxation system in the same way that China did.

Since the Household Responsibility System was implemented in the 1980s, the contribution of agriculture to national GDP has been declining. During the past two decades, China has seen four major changes to the agricultural taxation system. The results of each adjustment are shown in Figure 3.2.

The results of these reforms are remarkable. The percentage of agriculture and animal husbandry tax in the national revenue total was reduced to 0.92 per cent in 2004 from 29.3 per cent in 1950. In 2005, with the total abolition of the agriculture taxation system, farmer burdens were relieved further (Liao, 2006). In 2004, total agricultural tax revenue was CNY23.2 billion (about USD28 million). According to the State Administration of Taxation, cancelling agricultural taxation has resulted in an overall reduction in the tax burden for small farmers of CNY125 billion (almost USD20 billion) since 2006.

Because agricultural taxation systems in African countries vary greatly, it is difficult to reach uniform conclusions. However, in general the tax burden on poor people is quite heavy. According to Anderson and Masters (2008), when comparing farmers' tax burden between 1975–1979 and 2000–2004, it was found that the tax burden on farmers was reduced to a large extent in Ghana, Uganda, Tanzania, Cameroon, Senegal and Madagascar. Tax was changed to agricultural support in Mozambique, Kenya and Nigeria. High tax rates continued in Côte d'Ivoire, Zambia and Zimbabwe. Research on farmer tax burdens in 21 countries found that

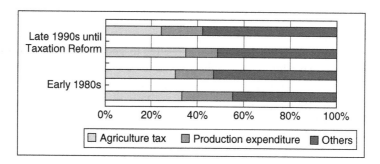

Figure 3.2 Taxation System Reform

it reached a peak value in the late 1970s[6] with an annual amount of more than USD10 billion, equal to a per-capita amount of USD134. From 2000 to 2004, the annual tax burden in China was USD6 billion, with each farmer carrying an average burden of USD41 (source: State Statistics Bureau of China).

The World Bank (2007) examined the agriculture tax burden in 11 African countries from the 1960s to the 1980s. For nine countries (Kenya, Uganda, Madagascar, Cameroon, Sudan, Ghana, Ethiopia, Tanzania and Côte d'Ivoire) the agricultural tax burden declined, and only in Nigeria and Zambia did it increase. For countries that experienced agricultural tax reduction, although the tax burdens for cash crops such as tobacco, peanuts and cocoa were largely reduced, the actual tax ratio was still very high (Box 3.7).

Changes in agricultural taxation policies in China and African countries reflect the character of different agricultural development phases. In the early years of the PRC, agriculture contributed to national capital accumulation for investment in industry and other production sectors. The 'price scissors' strategy (*jiandao cha*) meant that agricultural product prices were kept low to ensure low input costs for industry, and agricultural land policy and taxation policy supported this. Food security was made a priority, with smallholders sacrificing economic benefits for the cause of overall national economic development. When agriculture and the entire economy began to grow, China made concrete efforts to support smallholders and food crop production through the cancellation of agricultural taxes and fees. This opened up a new phase of emphasizing the twin objectives of food security and increasing incomes in the Chinese agricultural development strategy. At the same time, African countries still needed to ensure accumulation from agriculture to meet development objectives. Currently, agricultural taxation and trade policies attract the majority of investment to commercial agriculture and in particular export-oriented agriculture, with only limited linkages to smallholders.

Purchasing Policy for Agricultural Products in China

Consistent with agricultural development policy, the goal of purchasing policy for agricultural products in the early days of the PRC was to provide accumulation for industrialization. The state monopoly on the purchasing and marketing of grain was officially established in 1953, aiming to contribute to a national grain purchasing plan and assure industrialization. Although the ratio of government purchase to gross grain output decreased after three years of natural disasters, the government purchase price was maintained at a lower level from 1967 to 1978. Even according to the most conservative estimate, the surplus value circulation system has experienced different phases such as state monopoly for purchasing and marketing, contract purchase and open quotas with stable prices, with market orientation gradually assuming a clearer role. The influence of marketing mechanisms on the allocation of resources for grain production and grain prices has become stronger, which also causes prices to fluctuate widely (Hu *et al.*, 2000). In 2008, the Decision on the 3rd Plenary Session of the 17th Communist Party of China Central Committee strived to complete the agricultural products protection system and improve the price formation mechanism for major agricultural products such as grain.

BOX 3.7 AGRICULTURAL TAXATION POLICIES IN AFRICAN COUNTRIES

Zimbabwe

In order to promote diversification and counter the global financial crisis and its own financial problems (94 per cent unemployment), Zimbabwe cancelled additional taxes on agricultural machinery including motor cycles and their spare parts, tractors below 60 horsepower, furrows, harrows, disc harrows, seeding machines, threshing machines, harvesters and water pumps. In the meantime, taxes on windmills and corn husking machines were also cancelled as a measure to promote development of the local processing industry (Munthali and Mulenga, 2009).

Zambia

According to the Investment Law of Zambia, enterprises can obtain the following preferential policies by investing in agriculture:

- reduction of business income tax to 15 per cent, which is 25 per cent for other sectors;
- exemption from dividend tax in the first five years for large-scale agricultural investors;
- for enterprises producing coffee, tea, bananas, oranges and other fruit, taxes are paid after deducting 10 per cent of taxable revenue or profit;
- the majority of imported capital goods and mechanical equipment for agriculture were exempted from import duty (United Nations, 2006).

Ethiopia

Ethiopia has cancelled value added tax (VAT) on agricultural products. However, traders are required to show relevant papers to apply for reimbursement and report the categories and quantities of exported products. This process can be lengthy and bureaucratic.

Mozambique

Export duty on soybeans is not required, and income tax on investments in agricultural infrastructure is exempted for the first five years; the income tax on agricultural projects is 10 per cent. Investment enterprises can enjoy 50 to 80 per cent exemption from income tax when recouping capital outlay (within ten years) (source: Commercial Counsellor's Office of the Chinese Embassy in the Republic of Mozambique: http://mz.mofcom.gov.cn/).

Tanzania

Agricultural products are exempted from import duties, VAT on unprocessed agricultural products and animal products are exempted including unprocessed meat, fish and all agricultural products. VAT is exempted on all imported agricultural and fishery products, including pesticide and fertilizer, also on farmer cooperatives registered for export business and farming households in production associations; stamp duties on agricultural, animal and fishing products are exempted and many kinds of expenses levied by the government are exempted (source: website for the Ministry of Finance of Tanzania, http://www.mof.go.tz/). However, involuntary donations to school boards and village councils are also considered as charges to small-scale farmers, and this has increased their burden.

Sierra Leone

Although export tariffs on agricultural products have been cancelled, there are still quota limitations on some products, such as palm oil and fishing products (which is why smuggling to adjacent Liberia and Guinea prevails). Sierra Leone levies 5 per cent import duty on basic materials such as raw and input materials, which is a relatively low duty and helpful in reducing producers' costs. Other taxation regulations include a 5 per cent tax on agricultural machinery, 15 per cent import duty on rice, then years of tax exemption on income from rice planting and no double duty on input materials and finished products in agriculture.

After independence, some African countries implemented a price protection system for grain crops in order to ensure increases in grain production. African countries applied national purchase prices in order to control prices. For those countries highly reliant on export commodities, different policy measures were necessary for grain crops and export crops. Some states experienced severe food price crises and gradually cancelled price controls and reformed markets for agricultural products (Box 3.8).

BOX 3.8 PURCHASING AND SELLING POLICIES IN AFRICAN COUNTRIES

Madagascar

In order to trigger farmer enthusiasm for planting rice, the Government of Madagascar made a decision to raise the purchasing price of rice in 1977. As a result, rice output reached 244,000 tonnes in 1977 – an increase of 55,000 tonnes on 1976.

Tanzania

During the *Ujamaa* period in Tanzania, the government abolished traditional businesses and requested farmers to sell all products to their village committee. Due to low purchasing prices, farmers were satisfied to be self-sufficient and reluctant to engage in additional production, which resulted in a dramatic decrease in grain and economic crop output in Tanzania (Zhang *et al.*, 2003).

As requested by the IMF, the Tanzanian government raised the purchasing price of major economic crops as well as grain and oil crops in 1986/87 by 30 to 80 per cent and 5 to 10 per cent, respectively. The purchasing prices for ten kinds of agricultural products were raised in 1987/88.

Côte d'Ivoire and Senegal

Against internal and external pressures, especially harsh conditions imposed by the IMF, the Côte d'Ivoire government decided to reduce the production of cocoa. However, in order to protect the income of farmers producing cocoa, the government announced that the purchasing price for cocoa would remain unchanged in 1988/89 (Liu, 1989).

In order to encourage grain crop production, the Government of Senegal raised purchasing prices of grain by 100 per cent. Peanut prices were also raised (Xiang, 1987).

Regarding cash crops, countries such as Côte d'Ivoire and Senegal regulate minimum purchasing prices for crops for export. If the international market price rises, the government will raise purchasing prices accordingly, and if the international market price declines, the government will absorb losses by purchasing from farmers at the original price (Lu, 2000).

Malawi

Through the state-owned agricultural development and marketing company, the Malawi government guarantees a 15 per cent profit for small-scale farmers and at least 10 per cent profit for poor households by purchasing at appropriate prices (Wang, 1988).

Price protection of agricultural products in China and African countries aims to encourage farmers to engage in agricultural development. The difference is that many African countries have planned for export-orientated agricultural development. The policies of African countries were strongly influenced by international donor institutions, and thus are vulnerable to changes in trade conditions (Box 3.9). At the same time, China implemented many regulations focusing on smallholder food production to ensure food security.

BOX 3.9 LIBERALIZATION REFORMS IN AFRICAN COUNTRIES

Mozambique

Mozambique gradually decreased production and selling prices for agricultural products after 1988. Prices of 22 types of agricultural products were liberalized in 1993, with only the selling price of bread and flour still under control. In 1997, reserve prices for grain crops were cancelled (Lu, 2000).

Tanzania

The Tanzanian government relaxed grain prices when the Grain Security Law was issued in 1991. Later on, the Land Security Department under the Ministry of Agriculture and Food Security was established. The government took the following measures to encourage agricultural trade:

- development of unconventional export crops to take advantage of trade liberalization;
- support for research and extension;
- promotion of private sector involvement in production, processing, storage, supply and marketing;

- improvement of rural infrastructure to promote bilateral trade and export with neighbouring countries;
- improvements in post-harvest management;
- conduct of periodic supervision and evaluation of rural grain production status through an early phase monitoring system for crops;
- re-evaluation of legislation on the involvement of the private sector in agricultural production and marketing; and
- revision and implemention effectively of a grain reserve strategy.

Currently, 95 per cent of grain production is managed by the private sector, and less than 5 per cent is managed by the national management company. The role of government is limited to providing market information and co-ordinating and standardizing the market. However, the market is still very ineffective due to a lack of standardized mechanisms, poor agricultural infra-structure (such as feeder roads, markets and production and storage facilities) and a general lack of organization.

Zimbabwe

Since 1994, the Government of Zimbabwe has gradually introduced market reforms for agricultural marketing, including agricultural products from four key state-owned enterprises. The principal measures include reform of purchasing and sales policy for agricultural products by eliminating price restrictions for maize, cotton, sunflower seeds, soybeans, peanuts and wheat. Free import and export is allowed for all grains except maize, and the private sector is permitted to engage in wheat imports; the Agriculture Marketing Board has been abol-ished, alongside privatization of major state-owned enterprises, which were formerly managed by the Board.

Agricultural Subsidy Policy

Due to low levels of agricultural development, agriculture subsidies in China and many African countries were implemented relatively late and slowly, with limited coverage. This section will provide analysis only using the definition of subsidy in the World Trade Organization's (WTO) multilateral agreement framework, the 'Yellow Box Policy'. This refers to subsidies for grain and other agricultural products in the form of price subsidies, export subsidies and others including direct government price invention in agricultural product markets, subsidies for agricultural inputs such as seeds, fertilizer and irrigation, marketing subsidies and subsidies for land management.

China's agricultural subsidies started in the 1950s with quota subsidies for trac-tor ploughing losses, which was gradually expanded to support for agricultural production materials, subsidies for agricultural electricity use and preferential access to finance. Lu (2007) has observed that China's agricultural subsidy policy evolved through three phases since 1978. Between 1978 and 1992, subsidy policy was focused on production materials, as well as food subsidies to urban residents; from 1993 to 2002, protection prices for grains and input subsidies were implemented to accelerate the marketization process for agricultural products. Since 2003, agricultural taxes and fees have been reformed, the main feature of which is abolition of the agricultural tax. The 2004 No. 1 Document issued by central government promoted 'Two Reductions and Three Subsidies', which have switched hidden subsidies to direct subsidies to farmers (Box 3.10).

BOX 3.10 AGRICULTURAL SUBSIDIES IN CHINA

Currently, the principal agricultural subsidies include the high-quality seeds subsidy, the direct grain subsidy, the subsidy for purchasing agricultural machinery and a comprehensive subsidy for agricultural materials (Table 3.1).

1   Since 2002, subsidies have been provided to farms that use high-quality seeds and advanced technologies. High-quality seed extension demonstration plots encourage farmers to use high-quality seeds and increase agricultural production, promoting agricultural regionalization, correct planting, standardized management and industrialized operations. Presently, this subsidy applies to four grain crops: rice, wheat, maize, soybeans, and two economic crops: cotton and grapes.
2   The China grain risk fund system was established in 1994 with the aim of stabilizing grain market prices, subsidizing the grain resold to farmers, promoting a stabilized increase of grain production and maintaining normal grain circulation. Since 2004, the government has adjusted usage of the grain risk fund from consumption to production through direct subsidies for grain farmers.
3   In 2004, the subsidy for agricultural machinery was implemented to accelerate the mechanization of agriculture, promote the development of the agricultural machinery industry, expand domestic demand and maintain steady and rapid economic growth.
4   Since 2004, grain production costs for farmers have been rising due to higher electricity, fertilizer and pesticide costs. In order to encourage farmers to plant more good-quality grain, a direct subsidy policy for agricultural inputs was promoted from 2006.

Further to this, farmers enjoy other subsidies such as pig and dairy cow insurance subsidies, dairy cow importation subsidies, biogas subsidies, a subsidy for returning cultivated land to forest cover and home appliance subsidies.

TABLE 3.1 Agriculture Subsidy Projects and Amounts (Unit: CNY100 million)

Projects	2003	2004	2005	2006	2007	2008
High-quality seed subsidy	3	28.5	38.7	41.5	51.9	120
Direct grain subsidy	–	100	132	142	151	151
Agricultural machinery purchase subsidy	–	4.1	3	6	28	40
Comprehensive agricultural materials subsidy	–	–	–	120	276	482

Source: Based on data from the Ministry of Agriculture and Ministry of Finance websites

In order to promote grain production, African countries normally try to provide subsidies through price control of production materials such as fertilizer, seeds and machinery. Due to limited access to data, this sector takes fertilizer subsidy as an example to illustrate this phenomenon. Soon after independence, most African countries (such as Ghana) tried to encourage farmers to engage in agricultural production by providing seeds, fertilizer and pesticides at low cost: often half-price or completely free (Lu, 2000). From the late 1970s to the early 1980s, fertilizer subsidies were judged to cause price distortions. With only a limited range of fertilizer options available, the majority of the benefit from fertilizer subsidies went to large-scale farmers. Reforms were initiated in the 1980s. Due to cancellation of the fertilizer subsidy and currency depreciation, the price of fertilizer increased by 200 per cent to 300 per cent, causing several countries to reverse reforms and reissue fertilizer subsidies. As shown in Figure 3.3, 38 per cent of Zambia's national budget on agriculture was spent on fertilizer subsidies in 2004/05.

In June 2006, the African Fertilizer Summit was held in Nigeria. Its aim was to initiate a Green Revolution in Africa, improve the usage of fertilizer and create an Africa Fertilizer Action Plan to promote the utilization of fertilizers and other agricultural inputs by small-scale farmers.[7] One outcome of the summit was the establishment of an African Fertilizer Development Financing Mechanism in October 2007. The objective of this mechanism is to mobilize relevant resources to

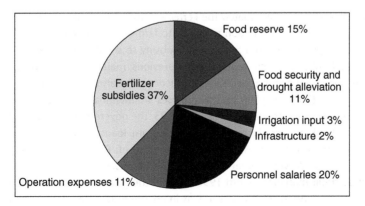

Figure 3.3 National Budget Distribution for Zambia in 2004/05

raise funds for developing the fertilizer industry in Africa, and to respond to the Abuja Declaration target to increase the usage of fertilizer from the current 8kg per hectare to 50kg per hectare by 2015 (Africa Fertilizer Development Financing Mechanism, 2007). On 16 May 2007, the African Development Bank ratified the Mechanism and its objective of providing fertilizer subsidies to small-scale farmers.

BOX 3.11 FERTILIZER SUBSIDIES IN AFRICAN COUNTRIES

Malawi

Between 2008 and 2009, Malawi spent USD186 million on fertilizer and seed subsidies, about three times the amount in the previous year. Such measures contributed to Malawi's transformation into a grain exporting country with stable grain prices. The president of Malawi was lauded by the FAO for this achievement. However, some experts warn that attention should be placed on the impacts of fertilizer on the environment and the costs involved in importing non-organic fertilizers. Maize production in Malawi went up to 3.4 million tonnes in 2007/08 from 1.2 million tonnes in 2005. Previously, Malawi had implemented fertilizer and seed subsidies (in 1999) but the new subsidy, started in 2005, enables local households to purchase 50kg of fertilizer with USD7, one-fifth of the market price. The government also provides cash coupons with which households can purchase enough seeds for half a hectare. As a result, average household output has risen from 0.8 tonnes to 2 tonnes a year. In 2007–2008 the government spent USD62 million, 6.5 per cent of the government budget, on fertilizer. In contrast, Malawi spent USD120 million importing grain for food security purposes, which means that fertilizer expenditure was still relatively small.

Zambia

The Zambian government initiated the Fertilizer Support Programme in 2002 to provide agricultural production materials to farmers such as fertilizers and seeds. The project provided a 50 per cent subsidy to small-scale farmers for purchasing fertilizer, which replaced the previous maize import subsidy. Electricity and diesel oil for agricultural production were also subsidized.

Minde *et al.* (2008) explain that five phases are identifiable in relation to fertilizer subsidies in Zambia. From 1991 to1993, the government designated a few state bank and credit organizations to grant loans for fertilizer. The repayment rate on these loans was less than 5 per cent. From 1994 to 1996, the government allowed several large private enterprises to import and sell fertilizer as credit managers. From 1996 to 1999 the government established the Food Reserve Agency; this bureau was in charge of fertilizer imports and distribution to agents. The Agency designated agents from the private sector to sell fertilizer to households and cooperatives. This mode of operation was easily influenced by political intervention. From 1999 to 2000, under pressure from donors, the government signed contracts with several large private companies to sell approximately three-quarters of fertilizer to small-scale farmers. The fifth phase started with implementation of the Fertilizer Support Programme, during the first four years of which the government provided an annual average of 66 billion tonnes of fertilizer. Small-scale farm households did not benefit as much as large farms. The government targeted more capitalized farmers who could utilize fertilizer more effectively and contribute more to national maize production and food security.

According to statistics from the Central Statistical Bureau of Zambia, 13.9 per cent of households obtained fertilizer from the Programme in 2003 with an annual household income of ZMK804,000 (around USD165), while the annual household income of those who did not was only ZMK266,000. The respective land holdings for receivers and non-receivers were 0.23 hectares and 0.15 hectares, and for fixed assets ZMK435,000 and ZMK173,000. The distances of their farms to towns were 29.8km and 35.2km, respectively.

Differences in agricultural subsidy policies between China and African countries reflect different stages in the agricultural development process. From the founding of the PRC to the early stages of reform, a development strategy of modernization and mechanization was followed: China offered subsidies on production materials and expanded these to all aspects of agricultural production, including subsidies to different producers to maintain grain market stability and promote scale effects in agricultural development. In contrast, African countries have been focusing on subsidies for seeds and fertilizer, with the purpose of improving land productivity through increasing investment in production inputs (Box 3.11). One fundamental problem with increasing fertilizer through subsidies is that in most countries in Africa, fertilizer needs to be imported and is expensive.

Trade Policy for Agricultural Products

In the early years of the PRC, China maintained low exchange rates for the Yuan Renminbi, which disadvantaged agricultural production for export. However, following reform and a period of opening up, China depreciated its currency 400 per cent (between 1978 and 1992). Export products became more competitive and contributed significantly to rapid export growth (particularly for non-grain products) as well as the good performance of the national economy in the 1980s (J. Huang, 2008). The effective exchange rate for the Yuan Renminbi increased 30 per cent between 1992 and 1997.

Joining the WTO was an excellent opportunity for China to change its agricultural trade policy (Box 3.12). Before joining, import duty on grain was maintained at a low level. The government did not allow organizations or companies without management rights and quotas to import grain. Meanwhile, the government only charged 3 per cent import duty for grain within quotas, but import duty charged to grain without quotas was as high as 114 per cent. Although China made efforts to commercialize the grain trade, trade liberalization for maize and cotton remained very slow (Huang and Rozelle, 1998): for example, China had been implementing export subsidies to increase the export of maize and cotton before joining the WTO. While subsidizing corn exporters, the domestic price was also raised, which effectively protected domestic producers.

BOX 3.12 AGRICULTURAL TRADE POLICIES IN CHINA SINCE ENTRY INTO THE WTO

There are five main aspects of the way that China has adjusted agricultural trade policy since joining the WTO in 2001. First, it China has cancelled non-duty measures such as import permits and quantity limitations, and has gradually reduced duty on agricultural products. The average rate of duty on agricultural products was reduced to 15.2 per cent in 2004, contrasting with the 21 per cent rate prior to WTO accession. Second, with customs duty with quotas ranging from 1 to 15 per cent, China has implemented tariff quota policies for ten major agricultural products including grain, cotton, oil and sugar, among others. The quota management system has gradually improved and the quota ratio for non-state enterprises has increased. In 2006, tariff quotas for vegetable oils were cancelled and replaced by a flat 9 per cent tariff. Third, export subsidies on all agricultural products have been cancelled and replaced by supportive domestic policies that have no or minimal distorting effects on trade. Fourth, China has been actively engaged in revising agricultural laws and regulations to make them consistent with WTO rules. Some laws have been revised, and transparency in the implementation of laws and regulations has been increased. Finally, scientific inspection and quarantine standards have been applied to imported animal and vegetable products (Niu, 2009).

Compared with China, African countries have engaged less favourably with international trade patterns and are highly dependent on the export of primary products. As substitutes have emerged in global markets, demand for African exported products has decreased, causing a slump in prices. Meanwhile, many developed countries have protected their own agricultural sectors and distorted world markets by the use of price subsidies. Dumping surplus agricultural products on foreign countries has created catastrophic effects for the development of agriculture in Africa. African countries have yet to overcome the effects of import barriers and tariffs imposed by developed countries. Export volumes are reduced and the export of surplus agricultural products by developed countries further limits the capture of surplus value by African farmers, as oversupply causes prices to fall and decreases export income.

These issues compound problems caused by a view held in many African countries that planting grain is no better than purchasing grain, and that cash crops are more important than grain crops. Moreover, many developed countries only import cheap raw materials from Africa, which can have a distorting effect on economic structures (Yao, 2002). Tanzania, for example, has had an export strategy which aims to promote the diversification of export products, focusing on improving quality and capturing more value-added through processing. Although crop and livestock product markets have been liberalized and the grain trade has been fully privatized (excluding the strategic grain reserve), agricultural trade is still insufficiently diversified and dependent on traditional export markets, accounting for approximately 50 per cent of export income. Therefore, price fluctuations on the world market and declining terms of trade continue to have a negative effect.

Many African countries have been through extended periods of market and trade liberalization. However, reforms have not always been consistent, and often interventionist measures have remained alongside liberalization reforms for reasons that are not always clear. For example, even while loosening restrictions on rice imports, cancelling price controls on tea and abolishing the monopoly power of cotton purchasing, Kenya still maintains state control of main grain production (maize, wheat and beans) through the National Grain Production Bureau (Lu, 2000).

Economic liberalization has brought about challenges for African producers. At the same time as price controls have been removed and the market has opened, farmers' production costs have increased. Some farmers are losing incentive to invest in the land. Many West African countries are highly dependent on cotton production. Cotton accounts for 5 to 10 per cent of GDP in Benin, Burkina Faso, Chad and Mali, and there are about 2 million cotton farmers in West and Central Africa. Cotton accounts for approximately 30 per cent of total export income and about 60 per cent of total agricultural income. African countries have been highly disadvantaged by the subsidies paid to cotton farmers in developed countries (see Gillson, 2005).

Furthermore, increases in international prices for agricultural products have had different impacts on African countries. Grain importers have to spend a higher proportion of export income on grain imports. Countries such as Benin, Burundi, Ethiopia, Mozambique, Nigeria, Rwanda and Sudan spend 10 per cent of their export income on grain imports; for Burkina Faso this figure is 20 per cent.

During the process of integration into the world economy the trade policies of both China and Africa have been greatly influenced by international markets. China has been perfecting laws and regulations and actively adjusting its economic structures to meet world market demand effectively. For African countries, due to insufficient internal demand and high reliance on global trade, adjustments to trade policies struggle with protecting existing benefits and world market share, which are even more vulnerable to fluctuations in international markets and events such as the global financial crisis.

Another factor that makes Africa countries different from China in trade policy is that Africa has engaged in accelerating processes of regional economic and trade integration. Examples include the East African Community, the Common Market for Eastern and Southern Africa and the Southern African Development Community. These held a joint summit conference in October 2008 with the aim to establish a united regional economic community, engaging 26 eastern and southern African countries, whose aim in turn would be to improve development prospects by regional integration. Regional trade cooperation can solve issues that are not included in the agenda of multilateral WTO trade agreements. For example, regional cooperation could improve regional political stability and increase scale effects from regional infrastructures. For the Sub-Saharan African region, which consists of many small countries, regional trade cooperation is very important and more realistic to achieve than multilateral agreements (for example, the WTO Doha Round). Currently there are four regional trade agreements in Africa, but internal trade volume remains small and only accounts for 17 per cent of total trade volume. In recent years, the economic integration process in Africa has accelerated, but African countries have been slow to unify tariff procedures, reduce tariff and non-tariff barriers and improve transportation and communications.

Rural Credit Policy

When the PRC was founded, the banking system was still poorly organized. Only a certain number of agricultural loans could be granted. Administrative power was the means to recover and develop production and solve the livelihood problems of China's large farming population. In 1951, the People's Bank of China issued rural finance guidelines, setting the objective of 'going into rural areas, to help farmers to relieve their difficulties and to help develop production'. At that moment, the government had limited financial power and the agricultural surplus was the source of accumulation for industrial development. The government and banks were focused on mobilizing and utilizing social funds in order to solve resource and grain shortages by means of rural private credit and cooperatives. Since then, two characteristics of the cooperative financial system have spread widely, albeit with several rounds of reform since the 1980s (Box 3.13). The first has been to emphasize the use of preferential loans; the second has been to work primarily through formal financial services.[8]

BOX 3.13 RURAL FINANCE POLICY REFORMS IN CHINA SINCE THE 1980S

Credit cooperative structures and functions were reorganized during a series of reforms in the 1980s, which promoted new management and ownership systems. Two consecutive No. 1 Documents released by central government in 2004 and 2005 proposed 'rural finance system innovations with multiple forms of ownership'.

The No. 1 Document of 2006 argued the need to establish 'community finance institutions with multiple forms of ownership in counties . . . guide households in developing mutual aid associations and standardize private loans'.

The No. 1 Document of 2007 identified that the direction of reforms was to 'expedite the establishment of an integral rural finance reform plan and development of a rural finance system with complete functions in which business finance, cooperative finance, policy finance and microcredit organizations are complementary to each other'.

The No. 1 Document of 2008 indicated the need to 'solve problems of insufficient funding for some rural credit cooperatives and new rural finance institutions through measures such as wholesale and transfer lending'.

The No. 1 Document of 2009 demanded an improvement in capacity to deliver rural financial services, indicating the need to 'encourage and support innovation by financial institutions in rural financial products and services including microcredit and microfinance services, allowing rural microfinance institutions to introduce funds from financial institutions in diverse ways'. While the current round of reforms are now complete, rural finance remains the weak point in China's fiscal system. Cai *et al.* (2008) note that 7 per cent of towns in China (and therefore also the rural areas that they administer) are still without any financial institutions.

Financial policy incorporates agricultural production insurance. Agriculture insurance initiated in 1982 is guided by the principle of 'achieving balance between income and expenditure with some profit and preparedness for disasters'. As with other supportive agricultural policies, agriculture insurance has been through fluctuations and was almost cancelled as an indiscriminate charge. In 2004, the Opinions of the State Council Concerning Several Policies for Promoting Increases in Farmer Income argued for the establishment of a policy-oriented agriculture insurance system. Since then, agriculture insurance issues have received wide attention. The China Insurance Regulatory Commission has carried out trials of agricultural insurance in nine provinces and cities. Subsequently, trials were carried out in 90 per cent of all provinces and cities and five operation modes were identified, including a professional agriculture insurance company, a self-operating commercial insurance company, an agent-operated commercial insurance company, a joint venture between government and companies, and a co-insurance operation. In 2008, new changes to the agriculture insurance policy were made. The agricultural insurance policy is another important supportive policy for farmers alongside the cancellation of agricultural tax and the direct grain subsidy. In 2008, agriculture insurance revenue reached CNY11 billion (USD1.5 billon), increasing by 112.5 per cent over the previous year. Agriculture insurance has become the third largest insurance code within the property insurance sector.

Financial liberalization is one of the key pillars of Strategy Action Plans in most of Africa. For example, Kenya abolished credit guidelines in December 1993 (which had been in existence since 1975) in favour of agriculture. Entering the twenty-first century, NEPAD emphasized the following points in relation to rural financial policies and financial services. First, financial services for rural people need to improve. There needs to be access to finance to increase the productivity of assets, to improve rural people's capacity to use existing resources effectively and efficiently through land use, application of human capital and development of management capacity. Second, it is important to improve institutions to encourage domestic savings and improved accessibility for rural households. Financial organizations need to cover more of the costs and take on risk, allowing low-cost financial services for smallholders.

Most commercial banks in Africa are private institutions and often controlled by foreign owners. This means that there is a limit to the degree to which governments can influence lending behaviour. Private banks direct their services at commercial farms and plantations, many of which are operated and owned by foreign investors. For most of Africa, a land contract is the only collateral accepted by banks. However, because small-scale farmers normally do not have land contracts, they are unable to receive loans. Under these circumstances governments have to establish professional agricultural banks or set up other financing measures to ensure that farmers can have access to credit. Funds for state agricultural banks are sourced from the government budget and low-interest loans and financial aid from foreign countries. However, these funds are insufficient to meet the large demand from the agricultural sector. Therefore, some African countries require that private banks provide a certain percentage of loans to the agricultural sector. As described by Ijioma (1996), the major features of agriculture credit in Africa are short-term agriculture loans, loans highly concentrated towards a few types of crops, a low interest policy in state agricultural banks, and a low repayment rate and high percentage of idle loans. This situation has not significantly improved as African governments cannot afford to provide more cheap loans; the private sector only grants loans to a small number of large-scale farmers and is unwilling to grant loans on grain production.

Regional financial organizations are an important component of the integration process in Africa. The African Development Bank granted USD2.7 billion between 1967 and 2007, of which 30 per cent of the investments were in agricultural and rural projects (128 in total). The African Rural and Agricultural Credit Association established in 1977 is a union consisting of banks and other financial institutions which provides direct or indirect financial services to the agricultural sector in Africa. It maintains close cooperation with the FAO and currently operates in Zimbabwe, Nigeria, Burkina Faso, Uganda and Cameroon.

In terms of financial policies, the major difference between African countries and China is that China has financial institutions which serve both agriculture and rural development. Although some informal financial products and services have been introduced, financial services for small-scale farmers are still provided mainly by the government and public agencies. In African countries, governments lack resources to provide access to finance for the small-holder sector. Despite the clear progress made in strengthening the African financial sector through a wave of reforms and the privatization of national financial institutions, there remain many challenges to overcome (Box 3.14). Only 20 per cent of people in Sub-Saharan Africa have a bank account (German International Cooperation (GIZ), 2009). Limited access to finance restricts the growth of private companies, and the high cost of credit generally discourages them from tapping investment funds. Having gone through the cycle of nationalizing and privatizing their banking systems, more than half of the region's countries have a banking market with either a dominant or significant share of foreign-owned financial institutions (Beck *et al.*, 2009).

BOX 3.14 RURAL FINANCE POLICIES IN AFRICAN COUNTRIES

Zambia

To promote savings and provide financial services to members of cooperatives, Zambia enacted legislation on cooperatives in 1998. The State Agricultural Policy for 2004–2015 sets out the overall objectives of agricultural credit as being 'to establish and standardize a rural credit and finance system that is efficient, effective, demand-driven and sustainably coordinated with financial institutions'. Specific goals include:

- developing small credit institutions;
- broadening the coverage of savings institutions;
- encouraging short-term and mid-term seasonal credit and financial services for male and female farmers;
- facilitating private sector involvement in household credit; and
- guaranteeing financial channels for farmer investment.

Mozambique

Banks impose 35 per cent interest on agricultural loans and this impedes the development of agriculture. For the majority of households, particularly low-productivity grain producers, the high level of interest is not affordable.

Liberia

To allow smaller farmers to effectively sell their products the Agricultural Cooperative and Development Bank was established in Liberia. This bank has operated successfully for many years, providing short-term loans to farmer cooperatives, farmer associations and individual farmers which enables them to buy cash crop seeds (mainly coffee, cocoa, rubber and palm oil). However, the bank was subject to political and management problems and is no longer in operation, so small-scale farmers, cooperatives, farmer associations and collective or private agricultural enterprises are no longer able to receive loans from this bank. Presently, there are six commercial banks in Liberia, only two of which are still carrying on business outside the capital, Monrovia. These commercial banks provide loans to well-operated farmer cooperatives and associations rather than individual small farmers, which can reduce repayment risk. The government and donors could encourage these banks to fill the space left by the demise of the Agricultural Cooperative and Development Bank in granting small loans to farmer organizations.

Sierra Leone

Since only a few commercial banks in Sierra Leone provide services to agriculture, the majority of farmers in rural areas can receive loans only via informal channels with high interest rates. Currently, the government is exploring good methods for providing credit support to rural areas and agriculture: community banking is one such attempt.

Implementation of Agricultural Policies

Contexts for Implementation of Agricultural Policies

Many similarities can be noted between agricultural strategies and policies in China and African countries: this is particularly the case at the level of objectives, and the reforms conducted in China in the 1970s and those in Africa in the 1990s illustrate this well. Objectives include:

1   promoting productivity by virtue of market power, including privatizing state-owned enterprises;

2   increasing production and employment opportunities while balancing equity and efficiency, making agriculture the basis of the national economy, supporting farmers and adjusting agriculture with social policies including poverty reduction and provision of social services; and

3   encouraging investment in agricultural infrastructure and production through state intervention in the market, adopting measures such as subsidy and price controls to manipulate the price of land, means of production and labour.

Similarly, African countries have been prioritizing food security within their agricultural strategies in the 2000s. However, the specific ways in which strategies and policies are implemented in China and Africa differ greatly.

Agricultural strategies in China always have been in line with national economic development. The priority since 1978 has been socialist modernization, with the reform and opening process creating desirable conditions for development in the agricultural sector. A series of policies catered to farmers in the 2000s; at the same time, macro policies such as the Scientific Development Approach, and Construction of a Harmonious Society proposed in the Third Plenary Session of the Sixteenth Central Committee in 2003, which rejected the pursuit of unconditional GDP growth, has as its primary policy goal helping farmers through greater emphasis on social equality.

Africa has been severely confined by external conditions through every stage of development strategy formulation, such that policy consistency has been difficult to maintain. It is safe to say that drivers of agricultural strategy and policy adjustment in China have been domestic political and cultural factors. In Africa, the international political and global economic environment has been more salient.

China's core emphasis on food security within its agricultural strategy is a good example. Although facing grievous food shortages and malnutrition, African approaches to food security have been strongly influenced by the donor community. One example of this is the FAO Special Programme on Food Security in 1994, approved at the World Food Summit in November 1996 (Box 3.15). From 2002, the African Union has supported a national round-table agenda on food security activities under the Comprehensive African Agricultural Development Plan (CAADP). Currently, Nigeria and Tanzania have conducted all the activities prescribed in the national food security plan linked to CAADP, while Chad, Congo, Kenya, Madagascar, Malawi, Mali and Sierra Leone have carried out some steps. At the regional level, the Union Economique et Monétaire Ouest-Africaine has undertaken some initiatives on food security, and the Community of Sahel-Saharan States has approved a regional food security plan; the Common Market for Eastern and Southern Africa (COMESA) is developing similar plans as well.

Economic conditions are an essential component affecting policy implementation. In comparison with Africa, agricultural investment in China has accounted for a much larger proportion of the national budget (see Chapter 5). However, African countries cannot afford high levels of investment and have to rely on external support. For example, in Tanzania only 11.25 per cent of the research and development (R&D) budget has come from government revenue and the remaining 88.75 per cent from external sources. External funds support all research and extension activities as well as food security and tea and coffee research institutes. Domestic funds are used mainly for irrigation (63.3 per cent) and other agricultural production projects.

BOX 3.15 AFRICAN NATIONAL FOOD SECURITY PLANS UNDER THE FAO SPECIAL PROGRAMME ON FOOD SECURITY

Malawi

The Malawi government outlined the Strategic Framework for National Food Security and Nutrition Action Plan under the FAO's assistance in 2005. This is the Malawian version of a national food security plan. This document introduced actions to be taken to meet the food demands of the landless, in light of experience gained in the pilot phase of the Special Programme on Food Security of how to improve small farmer productivity. Some activities of great importance have been chosen and put into practice, and many have been included in the Malawi Growth and Development Strategy issued in November 2002, which is a framework for cross-sectoral and intra-sectoral development planning. The Malawi government and its development partners set down and approved an agricultural development plan within this framework. The plan adopted the pattern advocated by CAADP, and the food security pillar activities have become the National Food Security Plan.

Togo

The National Food Security Plan in Togo was sanctioned in December 2008 after a broad consultation process involving stakeholders at various levels. This plan is viewed as a cross-sector food security strategy concerning four aspects of food security. It is also a prioritized action and investment plan (2008–2015), and now part of the Poverty Reduction Strategic Framework. An agricultural investment plan has been developed based on CAADP, with five out of six parts in the National Food Security Plan fitting with the CAADP framework. However, an additional food and nutrition security plan is needed to ensure that all four aspects of food security mentioned in CAADP are covered.

Implementation Agencies for Agricultural Policies

The agriculture ministry plays a key role in agricultural strategy implementation. In China there were specific officials responsible for agriculture and water conservancy during the Yao Era (4,000 years BC). From the Qin Dynasty (2,000 years BC), granaries were set up at the county level and food storage was controlled by central governments. A taxation system was set up, going down to the township level.

In modern times, government capacity to control and mobilize populations for agricultural production is clearly dependent on the way that institutions are configured. The Central Rural Work Leadership Group is responsible for planning China's agriculture development, and involves all departments relating to agriculture. Different policies made by the Department of Policy and Law under the Ministry of Agriculture, or by provincial departments of agriculture and city agricultural bureaus, or even in the No. 1 Document released in January each year, can be carried out quickly by the farmers in their villages through the dual system of Communist Party and government administration. At the village level, policies are transferred to farmers through Party meetings, public announcements, village meetings, village congress meetings and other channels. Training is held on important policies at village, county, municipality, province and central levels, and policy implementation and feedback are guaranteed through surveys, interviews and other methods. This top-down administrative arrangement creates space for farmers' needs and for voices to be integrated into the decision-making process. A significant example of this mechanism is the Farmer Responsibility System, which has been transferred from local to central government and then disseminated throughout China.

As the organization responsible for setting and implementing agricultural policy, the Ministry of Agriculture has two major characteristics: it has clearly defined functions and tasks; and business departments have a key role to play. In addition, agricultural reforms are embodied in the organizational set-up of the Ministry, with specialized departments including the Bureau for Town and Village Enterprises, which is responsible for administering township enterprises, the Department of Rural Economy and Management Administration, which is responsible for rural operations (including land contracts, cooperative organizations and the agriculture socialization services system) for farmer tax and fee issues, and the Department of Development and Planning is responsible for resource allocation and industry development. The Department of Market and Economic Information is responsible for standardizing and improving market institutions for agricultural products, the Bureau of Agricultural Products' Quality and Safety Supervision is responsible for the certification of quality and safety of agricultural products and the agricultural quality system. The State Council Leading Group on Poverty Alleviation and Development was separated from the Ministry of Agriculture in 2002 and has responsibility for poverty reduction strategies in China.

Agriculture is the foundation of the national economy. The development of agriculture requires coordination between finance, agriculture and social security departments, among others. China has chosen to bring agriculture into the Five-Year Development Plan and supported it with public finance. The Department of Agriculture and Forestry in the National Development and Reform Commission is in charge of agricultural development, while supportive departments under corresponding ministries are responsible for inter-sectoral coordination. For example, the brief of the Department of Rural Water Resources in the Ministry of Water Resources is to provide support to farmland water conservation; the Agricultural Research Team, under the State Statistical Bureau, provides effective information support on farmer, rural areas and agriculture (*San Nong*) issues; the Department of Agriculture in the Ministry of Finance deals with financial policies towards farmers and participates in the design of agricultural development plans. Therefore, institutions are well coordinated to tackle farmer, agriculture and rural area issues.

In addition, numerous research institutes exist that are affiliated to official agencies in order to study agricultural policies, including some directly under the State Council, such as the Rural Department in the Development and Research Centre, Rural Division in the Research Office of the State Council, and the Rural Division of the Central Research Office. There are also many other independent research institutes acting as think tanks, such as the Academies of Social Sciences, Agricultural Sciences and Agriculture as well as forestry colleges at different levels of state. Thus specialized talent equipped with technologies is available at different administrative levels to contribute to the formation and implementation of agricultural policies.

Agricultural institutions in African countries are not nearly as diverse in function and numerous as those in China. At the micro-level the contrast is particularly evident. In Tanzania, secretaries in each village assigned by the state are supposed to shoulder responsibility for organizing agricultural production and extension, acting on the orders and instructions of their agricultural officers, but in local communities the actual leader is the chairperson voted in by the villagers. Government power is limited by this kind of arrangement. In some villages of the Kilosa District, no land survey has ever been undertaken, not to mention tasks such as village development planning, which has been carried out widely in China.

African agricultural colleges have never belonged to functional departments or ministries. It is noticeable that agriculture, forestry and mining colleges, relevant research institutes and colleges specializing in crop cultivation and breeding in China were all attached to different departments and ministries (following the Soviet system) prior to reform of the educational system in 1998, when most universities were transferred to attach to the Ministry of Education or provincial government. The linkage was loosened somewhat after reform, but the relationship between research institutes and official agencies responsible for policy formation remains quite intimate, enabling the former to get continuous support and subsidies to carry out policy studies as well as other research activities, and the latter to conduct effective policy analysis.

Implementation Processes for Agricultural Policies

The Communist Party of China followed a principle of 'from the grass roots and for the grass roots' in rural affairs prior to the Revolution in 1949. It can be safely argued that massive adjustments to agricultural policies throughout history were accomplished through political mobilization and mass movements. The centralized political structure facilitated top-down dissemination of policy and mobilization of resources. Meanwhile, the pilot study is a feature notable in successful policy implementation in China. When certain policy issues arise, some typical and representative areas will be identified, which might form the basis of useful lessons and experiences for the final formation of policy documents and implementation of policy schemes. In some cases, the practices trialled by the grass roots were scaled up and eventually became national policies: for example, the peasants in Xiaogang Village in Fengyang County, Anhui Province, signed an all-around contract (breaking free of collective production) in 1978 and tripled total grain output in 1979, with the result that income per capita in the village rose more than 20 times. Debate about this reform started at county level and aroused the interest of the provincial government. Encouraged by the then Provincial Party Secretary, Wan Li, reform was conducted first in Anhui Province, and later in the country as a whole with the support of the central government. Contracting land to each household became government policy and initiated a new round of national agricultural development. In contrast, agricultural policies have hardly benefited small farmers in Africa, and often are not effectively implemented at the local level – even when the intention is good.

As for disseminating and supervising agricultural policy, China can easily push implementation and reform forward through central government documents, cross-sector coordination and top-down policy implementation. However, African countries are not able to do this, being circumscribed by weak domestic economies and heavy dependence on external markets. In China, agricultural subsidy policy was enshrined in the No. 1 Document of every year and guaranteed financially by fiscal budgets at various administrative levels. In addition, the country can ensure that small farmers benefit from agricultural policies in just, fair and open ways, with the help of village autonomous organizations and grass roots government agencies. In terms of administrative institutions, various information systems have been set up, including one for the subsidy for procuring agricultural machinery established by the Ministry of Agriculture. In addition, relevant information was released on the agricultural mechanization website by provincial government. Furthermore, both the county department in charge of agricultural machinery and the enterprises involved have to collect and report procurement information to the corresponding provincial department, which may apply for settlement of the balance only when the information from the two sources matches. The provincial finance department has to audit the settlement list before the capital is transferred. All these measures are taken to prevent fraud, ensure the security of capital and guarantee that small-scale farmers gain benefits from subsidy policies.

However, cases from African countries reveal that this kind of supervision seldom happens. Allocation and termination of subsidies may cause social problems: for example, Tanzania initiated a subsidy for agricultural investment projects in 2003 and invested TZS146 billion (around USD0.12 billion), for the purpose of benefiting smallholders through the sales system. A household investigation showed that nobody went to the village office to apply for a certificate, with which they could purchase fertilizer worth TZS60,000 for only TZS10,000 (according to the fertilizer subsidy policy of 2008). The majority of households interviewed for this research reported that they had never benefited from this kind of project and had only obtained some seeds for free, which reflected how unsatisfactory policy dissemination and mobilization was in that particular case.

Effectiveness of Implementation of Agricultural Policies

The effects of agricultural policies in China and Africa differ widely due to the different policy resources that can be mobilized and the types of measures that can be taken. Generally speaking, China has solved the problem of food shortages successfully, and agriculture has had a major role in poverty alleviation. Growing support for agriculture and the countryside in recent years has contributed to the formation and development of a policy framework that strengthens agriculture and favours farmers, thus farmers' enthusiasm and innovation have been greatly promoted.

Of the various policies catering to farmers, the most dominant economic and social effects have been achieved by various agricultural subsidy policies, which have been continually proposed and improved. As mentioned previously, although the land tenure system in China has undergone several reforms, it has failed to solve the problem of the fundamental separation of ownership and operation rights, which results in a relatively low labour productivity. As a consequence, farmers cannot gain economic profit directly from comparatively high land productivity, given the low prices for agricultural produce. Moreover, the previous land reforms were productivity-oriented and unable to improve farmer income. It can be contended that the growth of income in the new century for Chinese farmers derives from the cancellation of longstanding agricultural taxes and improved agricultural subsidies (Boxes 3.16 and 3.17).

BOX 3.16 INCOME INCREASES FROM HIGHER SUBSIDIES

Taking one village in Guizhou as an example, the main source of this village's finance is from state financial transfer payments, which amounted to CNY20,000 (about USD2,500) per year, after the cancellation of the agricultural tax in this village in 2006. In 2008, one farm household from this village harvested 1,000kg rice and 2,500kg maize, and the gross income was around CNY7,000 (about USD1,000). Production input costs were about CNY2,000 (about USD300).

In the same year, this household received CNY2,400 (about USD350) of subsidies in total, comprising the following:

- subsidies for conversion from farming land to forestry programme – the standard is 75kg grain per mu (1,125kg grain per hectare), equivalent to CNY240 (USD34), and the total for the sample household was CNY1200 (USD170);

- direct subsidy to grain producers – the standard is CNY20 (USD3) per mu (CNY300; USD43 per hectare), and the total for this household was CNY80 (USD12);
- subsidies for growing good quality varieties – the standard is CNY10 (USD1.43) per mu (CNY150 per hectare), the total for this household is CNY50 (USD7);
- subsidies for natural disaster relief for crop production – the standard is CNY21.08 (USD3) per mu (CNY316.2; USD45 per hectare), the total was CNY105.40 (USD15);
- subsidies for good-quality rice varieties – the standard is CNY15 (USD2.1) per mu (CNY225; USD32 per hectare), the total was CNY720 (USD103);
- subsidies for replacement sows – the standard is CNY90 (USD12.8) per sow, the total is CNY180 (USD25.7).

In addition, the sample household received subsidies for purchasing agricultural machinery, buying ploughs, etc. The household also received reimbursement subsidies for participating in the new Rural Cooperative Medical System.

BOX 3.17 CHANGES IN PURCHASING POLICIES IN CHINA SINCE 1978

Agricultural production is very sensitive to the purchase price of inputs. In the early phases of reform, the central government raised the purchasing price for agricultural products by large margins and then adopted a dual pricing system (1985–1994), which means that it would purchase contracted grain at the contract price and purchase grain above quota at a higher price. As a result in 1984, China achieved the biggest harvest since the foundation of the PRC. After that, the government cancelled the bonus price for grain purchases above quota and changed the system to purchase all grain at the average of the quota price and the above-quota price, which resulted in a steep decline in grain harvests in 1985.

In 1988, the government applied a protection price to purchasing surplus grain from farmers, causing grain output to increase dramatically for several years afterwards and reaching a peak of 620 million tonnes. Later, the government decided to cancel the protection price, which again resulted in lower grain prices, followed by a reduction in grain output which, at its lowest, was only 430 million tonnes (Wang, 2008a).

From 2001 to 2002, the government began to cancel national purchase orders and intervention in the market. Then from 2003 to 2004, it began to

> expand reform to the main grain production areas. A policy was announced in 2004 that determined the complete market system for grain (Huang, 2008). In order to encourage grain production and protect the interests of grain producers, the government carried out a minimum purchase price policy.
>
> In 2006, the market price for grain was low. The government then initiated the pre-arranged plan for minimum purchasing price of wheat and rice, sub-sidizing CNY5.9 billion (around USD0.8 billion) from state revenue, paying a CNY0.2 per kg increase in the grain price. This led to a CNY23 billion (USD3 billion) increase in farmer income (Ministry of Finance).

In contrast, the agricultural sector in African countries has failed to eliminate poverty or to feed its growing population. Agriculture in China has played a fundamental role in dealing with financial crisis, but agricultural sectors in Africa were most affected by the financial crisis when examined in terms of impacts on the overall economy. According to monitoring data from the FAO, rice prices in Africa in 2008 increased by 50 per cent in Côte d'Ivoire and Central African Republic, 39 per cent in Cameroon, 45 per cent in Senegal, 60 per cent in Guinea Bissau, 42 per cent in Mauritania and 300 per cent in Sierra Leone. In China, the agricultural sector buffered negative impacts on income generation and employment in the financial crisis, while the weak foundation of African agriculture was weakened further.

Another distinct characteristic of many African countries' agricultural policies is a tendency to strong declaration of intent but weak implementation. The Lagos Plan of Action in the 1980s, for example, failed to be implemented for a number of reasons, including a lack of political commitment, synergy with the required political and economic reforms, ownership, political will and resources (Hope, 2002). Another example is the implementation of the Maputo Declaration on Agriculture and Food Security 2003, in which countries in the African Union promised to spend 10 per cent of the national budget to support agriculture and rural development within the next five years. However, a preliminary investigation of 19 sampled countries shows that 63 per cent of the countries spent less than 5 per cent of their national budgets, 21 per cent of the countries spent 5 to 10 per cent, and only 16 per cent appropriated not less than 10 per cent (NEPAD, 2006).

Looking at the regional development strategy of Chongwe District in Zambia, the plan for agriculture is to support the sustainable and competitive development of agriculture to ensure household and regional food security, and to maximize regional food contributions to the whole province and country. Its specific goals include:

- improving agricultural productivity and diversifying production;
- improving the efficiency and marketing system for breeding, crops and fisheries;
- improving the production efficiency of livestock breeding, especially in the rural sector;

- promoting the sustainable development of domestic and foreign markets for agricultural products driven by the private sector;
- promoting the development of fisheries; and
- promoting the development of aquaculture.

From its investment in projects in the agricultural sector, we can see that besides a large percentage of investment in irrigation and infrastructure, a substantial percentage has been invested in participatory community empowerment and poverty reduction, human capacity-building and management and coordination, indicating the attention to internal structural adjustment of agriculture and consideration for the social aspects of agriculture, at least during development planning (Table 3.2). From our survey in a village near Lusaka in 2009, it was found that nobody had received subsidies from the government, although some of them had heard about the fertilizer subsidy programme. Although implementing the plan will overcome many obstacles, for example institutional and fiscal capacity enhancement, this could be still optimistic from the experiences of Malawi (Juma, 2011).

Agricultural credit is another example. In the 2007/08 fiscal year, the Agricultural Input Trust Fund of Tanzania provided TZS4.4 billion (Ministry of Agriculture,

TABLE 3.2 Estimated Investment on Agricultural Projects in Chongwe, 2006–2011 (Unit: ZMK millions)

Project Field	Invested Funds
Livestock development and disease control	8427.55
Participatory community empowerment and poverty reduction	7290.00
Human resources development	5784.50
Irrigation and land use	5152.90
Management and coordination	4932.65
Infrastructure development	2860.40
Chalimbana Farm Institute support	2860.40
Aquaculture development	1354.80
Micro savings and credit development	1050.50
Cooperatives promotion and development	703.08
Block and camp operations	598.14
Crop diversification and development	546.30
Agricultural information services	371.50
HIV/AIDS and gender integration	315.92
Fisheries development	277.86
Agricultural marketing trade	234.35
Entrepreneurship development	213.36
Seed multiplication development	176.92
Participatory farming systems development	158.60
Farm power mechanization	119.50
Total	43,429.23

Source: Chongwe District Development Plan 2006–2011, Republic of Zambia

Food Security and Cooperatives, 2008). However, in Morogoro, only 4.4 per cent of rural households received credit and only 32 per cent of these were female-headed (Morogoro Report of Tanzania, 2008). In Kilosa, only male labour claimed that they were able to access official credit. In Pea Pea village, one of the field sites for the study of this book, no family received any credit.

The Economic Commission for Africa (2005) found that, related to economic inputs, in the 19 countries surveyed on agricultural issues, 51 per cent of household respondents said that they lacked access to agricultural extension services, 61 per cent lacked government credit for agriculture, and 57 per cent lacked access to irrigation facilities.

Conclusion

Both the Chinese government and governments in many African countries have adopted a development strategy that prioritizes industrialization and urbanization. At the same time agriculture is seen as the foundation of the national economy and responsible for providing a surplus for the industrialization and urbanization process. What differs between China and African countries is that China has been focusing on food security while ensuring adequate basic accumulation for industry: an approach that remains at the core of Chinese agricultural development policies. Specifically, China has set up a package of policy systems and relevant measures to ensure food production-oriented agricultural development in terms of land tenure, pricing policy, investment in science and technology, subsidies to agriculture and provision of agricultural infrastructure. In contrast, many African states treat agriculture as the capital source for industrialization and give priority to export-oriented economic crop production, ignoring domestic food production and national food security. The absence of endogenous agricultural development strategies has led to a heavy reliance on external support and a weak capacity to develop and implement locally-owned agricultural policies. Sadly, agricultural growth in Africa has been stagnant for several decades.

In order to ensure that agriculture supported the development of industry and other sectors, the Chinese government used a 'price scissor' strategy and kept the price of agricultural produce low, partly by keeping production costs low. It organized the agricultural cooperative movement so that a low-cost labour force could substitute for other high-cost production factors. The planned economy also enabled agricultural surplus to be invested directly into industrial production, bypassing the market. The country is now gradually adjusting this orientation so that rural areas, farmers and the agricultural sector (*San Nong*) can benefit from industrial and urban development. China is in a phase of integrated urban–rural development, subsidizing agriculture by using profits from industry. The high centralization of state power has guaranteed the consistency and continuity of policy during this transition.

In comparison with China, African countries have been able to accumulate resources for industrialization only through reliance on economic crops and export of agricultural products. However, this strategy has not guaranteed national food security or provided sufficient accumulation for industrialization. Key challenges have been economic downturns and social instability, as well as more specific problems such as inadequate foreign exchange to meet the balance of payments, neglect of smallholder production, an inability to plan and control the value produced by export-oriented agricultural production, limited support for industry, failure to mobilize people and organize the labour force to substitute high-cost productive factors, and inconsistency and interruption of development strategies due to pressure from both donor countries and local demands.

China has a full administrative system for the implementation of agricultural development strategies and policies. Every level of the government, including villages, can be easily informed and mobilized. Meanwhile the agriculture education, research and extension system, which is led by official departments and has a think-tank function for government, has been playing an important part in the cycle of developing, experimenting, implementing and providing feedback to policies. This effective policymaking, implementation and feedback system ensures that agricultural strategies and policies in China are continually rectified and adjusted until they fit well with farmer needs and realities.

By contrast, Africa has never had a hierarchical residential registration system or land tenure system, and national government has limited control over both society and capability to mobilize people. As a relatively disadvantaged sector, agriculture is generally not at the heart of government thinking. Agricultural policies barely reach the scattered small farmers who actually produce most of the food crops. Systematic reflection on strategic orientation and adjustment of agricultural policies is often lacking. However, researchers have questioned the obstacles of institutions under governmental lines. Bloom and Sachs (1998) stress that the emphasis on policy and institutions as the determinants of Africa's growth is exaggerated. They suggest instead that 60 to 90 per cent of Africa's slow growth is attributable to geography and demography – tropical climate and a tropical disease burden, hostile and unfertile soil quality, a high youth dependency ratio and a semi-arid climate with rainfall subject to long cycles and unpredictable failure, among others. Other aspects of geography and exogenous factors emphasized include low population density, which exacerbates high transport costs, a colonial heritage that artificially subdivides Africa into many unviable states with the median country's GDP averaging USD2 billion, many of its countries are landlocked, and have a higher ethno-linguistic diversity than in any other region.

Different policy effects can be identified in China and Africa where similar agricultural strategies and policies have been devised but implemented through different measures. Agriculture in China has contributed a lot to the solution of food security problems as well as the establishment of an industrial foundation within a short period of time. In this day and age, agriculture in China has become a buffer for the economic crisis and continues to ensure food security. Although African countries have similar agricultural strategies compared with China, and government functions and policies have been reformed more than once, food security has never been fully guaranteed and social problems remain entrenched. Constrained by limited internal authority and capacity and unreliable external conditions, African countries are neither capable of providing more support to agriculture, nor can they guarantee the long-term implementation and supervision of policies. Quite a few policies, particularly supportive ones, are merely nominal and are difficult to enact.

Undoubtedly, important lessons emerge from reflection on agricultural development strategies and policies in China and Africa. China has prioritized the development of industry and urban areas for several decades, and this has led to numerous social problems during a transition period relating to income disparity between urban and rural residents. China has emphasized food security and promoted land productivity through a land tenure system which separates ownership and use rights, and a residential registration system which creates a dual urban/rural dichotomy. Agricultural livelihoods have come under pressure in China, leading to widespread out-migration from rural areas and the creation of a surplus labour force of migrant labourers (the 'floating population'). Additionally, rapid investment in agricultural production has given rise to severe ecological problems and degrading of natural resources. Offsetting the negative externalities caused by past polices comes at a huge economic price. Similar to China, Africa has sacrificed agriculture for urbanization and industrialization. It is notable that Africa is endowed with many natural resources and has great potential for a vibrant farming sector. In the future, sustainable agricultural development may occur through effective policies to reallocate resources and mobilize society. The lessons and experiences from China in agricultural development may be relevant, although it will be important to adapt them to the different contexts found in diverse African states.

4

COMPARISON OF AGRICULTURAL PRODUCTION CONDITIONS IN CHINA AND AFRICA

Africa has sufficient land and water resources for grain production. If Africa's agricultural potential could be fully developed, it would not only solve its own grain needs, but also help to meet demand in other regions (25th Africa District Meeting of the United Nations Food and Agricultural Organization (FAO, 2008a). Besides abundant land and water resources, 95 per cent of areas in Africa are located in tropical or subtropical climatic zones, providing a cumulatively good temperature (heat units) for the perennial growth of crops. In terms of basic agricultural production conditions, China as a whole is inferior to Africa. However, Africa remains at a lower level when it comes to land quality, water resource utilization efficiency and the resilience to recover from natural disasters, all of which are related to limited investment in agriculture over a long period and to low output efficiency compared to factor inputs (Eswaran *et al.*, 1997). In Africa, relatively poor agricultural production conditions have restricted the development of agriculture. China, with a variety of types of land and seasons which are matched by a diversity of agricultural production modes and types and high market integration, possesses a great capacity for agricultural production and regulation of supply within the region. Meanwhile, with large differences in production between different countries in Africa and with regional cooperation organizations unable to coordinate discrepancies in production or encourage balanced trade between states, African countries find it hard to make an overall plan for regulating and utilizing internal production conditions, which ultimately restricts the improvement of resource utilization efficiency.

Natural Conditions for Agricultural Production

How Land Resources Are Utilized in China and Africa for Agricultural Development

Africa has more abundant land resources than China, first of all in the total area of cultivable land. As Figure 4.1 shows, in 2004 the Sub-Saharan Africa region had 166 million hectares of farmland, which is far more than the 122 million hectares of farmland in China. Per-capita cultivable farmland in the Sub-Saharan Africa region is 0.25 hectares; in China this figure is just 0.15 hectares (see Figure 4.2). The most critical difference is the proportion of utilized cultivable land, which has now almost reached saturation point[1] in China, while there is a vast quantity of land in Africa which has neither been developed nor currently utilized. According to 2002 statistics, Africa had 771 million hectares of cultivable land, with an actual arable land area of 204 million hectares under cultivation, accounting for 26 per cent of the total. Zambia, for example, covers an area of 75,200km^2, 58 per cent of which is arable land, however, only 14 per cent of that arable land has been developed (Zambia Fifth National Development Plan, 2006–2010). Even Mozambique, which is much more efficient in the development and utilization of arable land, utilizes less than one-fifth of its available arable area. It can be seen from this indicator that African land resources still have a huge potential for extensive development.

The trend in the change of the total arable land area indicates that arable land use in both China and Africa has been on the increase, especially in Africa where the arable land area utilized rose for 25 years from 1980 to 2004, while in China it began to decline slightly after reaching its maximum in 2000. In China there is a relationship between the increase in total cultivable area and population density; historically, the founders of dynasties mostly improved and adjusted the relationship between land and population by reclaiming wasteland and developing farmland (Li, 2010). After the founding of the People's Republic of China (PRC) in 1949, China largely reclaimed wasteland and developed farmlands, with agricultural acreage reaching 107 million hectares in 1952. Under the national policy of ensuring food security, agricultural acreage soared to 130 million hectares until 1996 and this continued until 2000, when it reached 137 million hectares, the maximum in history (see Figure 4.1). Due to the appropriation of farmland for construction, arable land ruined by disasters, the return of farmland for ecological protection and adjustment of agricultural production structures, agricultural acreage began to decrease to 121.8 million hectares by 2006, with a per-capita arable area of 0.09 hectares. The growth of the total cultivated area in Africa also correlates with that of its total population; however, with a relatively bigger base of arable land, its total cultivated area increased notably, with an increase of nearly 40 per cent from 1980 to 2004.

Although the cultivated area in both China and Africa is growing, the growth rate is lower than the population growth rate. The per-capita area of cultivated farmland in China reached 0.19 hectares in 1952, which is the highest level since the founding of the PRC, after which it continued to decline and has remained at a steady but low level since 1980. This figure declined to 0.1 hectares in 1996 and further to 0.09 hectares in 2005, which is only equal to 40 per cent of the world average. In Africa, although the total cultivated area expanded due to more rapid growth in population, the per-capita cultivated farmland area declined noticeably, decreasing by 34 per cent from 1980 to 2000. During the period from 1980 to 2000, growth of the total cultivated area was not as high as it was between 2000 and 2004, while the population growth in the two periods was relatively similar, about 2 to 3 per cent. Therefore, after the per-capita area of cultivated farmland declined from 0.38 hectares in 1980 to 0.25 hectares in 2000, the figure remained at a relatively steady level of 0.25 to 0.27 hectares[2] in the period from 2000 to 2004. The total cultivated area of Africa has grown much faster than that of China, with a 15 per cent difference between Africa and China during the period between 1980 and 2004, but there is no noticeable gap between these two regions as the population of Africa grew at a higher rate than China. The annual growth rate for Africa was 2.8 per cent from 1987 to 1997 and 2.5 per cent from 1997 to 2007, while the figure in China was 1.2 per cent and 0.7 per cent respectively in the corresponding periods (World Health Organization (WHO), 2009).

Although Africa's cultivated land expanded much more slowly than its population, according to the data from the World Bank (2002) the growth of agricultural output in Sub-Saharan Africa primarily derived from the growth of cultivated land area in the period from 1961 to 2001. The FAO indicated that since the 1960s the grain-growing area in Sub-Saharan Africa had doubled, but the per-unit yield of grain remained almost unchanged. In the meantime, data from China showed that cultivated land expansion made little contribution to agricultural development in China. As indicated by Table 4.1, of all the inputs to agriculture, the contribution of cultivated land area expansion to growth of total agricultural output was negative and the situation was even worse in the period from 1984 to 1987 than in the period from 1978 to 1983.

If only land utilization is taken into account, the difference in styles of land management would be the main reason for the discrepancy in agricultural output

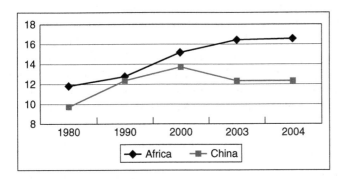

Figure 4.1 Comparison of Total Cultivated Farmland in China and the Sub-Saharan Africa Region (Unit: million ha)

Source: FAOSTAT

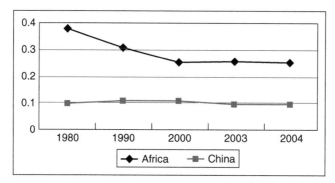

Figure 4.2 Comparison of the Per-capita Area of Cultivated Farmland in China and the Sub-Saharan Africa Region (Unit: ha)

Source: FAOSTAT

between China and Africa. In China, intensive land utilization over a long period of time has a very important position in history. While this method can greatly increase land productivity, it results in excessive reclamation of forest land, grassland and wetlands, and negatively impacts on the climate and environment. In the Ming Dynasty and the Qing Dynasty (1368–1911), in response to an exploding population, the government had to reclaim land to expand agricultural acreage. The efforts made in both dynasties to transform the Yellow River and Huai River into farmland is a good example. By 1855, a total of 10,000km² of land was created, with the mouth of the river extending 90km into the sea (Lu *et al.*, 2007). However, from 1700 to 1949 the forested area in China decreased from 248 million hectares to 109 million hectares.[3] China has implemented measures such as planting trees and foresting bare mountains, which has resulted in an increase in the forested area to 175 million hectares;[4] however, tropical rainforests and virgin forests have been irrevocably destroyed. In addition, arable land expansion has resulted in a drastic reduction of wetland acreage and the deterioration of natural grasslands, which has not been effectively resolved. For example, in Qinghai Province there are 547 million hectares of natural grassland, and 90 per cent are moderately degraded. According to farmers' reports in the Xianghai National Natural Reserve, which is located in the Keerqin Sands in Jilin Province, the water table has dropped by nearly 20 metres over the past decade. This is costly: by the end of 2006, China had totally invested more than CNY130 billion in programmes to return farmland to forests. In 2007, an additional cycle was extended with further investment of CNY206 billion. At the same time, the Natural Forest Protection Programme initiated in 1998 has cost a total of CNY94.58 billion. The Beijing-Tianjin Sandstorm Control Programme and the programme of converting grazing areas to grassland initiated in 2000 have cost CNY6.52 billion in total.

Often, land tenure in Africa is not formally specified, and this can encourage extensive use of land (see Box 4.1). However, with the growth of population pressure, the manner of utilizing land in Africa has been changing with, for example, shortened fallow periods, blind crop rotation and intensive use of pasture land. These trends can result in land desertification and erosion and loss of farmland. Due to the large scale of land resource development, the tropical rainforest area declined sharply to 6.4 per cent. The area of remaining forest is also declining by 300,000 hectares (5 per cent) every year (Lu, 2000).

According to statistics, about half of the desertification in Africa is caused by overgrazing. Deforestation, over-cutting and irrational agricultural economic activity are resulting in increasing land impoverishment and undermining food security. In 2002–2004, about 85 per cent of arable land had lost nutrients equivalent to 30kg/ha annually, with 40 per cent of the land losing more than 60kg/ha, equivalent to a loss of USD4 billion (Economic and Commercial Counsellor's Office of the Embassy of the People's Republic of China in the Republic of Guinea, 2006).

The status of energy shortage in rural Africa is the most serious for all the world's continents: 80 to 90 per cent of energy consumption is from wood fuel, crop straw and animal waste. The use of natural resources as energy in rural areas has resulted in increasingly serious damage to natural vegetation (mainly forest), which is beyond the natural regeneration rate. According to United Nations Environment Programme (UNEP) data, Africa is losing 4 million hectares of forest each year, which is twice the world average as well as more than 250 million hectares of tropical grassland; 65 per cent of African land degradation comes from the erosion and damage from chemical and physical properties (Jiang, 2008).

TABLE 4.1 Contribution of Various Factors to Agricultural Growth in China

Production Function Approach	1978– 1984	1984– 1987	Supply Response Function Approach	1978– 1984	1984– 1987
Input	45.79	−9.97	Relative market price	−0.76	127.32
Land	−1.75	−38.24	Relative acquisition price	15.98	−119.72
Labour	4.52	−70.07			
Capital	10.82	44.73	Time trend	29.84	149.64
Fertilizer	32.2	53.71			
Productivity	48.64	48.71			
Household contract system	46.89	0.00	Household contract system	42.20	0.00
Multiple-crop index	−1.94	20.90			
Proportion of non-grain crops	3.69	27.79			
Residual error	5.57	61.28	Residual error	12.74	−57.24
Total	100.00	100.00	Total	100.00	100.00

Source: Lin (1992)

BOX 4.1 MANNER OF LAND CULTIVATION IN MUSEKE VILLAGE, CHONGWE DISTRICT, ZAMBIA

Olipah Kaseba in Museke Village has seven children, the family has about 3.5 hectares of farmland (0.5 hectare per capita); however, her family owns 10 hectares of land. She claims that due to lack of labour they have not fully cultivated the land, therefore, she does not worry about land issues and even if the children still live in the village when they grow up, they will have sufficient land. Even then, if 10 hectares of land is insufficient, they can apply to the village head and claim other wasteland. Although she claims that they already adopt conservation tillage, according to this procedure some tillage activities should be made in the beginning of the hot and dry season: in actual fact, in the dry season they still do not use labour on their lands. According to the introduction made by Museke, the village chief, each household in the village actually can be allocated 3 hectares out of the total land of the village, which will be sufficient.

One of the important experiences that China has had in land utilization is to make more of the cultivated area by enhancing the multiple-cropping index so as to enhance land utilization efficiency. In the early 1970s, the arable area in China declined by 0.2 per cent every year, but the cultivated area increased by nearly 1 per cent each year. Since 1978, the grain cultivation area continued to decline and reached the lowest level in 1988. In the period 1978–1992, the cultivated area of industrial crops increased by 3.4 per cent every year (*China Statistical Yearbook*, 1995) (see Figure 4.3 for the change in the cultivated area and multiple-cropping index).

China's Experience Can Inform Land Utilization Efficiency in Africa

China's experience in water and land conservation can be used as a reference to enhance land utilization efficiency in Africa. Although there are abundant land resources on the African continent, soil quality is relatively poor: 20 per cent of the soil in the West African Sahel is severely desertified and eroded; meanwhile, the soil in tropical areas is acidic, 18 per cent of lands are relatively infertile and 22 per cent of the African continent is a desert in which no cultivation activities can be undertaken. With plenty of precipitation, most African countries enjoy rainfall between 900mm and 1750mm but droughts occur frequently, with 66 per cent of areas often suffering from drought and only 4 per cent of lands under irrigation (World Bank, 2008). A study by the FAO shows that 46 per cent of African land is unable to develop rain-fed agriculture, 24 per cent of land is too humid, and only 30 per cent of land is suitable for rain-fed agriculture. Population pressure in Africa is gradually increasing but it is not feasible to extend the cultivated area. In addition,

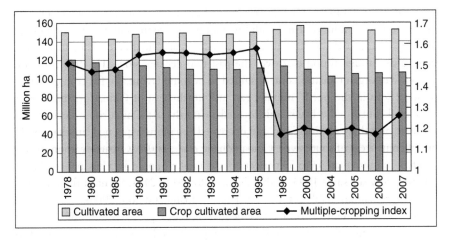

Figure 4.3 Change in Cultivated Area of Agricultural Product and Multiple-cropping Index since Chinese Reform (Unit: million ha)

Source: *China Statistical Yearbook* (1995, 1996, 2008)

soil fertility decline is a serious issue: in the last 10 years, increasing attention has been paid to the soil degradation issue and the sustainable utilization of lands (Wopereis *et al.*, 2006). However, China has been able to maintain soil fertility because of various intensive labour inputs, fine cultivation techniques and continuous fertilizer inputs. The difference in land productivity between China and Africa is the main reason for marked differences in agricultural output levels. Research suggests that land quality, labour quality and government efficiency significantly contribute to the productivity of African agriculture (Ajao, 2008), whereas the enhancement of agricultural land productivity in China is mainly derived from technological advances, systematic innovation and input of capital and labour (Huang, 2003). In addition, soil management technologies have promoted improvements in soil quality. These include the vertical cultivation model, green manure, dry soil rice cultivation, deep tillage and mulching, all of which have contributed to a fertile soil structure (Sandrey and Edinger, 2009).

Seventy-two per cent of arable land and 31 per cent of grasslands suffer from degraded soil quality. In addition to an inherent lack of fertility in many soils, nutrient mining is argued by many researchers as a primary cause for declining soil fertility. This occurs through processes such as leaching and inadequate replacement of nutrients removed by cultivation. Some commentators argue that the major nutrients nitrogen, phosphorus and potassium have all declined over the last 30 years.[5] Some studies indicate that the loss of these three nutrients in many countries reaches 60kgs per hectare each year (Smaling *et al.,* 1997; De Jager *et al.*, 1998; van den Bosch *et al.*, 1998; Wortmanna and Kaizzi, 1998; Nkonya and Kaizzi, 2003). It is noted that figures on African soil fertility are disputed, given limitations in methodologies in extrapolating from small to large areas and great variability at plot, farm, regional and national scales (Scoones, 2001; Keeley and Scoones, 2003).

Changes in Chinese soil organic matter have been relatively positive. Due to highly intensive utilization and with low inputs, the second soil investigation in the late 1970s and early 1980s showed low soil organic matter content in China's farmlands. Studies found that over the past two decades since the 1980s, the soil with lower organic matter content shifted to become favourable for crop growing: in most soils in the north, middle, east and north-west of China, organic matter increased, but for the black soils located in north-east China some decline was evident, and there are increased and decreased situations happened simultaneously in different areas of south-west China (Zhang *et al.*, 2007). Organic carbon matter content in more than 53 to 59 per cent of the total cropping area has increased over the past 20 years since 1993, with a decrease for 30 to 31 per cent of the cropping area and remaining stable for 4 to 6 per cent (Huang and Sun, 2006).

The advancement of soil management technology provides an improved basis for maintaining soil fertility. Some technologies have been extensively applied to agricultural production in Africa such as the intercropping model, which has been adopted in many places. Moreover, many land management technologies do not require a large amount of capital input, but plenty of labour input such as conservation tillage, as mentioned previously. In China, agriculture became both technology-intensive and labour-intensive over time, which compensated for an insufficiency of land resources and allowed for high levels of unit land output.

However, fertilizer utilization demonstrated negative impacts on the environment, particularly due to overuse. Currently, the effectiveness of nitrogenous fertilizer utilization is only 28.3 per cent, 28.2 per cent and 27.5 per cent respectively for rice, wheat and maize production, and the average is 27.5 per cent (Zhang, 2007). According to research in China (Vitousek *et al.*, 2009), severe acidity has occurred in farming land during the past 20 years, while nitrogen is the major factor to blame. China is now consuming 35 per cent of global nitrogen on its 7 per cent of arable land. This has resulted in different levels of direct soil acidification in up to 90 per cent of arable land in China. According to this research, nitrogen has decreased soil pH value by 0.5 on average, whereas naturally it would take hundreds of years to be there without human interference. For the grain crop system, nitrogen overuse contributes to 60 per cent of soil acidification; while for the cash crop system as greenhouse vegetables and fruits, the number can be as high as 90 per cent.

These accelerated factors, including subsidies on fertilizer for smallholder production in China, should be reviewed seriously while they are proposed as a reference for the intensification of agriculture in Africa.

In Africa, if basic technological innovations are adopted, such as greater usage of fertilizer, about 43 per cent of land can reach a medium sustainable level (see Table 4.2). If inputs can be increased and farmers provided with training, then potentially 10 million km^2 (35 per cent) of land could achieve sustainable agricultural development (Eswaran *et al.*, 1997).

TABLE 4.2 Proportion of Land Area to Input Levels in Africa, Based on Sustainable
Utilization Potential (%)

Potential of Sustainable Utilization	Low Input	Medium Input	High Input
High	0	21.8	35.2
Medium	43.2	13.5	8.9
Low	2.2	19.6	10.6
Very low	53.7	44.4	44.4
Water bodies	0.9	0.9	0.9
Total	100	100	100

Source: Eswaran *et al.* (1997)

Climatic Resources Impact Significantly on Agricultural Development in China and Africa

Climatic resources such as rain and temperature have a significant impact on
agricultural development in both countries, and determine the main methods of
agricultural production. China possesses many types of climate with significant
effects on agricultural production systems. These include tropical, sub-tropical and
temperate climates, and an eastern monsoonal region abundant in water resources
and with high temperatures. In this area, where the rainy season and the hot season
occur simultaneously, growth of various types of crops is possible. For example, in
China there are six different rice production zones between the north and south of
the country. The cropping system and selection of varieties for each zone differ
markedly (see Table 4.3), reflecting differences in annual cumulative temperature
and rainfall.

Africa is located between latitude 35°S and 37°N: 75 per cent of the African
landmass is within the Tropic of Capricorn and the Tropic of Cancer, tropical and
sub-tropical climates dominate and the average temperature is above 20°C. The
average temperature is only below 20°C at the northernmost and southernmost tips
of the continent and in some mountainous areas. Southern Africa is generally rich
in sunshine, with an annual average duration of 2,400 to 3,200 hours. From the
south-east coast to the north-west inland areas, average sunshine duration gradually
increases, making this area suitable for farming. Most areas are suitable for two or
three crops per year (Jiang, 2008).

As mentioned previously, lying in the tropical climatic zone, 95 per cent of
African regions are characterized by tropical and sub-tropical climates, with an
annual average temperature above 20°C, while an average below 20°C only occurs
in the southern and northern extremes of the continent and some mountainous
regions. The climate in Africa is greatly affected by its position straddling the
equator. The southern and northern tropical zones in Africa enjoy high temperatures
most of the year, mitigated to some extent by high mountains and ocean tidal

TABLE 4.3 China's Rice Growing Zone

Name	Area	≥10 °C		Rainfall (mm)	Total Amount of Solar Radiation kJ/cm²	Annual Hours of Solar Radiation	Cropping System and Variety Selection Resulting from Difference in Annual Cumulative Temperature
		Annual Cumulative Temperature °C	Days				
South China – temperate and tropical double-cropping rice production zone	South of Nanling and Taiwan	5800–9300	260–365	1200–2500	377–502	1500–2600	Double cropping, 3 harvests
Mid-China temperate and humid single and double-cropping rice production zone	North of Nanling, South of Qingling and Huaihe	4500–6500	210–260	800–2000	209–482	1200–2300	Double cropping, 3 harvests and single cropping, 2 harvests
South-west China Plateau – humid single-cropping rice production zone	Yunnan and Guizhou Plateau and Tibetan Plateau	2900–8000	180–260	800–1400	293–461	1200–2600	Single cropping

North China – semi-humid single cropping rice production zone	South of Great Wall, North of Qinling and Huaihe	4000–5000	170–210	580–1000	461–565	2000–3000	Single cropping, 2 harvests; 3 harvests in 2 year; 1 harvest in a year
North-east China – semi-humid single-cropping zone	North of Great Wall, East of Daxinganling	2000–3700	110–200	350–1100	419–611	2200–3100	Single harvest
North-west China – arid single cropping	West of Hexi Corridor, North of Qilan Mountain	2000–4250	110–250	50–600	544–628	2500–3400	Single harvest

Source: Chinese Rice Research Institute (1989)

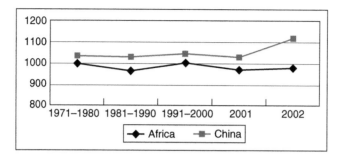

Figure 4.4 Rainfall in China and Africa (Unit: mm)

currents along the coast, such as the cool Benguela current (in the south-west) and warm Mozambique current (in the south-east). The entire continent of Africa is divided into eight climatic regions: hot desert, semi-arid, tropical wet and dry climate, tropical humid (Equator) region, Mediterranean region, sub-tropical humid ocean region, warm temperate plateau region and mountainous region.

Total flow volume for rivers in Africa amounts to 4,657m³, accounting for 12 per cent of the global total and ranking third only after Asia and South America. This means that Africa enjoys sufficient irrigation water, particularly if lakes, marshes and underground water are counted. Recyclable water resources in Africa reach nearly 4 trillion m³, accounting for 9 per cent of the global total, with per-capita water standing at 4,600m³ in 2003. China only enjoys total fresh water resources of 2.8 trillion m³, accounting for 6 per cent of the global total, with per-capita water amounting to 2100m³, less than one-third of the world average of 6900m³. China is one of the most limited countries in the world in terms of per-capita water resource availability:[6] the difference in water resource distribution between south and north China is particularly acute. Of the total Chinese population, 54 per cent live in the Yangtze River region and south of the Yangtze, and this area enjoys 81 per cent of total Chinese water resources. Meanwhile, 46 per cent of the Chinese population live in the north of the country, but this area only enjoys 19 per cent of total water resources (Xinhua Net, 2005). However, compared to Africa, China has a better combination of water resource and climatic conditions. Monsoonal rains in the warm months enable double-cropping in the region around the Yangtze (Stavrianos, 1999). In addition, mean precipitation in China is relatively higher than in Africa (Figure 4.4).

Climate change has important impacts on agricultural output. Rainfall, soil moisture, daily precipitation and evaporation all affect agricultural output. These impacts vary with different types of crops. However, judging from the correlation between precipitation and output, these impacts can be detected to some extent.

As in China, countries in the Sub-Saharan African region also have an imbalance of precipitation distribution (Figure 4.5). Distribution of precipitation is influenced by terrain, land and sea locations, ocean currents and other factors. This means that eastern and southern Africa, which are more mountainous, have more complicated

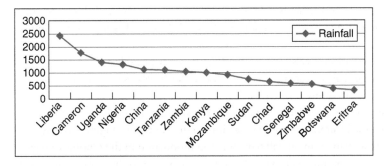

Figure 4.5 Rainfall Comparison between China and Selected African Countries
(Unit: mm)

Source: FAOSTAT

rainfall distribution patterns than West Africa (Zeng, 1984). The clear rainy season
in much of Africa can be associated with concentrated rainfall causing loss of soil
nutrients, which is not conducive to crop production (Zungu, 1984).

Annual rainfall distribution in most countries is extremely uneven, making it
impossible to cultivate crops only by depending on natural rainfall over the whole
year without irrigation facilities. Figure 4.6 shows Zambia's climatic change in one
year: the rainfall from April to October is less than 22mm, which cannot meet the
demand of grain growth, while there is almost no rain in July and August.

It can be discovered from analysing both rainfall and output in these countries
that they have a certain correlation: for example, in Botswana where there is less
rainfall, the unit crop production is lowest; while in Tanzania and Uganda, where
there is moderate rainfall, unit crop production is relatively high. However, due to
complicated agricultural production conditions and variability in input use, the

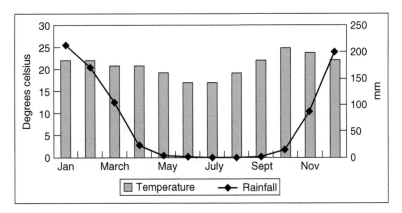

Figure 4.6 Air Temperature and Rainfall Distribution of Lusaka, Zambia in a Year by
Monthly Average

Source: http://www.studentsoftheworld.info/pageinfo_pays.php3?Pays=ZAM&Opt=climate

influence of rainfall on agricultural production has to be considered alongside other factors, such as availability of irrigation. Hence Algeria and Kenya, for example, maintain high unit crop outputs of 3,348kg and 1,512.6kg per hectare respectively at lower precipitation levels (see Figure 4.7). It is not possible to generate a conclusion from Zimbabwe data in 2002, because it mostly relates to political instability and the exodus of commercial farms.

There are strong links between rainfall patterns and crop production in much of Africa, given the limited amount of irrigation on the continent. Figure 4.8 illustrates the impact that changes in rainfall have on crop production in the Chongwe region of Zambia. Comparing Tengxian County, Guangxi Province in China with Chongwe, both of which have unstable precipitation, Tengxian County is much less affected than Chongwe. Hit by flood disasters occurring in the Xunjiang region on 12–16 June 2008, Tengxian County[7] only yielded summer grain of 27kg/ha which was calculated by sowing area – a reduction of 2.91 per cent on the previous year. For grain, early rice reached 29kg/ha, remaining at the same level as 2006 but decreasing by 2.47 per cent when compared with that of 2007. Other grain crops were less impacted by the disasters, so their unit production changed little: corn production per mu grew by 2.37 per cent, soybean production per mu grew by 3.99 per cent, green bean production per hectare grew by 2.17 per cent, mixed bean production per hectare grew by 3.89 per cent, and sweet potato production per hectare grew by 0.81 per cent. We can get a better view of the present water irrigation conditions in Zambia by going back several decades, when crop production conditions in the Guangxi Autonomous Region of China were similar to Chongwe at present. In view of this, we know that the input of other production facilities, such as improving water irrigation facilities, plays a significant role in compensating for a lack of favourable natural resource conditions.

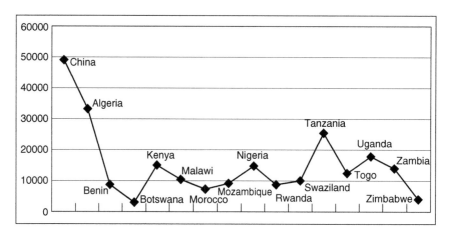

Figure 4.7 Crop Output in China and Some Countries in Sub-Saharan Africa in 2002 (kg/ha)

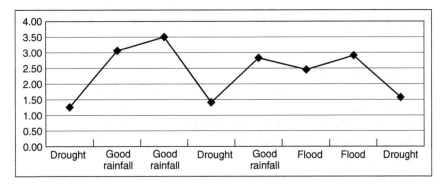

Figure 4.8 Units of Corn Production of Chongwe Region, Zambia under Different Rainfall Conditions, 2001–2002 to 2008–2009 (Unit: Tonnes)

Source: Ministry of Agriculture and Cooperatives, Chongwe District

Africa still has irrigation potential that needs to be brought into full play, especially as out of 42.5 million hectares of potentially irrigable lands, only 12.7 million hectares (30 per cent) have been irrigated (InterAcademy Council, 2004). FAO (2007a) data show that 40 per cent of irrigated land in Africa was in North Africa, while the large Sub-Saharan Africa region had 9 million hectares of irrigated and cultivated areas, only accounting for 5 per cent of the total; 60 per cent of the expected irrigable regions were in humid regions, nearly 25 per cent of which were in the Congo basin. Due to abundant rainfall, irrigation only serves as a supplement: for example, in Zambia, as long as rainfall in the warm and humid season remains at the normal level of 800mm, underground water in the dry season is sufficient for crop production. Compared with Asia, Africa requires higher investment in irrigation facility construction, ranging from USD5,000 per hectare to USD25,000 per hectare (InterAcademy Council 2004). As indicated by the FAO (1995), water resource development costs for medium and large-scale irrigation were USD8,300 per hectare in the Sub-Saharan Africa region and USD6,800 per hectare in northern Africa. The direct cost of social infrastructure construction, such as roads, buildings, cables and public facilities, is relatively high. Research suggests that the average irrigation cost per hectare in the Sub-Saharan Africa region is around USD18,300 (Rosegrant *et al.*, 2002). Based on AQUASTAT Database on Investment in Irrigation Projects,[8] we calculated the approximate cost of irrigation investment on rehabilitation (i.e. restoration of an existing irrigation system into good or working condition) and modernization (i.e. upgrading the system with more modern technologies and management) with surface irrigation technology: the average cost in ten projects in China is USD372, and the average cost in three projects in Ghana, one project in Niger, one project in Senegal and one project in Sudan is USD3,205. The calculation applies to the years of the project around 1997–2000 and uses the price in 2000.[9]

The input and maintenance of irrigation facilities requires guaranteed land ownership and water rights. Meanwhile, utilization of water resources requires the support of other factors such as:

- proper crop varieties
- supplementary input of fertilizer (as additional fertilizer is needed when watering times increase)
- an available labour force at busy points in the agricultural calendar
- demand for irrigated products
- market access
- incentives to agricultural intensification
- favourable topography
- good–quality soil
- adequate policy environments.

However, these preconditions have been difficult to meet in many African settings (Rosegrant and Perez, 1997; FAO, 2006, 2008b). Although the cost of irrigation projects implemented in developing countries have generally decreased over the last four decades, and the performance of irrigation projects has improved (Inocencio *et al.*, 2007), the situation in Sub-Saharan Africa is different. This region has higher costs than other regions in terms of simple averages, although some projects have been implemented successfully with lower costs compared to other regions (Calzadilla *et al.*, 2009). This means that rain-fed agriculture is dominant in Africa. The 2005 AQUASTAT update for Africa estimates that out of 182,645,012 hectares of cultivated land in Sub-Saharan Africa, only 7,105,119 hectares (4 per cent) are equipped for some form of irrigation, and only another 2 million hectares are cultivated as non-equipped wetlands/valley bottoms/flood recession (FAO, 2006). According to Rosegrant and colleagues, the situation will remain unchanged until 2025 (Rosegrant *et al.*, 2002).

If there is no irrigation, grain production in Africa will be greatly impacted by changes in rainfall, air temperature and climate. This is very serious for both case and food crops. According to studies by Barrios *et al.* (2008), geographic conditions and agricultural production systems in Sub-Saharan Africa make it more sensitive to climate change impacts. The Intergovernmental Panel on Climate Change (IPCC, 2007) reports that countries in Sub-Saharan Africa are likely to be severely affected by climate change and variability. Projections show that extreme heat and heavy precipitation are likely to become more frequent, affecting the ability of an already stressed area to produce cash as well as food crops. Given the likely gradual decline in rainfall, it is very important for policymakers to adopt appropriate policies in order to mitigate impacts on the agricultural sector.

Impact of Agricultural Disasters on Agricultural Development in China and Africa

China is one of the countries in the world that suffers from the most frequent and severe disasters. In 2006, it was hit by 38 natural disasters, affecting a population of 88.74 million and causing direct economic losses of USD13.6 billion, ranking first in the world. Seven out of the top 10 natural disasters in the world that have caused great economic loss occurred in China. The top five natural disasters all happened in China (Centre for Research on the Epidemiology of Disasters, 2007). From 1991 to 2006, the total annual cultivated area for agricultural crops in China averaged 153 million hectares; according to statistics from the Ministry for Civil Affairs, the disaster-hit cropland area in China was 49.95 million hectares, accounting for 31.93 per cent of the total cultivated area; the damaged area (where production was reduced by 30 per cent) was 25.29 million hectares, accounting for 16.53 per cent of the total cultivated area and 51.77 per cent of the disaster-hit area; and the area where crops failed (with production reduced by 80 per cent) was 6.4 million hectares, accounting for 4.18 per cent of the total cultivated area, 13.09 per cent of the disaster-hit area and 25.29 per cent of the disaster area.

With a vast expanse of territory, complicated terrain and a transparent monsoonal climate, China often incurs climatic disasters. Droughts, floods and extreme cold are the major challenges. Droughts can be classified as spring, summer and autumn droughts. China has different types of droughts in different areas. The Yellow River–Huai River region mainly has spring droughts, and the Yangtze River mainly has summer droughts and sometimes autumn droughts. Shocks from extreme cold period mainly happen in northeastern and northern China, causing damage to rice, sorghum, corn, soybeans and other crops.

Cold weather can cause wind, rain, snow and frost, and these cause most damage for crops in spring and autumn: for example, in the 1950s the wheat region in north China was hit by very severe frosts, causing about 3 billion kilograms of wheat harvest loss. In the last 30 years, drought disasters in each period have continued to intensify (Table 4.4). The proportion of areas damaged by drought remained consistent through the 1980s and 1990s, but the figure has risen extensively since 2000. During this period, annual grain loss nationwide has been 37 million tonnes, about double that for the 1980s and a figure equivalent to around 8 per cent of grain production. In 2000, the drought-hit area nationwide reached 40 million hectares, accounting for 25.9 per cent of the cultivated area and 1.6 times the average disaster-hit area. The damaged area was 27 million hectares, accounting for 66.1 per cent of the total national disaster-hit area, and twice the average damaged area. Grain loss due to drought was nearly 60 million tonnes, about 2.5 times the average due to drought in previous years and accounting for 13 per cent of total grain production.

The harm to agriculture from agricultural pests is only second to that of drought. Before the 1980s, the Chinese government not only emphasized the alleviation and prevention of pests through agricultural chemicals, but also focused on the development of biological technologies, such as using white muscardine fungi to prevent longicorn beetle from attacking crops. At present, the development of

TABLE 4.4 The Effects of Drought on Agriculture in China between 1980 and 2007

Year	1980–1989	1990–1999	2000–2007
Annual average drought-hit area	3.68	3.37	3.93
Annual average drought-damaged area (10^8 mu; one mu = 1/15 ha)	1.76	1.79	2.33
Annual total crop failure area (10^8mu)	0.39	0.33	0.54
The proportion of drought-damaged area in disaster area (%)	47.9	48	59.3
Annual average grain loss due to drought (10^4t)	1921.9	2065.3	3728.4
Proportion of grain loss due to drought in total production (%)	5.1	4.4	7.7

Source: Zhang and Qu (2008)

biopesticides in China has achieved great progress; meanwhile, great attention also has been paid to developing and applying agribiotechnologies: for example, by using tissue culture to undertake the propagation of virus-free fruit trees, flowers, vegetables and potatoes. So far, China has made world-class achievements in the development of transgenic insect-resistant cotton and in the prevention of locusts and other similar large pests. In the last 30 years, China has not suffered large-scale agricultural pest disasters; to a certain extent this explains the steady growth in grain production.

Natural disasters in Africa are also very frequent. According to relevant statistics, the population in the African continent affected by floods averaged 5.2 million in the 1960s and 15.4 million in the 1970s. The population affected by drought was 18.5 million in the 1960s, 24.4 million in the 1970s and exceeded 30 million in 1985. The African continent suffers from serious drought almost once every 10 years (Lu, 2000). African agriculture is greatly affected by drought and one of the biggest challenges facing small farmers is the risk of crop loss due to different rainfall and drought, which endangers food security. Even in a year of generally sufficient rainfall, disastrous consequences befall on agriculture due to late or early rainfall (World Bank, 2004). In the drought and semi-drought-prone agro-ecological regions, climate change is increasingly a challenge that needs an appropriate response.

Pest disasters impact on agricultural production and increase livelihood vulnerability for farmers in Africa. Locust disasters are very catastrophic and happen frequently, especially those caused by desert locusts, found particularly in areas adjacent to the Sahara Desert in West Africa. Major grain crop losses are caused by disease (15.6 per cent), pests and birds (16.3 per cent) and weeds (16.6 per cent), equalling 48.5 per cent of all losses.

Africa has long-established research institutions focusing on locusts, including the International Centre for Insect Physiology and Ecology in Nairobi, Kenya and the Centre de Lutte Antiacridienne for locusts in Nouakchott, Mauritania. Other regional international institutions include the Desert Locust Control Organisation for Eastern Africa and the International Red Locust Control Organization for Central and Southern Africa. Besides locusts, these organizations also monitor and take action against the cabbage army worm, tsetse fly and quelea bird (a rice pest in the Sahel). They cooperate with neighbouring countries, provide funds and information and undertake treatment and prevention under the instruction of experts.

Although both China and Africa are equipped with disaster prevention and rescue facilities supported by government, the utilization of these facilities and inputs is comparatively more efficient in China. For example, during the relatively severe natural disaster of 2007, the central government responded and transferred CNY13.3 billion (USD1.95 billion) to support the disaster response; local government also actively arranged funds (Ministry of Finance, 2008a, 2008b). At the beginning of 2008, central government transferred CNY47.91 billion (USD7 billion) of disaster rescue funds, making efforts to protect against snow and cold weather in southern regions and to strengthen temporary support for disaster-hit people, energetically supporting the recovery of agricultural production, rebuilding of collapsed civil buildings and recovery of electricity networks, transportation and education. In 2001, the Ministry of Finance formed the Fund Management Method for Agricultural Disaster Prevention and Relief to utilize disaster prevention and relief funds in order to reduce disaster loss. In Africa, fiscal constraints mean that disaster prevention inputs and relief mainly derive from international aid. In June 2009, the International Red Locust Control Organization in East Africa and South Africa successfully curbed severe locust disasters in Tanzania using biological disinfectants. The affected countries requested aid from the FAO, as resources were lacking to respond to this problem. The UN's Central Emergency Response Fund donated about USD2 million, and the FAO provided about USD1 million from its emergency fund. If there were no such support, the locust disaster would have affected 15 million grain producers (FAO Media Centre, 2009).

Compared with China, losses caused directly by drought and pests in Africa are inevitable. However, disaster prevention and relief could reduce losses to a large extent when disasters happen.

Comparison of Capacity to Balance and Coordinate Resources and Production Supply within the Region

The UN divides Africa into five regions: north, east, south, west and central. There is a large discrepancy in terms of agricultural resources between these regions: the structure of agricultural production differs from one region to another, and within regions as well as within countries. In Zambia, for example, there are several agro-ecological regions (see Box 4.2).

One problem across the African continent is a lack of infrastructure, as well as market barriers between countries that limit the flow of resources and products. Although natural conditions for agriculture are generally good, the 53 countries in the continent face different natural conditions, which result in very different agricultural production capabilities. Although some regional cooperation organizations have been established to promote integration among African countries, their functioning remains limited and their capacity to adjust production and supply within regions remains relatively poor.

BOX 4.2 ZAMBIA'S THREE AGRO-ECOLOGICAL REGIONS

Zambia can be divided into three major agro-ecological areas reflecting different climatic conditions and soil types.

Region I

The rainfall in this region is no more than 800mm. The region accounts for 12 per cent of Zambia's land area, and covers some of the southern province and parts of the eastern and western provinces. The region is suitable for growing crops that are strongly resistant to drought, such as cotton, sesame, sorghum and chestnuts. Some regions are suitable for growing cassava. Much of this area is low-lying, humid and hot, with a widespread prevalence of tsetse fly: as such, these regions are not suitable for raising livestock.

Region II

This region with rainfall between 800 and 1,000mm accounts for 42 per cent of the Zambian land area. The region can be divided into sub-regions IIa and IIb. Sub-region IIa includes the middle province, Lusaka, southern province and the plateau in the eastern province, all of which are very fertile. Large amounts of medium and long-term investment have been made to promote the development of agriculture in the region. A variety of grain crops are planted, including maize, cotton, tobacco, sunflower, wheat and peanuts as well as other crops. The region is also suitable for planting flowers, red peppers and vegetables. Region IIb mainly refers to the western province and is primarily a sandy region. This region is suitable for growing cashews, rice, cassava, millet, vegetable and forestry products, as well as raising beef cattle, dairy cows, chickens and laying hens.

Region III

This region's annual rainfall of 1,000–1,500mm accounts for 46 per cent of the territory in Zambia, and mainly includes the Copperbelt Province, Luapula Province, northern province and northwestern province. With the exception of

Copperbelt Province, the soil in the region is mainly acidic soil, with great potential for planting millet, cassava, sorghum, soybeans and peanuts. The region also could grow coffee, sugarcane, rice and pineapples. If treated with limestone, the agricultural potential in the region could be further strengthened. Water resources are suitable for the region to develop small farmland irrigation systems.

Source: Zambian Fifth National Development Plan, 2006–2010

Mainland China has different lands and season types for agricultural production, especially for grain production. Grains are harvested in both summer and autumn. Key agricultural production modes include rain-fed, dryland and irrigated agriculture. Since the reform and opening up in 1978, market integration has occurred and capacity to adjust grain production and supply has increased. Administrative adjustment and control rely on central government, whereas local government independently develops production within a centrally determined framework. The highly integrated market system provides a conducive economic and social environment for resource distribution and production decision-making in different regions.

According to a study by Qian (2002) and other researchers, Chinese rural reforms under a 'double-track system' not only promote the market process, but also mitigate impacts on potential losers. Introducing the market system benefits farmers, but grain acquisition under the planning system and the system of 'three deductions and five charges' means that evolving the income distribution system has been a gradual process, reducing resistance to reform. With the progress of market liberalization the planning function gradually declines and the role of the market increases. At the beginning of the twenty-first century, restrictions on market transactions, such as government interference with grain prices, were eliminated. After 20 years of efforts, China's policy fully accepted the market and the effect of the market system for resource distribution and production decision-making. This removed the situation of separation between regions and enabled the flow of agricultural products and agricultural production factors between regions. Market integration could be mostly reflected by the integration of prices in different regions.

Conclusion

Compared with China, the Sub-Saharan African region has an obvious advantage in terms of total cultivated area and per-capita cultivated area. First, growth in agriculture in Africa is driven mainly by expansion of cultivated land area. Although the total cultivated area in the Sub-Saharan Africa region has continued to grow since the 1980s, due to rapid population growth per-capita cultivated farmland area in Africa has been on the decline since 1980s. At the same time, per-capita agricultural output has been declining. China developed farming systems that could take full advantage of land, sunlight, temperatures and other natural conditions through, for example, intensive cultivation, water and soil conservation and inter-cropping. Most African countries however focus on extensive cultivation with the exception of some large farms.

Second, farmers in China have developed methods for managing soil nutrients, but in African countries, extensive production models and the pressure of population growth have meant that in many areas soil quality has declined, which impacts agricultural production. By contrast, China's modern soil maintenance technologies and long tradition of sustainable farming and land management have enabled basic maintenance and enhancement of soil fertility. This experience could be instructive for African agricultural development.

Third, lack of irrigation and climatic and rainfall fluctuations have impacts on agricultural production. This is the major reason why farm productivity in Sub-Saharan Africa has been limited. China has diverse climates and uneven distribution of rainfall, as well as many agricultural disasters such as drought and locusts. However, it has a strong ability to control these natural factors, so losses in agricultural production caused by them are far less than those experienced by African states.

In conclusion, in order to further promote the development of African agriculture, Africa should improve agricultural production conditions in order to exploit the potential of its land, climate and water resources. Overall, it can be argued that China has accumulated rich experience in these critical areas for farming and food security, and that through appropriate exchanges, these can be used as a reference by African policymakers in planning for agricultural development.

5

COMPARISON OF AGRICULTURAL PRODUCTION INPUTS IN CHINA AND AFRICA

Agriculture accounts for 9 to 12 per cent of China's total fiscal expenditure. Labour engaged in the construction of farmland water conservation infrastructure contributed 54 per cent of the growth in gross value of agricultural output prior to reform in 1978. Capital inputs at the time were still lower than those made by technical inputs, which stood at 61.3 per cent; but the contribution to the value of agricultural output growth from capital and fertilizer increments reached 44.7 per cent and 53.7 per cent respectively between 1983 and 1987; increases in the multiple-cropping index added about 20 per cent (see Table 5.1). Subsequently, China has been making comprehensive, large-scale investments in water conservancy construction, fertilizer production and utilization, improvements in crop varieties and animal breeds, road transportation and market facility construction. Institutional reform alongside market liberalization has supported all these efforts. In contrast, owing to financial weakness and a comparative lack of macro-development strategies, the agricultural input of African nations accounted for only 5 per cent or so of their fiscal budgets. Added to this, these low budgets have been directed primarily at export-orientated economic crop production rather than food crops that play key roles in food security maintenance. The Chinese example demonstrates that fiscal support for farming and rural areas is the foundation for sustainable agricultural development.

Comparison of Fiscal Inputs to Agriculture

During the 29 years prior to 1978, Chinese agriculture grew 2.2 per cent annually on average and the government's fiscal investment in agriculture totalled CNY157.7 billion (USD23 billion), while spending on agriculture continued at around 9 to 12 per cent of fiscal expenditure. Steady increases in agricultural investment have made possible the construction of large-scale projects and the establishment of a strong agricultural science base. Capital investment in land has been quite limited and for this reason China supported labour mobilization for construction of farm water conservation infrastructure. It is estimated that in the 29 years from 1950 to 1978, cumulative labour investments amounted to CNY100 billion (USD14.6 billion), equivalent to the government's total fiscal expenditure on agriculture over the same period. The Douglas production function calculated between labour input, capital input and gross agricultural output value between 1952 and 1978 shows that labour force investment contributed 54 per cent to the growth of gross agricultural output value. Chinese agriculture grew at 7.4 per cent on average each year between 1978 and 1984 and soared to 10.9 per cent in the three years from 1981 to 1984, when the Household Responsibility System was gradually introduced. Since then, inputs to agriculture have increased year-on-year and the proportion of agricultural fiscal expenditure within agricultural gross domestic product (GDP) has continued to increase, exceeding 10 per cent in 2003 (Table 5.1). Continual increases in investment, particularly farmland water conservation, have improved agricultural production conditions. The national irrigated area covered 45 per cent of the total farmland area in 2005, up from 18 per cent in 1952. Meanwhile, improvements in road transportation, access to electricity, healthcare, education, drinking water supply and other public services and living conditions also contributed to the transformation of agricultural production. According to Lin (1992), this amazing growth resulted largely from investment increases and system reform. Investment increments made a contribution of 45.79 per cent to the growth of the gross output value of agriculture, 48.64 per cent to efficiency improvement and 5.57 per cent to technological change between 1978 and 1984. Among all the factors, system reform was responsible for a remarkable contribution of 46.89 per cent (of growth in agriculture), compared with 4.5 per cent made by the labour force between 1978 and 1984 (Table 4.1).

Reportedly, annual public spending per African rural resident is around USD10 (Bezemer and Headey, 2008). According to the International Food Policy Research Institute (Fan *et al.*, 2008), in order to attain the Millennium Development Goals all African governments will have to increase agricultural expenditure annually by 20 per cent. Ghana needs to add 9.5 per cent, which is comparatively easy to reach, but an increase of 33 per cent is virtually impossible for Madagascar. Zimbabwe, with worsening economic conditions, will have to reach around 50 per cent. It is estimated that USD32 to USD39 billion should be invested in Africa each year, but in 2004 only USD9.789 billion dollars were put in place (Fan *et al.*, 2008). In contrast, subsidies for improved varieties and production for each farmer in China reached CNY66.75 (USD10), with a total government subsidy of CNY26.7 billion (USD3.9 billion), equivalent to the total spending of all rural Africans. Moreover, China invests CNY100 billion (USD14.6 billion) in hydropower and water conservancy facility construction each year. The investment of Chinese farmers' in their own production adds more than as much again to the government subsidy figure.

The issue of investment is both a matter of development strategy and government financial capacity. Many African countries appear not to have prioritized agricultural development. In the period after independence some states began to move away from reliance on a single export crop and sought to boost grain production; however, investment in real terms was limited. For many nations, investment in agriculture was only 5 to 6 per cent of the fiscal budget between 1967 and 1973 and only 4 per cent in 2004 (Lu, 2000; World Bank, 2008). The reasons for such low investment in agricultural production include unfavourable agricultural policies and low capital availability (World Bank, 2008). In recent years, some African nations have begun to emphasize agricultural production, but the results to date in most instances have not been remarkable. The African Union signed the Maputo Declaration on African Agriculture and Grain Security in 2003, pledging to lift each nation's investment in agriculture to more than 10 per cent of their fiscal budget within five years. However, according to UN Food and Agriculture Organization (FAO) figures, of all 53 African countries, only six had reached the goal by 2008. At present, agricultural investment in Sub-Saharan Africa is insufficient to meet the challenge of promoting sustainable development (World Bank, 2008).

TABLE 5.1 China's Agricultural Expenditure and Share

Year	Total Agricultural Expenditure (CNY100 million)	Agricultural GDP (CNY100 million)	Agricultural Expenditure Share of Agricultural GDP (%)	Agricultural Expenditure Share of Total Fiscal Expenditure (%)
1978	151	1027.5	14.7	13.4
1980	150	1371.6	10.9	12.2
1985	154	2564.4	6.0	7.7
1990	308	5062.0	6.1	10.0
1991	348	5342.2	6.5	10.3
1992	376	5866.6	6.4	10.0
1993	440	6963.8	6.3	9.5
1994	533	9572.7	5.6	9.2
1995	575	12135.8	4.7	8.4
1996	700	14015.4	5.0	8.8
1997	766	14441.9	5.3	8.3
1998	1,155	14817.6	7.8	10.7
1999	1,086	14770.0	7.4	8.2
2000	1,232	14944.7	8.2	7.8
2001	1,457	15781.3	9.2	7.7
2002	1,581	16537.0	9.6	7.2
2003	1,754	17381.7	10.1	7.1
2004	2,338	21412.7	10.9	9.7
2005	2,450	23070.4	10.6	7.2
2006	3,173	24737.0	12.8	7.9

Source: *China Statistical Yearbook*, 2007

Low investment has hindered the development of agriculture in Africa and failure to support food grain security adequately has had serious consequences. As noted previously, many African countries focus investment primarily on export crops. For example, Côte d'lvoire allocated less than one-quarter of its agricultural budget to grain production between 1970 and 1980. A number of African nations advocate improvements in agricultural productivity, but fail to achieve sustained success (World Bank, 2008). This shows the gap between agricultural strategies and development achievements in African countries. Meanwhile in China, strategies, policies and implementation measures have been relatively consistent.

Analysis of China's fiscal investment in agriculture and the growth of agricultural GDP over the last three decades show a close relationship between the two. Agricultural GDP is not as sensitive to changes in agricultural investment as a percentage of GDP. However a comparison of different countries, as shown in Figure 5.1, indicates a positive relationship between agricultural GDP per capita and the share of fiscal expenditure going into agriculture. For example, Namibia and Zimbabwe reported high fiscal agricultural expenditure and agricultural GDP per capita at the same time. Agricultural GDP per capita for Namibia was USD166 and

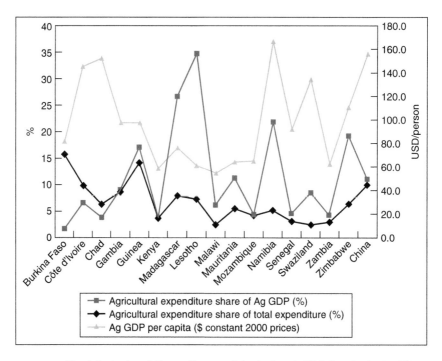

Figure 5.1 Fiscal Agricultural Expenditure and Agricultural GDP Per Capita in China, Sub-Saharan Africa and Countries in Sub-Saharan Africa, 2004[a]

[a] Where agricultural GDP accounts for between 10% and 35% of total GDP

Source: *China Statistical Yearbook,* 2007; Fan *et al.* (2008)

Zimbabwe USD109 in 2004, compared with USD155 registered in China in the same year. Nonetheless, high fiscal agricultural expenditure does not necessarily mean high agricultural GDP per capita, as is the case in Lesotho and Madagascar, for example. Conversely, Malawi's magnificent progress in agriculture presented how aggressive agricultural investment (16 per cent of government spending) can yield increased production and results (Juma, 2011).

Agricultural Labour Force

The labour force is a key factor in agricultural production. For both China and the Sub-Saharan African region the agricultural labour force is above 60 per cent of the total population (China has a higher percentage), but this has been decreasing gradually, as shown in Table 5.2. China's agricultural population was 742 million (73.9 per cent of its total population) in 1979–1981 and increased to 849 million (64 per cent of the total population) in 2004. Sub-Saharan Africa's total population also increased between 1979 and 2004, starting from 310 million in 1979, 225 million of whom were rural people (72.6 per cent of the total). Twenty-five years later, the agricultural population had increased to 407 million, equal to 62 per cent of the total population of 659 million (Table 5.2).

Figure 5.2 shows that between 1979 and 2004, the percentage of agricultural labourers in the total economically active population declined in both China and Sub-Saharan Africa. The agricultural labour population was 408 million in China and 104 million in Africa in 1979, accounting for 74 per cent and 71 per cent of the

TABLE 5.2 Agricultural Populations of China and Sub-Saharan Africa and Their Proportion of the Total Population

	1979–1981	1989–1991	1999–2001	2003	2004
China					
Agricultural population (Unit: 1,000)	742,341	833,139	853,602	851,028	849,417
Total population (Unit: 1,000)	1,004,204	1,160,914	1,282,320	1,311,709	1,320,892
Percentage (%)	79	72	67	65	64
Sub-Saharan Africa					
Agricultural population (Unit: 1,000)	225,138	281,379	384,431	401,947	407,630
Total population (Unit: 1,000)	309,913	414,477	599,432	644,189	659,467
Percentage (%)	73	68	64	62	62

Source: FAOSTAT

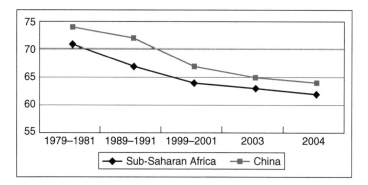

Figure 5.2 Proportion of the Agricultural Population in China and Sub-Saharan Africa in the Total Economically Active Population

Source: FAOSTAT

total population, respectively. This increased to 510 million and 188 million respectively by 2004, or 64 per cent of the Chinese population and 62 per cent of the African population. The marginal contribution of the Chinese agricultural labour force to agricultural GDP was negative between 1983 and 1987, reflecting a high level of surplus labour. For a long period, the opportunity cost of agricultural labour in China was kept at a very low level, hence agricultural labour has provided low-cost inputs for agricultural infrastructure construction, substituting for inadequacies in capital inputs. This kind of substitution happened under the state-controlled resource mobilization system in China, which is known as '*Liang Gong*' ('Two Labour system) and refers to 'compulsory input of work days' and 'cumulative input of work days'. Statistics from the Ministry of Water Resources show that more than 10 billion work days had been put into the construction of rural water facilities prior to reform of the Chinese rural tax system in 2004, when all agricultural taxes on farmers were cancelled. The state had invested CNY76.3 billion in water resource facilities prior to China's reform and another CNY58 billion had been mobilized by rural communities and *Liang Gong*. After reform, labour input is still the main input in the construction of rural infrastructure. In the 10 years between 1990 and 1999, an average of 7.5 billion work days were put into the construction of rural water facilities annually, which can be valued at CNY7.5 billion (calculated at CNY10 per work day). The main use of this investment was the construction and maintenance of small-scale rural water facilities (China Irrigation and Drainage Development Centre, 2008). Even after the *Liang Gong* system was terminated, 4.7 compulsory work days had to be committed to the construction of rural water facilities in 2003. This represented a 70 per cent decrease compared with 1998–1999 (Zheng *et al.*, 2009).

The transfer of surplus labour in China was accomplished through system reform. In the 1980s, adoption of the Household Responsibility System improved agricultural productivity remarkably. Between 1978 and 1983 farming became increasingly diversified. Later, in order to guarantee the employment of labourers moving out of farming and avoid the large-scale migration of rural people to urban areas, local governments at all levels encouraged the development of rural Town and Village Enterprises. As a result, labour absorbed by township enterprises ballooned to a record high of 135 million in 1996 from 92.7 million in 1990, 52 million in 1984 and 30 million in 1980 (*China Statistical Yearbook*, successive years). In this period large-scale occupational shifts were realized within the rural economic system, rather than through simple rural to urban transfer. With increasing demand for labour in urban areas in the 1980s and the release of the State Council's Decision on the Settlement in Urban Areas of Farmers, the number of migrant workers increased by 25 million in 1988. These numbers rose especially after 1992, reaching 64 million in 1994, 80 million in 1998 and 137 million in 2007, accounting for 46.7 per cent of the total urban labour force (194 million). While the marginal productivity of agricultural labour was improving, the main body of agricultural production underwent dramatic changes. Women increasingly made up the majority of agricultural labourers, along with the elderly and the less well-educated (Table 5.3).

The transfer of labour out of agriculture in Africa is often limited by low levels of industrialization and urbanization. Surplus labour in the countryside limits labour productivity. At the same time, without a similar state-controlled resource mobilization system, African countries have not been able to turn labour resources into capital resources, thereby failing to overcome existing agricultural input constraints. Some African countries such as Tanzania have experimented with forms of collectivist agriculture (part of the *Ujamaa* policy). However, in practice this kind of social engineering has not been successful for a variety of reasons. One factor was that this

TABLE 5.3 Comparison between Chinese Agricultural Labours and Migrant Workers

	Agricultural Labourers	*Migrant Workers*
Number (Unit: 10,000)	34,874	13,181
Gender (%)		
Male	46.8	64
Female	53.2	36
Age (%)		
<20	5.3	16.1
21–30	14.9	36.5
31–40	24.2	29.5
41–50	23.1	12.8
>51	32.5	5.1
Education (%)		
Illiterate	9.5	1.2
Primary school education	41.1	18.7
Junior school education	45.1	70.1
Secondary school education	4.1	8.7
Sixth-form and university education and above	0.2	1.3

Source: China State Statistics Bureau (2008)

type of resource mobilization mechanism requires a form of farmer submission to the state, something that has been experienced in China but which has been difficult to realize in the African context. At the same time a significant amount of labour entered into cities to take unskilled work, but failed to deliver either adequate remittances or secure enough income to cover their own subsistence. Most migrant workers are young and middle-aged educated men, while those left at home are mostly uneducated women and the elderly, therefore Africa has also experienced a feminization of agriculture and ageing of the agricultural workforce (Lu, 2000; Anríquez, 2007; Anríquez and Stloukal, 2008). The female share of the economically active in agriculture in Sub-Saharan Africa was 46 per cent, 47.1 per cent and 48.7 per cent in 1980, 1995 and 2010 respectively, with a similar trend of change at 45.8 per cent, 47.6 per cent and 47.9 per cent in China (FAO, 2011). The dependency ratio in rural is 1.02 in Sub-Saharan Africa, which is much higher than 0.76 in urban and the share of population aged over 60 in rural is 6.6 per cent, which is also much higher than 4.4 per cent in urban (Anríquez and Stloukal, 2008).

In addition, improving agricultural productivity is linked to human capital investment in agricultural labour. The proportion of Chinese rural labourers who were either illiterate or semi-literate fell to just under 8 per cent in 2003 from 28 per cent in 1985; at the same time, those with primary and secondary school education and technical secondary education expanded. The average number of years of education of the rural population increased to just under eight in 2003, from under six in 1985. In China, the anti-illiteracy movement made a big difference in raising the adult literacy rate from 20 per cent in 1949 to much higher in the collectivized agriculture period and to 42.7 per cent in 1964 (Liu and Xie, 2006). By contrast, most agricultural labour is in less-educated settings in Sub-Saharan Africa and illiteracy rates were around 33.3 per cent in 2007. Farmers in the Sahel are not convinced of the benefit of free education starting in French, but illiteracy cuts them off from written information (whether it be reading a fertilizer label, or in the accounts of their *Groupement d'Interêt Economique*) and better-paying non-farm jobs (Tiffen, 2003).

TABLE 5.4 Changes in Education of the Chinese Rural Labour Force (%)

Year	Illiteracy and Semiliteracy	Primary School Education	Junior High School Education	Senior High School Education	Technical Secondary School Education	Sixth-form College Education and Above	Average Education Year
1985	27.87	37.13	27.69	6.96	0.29	0.06	5.88
1990	20.73	38.86	32.84	6.96	0.51	0.10	6.41
1995	13.47	36.62	40.10	8.61	0.96	0.24	7.13
2000	8.09	32.22	48.07	9.31	1.83	0.48	7.75
2003	7.41	29.70	50.33	9.87	2.11	0.58	7.84

Sources: *China Rural Household Survey Statistical Yearbook*, 2003; *China Rural Household Survey Statistical Yearbook, 2004*; Lu (2005)

Furthermore, insufficient food intake affects the quality of farm labour in many African countries. Most experts agree that a daily intake of 2,100 calories is enough for most people, but there is a big difference between different countries in calorie consumption. For example, an average American takes in 3,800 calories, while an average Ethiopian consumes only 1,520 calories, less than half of an average American (WFP, 2007). Low calorie intake can result in physical weakness. Table 5.5 indicates that African adult mortality increased from 37.4 per cent in 1990 to 40.1 per cent in 2007. The morbidity of lung disease also increased from 168 per 100,000 in 1990 to 363 per 100,000 in 2007. According to the Joint United Nations Programme on HIV/AIDS (UNAIDS) and the World Health Organization (WHO), 25.3 out of 36.1 million HIV/AIDS sufferers in the world are from the Sub-Saharan African region: this is equivalent to 70 per cent of the world's total adult sufferers and 80 per cent of child sufferers. One of the most serious impacts of HIV/AIDS in Africa is the impact on the labour force. About one-third of the working rural population has been lost to HIV/AIDS in many African countries (FAO, 2007a). As indicated in Table 5.5, HIV/AIDS affects a significant part of the population aged between 15 and 49 in many African countries, with negative impacts on agricultural production and social stability. Other diseases also pose challenges to labour and agricultural production. The longitudinal dataset in Kenya (Yamano and Jayne, 2004) shows that the death of an adult male head of household is associated with a larger negative impact on household crop production, non-farmer income and crop production than any other kind of adult death. In addition, the Kenya data show that the impact of adult mortality on household welfare is more

TABLE 5.5 Comparison of Key Health and Mortality Indicators for China and Africa

Basic Quality of Life Indicators	Year	China	Africa
Life expectancy at birth (year)	1990	68	51
	2000	71	51
	2007	74	52
Adult mortality (possible mortality of 15- to 60-year-old adults per 1,000 persons)	1990	172	374
	2000	135	414
	2007	115	401
Lung disease incidence rate (per 100,000 population)	1990	116	168
	2000	105	319
	2007	98	363
HIV/AIDS infection rate (>15-year-old people per 100,000 population)	2007	65	4735
Adult literacy rate (%)	1990–1999	77.8	51.8
	2000–2007	93.3	63.4

Source: World Health Statistics (2009)

severe for households in the lower half of per-capita income distribution (Binswanger-Mkhize, 2009).

Research on Chinese agricultural development shows that at certain stages, labour inputs can play a bigger role than capital inputs or other factors in agricultural production. Reportedly, total factor productivity decreased in the early collectivization period between 1955 and 1957, and fell to a record low in 1960, when China experienced serious famine during the 'Great Leap Forward'. It then rose slightly but fell later and maintained the level recorded in the famine period until agricultural reform in 1978, then returned to the 1958 level in 1984, suggesting that agricultural growth during the collective agriculture period could not be solely attributed to efficient utilization of the labour force, land or other inputs. Naughton (2007) found that during 1953–1978, days of labour input to rice production jumped by 68.4 per cent, inputs for cotton doubled and for wheat, almost trebled. Labour force increases arguably made the greatest contribution to agricultural production growth.

Comparing with that in 1978, rice, cotton and wheat yields continued to rise in 1985, despite a fall in labour input days of 22 per cent, 29 per cent and 53 per cent respectively, indicating that total factor productivity was raised. Although labour force inputs are directly related to output growth, too much input is wasted when low-efficiency policies are adopted. Therefore, grain output per capita remained unchanged from 1952 to 1978 in China, although with apparent increasing labour inputs. This also explains why agriculture shrunk during the latter part of the People's Commune period, as well as during Tanzania's implementation of the *Ujamaa* system.

African total factor productivity remains low, and labour inputs have not improved. As a result, African agricultural production still lags behind that of China.

Agricultural Production Factor Input

Fertilizer, seeds and pesticides can all be seen as significant elements in the development of agriculture, although there are of course negative consequences associated with the misuse and overuse of agrochemicals. The next section compares patterns of fertilizer use in China and Africa.[1]

According to the FAO (Figure 5.3), there is a sharp discrepancy in levels of fertilizer usage between China and Africa. China's usage increased by 158 per cent

TABLE 5.6 Days of Labour per Unit of Land in China (Unit: mu = 1/15th hectare)

Crop	1953	1978	1985
Rice	250	421	328
Cotton	300	908	643
Wheat	120	461	218

Source: Yao (2008), quoted in Naughton (2007)

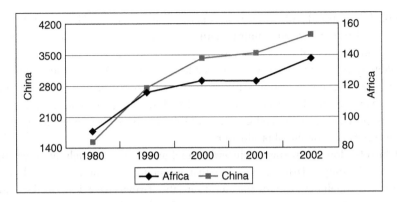

Figure 5.3 Usage of Fertilizer in China and Africa (Unit: 10,000 t)

Source: FAOSTAT

to nearly 40 million tonnes in 2002 from 15 million tonnes in 1980; Africa saw a rise of 52 per cent to 1.3 million tonnes, which is only 3 per cent of China's usage. In 1980, China's usage was 158kg/ha, compared with a Sub-Saharan African average of 5.3kg/ha. By 2002 Chinese fertilizer use averaged 323kg/ha, 47.5 times higher than that for Africa (6.8kg/ha) in the same period. The FAO estimated that Africa's fertilizer usage was lower than 10kg/ha, about 1 per cent of total global usage. It is predicted that this status will last until 2030 (Table 5.7). Fertilizer has exerted a great effect on the growth of grain output in China and guaranteed high production levels. According to Lin (1992) (see also Table 4.1), fertilizer contributed 32.2 per cent to the growth of gross agricultural output value in China during the first phase of the reform and opening up from 1978 to 1983 and rose to 53.71 per cent in the second from 1984 to 1987.

Most African countries rely heavily on imported fertilizer, and thus have to shoulder high and fluctuating global fertilizer prices. Poor infrastructure increases transport costs, making fertilizer unaffordable for many farmers. Fertilizer per ton costs USD336 in Nigeria, USD321 in Malawi, USD333 in Zambia and USD828

TABLE 5.7 Fertilizer Real Consumption and Expected Consumption

	Kg/ha (Arable Land)					Rate of Change (%)		
	1961–1963	1979–1981	1997–1999	2015	2030	1961–1999	1989–1999	1997/1999–2030
Sub-Saharan Africa	1	7	5	7	9	4.5	−2.4	1.9
The World	25	80	92			3.3	0.1	

Source: FAOSTAT

in Angola, compared with USD227 in America (Eilitta, 2006) and less than USD170 in China. In most African countries, farmers relied on subsidies before economic reform; afterwards, subsidies were cancelled and fertilizer prices soared accordingly. In addition, water shortage has constrained fertilizer use in Africa because adopting it without sufficient irrigation will not improve output very much (Camara and Heinemann, 2006; Havnevik *et al.*, 2007). In China, improvements in both small farmers' purchasing power and government subsidies have encouraged increases in factor inputs to agricultural production.

China has long been engaged in agricultural production through intensive cultivation, forming a farming tradition that integrates land utilization and conservation through the use of organic fertilizers, thus farmers have developed specific technologies for the effective use of a range of fertilizers. From the Ming and Qing Dynasties (1368–1644 and 1644–1912) considerable progress has been made in ways of making fertilizer: as explained elsewhere, this was partly due to scarcity of land resources. As possibilities for further geographic expansion declined, China became more reliant on intensive cultivation to meet the demand of its soaring population, and as chemical fertilizers replaced organic fertilizers, a range of waste and pollution problems became evident. China's demonstration sites extension system used various subsidies as basic tools to mobilize resources to disseminate production materials, particularly chemical fertilizer and pesticide inputs. However, the overuse of fertilizer has led to a decline in farmland productivity. This vicious circle has led to environmental pollution, decline in crop resistance to disease and decrease in soil quality. Research results from the Nanjing Soil Research Institute, under the Chinese Academy of Sciences on Agricultural Non-point Source Pollution in Taihu Lake, shows that industrial pollution accounts for only a small proportion of total pollution, about 10 to 16 per cent. Meanwhile, agricultural non-point source pollution is responsible for 59 per cent of the pollution. However, at the same time the effective utilization rate of fertilizer and pesticides is less than 35 per cent.

On the one hand, inputs of fertilizer, pesticides and other agrochemicals are relatively low in African countries, which means that Africa may well be more suited to the development of organic agriculture (United Nations Conference on Trade and Development (UNCTAD) and United Nations Environment programme (UNEP), 2008). On the other hand, some specificities of the natural resource base – namely local homogeneity and spatial diversity of the predominant Basement Complex soils – imply that simple fertilizer strategies may not produce the yield increases obtained elsewhere (Voortman *et al.*, 2003). There is already some best practice in organic agriculture in Sub-Saharan Africa. A large survey of sustainable agricultural practices and technologies in developing countries (Pretty *et al.*, 2003) found that in Sub-Saharan Africa, water harvesting is transforming barren lands and the technologies are not complex and costly. It was found that in central Burkina Faso, 130,000 hectares of abandoned and degraded lands have been restored with the adoption of *tassas* and *zaï*, which are 20–30cm holes dug in soil that has been sealed by a surface layer of salt and hardened by wind and water erosion. The holes are filled with manure to promote termite activity and enhance infiltration. When it rains, water is channelled by simple stone bunds to the holes, which fill with water and into which millet or sorghum seeds are planted. Cereal yields in these regions rarely exceed 300kg per hectare, yet these improved lands now produce 700–1,000kg per hectare. Reij *et al.* (1996) calculated that the average family in Burkina Faso using these technologies had shifted from being in annual cereal deficit amounting to 650kg – equivalent to six-and-a-half months of food shortage – to producing a surplus of 150kg per year. Furthermore, *tassas* are best suited to landholdings where family labour is available or where farm labour can be hired, such that this labour-intensive soil and water conservation method has led to a market for young day labourers who, rather than migrate away, now earn money by building these structures. With the low ratio of cultivated land to total arable land, there is scope to promote organic agriculture on large areas of uncultivated land, although care should be taken to investigate competing land use claims.

China started its organic agriculture in 1999 and now nearly 10 million tonnes of organic fertilizer are used. There were 2.1 million hectares of land certified for organic agriculture and 2.08 million hectares of land carrying out organic certification with 'wild collection' (Institute for Market Ecology and Klaus Dürbeck Consulting, 2005: 5), and 1.1 million hectares of land that was organic conversion land in 2006, accounting for 4 per cent of total cultivated land area (Scoones, 2008). However, given the total arable land area and current farming methods, organic agricultural production will not exceed 3 per cent of total farm production.

Agricultural Mechanization

The small-scale farming system in both African countries and China suggests that agricultural mechanization could be a long-term objective. However, the gradual change towards mechanization can show to some extent the trend and possibility of agricultural production pattern transition. Most places in Africa continue to utilize traditional production methods; in some areas, 'slash and burn' cultivation systems persist. In Sub-Saharan Africa, in overall terms, humans are the principle source of power, cultivating 65 per cent of the total area under cultivation, with animals cultivating 25 per cent and tractors 10 per cent only (FAO, 2007a). Within the Sub-Saharan African region, there are marked differences in the levels of mechanization in central, western, eastern and southern regions (Table 5.8). In 2000, it was estimated that the number of tractors used in agricultural production in Sub-Saharan Africa was 221,000 units (FAO, 2007a). As shown in Figure 5.4, the number of tractors per hectare of arable land in China decreased moderately to 7 in 2003 from 1979, while that in Africa shrunk to 3.1 from 5.

As shown in Figure 5.5, China's usage of reaper-threshers per 100 hectares increased from 30 in 1979 to 250 in 2003, compared with Africa's 2.6 to 3.7, suggesting a rather low level of agricultural mechanization for many countries in Africa.

TABLE 5.8 Levels of Mechanization in Sub-Saharan Africa

Sub-Saharan Africa Region	% Land Cultivated		
	By Hand	By Animals	By Tractor
Central	85	11	4
Western	70	22	8
Eastern	50	32	17
Southern	54	21	25

Source: FAO (2007b)

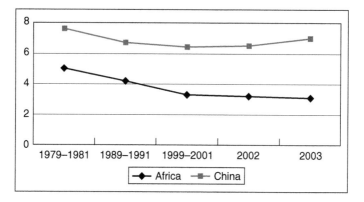

Figure 5.4 Number of Tractors Per Hectare in China and Africa

Source: FAOSTAT

China's experience is worth studying: utilization of agricultural machinery should comply with specific natural conditions, and the utmost use of comparative advantage should be made. However, external support takes an important role in China's case. For example, the Law on Promotion of Agricultural Mechanization, which was adopted at the 10th Meeting of the Standing Committee of the Tenth National people's Congress on 25 June 2004, supported various methods of mechanization services and facilitated the emergence of specific subsidy policies. The total subsidies for agricultural mechanization amounted to CNY17.5 billion in 2011, an increase of 250 times compared to CNY70 million in 2004. Africa has a substantial land area as a foundation for the utilization of agricultural machinery (Zhu and Zhao, 2011), but capital limitations cannot be ignored; thus livestock remains the alternative to labour for agricultural production in Africa.

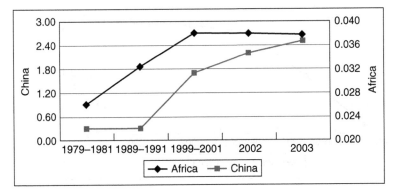

Figure 5.5 Reaper-threshers Used per Hectare in China and Africa (Unit: set/ha)

Source: FAOSTAT

Agricultural Infrastructure

Water Conservancy

In addition to capital insufficiency, ineffective utilization of water resources constrains grain production in Africa. Rain-fed agricultural production is much higher as a percentage of total production than anywhere else in the world: 69 per cent of the world's grain yielding areas are rain-fed, yielding 40 per cent of the total global rice harvest, 66 per cent for wheat and 82 per cent for maize; 86 per cent of the harvest for remaining grains are rain-fed. The world's output of rainfed grain is estimated to be 2.2 tonnes per hectare, 65 per cent of the unit output of irrigated land. This amounts to 58 per cent of the world's total grain output, while the output from irrigated lands is 42 per cent (Rosegrant *et al.*, 2005).

In Africa, irrigated acreage is less than 5 million hectares, only 4.9 per cent of arable land. Two countries, Madagascar and Sudan (Wiggins, 2000) alone account for 3 million hectares of total irrigated acreage. As Figure 5.7 shows for 1980, Sub-Saharan Africa's irrigation acreage made up 2 per cent of total arable land, rising to 3.7 per cent in 2003. During 1965–1980, irrigation acreage expanded by more than 4.4 per cent annually on average in Africa, but the growth rate has been at a standstill since 1980 (FAO, 2002).

Improvement in water resource management has been an important factor in the increase of China's total grain output. National irrigation acreage accounted for 45 per cent of total arable land area in 1979–1981, up from 18 per cent in 1952 (FAO, 2004). In 1950, most water conservancy projects were either small-scale and constructed by local government, or of large size and invested in by central government. At the end of the 1960 and 1970s, mechanical advancement promoted the utilization of groundwater irrigation technology. Since the 1970s, a batch of new medium and large-scale water conservancy projects have been implemented, but in the latter period of reform and opening, the state's investment in water conservancy infra-

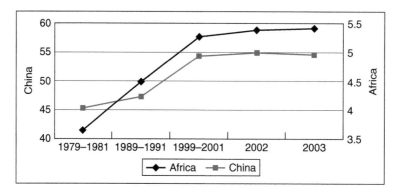

Figure 5.6 Comparison of Irrigation Areas in China and Sub-Saharan Africa
Source: FAOSTAT

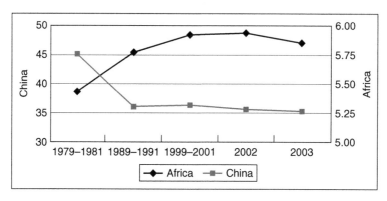

Figure 5.7 Comparison of the Proportion of Irrigated Land Area in the Total Arable Land Area in China and Sub-Saharan Africa
Source: FAOSTAT

structure declined and did not recover until the early 1990s. Irrigated acreage increased to 54 million hectares in 2003 (FAO, 2004), occupying 35.3 per cent of total arable land and permanent cropping land, below the 45 per cent recorded in the early phase of the reform and opening period.

Irrigation costs vary in different irrigation districts. A field survey in Erdos in Inner Mongolia showed that irrigation costs were CNY5,790 per hectare, including electricity costs of CNY300 for maize growing using well water; the annual net return was CNY6,810 per hectare (Liu and Qi, 2010). In Jinghuiqu Irrigation District, Shaanxi Province, maize growing cost CNY2,686 per hectare including CNY486 of irrigation costs; the net return was CNY3,624 per hectare on average. In Shijin Irrigation District on the North China Plain, maize growing costs were CNY1,750 per hectare, including CNY309 of irrigation costs; the net return was CNY5,679 (Liao, 2009).

The coverage rate of irrigation facilities in Africa is rather low, which is largely attributed to high costs (around USD5,000–25,000 per hectare) (International Food Policy Research Institute, 2010). Production in some irrigated areas is unsatisfactory due to poor facility maintenance and low usage of agricultural inputs and other resources (Peacock *et al.*, 2007).

The Chinese practice shows that small water conservancy irrigation could be an alternative when capital is limited. As small-scale irrigation mainly depends on community cooperation for labour input, maintenance problems can be averted; in addition, water harvesting using small reservoirs can serve the purpose of irrigation. Furthermore, terrace cropping on dry land, deep tillage and water preserving, no-tillage with mulching and the use of green manure rotation can help address the moisture needs of crops. Deep tillage on flat land could lift output by 30 to 40 per cent. In addition, Chinese experience suggests that a 50m^3 cistern could be a replacement for irrigation on dryland in some circumstances.

Transport Linkages in Rural Areas

Rural roads are important for agricultural production and farm product trade. Since the 1990s the Chinese government has invested consistently in transport infra-structure, including roads. By the end of 2006, more than 3 million kilometres of rural roads had been built, more than 60 per cent of villages could be accessed by a cement road, and nearly 100 per cent of townships and towns (the lowest level of government, responsible for managing villages) were connected to a main road (Du, 2008).

In sharp contrast, transport infrastructure is rather poor in rural Africa. According to statistics from 1988, Africa had more than 1.5 million kilometres of roads; the regional average density was 5.06km per 100km, compared with the average popu-lation density of 25.18km per 10,000 people. Moreover, the regional distribution of main roads was uneven. Highway density for south-east South Africa, the coastal areas of the Gulf of Guinea, West and North Africa and parts of East Africa was relatively high, while for inland areas in Central Africa, the Congo Basin rainforest, South Africa's *kgalagadi* areas and the Sahara Highway, prevalence was pretty low. Of all highway stretches, only 380,000km were hard-surfaced, one-quarter of the total length; others were sand-surfaced or earthen roads. Even hard-surfaced roads were poorly maintained. Botswana and Mauritius had the highest road density (1977km and 1549km per 1 million people) with more than 90 per cent of roads in sound condition (Li, 1998).

Hine and Rutter's (2000) analysis of farmers' degree of isolation shows that 51 per cent of villages in Ghana and 60 per cent in Malawi are more than two kilo-metres away from the nearest place, with access to motorcycle transportation and 10 per cent of them above 10km away. The Independent Evaluation Group (2007) reported that Africa's transport costs represented 11.5 per cent of its total imports, while those of Asia and North America were only 7.2 per cent and 6.7 per cent, respectively. Many African countries have had to pay transport costs of 20 per cent out of their total export expenditure; the amount in some inland countries such as Malawi reached 55 per cent.

This of course impacts negatively on commodity trading for these countries. High transport costs in African markets mean that even if markets are competitive, the final costs to consumers during national production shortfalls can be high (Poulton, 2006; Tostau and Brorsen, 2005).

Rural Markets

In most African countries, less than one-third of the food produced by farmers is traded in the market (Sasakawa Africa Association, 2004). In contrast, in China since the reform period began, nearly 53.3 per cent of agricultural products were traded in the market in 1984. Under the planned economy, agricultural product trade was strictly prohibited. The reform of agricultural policy and ensuing market opening have provided a foundation for trade in agricultural surplus products. During 1980–1992, rural markets expanded by 71 per cent from 37,890 to 64,678, and trading volume jumped to CNY6,688 million – more than double that in the early stages of the reform period.

The successful development of Chinese rural markets after reform can be largely attributed to careful policy choice. First, the transformation of agricultural production methods, especially the implementation of the Household Responsibility System, promoted the output of surplus farm products. Second, the traditional micro-free market helped lower trade costs and further promoted exchange between farmers. Some experts believe that price increases and trade reforms directly stimulated agricultural production in the early stages of agricultural reform (Secular, 1992).

Small markets also played an important role in the development of agriculture in Africa following implementation of market reforms, but low population density and a limited market for farm products often curtailed the effectiveness of these measures associated with Structural Adjustment Programmes. As price mechanisms rely on sound infrastructure, all-round market information and price transmission systems, small farmers in remote areas with poor communication and transport facilities are incapable of transporting their products to the market, even when if they have received certain price signals. Sicular (1992) held that transport improvement was significant in advancing agricultural product market reform in the early reform period. Park et al. (2002) also noted that infrastructure investment was one of the major policies that the Chinese government created in order to maximize benefits from the liberalization of agricultural markets. In addition, the construction of railways and highways furthered regional trade in agricultural products after the mid-1980s.

Reform of the market for agricultural production factors such as fertilizer and pesticides came after the reform of agricultural product markets. Reform of agricultural machinery, pesticide and agricultural plastic film markets was launched in the mid-1980s. Liberalization of fertilizer and seed markets started in the early and late 1990s, respectively. Chinese farmers were no longer able to access cheap fertilizer from the state, but fertilizer prices fell with the removal of price controls and a greater role for the private sector. Meanwhile, fierce competition has greatly improved market efficiency and sharpened traders' sensitivity to market demand and cost, and farmers have responded by boosting sales and production. Following reform of the fertilizer market, Chinese farmers spend only 15 per cent of income on fertilizer. By contrast, as African farm income has remained low despite market liberalization, purchase of adequate amounts of fertilizer has often been impossible. Moreover, underdeveloped agricultural industries have compounded these issues. Sharp hikes in fertilizer prices occurred in China's market reform process, doubling between 1993 and 1996. The retail price for urea tumbled to CNY1,361 per ton in 2001 from CNY2,209 per ton in 1996. China's fertilizer output accounted for 21.6 per cent of the global total in 2002, up 12 per cent from 1980. Sub-Saharan African yields have remained unchanged or even shrunk since 1979, and most African countries even ceased fertilizer production. African fertilizer output was only 0.26 per cent of global output in 2002 (Figure 5.8).

Conclusion

During the process of Chinese agricultural development, the government's support for and adoption of market mechanisms boosted agricultural production, while in Africa, insufficient aid from the government and radical market liberalization policies were unable to provide farmers with access to key resources, and the use of agricultural inputs remained at a low level.

The lack of adequate fiscal support for agriculture in Central Africa explains the low levels of agricultural infrastructure (particularly irrigation coverage) and agricultural technology adoption, and the limited availability of subsidies for production inputs. However, because of land pressure, China has made good use of technology

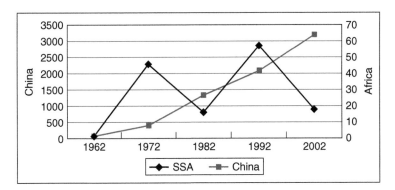

Figure 5.8 Comparison of Fertilizer Output for China and Sub-Saharan Africa (excluding South Africa) (Unit: 10,000 tonnes)

Source: FAOSTAT

to substitute for land resources, and inputs of fertilizer and irrigation have become important factors in agricultural development.

The key characteristic of China's agricultural input system is a capacity to turn labour surplus into capital, making up for lack of financial capital. African countries in general do not have a similar system, so while there is an agricultural labour surplus, highly-skilled labour cannot be fully employed and effectively mobilized. Understanding the contribution of labour to agricultural output growth prior to reform in China would be useful for analysts of African agriculture, given current capital limitations and low efficiency of resource use. Labour force inputs, as well as full utilization of livestock and water resources, are critical for the development of long-term productive and sustainable farming in Africa.

China's progressive marketization also provides some guidance for Africa on the matter of deepening market reform. Agricultural policy reform, construction of an agricultural product market infrastructure and the promotion of agricultural industry are indispensable components of the agricultural marketization processes. With a vast population and limited farmland, China has focused on intensive use of land and labour. African policymakers should consider how to make use of rich land resources and scarce labour through policies that make intensive use of limited capital resources possible and attractive.

6

COMPARISON OF AGRICULTURAL TECHNOLOGY DEVELOPMENT IN CHINA AND AFRICA

With a growing world population and shrinking water and land resources, future increases in agricultural output will need to be met by agricultural productivity growth. Technology is important for the improvement of agricultural productivity (World Bank, 2007). China has accumulated lots of valuable experience in developing agriculture through technological innovation. Since 1949 and especially since 1978, agricultural growth has been largely attributed to technological innovation. By 2008, the contribution of technology to agricultural productivity increase had reached 50 per cent (Ministry of Agriculture Rural Economy Research Center, 2009). Most African countries began to build agricultural technology research and development (R&D) and extension systems after their independence, but primarily depended on technology and scientific management introduced from western countries for the cultivation of high-yielding commercial crops. After a decade of stagnation during the 1990s, investment and human resource capacity in public agricultural R&D averaged more than 20 per cent growth in Sub-Saharan Africa during 2001–2008 (Beintema and Stads, 2011). However, most of the investment growth occurred in a handful of countries; in many other countries, investment levels have stagnated or fallen. Research capacity and funding depend overwhelmingly on often volatile, external funding sources in many countries: in particular those in francophone West Africa, which are threatened by extremely fragile funding systems, face fundamental capacity and investment challenges (Beintema and Stads, 2011). The uniqueness of African agro-ecologies limits the possibilities for benefits from international technology transfer. African countries also find it difficult to realize suitable economies of scale for research because of small populations. Low investment in scientific research and absorption of advanced technology are important explanations for poor maize output in the Sub-Saharan Africa region, relative to other regions of the world (World Bank, 2007).

Agricultural Technology Development in China and Africa

Agricultural technology development levels can be measured in many ways, including:

- adoption of improved varieties;
- adoption of agricultural biotechnologies;
- levels of input use;
- integration of agrarian techniques; and
- protection of the agricultural environment.

Around the world, the contribution of variety improvement to the growth of agricultural output was 21 per cent in the 1960s–1970s and 50 per cent in the 1980s–1990s. Without growth in agricultural output resulting from improved varieties, the global grain price would be 18–21 per cent higher than the market price in 2000, and the available calories per person in developed countries would be 4 to 7 per cent lower: there would be 15 million more malnourished children, with negative impacts on forested areas and fragile biological regions due to expansion of the agricultural frontier (World Bank, 2007).

China has long devoted itself to crop breeding and variety improvement. New varieties of key crops such as rice, wheat and corn have been repeatedly delivered by the research system. Output growth and acreage expansion for hybrid rice have been higher than for other crops. At present, the improvement and update of major crop varieties is speeding up in China, with crop varieties changing once every six to seven years, with new varieties likely to raise output by 15 per cent compared to older varieties.

About 30–40 per cent of the productivity increases for major crops is attributable to plant breeding (Jiang and Sun, 2001), which explains why agricultural technology advances have contributed greatly to poverty reduction in China. There are remarkable differences in the adoption of new varieties between China and Africa. First, the coverage of improved varieties of major crops such as rice, wheat, maize, sorghum and cassava in Sub-Saharan Africa takes up lower percentages of the respective planting area compared to other countries (World Bank, 2007). The planting acreage of improved corn and wheat varieties in the Sub-Saharan Africa region was in the region of 40 per cent and 60 per cent respectively, and for major crops such as rice, sorghum, cassava and potatoes was only 22 per cent, 17 per cent, 19 per cent and 15 per cent respectively. In China, the coverage rate of improved varieties for all major crops reached 100 per cent (Jiang and Sun, 2001). In addition, the promotion and adoption rate of improved varieties varies from country to country within Africa: for example, the planting area of hybrid maize accounts for 80 per cent and 74 per cent of the total cultivated area in Kenya and Zimbabwe respectively, 49 per cent in Zambia, 30 per cent in Malawi and 28 per cent in Tanzania (World Bank, 2007). Furthermore, the crop varieties being promoted are different. Almost all major improved crop varieties with high coverage areas are planted by small farmers in China, but these are not necessarily commonly planted by African farmers. For example wheat, which has an improved varieties application

TABLE 6.1 Planting Percentage of Improved Varieties for Key Crops in Total Planting Area (%)

	Tanzania	Zambia	Liberia	Sub-Saharan Africa	China
Rice	–	80	73	22	100
Wheat	–	100	–	70	100
Corn	28	49	–	43	100
Sorghum	–	20	–	17	100
Cassava	–	24	52	19	100
Potato	–	100	–	15	100

Source: Zambia and Liberia: data sourced from field sites; Sub-Saharan Africa: World Bank (2008); China: Jiang and Sun (2001)

of 70 per cent globally, is not one of the crops most often chosen by African farmers. The application of other improved crop varieties is also quite low in Africa.

Africa has begun to focus on the development and extension of new varieties in recent years. The Alliance for a Green Revolution in Africa (AGRA), established in 2006, aims to develop 1,000 new crop varieties with high-yield, drought tolerance, adaptation to poor soils and other environmental stress-resistance properties. At present, Africa has made significant achievements in the promotion of New Rice for Africa (NERICA) and mosaic-resistant cassava. The planting area of new rice and cassava varieties are of about 0.2 million and 0.25 million hectares respectively. The acreage of improved varieties in the Sub-Saharan Africa region keeps increasing, from 1 per cent in 1970, 4 per cent in 1980, 13 per cent in 1990 to 27 per cent in 1998 (Beintema and Stads, 2006).

There are many reasons for the lower application rate of improved varieties in Africa: underdeveloped agricultural R&D and extension systems result in outdated technologies; at the same time, poor infrastructure and inadequate inputs are bottlenecks to the application of new improved varieties. Conversely, China has developed a large number of advanced production technologies, such as 'One-Time Full-Thickness Fertilization' rice, double-cropping, super high-yielding wheat cultivation, super high-yielding maize production, plastic film covering, vertical cultivation, large-scale farming and high-quality comprehensive supporting technologies. Currently, multiple cropping is applied on one-third of the existing arable land area and on two-thirds of the cultivated area. Multiple-cropping indices have soared from 128 per cent in 1949 to 158 per cent, and even 250 per cent in some areas. Land utilization and agricultural comprehensive production capabilities have improved significantly (Zhang, 2005).

In contrast, small farmers in most African countries including Liberia, Tanzania and Zambia (visited during this research) rely on rain-fed agriculture with one harvest per year. Ninety per cent of African agricultural production still depends on manual tools, and pesticides and fertilizers are not widely used; in addition, agricultural mechanization and irrigation are not widespread (Yao, 2002). The utilization of pesticides, fertilizers and agricultural machinery in China has increased rapidly. In 1980, China's fertilizer application per hectare of arable land was 158kg, compared to 5.3kg in the Sub-Saharan Africa region. This number climbed to 323kg in 2002, 47.5 times the Sub-Saharan Africa region (6.8kg). According to the UN Food and Agriculture Organization (FAO), Africa uses only 1 per cent of the world's total fertilizers, less than 10kg per hectare. This situation is predicted to continue until 2030 (FAOSTAT). Africa lags far behind China in terms of applying improved varieties and comprehensive production technologies. Implementing the New Green Revolution project in Africa has to take into account the role of agricultural production technology in development, because improved varieties cannot work alone. Technological support or an effective extension system is also necessary. African households have limited influence on the discourse on research and extension, which further restricts the adoption of new varieties.

Nevertheless, there are already many encouraging cases showing the possibility for African states to apply advanced agricultural technologies, not only in producing high production but also without harming the environment. An investigation of 40 cases of existing projects from 20 African countries where sustainable intensification had been developed, promoted or practised in the 2000s (some with antecedence in the 1990s) include a range of different themes, comprising crop improvements, agro-forestry and soil conservation, conservation agriculture, integrated pest management, horticulture, livestock and fodder crops, aquaculture and novel policies and partnerships. By early 2010, the 40 projects had documented benefits for 10.4 million farmers and their families and improvements on nearly 13 million hectares (Pretty *et al.*, 2011).

Adoption of so-called advanced technologies is another indicator of the technological status of agricultural production systems. Nowadays, the utilization of genetically modified (GM) crop technology is considered by many to be significant for future agriculture development. Currently, the market for genetically modified crop cultivation, promotion and application is dominated by North America, Latin America and Australia. Asia has also launched GM crops in recent years, but as yet Africa has not. The nations growing GM plants on the largest field areas are the USA (64 million hectares), Brazil (21.4 million hectares), Argentina (21.3 million hectares), India (8.4 million hectares) and Canada (8.2 million hectares). As before in 2008, the 2009 International Service for the Acquisition of Agri-biotech Applications report lists 25 countries that commercially utilize GM plants. Costa Rica is a new entry to this list. Germany was removed from the list of 'gene technology countries' after the enactment of a cultivation ban in 2009. Fourteen million farmers use GM plants worldwide: the majority of these are in developing nations (13 million), and this figure has increased by 700,000 since 2008. China's hectares of GM crops was only 3.7 million (mostly *Bacillus thuringiensis* cotton), ranking the country sixth among the top eight countries in which the planting area of GM crops exceeds 1 million hectares (James, 2009). Figure 6.1 shows trends in the development of GM crops in different countries in 1996–2006; it also shows that GMO (Genetically Modified Organism) cultivation in Africa is lower than in any other continent. Africa's attitude toward GM crops is affected largely by donor countries, especially European countries, which are largely against the use of GMOs.

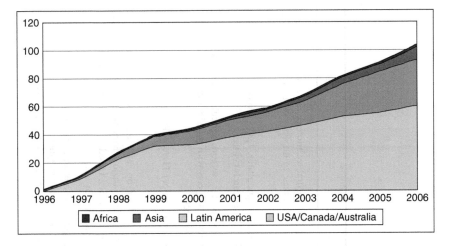

Figure 6.1 Area of Transgenic Crops in the World (1996–2006) (Unit: million ha)
Source: World Bank (2007, 2008)

Agricultural Technology Development Strategy and Policy in China and Africa

Since the late 1970s, the Chinese government has always attached great importance to science and technological progress and has launched the 'National Rejuvenation through Science and Education' and 'Agricultural Rejuvenation through Science and Education' strategies. In the National Medium-to-Long-Term Development Plan for Science and Technology, agricultural technology development is placed as a top priority.

China's strategy and policy for agricultural science and technology development was stated in the Outline of Agricultural Science and Technology Development 2001–2010. The goals are food security, improving farmer income, environmental and natural resource protection and increasing agricultural competitiveness. The focus of agricultural science and technology policies is shifting from basic agricultural technology to diverse agriculture-related technologies. Training and capacity-building for farmers are being strengthened through, for example: the Science and Technology for Household Programme, the Spark Programme, the Science and Technology Commissioner System and the Agricultural Technology 110 Programme. This shows that agricultural policies are strongly focused on improving farmer livelihoods through appropriate technologies.

The Chinese government's Outline of Agricultural Science and Technology Development 2001–2010 requires that agricultural science and technology development should meet four goals.

- Goal 1 is to increase agricultural production, guaranteeing food security from the present production capacity of 0.5 billion tons annually to meet the food

TABLE 6.2 Medium to Long-Term Development Plans of Science and Technology in China

Plans	Term	Document	Agricultural Projects
The First Plan (12 years)	1956–1967	One planning programme and four attachments	4 projects involving agricultural technology; 51 key problems involving 330 topics; to improve crop yield accounts for 50.6% of the total
The Second Plan (10 years)	1963–1972	One planning programme, five classified plans	19 specialities related to agriculture, 1,310 projects, 3,845 subjects, 10 pilot research centres
The Third Plan (8 years)	1978–1985	General planning programme and technical and scientific programme for basic science	Out of 108 key projects in 27 sectors, agriculture tops the list of 8 comprehensive subjects with priority influence and features in 17 key projects
The Fourth Plan (15 years)	1986–2000	One planning programme and 27 special plans	Spark Programme and Bumper Harvest Programme are released
The Fifth Plan (10 years)	1991–2000	Medium to long-term planning programme and 10-year planning programme	Cultivated about 250 new crop varieties, increasing output by more than 10%; updated major crops once; bred 120 kinds of improved new forest varieties; raised the popularity rate of improved aquatic varieties by about 30%
The Sixth Plan (10 years)	2001–2010	National technology development, 'Ninth Five Year Plan', and long-term planning programme until 2010	Providing strong technical support to ensure a stable supply of major agricultural and sideline products by the end of the twentieth century; accelerating the commercialization of

The Seventh Plan (15 years)	2006–2020	National medium to long-term technology development planning programme and 11 special development planning programmes	technologies and promoting new applicable technology as a top concern; tackling the remaining problems in improved seed cultivation, regional comprehensive management, pest prevention, resource management, processing and utilization, ecological and agro-industrial research–related issues; fundamental and high–tech research; technologies and equipment for comprehensive processing of agriculture and forestry products, raising added value by about 30% Agriculture and forestry biomass project; animal and plant breeding project; Science and Technology Project for Food Production; research and industrialization of key food processing technologies, pesticide project; key dairy technology research and demonstration, bird flu and other major animal disease prevention and control

Sources: Xu (2004); Ministry of Science and Technology website

needs of 1.6 billion people in 2030, with an annual per-capita grain production of 400 billion tons.

- Goal 2 is to increase farmer income by adjusting agricultural structures.
- Goal 3 is to protect the environment and deal with the shortage of natural resources.
- Goal 4 is to increase agricultural competitiveness. Primary agricultural product prices have been 20 per cent higher in China than on the international market, which indicates a low level of competitiveness for China's agricultural products.

TABLE 6.3 Agricultural Research Content of Chinese Technology Programmes

Programmes	Content
Scientific and Technological Research Programme of the Sixth Five-Year Plan	Out of 38 projects, 8 relate to agriculture: livestock breeding technology and breeding system; regional integrated technology for production increase; fodder development technology; fast-growing and high-yielding tree variety breeding and comprehensive utilization of wood; high-efficiency and low-residue pesticide development; increasing proportions of phosphate and potash in fertilizer applications; studies of South-to-North Water Transfer Project; food storage, preservation and processing techniques
Scientific and Technological Research Programme of the Seventh Five-Year Plan	Improved varieties breeding and conversion of grain into other products; improving grain, cotton and oil crops during the Seventh Five-Year period, improve quality, resistance and raise yields to more than 10%; conversion of grain into feedstuff, paying special attention to feed protein development, formula feeds and livestock and poultry disease prevention and control
Scientific and Technological Research Programme of the Eighth Five-Year Plan	Placing agricultural technology research as a top priority; 473 new improved varieties of grain and vegetables, with yields increased by more than 10%; raising the extension rate of major crops such as rice, wheat and corn to 1.28 billion mu; establishing 50 high-yield and high-efficiency demonstration research districts with a total area of more than 3.5 million mu and then extending to 0.2 billion mu, with grain output increasing by 6 billion kilograms
Scientific and Technological Research Programme of the Ninth Five-Year Plan	Raising the percentage contribution of technology to agricultural production to more than 50% through integrated research and demonstration; tackling a batch of key technological problems to raise the agricultural technology level and realize sustainable development in the twenty-first century; projects in total, more than 800 subjects, nearly 18,000 people engaged in tackling agricultural technology problems, cultivating 664 new crop varieties, developing 988 new products, establishing 1995 experimental bases and 4,807 demonstration sites

TABLE 6.3 Agricultural Research Content of Chinese Technology Programmes

Programmes	Content
Scientific and Technological Research Programme of the Tenth Five-Year Plan	Deep processing of agricultural products, high-quality and high-efficiency production of key crops, large-scale livestock production, desertification prevention and control, plant and animal pest and disease control, high-efficiency utilization of agricultural biomass, environmentally-friendly agricultural development; development of key technology and products needed for sustainable agricultural development progression, improving pre-, during- and post-production technology, optimizing agricultural structures, improving agricultural quality, profit and the competitiveness of agricultural products

Source: Ministry of Science and Technology

The National Medium to Long-Term Development Plan for Science and Technology provides overall guidelines for agricultural technology development in China. In addition, the Chinese government has formulated special Science and Technology Key Task Projects for the fulfilment of priority objectives and tasks. In these Projects, which are important guiding documents for agricultural technological research, the focal points of agricultural research are well defined and made top priorities. In 2006, the government launched the National Key Technology R&D Programme, based on the Scientific and Technological Key Task Projects in order to implement key policies on agricultural technological development.

In order to fulfil the Scientific and Technological Key Task Projects and adjust Science and Technology Support Projects, the government also formulated special research programmes, including the National Significant Science and Technology Special Programme, the National High Technology Research and Development Programme of China (863 Programme) and the National Basic Research Programme (973 Programme). To ensure the implementation of these programmes, the government authorized laboratories to carry out the research and gave them great support. Of all the plans, agriculture-related projects take up the highest proportion.

The Chinese government has attached much attention to the training, introduction and support of research talent in agriculture. China established 83 agricultural colleges or universities to train human resources for agricultural research and extension. Each year 97,000 agricultural students graduate from colleges or universities, and 12,000 postgraduate students graduate (Ministry of Education, 2010). Of the 5,000 students sent abroad each year, 353 are students studying in agriculture (CSC, 2010). China's agriculture teaching curriculum has been reformed and is now based on international standards.

China has formulated a series of development strategies for agricultural technology development and a comprehensive multi-department agricultural development strategy system, with specific development plans as well as sector development initiatives under the authorization of the Chinese Ministry of Science and Technology.

TABLE 6.4 Major Research Plans Made by the Chinese Government

	Year	*Agriculture-Related Plans*
National Significant Science and Technology Special Programme	2001	Out of the 12 programmes of the Tenth Five-Year Plan, four are related to agriculture: deep processing of major agricultural products, dairy industry development, food security and water-saving agricultural development. There is one agriculture-related project included among the 13 National Key Special Technological Plans in the Eleventh Five-Year Plan, which focuses on the cultivation of new transgenic crop varieties
High-Technology Research and Development Programme of China (863 Programme)	1986	Modern agricultural technology development is one of ten key important projects covered during the Eleventh Five-Year Plan period
National Basic Research Programme (973 Programme)	1997	Key orientations for agricultural research during the Eleventh Five-Year-Plan period include: research on the functional genomics of important agricultural plants and animals; quality improvement for important agricultural plants and animals; crop pest and disease control and animal disease prevention and control; agricultural biotechnology resource protection and utilization; agricultural resource and environmental protection, ecological systems protection; efficient utilization of water, nutrients and light in crop planting
National Key Laboratories	–	At least 21 national key laboratories are engaged in agricultural research

Furthermore, the Ministry of Agriculture and other functional departments have carried out agricultural development planning on the basis of National Technology Development Planning. In 1997, China formulated its Agricultural Science and Technology Policy for China, strengthening agricultural high-tech research and development and promoting major breakthroughs in high-tech research based on biotechnology and information technology. As mentioned previously, in 2001 the central government promulgated its Outline for the Development of Agricultural Science and Technology (2001–2010) and made it clear that the objective of agricultural technology development is to protect national food security, solve the problem of low peasant incomes, ease resource shortages, protect the ecological environment and increase agricultural competitiveness. The Ministry of Agriculture issued the National Programme for Agricultural Science and Technology (2006–2020) in 2007, and announced that ensuring national food security, accelerating agricultural modernization, speeding up the commercialization and application of agricultural technology and developing circular agriculture to improve competitiveness in global markets were the major targets in agricultural technology development.

In addition, effective incentive mechanisms have been formulated, facilitating the innovation and promotion of agricultural technology. Awards for agriculture, forestry, animal husbandry and fishery accounted for 16.7 per cent of total national awards for science and technology in 2003. In 2000, China extended the State Supreme Science and Technology Award for science and technology workers who have achieved significant breakthroughs at the forefront of modern science and technology, made outstanding achievements in science and technology development, or created great economic or social benefits through technology innovation, scientific and technological achievements and the commercialization and industrialization of high technology. The award goes to no more than two nominees each year. So far, of the 14 people who have received the award, there are two from the agricultural sector: Yuan Longping (winner of the first session in 2000) and Li Zhensheng (the only winner in 2006), who have made outstanding contributions to hybrid rice and hybrid wheat breeding, respectively. China gives high honours to agricultural researchers to offset comparatively low salaries.

The commercialization and extension of scientific and technological achievements is an important prerequisite for agricultural technology development. The central government unveiled a series of macro policies including the Spark Programme, Prairie Fire Programme and Bumper Harvest Programme in 1986, 1987 and 1988 successively. China had already enacted the Law on the Popularization of Agricultural Technology in July 1993, confirming legally for the first time the importance of agricultural technology promotion organizations for agricultural advancement, and encouraging and supporting rural organizations in popularizing science and technology. In addition, it called for agricultural organizations such as agricultural science research institutes, agricultural colleges, agricultural enterprises and supply and marketing cooperatives and others to participate actively in the extension of agricultural technology and build up a diversified social extension network in which the state, collectives and individuals are all involved.

The government has formulated a series of policies to ensure the implementation of the Developing Agriculture through Science and Technology strategy, which covers scientific frontier research and applied research related to people's livelihoods involving agriculture, aquaculture, industrialized farming, forestry and environmental protection, as well as science and technology, education, agriculture, forestry and environmental protection departments and scientific research institutions in different sectors. These provide institutional guarantees and funding mechanisms for the development of agricultural technology.

Many African countries also have formulated agricultural technology development strategies similar to those developed by China. Some states such as Uganda have formed independent agricultural technology development strategies. In 2005, Uganda enacted the National Agricultural Research Act and established a national agricultural research system that aims to improve agricultural research by tackling the problems arising from agricultural modernization and is focused on meeting the

TABLE 6.5 Main Objectives of Chinese Agricultural Technology Service Programmes

Programmes	Departments	Year	Content
Spark Programme	Ministry of Science and Technology	1986	Providing agricultural technological services for townships and farmers by establishing technology-intensive zones, regional pillar industries and training bases
Prairie Fire Programme	Ministry of Education	1988	Making use of comparative advantages in human resources and technologies in rural schools; together with the agriculture, science and technology sectors, actively developing vocational training on applied agricultural technology and skills closely linked with the local economy; carrying out experiments, training and information services based on applicable technologies
Harvest Programme	Ministry of Agriculture	1987	Through technical training, demonstrations and breeding, popularizing high-quality crop varieties including livestock and fisheries, special, excellent and new varieties and advancing mechanization in farming and fisheries

Source: Ministry of Science and Technology, Ministry of Education and Ministry of Agriculture

demands of the poor by creating opportunities for agricultural livelihoods. It involves:

- converting current agricultural production into a modern technology-based, market-oriented, high-efficiency, high-output and sustainable system that could contribute to poverty reduction;
- promoting the development of agriculture and related industries and improving people's living standards and livelihoods in an environmentally friendly way; and
- supporting development and implementation of national policies by information and knowledge systems.[1]

Some countries have integrated agricultural development into their own science and technology development strategies. South Africa, for example, set forth its Agricultural Research Act in the 1990s, integrating its agricultural technology development strategy into national technology development and designating special departments to carry out the agricultural technology development plan.

Some African nations integrate agricultural technology development into their overall agricultural development strategies. Zambia elaborated the National Agriculture Policy of the Republic of Zambia and Cooperation Ministry (2004–2015). This focuses on three aspects of agricultural technology development:

1   developing adaptable varieties and techniques such as crop protection, storage, processing and utilization techniques to prevent or minimize the loss from disease or pests;
2   developing appropriate land and water resource management techniques to ensure the sustainable production of agricultural products and improve sustainability-related technologies; and
3   reconfirming explicitly that developing and extending appropriate technology is the key to agricultural productivity – work needs to focus on the development and extension of appropriate agricultural machinery, tools, equipment, apparatus and fishing skills as well as seeds and seedlings, livestock breeds, fish and aquatic species; pest control research; the development of sustainable farming methods and the extension of appropriate biotechnology.

Both China and Africa have placed much emphasis on the development and application of agricultural technology, and have formulated related policies in the last several decades. China's agricultural policies are more sophisticated and diversified, including both macro and detailed sector dimensions. There are detailed regulations on policy implementation and the development of supporting systems.

Africa's agricultural technology policies are relatively simple and limited to general principles. The New Partnership for Africa's Development (NEPAD) has put forward the following agenda for agricultural development in Africa:

> 193. Expand the ambit and operation of the integrated action plan for land and water management for Africa. The project addresses the maintenance and upgrading of Africa's fragile agricultural natural resources base. Many African governments are already implementing these initiatives as part of this programme. Partners include the Global Environment Facility (GEF), the World Bank, the African Development Bank, the FAO and other bilateral donor agencies.
>
> 194. Strengthen and refocus the capacity of Africa's agricultural research and extension systems. The project addresses the issue of upgrading the physical and institutional infrastructure that supports Africa's agriculture. Technological innovation and technology diffusion hold enormous potential for accelerating agricultural output and productivity, but the continent lacks the research capacity necessary for major breakthroughs. Major players include the Forum for Agricultural Research in Africa (FARA), the World Bank, the FAO and the Consultative Group on International Agricultural Research (CGIAR). (NEPAD, 2003: 60–1)

These agendas are still agendas and their implementation largely relies on further elaboration by GEF, the World Bank, FAO, CGIAR and other international development agencies, and most importantly on African leaders with high commitment on this 'hope for Africa' (Hope, 2002).

Individual countries such as Zambia have put forth a target for agricultural technology development but failed to give a thorough description of the implementation process. In Uganda, the National Agricultural Research Act gives a full description of the agricultural research system, but does not specify how to ensure that it is implemented.

Comparison of China and Africa's Agricultural Research Capabilities

Comparison of Technological Research Input

Studies show that investment in agricultural scientific research can be very profitable, with returns of around 43 per cent at the global level. For developed countries the figure is 46 per cent, for developing countries 42 per cent, and for Sub-Saharan Africa 35 per cent (Alston et al., 2000; Evenson, 2003; Thirtle et al., 2003). As indicated in Figure 6.2, Asia registers the highest level at 50 per cent. Adequate and sustainable investment in scientific research is critically important for the development of agricultural technology.

China's total investment in agricultural science research is much higher than that in Africa. In 2000, China's public expenditure on agricultural research stood at USD3.15 billion, while in Africa it stood at USD1.46 billion. The growth rate of China's agricultural research investments may be the highest in the world, standing at an average of 4.86 per cent during 1981–2000, compared to the global average of 2.11 per cent in the same period, 3.14 per cent for developing countries, 1.10 per cent for developed countries, 0.99 per cent for Africa and 1 per cent for Sub-Saharan Africa during 1980–2003 (Alene and Coulibaly, 2009). The figure continues to rise in China but keeps getting smaller in Africa. The World Bank pointed out in the *World Development Report 2008* that during the past 20 years China's agricultural R&D investment almost doubled, whereas that of Sub-Saharan Africa

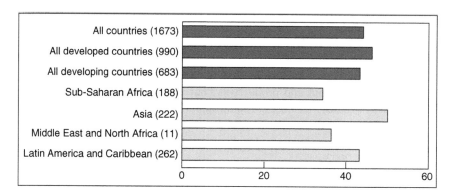

Figure 6.2 Rates of Return to Agricultural Technology Research Investment around the World (Unit: %)

Sources: Alston et al. (2000), World Bank (2008)

TABLE 6.10 CGIAR Investment in Agricultural Research in Sub-Saharan Africa

	1970s	*1980s*	*1990s*	*Since 2000*	*Total 2000–2004 in Sub-Saharan Africa*
Investment in Sub-Saharan Africa (USD1 million/year)	24	86	132	168	174
Percentage of total CGIAR investment	44%	41%	40%	44%	45%

Source: AusAID (2008)

overseas development assistance has not been able to address capacity-building problems at the local level. Large numbers of high-quality local experts are hired by international agricultural research programmes; this can weaken the research capacity of formal institutes in Africa. Attractive packages or consultancy rates offered by international organizations encourage highly-educated professionals to seek opportunities away from governmental agricultural research institutions. More importantly, although priority-setting for international development assistance takes Africa's practical needs into account, it is largely influenced by the donor countries' politics: in this sense, international programmes do not represent the agenda of African countries. A direct result is that it becomes more difficult for African agricultural research systems to give consistent consideration to food security, and Africa's attitude towards GM varieties is largely affected by donor countries whose understanding of modern agriculture is based on awareness of the costs or unanticipated consequences associated with industrialized agriculture. These states have sufficient funds to research and develop alternatives to aspects of the industrial agriculture model, but the problem is that Africa is in urgent need of conventional technologies to advance agricultural output. Therefore, some would question the relevance of promoting organic agriculture in Africa, although it can offer agro-ecological benefits and may be one way of capturing greater shares of local value in supply chains in some instances. Nonetheless, paradoxically, the decline in international aid money and the shift of priorities from agricultural research to environment, health, education, water and sanitation (NEPAD, 2003) has led to stagnation or even decline in agricultural R&D investment in Africa.

Agricultural Technological Institutions

Since the early 1950s, China has built 11 rural science and technology institutions, including seven research institutes for agricultural science in the north-east, north, east, mid-south, south, south-west and north-west and seven regional agricultural universities. After a long and complex process of adjustment, closure, rehabilitation and improvement, China has established a comprehensive agricultural science and technology research system with the world's largest number of workers (Xu, 2004). This system has the following characteristics. First, agricultural science research institutions are established at national, provincial and regional levels. State-level institutions are mainly responsible for the development of agricultural technology related to the overall development of the nation; the provincial agencies primarily provide services for agricultural development within the province and region or municipality; municipal institutions specialize in the research of localization of new varieties and new technologies. Second, there are both specialized research organizations and universities nationwide. Each province has at least one or two agricultural universities, with 65 in total nationwide. China has also set up academies of agricultural sciences, directly affiliated to the Ministry of Agriculture. The academies of agricultural sciences in each province (municipality and autonomous region), city and county are devoted to variety research and adaptation, experimentation, demonstration and extension. The Chinese Academy of Agricultural Sciences, the main force in agricultural scientific and technology development, has more than 1,000 divisions and more than 90,000 researchers.

Within the national agricultural development framework, different types of agricultural science and technology development strategies are embodied in various research programmes. State-level research institutions and universities receive research funding through open competition, as do their provincial counterparts. In addition to specialized agricultural research institutions, a growing number of R&D companies under the management of agricultural research institutions, state-owned and private agricultural enterprises, agricultural shareholder enterprises and multinational corporations, are involved in agricultural science and technology R&D in China. Agricultural research institutions have the primary role in agricultural R&D, but different types of companies are playing an increasingly important role in this respect. For example, in 1999 state-owned and private agricultural enterprises cultivated 86 kinds of new species, accounting for 2 per cent of the total new varieties that year (Fan *et al.*, 2006).

African agricultural research institutes fall under the umbrella of the National Agricultural Research System in each country. These systems in some regions of Africa are organized into sub-regional organizations. The following existed in 2011:

- West and Central African Council For Agricultural Research and Development (CORAF/WECARD)
- Association for Strengthening Agricultural Research in Eastern and Central Africa (ASARECA)
- Southern African Development Community's Food, Agriculture and Natural Resource Directorate (SADC/FANR)
- Currently, the sub-regional organization for northern Africa is being established.

TABLE 6.11 Chinese Agriculture Technology Research Organizations, 1999

	Total	Universities	Other[a]	Research Institutions in the Agricultural Sector[b]			
				Sub-total	State-level	Province-level	Regional
Number	1,635	312	104	1,219	56	451	712
Number of employees	131,439	10,200	12,457	108,782	10,706	51,609	46,467
Average number of institutions	80	33	120	89	191	114	65
Distribution of researchers	100%	8%	9%	83%	8%	39%	35%
				100%	10%	47%	43%

Source: Huang *et al.* (2002)

a 'Other' includes agricultural research institutions excluding agricultural universities and research institutions such as the Chinese Academy of Sciences, and research institutions affiliated to other non-government agricultural organizations.

b Agricultural research institutions at universities refer to those engaged in agricultural research; agricultural research staff refers to professors and lecturers engaged in agriculture and agriculture-related research; the number of employees refers to the total number, including staff of all specialties and ancillary workers.

The sub-regional organizations are expected to promote cooperation in agricultural research, and the European Union is currently a key funder for these. The Forum for Agricultural Research in Africa (FARA) was established in 2001 by three sub-regional organizations with a secretariat located in Ghana. The African Union and NEPAD have designated FARA as the agricultural research and extension coordination organization for the Comprehensive Africa Agricultural Development Programme (CAADP).

There are 300 universities in Africa, of which 96 public-owned universities teach agriculture and natural resource management. Of these there are 26 in Nigeria, 10 in South Africa, 6 in Sudan, 5 in Kenya, 3 in Ghana and 46 in other 40 countries (AusAID, 2008).

In most of the smaller countries, agricultural research is undertaken by a handful of government agencies and university faculties; systems in the large countries such as Ghana, Kenya, Nigeria, South Africa and Sudan are far more complex. Nevertheless, the majority of Sub-Saharan African countries have a single national agricultural research agency that accounts for the bulk of agricultural R&D capacity and investments. Examples include the National Agricultural Research Institute of Niger, the Togolese Agricultural Research Institute and the National Agricultural Research Institute in Eritrea. In some countries, an umbrella organization such as Ghana's Council for Scientific and Industrial Research or South Africa's Agricultural

Research Council oversees and coordinates the R&D activities of a large number of commodity or thematic centres, whereas in a country such as Mauritania, national crop, livestock and fisheries research agencies operate independently of each other without a coordinating body.

Overall, the government sector still dominates agricultural research in the region, but its relative share has declined over time (Beintema and Stads, 2011). Some nations such as Uganda, Sierra Leone and Zambia have built up government-led specialized agricultural research institutions. Uganda's national agricultural research system consists of public agricultural research institutions, universities and colleges, farmer groups, civil society organizations, the private sector, advisory services, regional or international organizations and other entities engaged in agricultural research services. The National Agricultural Research Organization is the leading agricultural research institution responsible for directing and coordinating all the research activities of the national agricultural research system in Uganda. The public agricultural organization system consists of national agricultural research institutes and regional agricultural research units. The national agricultural research institute is divided into departments for crops, fisheries, forestry, livestock, semi-arid areas and agricultural experiments. Each research institution has affiliates of its own, which is similar to the system of the Chinese Academy of Agricultural Sciences. Sierra Leone, another example, has an agricultural research institution that consists of food crop research stations among which the Rice Research Station is the most prominent division.

Zambia's agricultural research system is composed of public institutions, state-owned and private companies and universities, and in terms of research and study, it has different divisions with several foci. Zambia's public agricultural research institutions focus on agricultural management, while state-owned and private companies are engaged mainly in breeding research.

It is costly to establish agricultural R&D institutions. China enjoys vast land resources and a diversified ecological structure, which means that there are economies of scale in setting up a comprehensive range of research institutes. Cooperation between provinces is realized through overall planning by central government. Meanwhile, establishing different research institutions is expensive and unnecessary in Africa, however building agricultural research systems is important for integration. Most of the agricultural research institutions are replicas of similar institutions in other countries and cooperation is hard to achieve; outflow of talent and funding shortages limit the effectiveness of research institutions.

Agricultural Researchers

Due to lack of data on the numbers of personnel working with corporations and in the private sector, this section only discusses employment in scientific research institutions. The number of employees in China's agricultural scientific research institutions is very large: 92,300 employees (84 employees per institution) worked with 1,096 institutions of different levels in 2002, including 31,900 scientists and

TABLE 6.12 Comparison of Leading Agricultural Institutions in China and Uganda

	China	Uganda
Name	Chinese Academy of Agricultural Sciences	State Agricultural Research Institutions
Major research institutions	Crop Science Research Institute; Plant Protection Research Institute; Vegetable and Flower Institute of the Agricultural Environment and Sustainable Development Institute, Beijing; Animal Husbandry and Veterinary Research Institute; Institute of Apiculture; Feed Research Institute; Agro-Processing Institute; Institute of Biotechnology Research; Agricultural Economics and Development Institute; Division of Agricultural Resources and Agricultural Research Institute; Agricultural Information Institute; Agricultural Quality Standards and Testing Institute; Farmland Irrigation Research Institute; China National Rice Research Institute; Cotton Research Institute; Oil Crops Research Institute; Fibre Crops Research Institute, Institute for Sugar Beet; Fruit Institute; Zhengzhou Fruit Research Institute; Tea Research Institute; Harbin Veterinary Research Institute; Lanzhou Veterinary Research Institute; Lanzhou Institute of Animal Husbandry and Veterinary Drugs; Shanghai Veterinary Research Institute; Grassland Research Institute; Environmental Protection Scientific Research and Monitoring Institute; Methane Science Research Institute; Nanjing Agricultural Mechanization Research Institute; Tobacco Research Institute; Citrus Research Institute; Sericultural Research Institute; Agricultural Heritage Office: Buffalo Institute; Grassland Ecological Research Institute; Poultry Research Institute, Institute for Sweet Potato Research	National Crop Resources Research Institute: banana, bean, cassava, cereal, coffee, horticulture and sweet potato research institutes National Fisheries Resources Research Institute National Forestry Resources Research Institute: agriculture, forestry, forest management, non-timber forest products; Institute of Forest Protection National Livestock Resources Research Institute National Semi-Arid Resources Research Institute National Agricultural Research Laboratory: Agricultural Research Information Service, agro-meteorological research, appropriate technology and agricultural engineering centre, biological control research, food biotechnology research, National Agricultural Biotechnology Laboratory, plant genetic resources research and Entebbe Botanical Gardens, post-harvest services studies, soil research

Source: Chinese Academy of Agricultural Sciences and Uganda State Agricultural Research Institutions

TABLE 6.13 Agricultural Research Institutions of Zambia

Property	Organization
Public-invested agriculture research institutions	Soil and Crop Research Institute, Forestry Research Institute, Fisheries Research Institute, Livestock Research Centre, Water Resources Research Institute, Food Technology Research Institute
State-owned companies	Gold Valley Agricultural Research Trust, Cotton Development Trust
Private companies	Zambia Corn Research Institution, Zambia Dunavant Cotton Company
Schools	Agricultural departments in universities and colleges

Source: Pardey *et al.* (2006)

technicians (29 for each institution). Scientific researchers are highly concentrated at agricultural research institutions and higher-level agricultural colleges. There were 1,509 professionals in the China Agricultural University and 4,721 in the Chinese Academy of Agricultural Sciences. Such a high concentration of researchers is crucial for building an R&D coalition and advancing the progress of scientific research.

In contrast, Africa has far fewer agricultural researchers and the scale of research institutions is relatively small. There are only 8,746 agricultural research personnel through 27 nations in Sub-Saharan Africa. According to Beintema and Stads (2004), there are 400 agricultural R&D institutions in Africa, 40 per cent of which had fewer than five employees and 93 per cent had fewer than 50 workers. A shortage of researchers makes it hard to strengthen agricultural R&D capabilities on the African continent.

In China and Africa, agricultural researchers work primarily in scientific research institutions, especially governmental ones. In 1999, 90 per cent of agricultural researchers held positions within governmental institutions in China, and fewer than 10 per cent were in universities. About 80 per cent of agricultural researchers work

TABLE 6.14 Number of Researchers of Different Institutions in Africa

	Principal Government Agencies	Other Government Agencies	Higher Education Agencies	Non-profit Agencies	Private Agencies	Total
< 10	14	61	145	11	29	260
10–19	15	14	32	5		66
20–49	29	16	23	3		71
> 50	26	3		1		30
Total	84	94	200	20	29	427

Source: Beintema and Stads (2006)

TABLE 6.15 Distribution of African Agricultural Researchers

Institution	1971	1981	1991	2000	Annual Growth Rate
Government agencies	88.1	86.3	82.7	77.4	3.51
Higher education agencies	8.5	11.3	14.6	19.3	6.90
Non-profit agencies	3.4	2.5	2.7	3.3	4.33
Total	100	100	100	100	3.97

Source: Beintema and Stads (2006)

in governmental institutions in Africa. For example, in 2000, Zambia had 261 agricultural researchers, of which 204 were in governmental institutions and 57 in agricultural colleges and universities; of these, 60 were expatriate researchers. Meanwhile, Tanzania had 542 agricultural scientists and technicians, including 440 working in government research institutions (Beintema *et al.*, 2003).

The ratio of supporting staff and technical personnel in research institutions in African countries is higher than in China. The ratio of management to supporting staff and technicians in research organizations in 27 nations in Africa was 2.94:1 but only 0.8:1 in China, according to the Chinese Academy of Agricultural Sciences.

With regard to scientific researchers' educational background, 12 per cent of those in the Chinese Academy of Agricultural Sciences hold a doctorate. According to the *World Development Report 2008* (World Bank, 2008), 25 per cent of agricultural researchers in Africa have a doctorate (Zambia: 6 per cent; Liberia: 3 per cent), however this data may not accurately reflect reality in China and Africa due to different statistical standards. Africa may have a higher percentage than China as it has gained much support from international aid donors. The development of human resources has been highlighted ever since independence, suggesting that Africa has advantages in agricultural development, but unfortunately these advantages are not utilized to their fullest.

Agricultural Research Domains

Agricultural research priority setting is influenced by natural, economic and socio-political conditions. Developing countries attach much importance to conventional technologies to improve agricultural land quality, advance labour productivity and

TABLE 6.16 Comparison of Agricultural Science Researcher Educational Levels in China and Africa

	Zambia	Liberia	Sub-Saharan Africa	China
Number of researchers	321	25	12,224	181,927
PhD level (%)	6	3	25	12

Source: Data for Africa: World Bank (2008); China: Fan *et al.* (2006); Zambia and Liberia: field investigation data

achieve food security, while developed countries pay more attention to transgenic varieties (subject to intellectual property protection) and processed and functional foods, emphasizing food production systems (including organic production, animal welfare and certification of agro-food products), precision agriculture techniques, conservation agriculture technologies and bio-energy crops. Alston *et al.* (1999) argues that both public and private investment in developed countries into research on agricultural productivity has been gradually reduced, and that the focus has shifted towards sustainable agriculture, food safety and other fields.

With a vast population but limited farmland, China always gives top priority to food security, and central government has been devoted to investment in agricultural science and technology. More than 50 per cent of total agricultural research invest-ment goes to crops, in particular key grain crops. Meanwhile, China has been persisting in the development of multi-harvest and intensive cultivation: its high multiple-cropping index is an indicator of Chinese success in improving land productivity. China's agricultural technology system is based on the use of alternative inputs to compensate for scarcity of land resources. It must be pointed out that on the one hand, this system effectively increases land productivity by maximizing fertilizer and pesticide inputs; but on the other, negative environmental and eco-logical effects have already emerged, such as groundwater pollution and land degradation. In the context of global warming, this system may not be sustainable in the long run, but developing a more sustainable form of agricultural production is not straightforward.

Like China, Africa puts most research funds into arable crops. Sub-Saharan African countries have invested 45.5 per cent of total agricultural research funding in crop research, with southern Africa topping the list (Table 6.17). Zambia spends 50 per cent of total agricultural research funds on crops and 14 per cent on livestock raising, 10 per cent on post-harvest management and 10 per cent on natural resource management. Major governmental research institutions in Zambia invested nearly 70 per cent of their research budget on crop research (Beintema *et al.*, 2004). Most research expenditure on crops is invested in corn, rice, sorghum and cassava research. Zambia gives top priority (nearly 20 per cent of its total investment) to corn research (Beintema *et al.*, 2004).

According to data collected from Ministry of Agriculture in China, the breakdown of agricultural research expenditure at state-level is 51 per cent for crops, 10 per cent for forestry, 8 per cent for animal husbandry, 6 per cent for fishery, 10 per cent for water resources protection and 7 per cent for others. In the last few decades, this distribution has not seen obvious change except in the first seven years of the 1990s, where expenditure for animal husbandry accounted for 15 to 16 per cent.

To ensure food security and a steady increases in crop yields, China has carried out research on different aspects aside from breeding new varieties, including the following.

1   Planting and breeding technology development – such as the wheat indexation cultivation system and rice cultivation technology based on leaf age; and super

TABLE 6.17 Breakdown of Agricultural Research Funding in Africa

Fields	East Africa	Southern Africa	West Africa	Sub-Saharan Africa
Crop production	43.0	49.5	45.9	45.5
Husbandry	22.0	20.7	17.5	19.9
Natural resources	9.5	10.9	7.1	8.8
Forestry	7.6	3.2	6.9	6.4
Social economy	5.5	2.9	6.9	5.5
Fisheries	5.2	3.1	6.6	5.3
Agricultural products processing	2.6	6.4	6.1	4.8
Other	4.6	3.3	3.0	3.7

Source: Beintema and Stads (2006)

high-yielding theoretical models for wheat, corn, super rice, canola and other novel varieties. A supporting system for improved varieties has been studied and promoted, as well as intensive livestock, poultry and aquatic fauna raising to significantly improve productivity.

2   Land and water resources management – the application and extension of plastic film technologies, scientific fertilizer application and water-saving irrigation technology to increase yields.

3   Disease and pest control – the prevalence and incidence of migration for more than 30 kinds of major pests and diseases have been identified, as well as short and medium-term forecasting techniques for disease and pests; R&D has been carried out for more than 150 kinds of efficient low-residue pesticides and new spraying technologies; more than 60 kinds of animal disease vaccines have been developed: foot and mouth disease, avian influenza and other animal diseases have been effectively controlled, and cattle lung plague has been completely eradicated. Important breakthroughs have been achieved in research on principle aquatic disease pathologies and rapid diagnosis and control techniques.

4   Improvement of medium and low-yielding lands – conditions for crop production have been improved; scientific and technical research on the comprehensive management of medium and low-yielding fields has been carried out, regional agricultural development models as well as high-yield, high-quality and high-efficiency cultivation technology systems have been put forward.

5   Agricultural mechanization – the extension of new intelligent agricultural machinery technologies (People's Daily, 16 January 2009).

In order to give full play to biotechnology, China focuses on research, production condition improvements and the supply of adequate inputs and development of agro-industry.

Africa also pays much attention to varietal improvement. More than half of its total investment goes to crop breeding and related fields, and nearly 30 per cent of research is targeted at agricultural marketing. However, investment in improvements in production techniques has been inadequate: the funds spent on soil fertility research constitute only 3.96 per cent of total research funds. By relying solely on breeding it is impossible to solve the problem of low land productivity. According to the Inter Academy Council investigation in 2005, the improvement of agricultural productivity in Africa is more constrained by water resource and soil fertility management issues than crop variety improvement. This is because soil and water conditions do not allow farmers – especially small farmers – to adopt improved varieties. African countries for the most part have not made adequate investments in this regard.

Another major difference in agricultural technology development between China and Africa is in relation to GM crops. China's attitude in this regard is positive. Out of 13 key technological projects during the Eleventh Five-Year Plan, one is for transgenic crop breeding research. Moreover, transgenic studies have been prioritized in the new Medium and Long-Term Plan for Science and Technology. GM cotton (*Bacillus thuringiensis* cotton) is the most remarkable achievement that China has made, taken up by 7.1 million farmers. The planting area for *Bacillus thuringiensis* cotton accounts for more than 70 per cent of total cotton planting (China Cotton Research Institute, 2008). By 2009, only four out of 53 African countries had accepted GM crops: Burkina Faso, Egypt, South Africa and Kenya. Some argue that Africa's attitude towards GM crops is strongly influenced by international donors: multinationals are not very interested in researching priority crops for Africa, and Africans have developed their own reflections on GM crops which have contributed to scepticism on the subject.

The development of agricultural technology in Africa faces many challenges. On the one hand, due to the low level of industrialization in Africa, non-agricultural employment is relatively low; but on the other hand, the labour shortage problem has been increased by the impact of HIV/AIDS and ineffective migration from rural to urban areas. There has been a lack of adequate investment in the development of alternative technologies as a substitute for labour shortages. At the same time, land productivity is very low. Africa has no particular incentive to improve production conditions such as irrigation and fertilizer, or R&D for high-yielding varieties.

Thus, land resource potentials in Africa cannot be utilized fully because of labour and capital shortages; whereas in China, shortages of land and capital are overcome

TABLE 6.18 Investment Orientation for the Alliance for a Green Revolution in Africa (AGRA) Programme

	Varieties Improvement	*Varieties Improvement and Utilization*	*Seed Production*	*Market Construction Research*	*Soil Fertility Sales*	*Agricultural Product*
USD	1,842,4937	8,488,270	16,792,638	1,345,578	2,930,330	25,986,236
%	24.91%	11.48%	22.70%	1.82%	3.96%	35.13%

Source: http://www.agra-alliance.org/

by labour force advantages. This is a key characteristic of Chinese agricultural technology development.

Comparison of Agricultural Technology Extension in China and Africa

As early as 1951, China set up pilot agricultural extension stations in north-east and north China. In 1953, it built specialized agencies equipped with full-time staff to carry out agricultural technology extension nationwide. Agricultural stations were formed in various counties in 1962, and 29 county-level extension centres were launched by the Ministry of Agriculture in 1979. In 1982, the Communist Party of China Central Committee Document No. 1 called for 'building up county-level extension agencies, integrating institutions engaged in technology extension, plant protection, soil conservation, fertilizer application and other agricultural technology, to achieve a reasonable labour division under unified leadership'. Under these guidelines, county-level extension centres were given full play and the promotion of agricultural technology entered a stage of rapid progress. After several decades of development, China has formed a diversified agricultural technology extension system led by government, assisted by specialized farmers' cooperatives and market-oriented NGOs and research institutions, aiming to meet the needs of farmers in adopting different technologies.

The government-led extension system in China falls into two areas. The first is the extension station system, which covers state, provincial, municipal, county and township organizations, and is engaged in introducing agricultural technology to farmers and providing plant protection, soil and fertilizer and seed-related services. At the county or township level 173,000 extension agents work in the areas of crop production, animal husbandry, aquaculture, farm machinery technology and management. This includes 22,000 county-level agencies and 151,000 township-level institutions (*China Statistical Yearbook*, 2005; *China Agricultural Statistical Yearbook*, 2006), with a total of 1.03 million extension personnel (Lu, 2005).

The second is the technology agent system organized by the Ministry of Science and Technology. From 2002, central government dispatched special agents to provide technical services in rural areas. As of December 2007, the system has covered 1,039 counties (cities, districts, banners and groups) in 31 provinces (autonomous regions, municipalities and the Xinjiang Production and Construction Corps) in China. The number of agents reached 57,000, serving more than 14 million farmers in nearly 40,000 villages (Ministry of Science and Technology, 2008).

The private sector and NGOs play an increasingly important role in the agricultural extension system in China. Seed, pesticide and fertilizer firms promote their new products to farmers with advertisements, through government infor-mation platforms and their own sales systems. By 2001 China had built up more than 100,000 agricultural technology associations, more than 400,000 village-level service organizations, millions of technology demonstration households and numer-

TABLE 6.19 Genetically Modified Crop Cultivation in Africa and China

	Zambia	Liberia	Africa	China
Policies towards genetically-modified crops: Open, Conditionally open, Prohibited	Zero tolerance towards GMO and GMO products	Subject to domestic laws and the Cartagena Bio-safety Protocol if importing GMO	All countries have prohibited GM plant varieties except for Burkina Faso, Egypt, South Africa and Kenya	Only non-food GM crop varieties are permitted, although certain GM rice and maize varieties have recently been given bio-safety approval for cultivation subject to plant variety approval being granted
Which transgenic crop varieties can be cultivated?	0	Article 1.4(b) of the Plant and Quarantine Law 1973 allows the import of GMO *in vivo* for the purpose of testing, but prohibits the import of parasitic and infectious animals and plants, except those serving R&D, medical, experimentation and education purposes. The import of GMOs for experiments is allowed exclusively within the research region and institution. Biological, chemical, physical, space and environmental isolation in appropriate locations is required. Experiments can be carried out in fields or greenhouses. All details should be recorded (section 3.4.1 and 3.4.2)		Cotton, tomato, poplar, petunia, virus-resistant papaya and sweet pepper
How many transgenic varieties have been bred or introduced?	0	None		270 genetically modified cotton varieties (2008)
Planting area for GM crops	0	0		3.8 million hectares
Priority GM crop traits	n/a	High-yield, disease and weed-resistance		Insect-resistance

Source: China: China Cotton Research Institute (2008); Zambia and Liberia: field sites in 2009

ous agriculture-related enterprises. China's agricultural science research institutions also bear the important task of commercializing and extending technological achievements through experimental fields, pilot and demonstration sites and other methods. Since 2009, the Ministry of Agriculture has authorized 45 agricultural universities, colleges and research institutions as 'modern agricultural technology training bases' in order to strengthen fundamental R&D, update the knowledge of technicians and facilitate capacity building for grass roots technicians.

In addition to building a complete agricultural technology extension system, the Chinese government has made huge financial investments in the extension of agricultural technology. According to the Agricultural Extension Department in the Ministry of Agriculture, the government allocated CNY7,047 million (USD1,032 million) to extension in 1999 and CNY483 million (USD70 million) to the agent dispatch programme alone in 2007 – an increase of 22.9 per cent from 2006 (Ministry of Science and Technology, 2008).

In addition, China has established an agricultural extension system based on modern information technologies, and an agricultural long-distance education network relying on radio and television and schools of all levels. With the advancement of the To Every Village project, more villages will enjoy these services. Some provinces have used agricultural information and communication technologies to send useful agricultural science and technology messages to farmers through mobile phones. The information-based extension and government-funded mass media is playing an important role in agricultural technology extension. The Rural Economy Research Centre if the Ministry of Agriculture conducted a nationwide household survey on access to new agricultural technology, and the results showed that television and radio, books and other printed materials are major channels for farmers to adopt new production technology.

TABLE 6.20 Changes in the Funding of Chinese Agricultural Technology Promotion Departments (Unit: CNY1 million)

	Fiscal Allocation	Self-earned Profit?	Total
1990	2,132	7	2,139
1991	2,371	8	2,379
1992	2,589	10	2,599
1993	2,884	28	2,912
1994	3,484	27	3,511
1995	4,206	40	4,246
1996	5,130	70	5,200
1997	5,509	238	5,747
1998	6,330	1502	7,832
1999	7,047	1492	8,539

Sources: Development Research Centre of the State Council; Chinese Government Agricultural Capital Investment and Management System Reform Research, 2003

TABLE 6.21 Access to New Production Technologies by Farmers in China (%)

	2001	2002	2003	2004
Neighbours	38.6	38.8	28.6	35.3
Department of Agricultural Technology Promotion	22.0	23.3	28.1	24.5
Television and broadcasting	9.1	9.4	21.9	13.5
Farmers associations	1.1	1.4	1.0	1.2
Books and other media	13.8	14.7	8.4	12.3
Other	15.4	12.4	12.0	13.3
Number of surveyed farmers	1,012	1,154	1,608	1,258

Source: Rural Economic Research Centre of the Ministry of Agriculture, Investigation on Farmer Demand for Technology and Market Information, 2004

In addition, some African countries have formed government-led agricultural extension systems. Uganda's agricultural extension system includes the following.

1   The National Agricultural Advisory Services (NAADS), aims to improve the efficiency of agricultural extension. According to the National Agricultural Advisory Services Act 2001, NAADS aims to providing the farmers in poor living conditions (especially women, youth and the disabled), with a demand-oriented and farmer-led agricultural service system. NAADS is a semi-autonomous agency with five branches responsible for advisory and information services for farmers, technology development and marketing, quality monitoring and technical review, institutional building in the private sector and project management and assessment. Launched in 2002, NAADS' service network continues to expand towards new areas. To date, it works in 79 counties and 710 sub-counties.

2   The Agricultural Research and Extension Network (ARENET) is a website targeted at strengthening relationships between the national agricultural research system and national agricultural advisory services, and related extension organizations and their members. It provides information and knowledge about technology research and extension systems. ARENET is committed to helping individuals or organizations who want to improve agriculture production to obtain technology and trading information from both home and abroad as quickly as possible, assisting agricultural extension service personnel and agencies as well as rural development workers to solve the problems encountered by farmers with the help of research institutions and local governments.

3   The National Agricultural Education Strategy 2004–2015, issued in 2003 by the Ministry of Education and Sport, guides the country's agricultural education and training and aims to advance sustainable agriculture by providing high-quality formal or informal education and training at all levels.

Most African countries have not built unified agricultural extension systems; instead, they depend heavily upon international assistance (Alene and Coulibaly,

2009). The Chinese agricultural delegation to Sierra Leone reported[3] that by September 2002, Sierra Leone had not established specialized agricultural machinery management, extension and service agencies or teams. At present, agricultural technology promotion is reliant on the efforts of international donors, especially the countries suffering from civil disturbance: for example, Sierra Leone has increasingly encouraged NGOs and international agencies to provide substantial advisory services to meet its urgent need for development and reconstruction after the civil war. Rice technology extension is mainly undertaken by Chinese experts.

Farmer field schools (supported by the World Bank) are the major modality for promoting agricultural technology in Sierra Leone. Six farmer field schools (involving 14,550 farmers) were established in 14 districts in 2006. Government agriculture and food security, fisheries and aquatic resources departments, together with some international NGOs, established 520 schools and 66 agricultural schools.[4] Many African countries failed to build up government-led agricultural extension systems, and instead have conducted agricultural extension services in other ways. Farmer field schools are the main mode of agricultural extension and are funded largely by international agencies.

Field interviews reveal that Zambia spends USD4 million per annum on agricultural extension, while Liberia only spent USD1.5 million. China by contrast spent nearly USD700 million. With regard to extension methods, China has introduced new approaches to sharing information using the internet, distance education and mobile phones. Many parts of Africa rely exclusively on face-to-face extension, which has limited the availability of agricultural technology. However, the situation is changing: for example in Kenya, mobile-based extension is spreading quickly through the National Farmers Information Service (Gakuru et al., 2009), which is a comprehensive information service intended to serve farmers' needs throughout the country, including rural areas where internet access is limited. The service comprises a detailed website that is easily updated by extension officers, and a voice-based service containing summarized information that farmers can access via mobile phone. The voice service is available both in English (Kenyan Local dialect) and Kiswahili.[5]

One of the advantages of China's agricultural extension system is that China's arable land is organized under farming zones and owned collectively by village communities, yet managed by individual households. Farmers live in nucleated villages, which makes agricultural extension more convenient. African farmers do not necessarily live in villages next to their land: the diversity of land tenure and dwelling places do not favour agricultural extension. Many African farmers have not seen government researchers or extension staff for many years, according to a field survey by Scoones et al. (2005). Due to the character of villages and limitations of the capacities of the national extension system in African countries, there is an urgent need for an appropriate and diverse, not homogenous, approach to extension. Some novel approaches have demonstrated possible future directions: for example, university–industry linkages, wider institutional linkages and a self-organizing system, which has been analysed by Juma (2011).

TABLE 6.22 Agriculture Promotion Methods of Different African Nations

Country (approximate no. of agents where known)	Current Model(s)
Angola	Rural Development and Extension Programmes; farmer field schools
Benin	Participatory management approach, decentralized models; farmer field schools
Burkina Faso	Farmer field schools
Cameroon	National Agricultural Extension and Research Programme Support Project; Farmer field schools
Ethiopia (65,000)	Model based on Sasakawa Global 2000 approach (SG-2000); Participatory Demonstration and Training Extension System; farmer field schools
Ghana	Unified Extension System (modified Training and Visit); pluralistic, with NGOs and private companies part of the national extension system; decentralized; farmer field schools
Kenya	Pluralistic system including public, private, NGOs, farmer field schools, the stakeholder approach (National Agriculture and Livestock Programme); sector-wide, focal area, demand-driven, group-based approach
Malawi	Pluralistic, demand-driven, decentralized; 'one village, one product'; farmer field schools
Mali	Modified Training and Visit; both private and parastatal services for cotton; farmer field schools; SG-2000
Mozambique (1,068)	Government-led pluralistic extension; farmer field schools
Nigeria (5,252)	Farmer field schools; participatory; SG-2000
Rwanda	Participative, pluralistic, specialized, bottom-up approach; farmer field schools
Senegal	Farmer field schools; government-led demand-driven and pluralistic system
Tanzania (7000)	Farmer field schools; group-based approach; SG-2000; modified Farming Systems Research and Extension from Sokoine; University of Agriculture's Centre for Sustainable Rural Development; private extension; decentralized participatory district extension; pluralism
Uganda	Pluralistic; NAADS is demand-driven; client-oriented and farmer-led; SG-2000; farmer field schools
Zambia	Participatory Extension Approach; farmer field schools

Source: Davis (2009)

TABLE 6.23 Agricultural Extension Systems in Three Countries (Unit: 1,000 Agricultural Population)

	Zambia	Liberia	China
Government's extension expenditure (USD/year)	517.5	1000	906.8
Government extension institutions	0.21	0.01	0.23
Government extension personnel	0.27	0.06	1.38
NGOs	0.002	0.03	0.13
Private extension institution	0.003	0.007	–

Source: Zambia and Liberia: data sourced from fieldwork in 2009; China: Lu (2005). Liberia and Zambia: population data from UNICEF; China: National Economic and Social Development Statistical Communiqué, 2005

Conclusion

There are obvious differences in the adoption and development of agricultural technology between China and the African continent. With the impetus of the Green Revolution, China has made significant progress in the use of high-yielding improved varieties and fertilizer, pesticides and plastic film. In spite of declining arable land and crop cultivation areas, China's total grain output continues to increase and grain supply is sufficient to meet demand, meaning that national food security is basically ensured. Moreover, it has made great efforts in the development and advancement of high technology, especially GMO technology. Conversely, the African continent has been largely left behind by the Green Revolution for a variety of reasons, but many encouraging innovations have accumulated through long-term efforts by multi-stakeholders including farmers, agricultural research institutes and private sectors, with few national policies being directly influential.

China and Africa have attached great importance to agricultural science research. The Chinese government has made the Agriculture Rejuvenation Through Science and Education strategy a fundamental one for national development, with the support of related plans. A system involving development objectives, projects, measures, capital and human resource supplies has been established. Africa also has formulated agricultural technology development strategies, but no specific implementation plans. In addition, many agricultural technology strategies cannot be implemented due to Africa's economic and fiscal weakness.

Both China and Africa have built up agricultural research systems, with government-funded public research institutions as major components. China's agricultural research institutions have large numbers of personnel, and agricultural researchers are concentrated in national and provincial research institutes and agricultural universities, which makes it easy to develop coherent R&D plans. By contrast, most African agricultural research institutions are small-scale with low research capability.

Both Africa and China attach much importance to training agricultural researchers, introducing talent from abroad and sending agricultural talent overseas for training. In China, there is not only higher education in agriculture, but also medium and vocational agricultural education on a huge scale. China gives high honours to researchers, including agricultural researchers, to offset their relatively low salaries. This situation does not appear to be matched in Africa.

China's investment in agricultural research mainly comes from the public budget, which has increased rapidly year-on-year. Research institutions are gradually becoming more financially sustainable and even self-financing. Meanwhile, in most African states agricultural research investment is inadequate. A considerable number of states source their agricultural development funds from foreign countries, which results in instability and insecurity in agricultural research funding.

One of the advantages of the China's agricultural extension is that its arable land falls under farm zones and is collectively owned by village communities, yet individual households manage it. Farmers live in villages that favour agricultural extension, whereas African farmers do not necessarily live in villages close to their fields, such that diversity of land tenure and dwelling arrangements do not favour agricultural extension in Africa.

Both China and the African continent focus on crop planting related to food security. The difference is that China not only emphasizes the cultivation of new varieties, but also production technologies such as soil improvement, irrigation, pest and disease control and advanced field management, so that the whole farming system is updated. Africa puts most of its effort into variety breeding rather than other aspects related to production, which lowers the adaptability of new varieties and slows the extension of improved varieties. With a large population and limited land reserves, China has developed a technology system focused on land productivity improvement. In this way, labour force advantages can be used to their best ability. Africa is unable to form such a system due to capital and labour shortages, despite abundant land resources. However, at the same time intensive agriculture in China is facing serious environmental challenges; whereas in Africa there could be bright opportunities to transform traditional agriculture into a sustainable modern agriculture in a low-cost and environmentally friendly way.

China has built a complete, diversified and multi-layered extension system including government agencies, NGOs and the emerging private sector. Together with effective and stable funding from the state and modern agricultural technology transfer, China's agricultural technology extension capacity has been significantly improved. In contrast, only a few African countries have national agricultural technology extension systems. Most African countries have agricultural extension systems that depend on international assistance and are constrained by their own economic capacities and infrastructure conditions, which have greatly affected agricultural progress.

Some novel innovation approaches present a more diverse picture of the R&D system in Africa, which could be very different from China.

7

COMPARISON OF AGRICULTURAL PRODUCTION AT THE HOUSEHOLD LEVEL IN CHINA AND AFRICA

In 2007, China had more than 255 million rural households with a population of more than 949 million (*National Statistical Yearbook*, 2007). This population occupied 116 million hectares of farmland in total and 0.456 hectares per capita. There were also 1,885 state-owned farms in China managing more than 5 million hectares of land, equivalent to 4.4 per cent of the total area (*National Statistical Yearbook*, 2008). Clearly, smallholder family farms still form the backbone of China's agricultural production system.

In Africa, taking Liberia as an example, although plantations take up a large amount of land, some of them being more than 200 hectares, more than 80 per cent of the total national land area is in the hands of smallholders (who themselves make up 70 per cent of the population). The degree of urbanization is generally low in countries in Sub-Saharan Africa; about 72 per cent of the population live in rural areas and 70 per cent of the population is still engaged in agricultural production (Moussa, 2002). Agricultural production is mainly reliant on smallholder farmers.

As can be seen, African agriculture shares important structural characteristics with Chinese farming. Smallholder farms based on the family unit allocate production factors (including land use, labour and capital investment) at the household level. Judging from the current development situation, this kind of agricultural production system will persist for a long time in both China and Africa.

In terms of land resources, smallholders in Africa hold much larger plots of land than their Chinese counterparts (who own less than half a hectare per capita). On average, each farmer owns 13.20 hectares of land in Liberia, 3.64 hectares in Zambia and 1.19 hectares in Tanzania.

Agricultural development is directly affected by macroeconomic policies and science and technology investment, agricultural subsidies and other development policies. Ultimately, most agricultural policies must be implemented at household level; therefore, how these units organize agricultural production and resource allocation is fundamentally important. Landholding, labour force structure and skills, technology adoption, national agricultural policies, credit access and access to market information are all key in the organization and implementation of agricultural production at the household level.

Resource Utilization by Smallholder Farmers in China and Africa

Land Utilization

China is a vast country and its climatic conditions differ markedly between North and South China and between west and east. Farmers in different areas have their own ways of making full use of local resources. In South China, the rural population is concentrated mainly in mountainous areas, where land holdings are very small and often arranged on terraced hillsides, but the climate and rainfall conditions are favourable for multi-season farming. As shown in Table 7.1, intensive land utilization in South China is significant, making three harvests a year possible if early rice, late rice and early-maturing varieties of winter wheat are planted in succession. Smallholders in South China are heir to highly intensive cultivation traditions handed down from ancient China (see, for example, FAO, 2012). In contrast, land resources are relatively rich in North China, while rainfall and light conditions are less favourable for agricultural production compared to South China. For example, in Shui Village in the west of Gansu Province, farmers harvest only once a year because of the harsh climate – the frost-free period lasts for only 140 days (Tang, 2009).

In terms of planting seasons, Africa's climate is generally bimodal, characterized by wet and dry seasons, rather than the four seasons as experienced in China. Rainfall distribution is very uneven on the African continent. Of the three countries visited for field research, Liberia has the highest rainfall (up to 5,000mm) and comparatively frequent rainfall even in the dry season, making it very suitable for crop production. Smallholders harvest rice once a year in Liberia, but Chinese experts have concluded that they could grow three seasons of hybrid rice, given the favourable local climate.[1] Unlike China, landholding per capita in Africa is large and smallholders do not exploit land as intensively as in China. The national land utilization rate for Liberia is less than 15 per cent, meaning that a vast amount of land is still underutilized. The landholdings per household in three field sites in Tanzania (Village A), Zambia (Village B) and Liberia (Village C), are 1.19 ha, 3.64 ha and 13.20 ha respectively, all surpassing China's 2007 average household landholding of just under half a hectare. In terms of land usage, farmers in all three African villages allocate more than 80 per cent of arable land to food crops (corn or rice) and cash crops, leaving some land fallow. Cropping patterns or marketing choices are not the result of a single economic calculus, but the outcome of negotiation between husbands and wives, between co-wives and between parents and their children (Guyer and Peters, 1987).

In addition, African smallholders do not arrange their agricultural production activities according to a clear and logical timetable. For example, in Tanzania, maize sowing and harvesting run from March to August, and rice from December or January to April, meaning that there is an idle season from August to December or January. Moreover, smallholders in the three countries hardly adopt techniques such as inter-cropping or relay cropping, although they do practise crop rotation to sustain soil fertility. In areas with similar climatic conditions in China, cash crops are grown to exercise their comparative advantage based on abundant land resources and favourable climate conditions, but grain planting remains the dominant use of land. For example, in 2005, in Fulong Township, Baisha County in Hainan Province, with a population of 4,686 out of a total of 5,014 residents, and with 64.22 km^2 of land, the grain sowing area was 651.4 ha with an output of 2,965 tonnes, yielding the following:

- of the total rubber planting area of 646.53 ha, there were 271.6 ha of tapping area with an output of 285 tonnes of rubber;
- the cassava cultivation area was 216 ha with an output of 5,164 tonnes;
- the sugarcane cultivation area was 394.27 ha with an output of 15,000 tonnes; and
- the betel nut and bamboo areas covered around 20 ha and 40 ha respectively.[2]

These land use patterns took shape in the 1990s, driven by market opportunity and government support for cash crop development alongside rice production. Therefore, in China enhancing the potential for land productivity is exploited as quickly as possible at the household level (as discussed in earlier chapters).

Labour Distribution

In the three field villages visited in Africa, household size and labour resources are as follows:

- one household has an average of 4.27 people and 1.93 labourers in Village A in Tanzania;

TABLE 7.1 Seasonal Calendar for Main Crops in China and Africa

	Country			
	Tanzania	*Liberia*	*Zambia*	*South China[a]*
Corn	Sowing (Mar.) Harvest (Aug.)	Sowing (Apr.) Harvest (July)	Sowing (Nov.–Dec.) Harvest (Next Apr.)	Sowing (mid-Apr.) Harvest (mid-Sep.)
Rice	Sowing (Dec.–Jan.) Harvest (Apr.)	Sowing (May) Harvest (Oct.)	– –	Early rice: Sowing (late Feb.) Harvest (July) Late rice: Sowing (late June) Harvest (Nov.)

a Three harvests are possible when early rice, late rice and early-maturing winter wheat varieties are adopted.

- 4.80 people and 2.13 labourers in Village B in Zambia; and
- 5.03 members and 2.13 labourers in Village C in Liberia.

In China, the average number of people and labourers per household are 4.4 and 2.82, respectively (Zhong, 2006). Adequate labour is a prerequisite for agricultural production, while the quality of the labour force, in particular educational attainment, is equally important. The educational level of China's agricultural labour force has risen gradually since the 1980s. The semi-literacy and illiteracy rate for rural labour dropped from 27.87 per cent in 1985 to 6.34 per cent in 2007, while the proportion of the workforce with secondary school and technical secondary school education also increased; in particular the proportion of the labour force with a technical secondary school education or above rose from 0.35 per cent to 3.99 per cent (*China Agriculture Yearbook*, 2008).

In Africa, education for farmers is relatively poor and uneven in rural areas. In the three field sites, peasant illiteracy rates hovered at around 30 per cent, and very few farmers had finished high school or above. Furthermore, effective utilization of labour is undermined by the impact of disease.

China has taken advantage of an abundant labour force for agricultural infrastructure construction using voluntary labour inputs encouraged by governments at different levels. However, in Africa, labour force shortage restrains such government (or other organizational) attempts to improve land productivity (Table 7.3).

In China, the rural labour force has been able to migrate to non-agricultural sectors and urban areas since the beginning of the reform period. In recent years, the traditional male-led agricultural production system has changed significantly, as a large number of young rural male labourers have migrated to cities. At present, China's rural migrant workers have reached 225 million, and 47 million women are left behind in villages (Zhang, 2006),[3] causing a feminization of agriculture. There are historical antecedents for this. In 'Farmland in Lu Village' (2006[1945]) written by the anthropologist Fei Xiaotong, a clear gender division of labour for agricultural production was depicted vividly in the 1930s. In particularly, crop rotation practices for rice and beans involved women's work more than men (Fei, 2006[1945]). As a consequence it can be inferred that the feminization of the agricultural labour force emerged in villages like Lu Village (Hu, 2006; Wu, 2008). Driven by low return rates to agricultural production, and attracted by higher income from urban employment, the migration of a large numbers of young males has become a dominant pattern. That agriculture has become more of a female domain (and also of the elderly) is an inevitable consequence. Women in rural China shoulder a heavy burden, spending time on household chores alongside agricultural production (Gao, 1994; Li, 2001; Tong and Long, 2002) as well as looking after the elderly. According to Zhang (2009), in a total of 306 households with 1,426 people, where 910 labourers lived in eight randomly sampled villages in four provinces characterized by high labour mobility, there were 241 households with migrant labour. In the other 65 households, most of the male labourers were married and middle-aged; they were also engaged in farming during the busy season and part-time off-farm work during the slack season. While some male labourers are involved in sowing and harvesting, it is women who carry most of the responsibility for field management.

The extensive cultivation of African smallholders also affects household labour distribution and the gender division of labour. In Village A in Tanzania, Village B in Zambia and Village C in Liberia, 86 per cent, 91 per cent and 63 per cent of households respectively were reliant on male labour for sowing. Yet it is noteworthy that five rice planting procedures – namely, raising seedlings, transplanting, irrigation, fertilizer application and pesticide spraying – were not taking place in the three villages, suggesting huge differences in planting methods compared to China. Similarly, due to the relative shortage of labour, households in African countries are unable to improve land productivity through intensive labour inputs as in China. In terms of field management, weeding is the only heavy work carried out in the site villages: 90 per cent of families in Village C count on female labour for weeding, and 52 per cent of households in Village B. Of the households in Village C, 80 per cent rely on female labour (or children) for harvesting. In Village A, male labour in 92 per cent of households is responsible for harvesting, but attention should be paid to the fact that machinery usage rates are very low for sowing, weeding, harvesting and even processing. At present, machinery is adopted only to a relative low degree for land preparation. In Village A and Village B, only 20 per cent and 10 per cent respectively of households hired tractors for land preparation. In Village C, harvesting is practised mostly using manual tools, without any farm machinery.

To summarize, the biggest difference in labour distribution between China and Africa is that in China, the labour force pursues opportunities for off-farm employment while taking care of agricultural production. Along with rapid economic growth, an increasing number of rural labourers have migrated to cities for jobs created in the second and third sectors. In Africa, due to relatively low levels of urbanization and industrialization, it is difficult for migrant labourers to find jobs in cities or factories, so most farmers have to devote themselves to agricultural production and only a few have the opportunity to do part-time, seasonal, non-agricultural jobs (Anríquez and Stloukal, 2008).

As described previously, a large proportion of the young male labour force in China's rural areas work as migrants outside the village and female family members and the elderly are left behind to manage agricultural production.[4] In addition, labour-replacing machinery such as transplanters and harvesting machines are widely employed in rural China. Even small farm households hire machinery for procedures such as land preparation, sowing and harvesting. However, visits to the three village sites in Liberia, Tanzania and Zambia reveal that there are only a few male labourers taking up part-time small businesses such as charcoal selling during less busy periods in the agricultural year. Within families, men are mainly responsible for sowing, while women (and children) are responsible for weeding and harvesting.

In conclusion, land productivity in the main is not increased by intensive labour inputs. There are two possible explanations: first, the African labour force cannot carry out the necessary physical work associated with this type of intensive cultivation (from land preparation to crop planting) as found in China; second, farm machinery is relatively inaccessible for small farmers in Africa.

Rural Household Income Structure in China and Africa

Agricultural and non-agricultural incomes represent different proportions of household income structure in China and Africa. In 2007 the average net income of rural households in China was CNY4140 (USD607), of which 42 per cent came from agriculture (consisting of 1.4 per cent from forestry, 8.1 per cent from livestock raising and 1.1 per cent from fishing), 38.6 per cent from wages, 10.8 per cent from non-productive net income, 3.1 per cent from property income and 5.4 per cent from transfer income (China Agriculture Yearbook, 2008). Li (2006) investigated 500 households in five villages in Huaiyuan County, Anhui Province and concluded that farmer incomes came mainly from farming, accounting for as much as 30 to 50 per cent, with the rest from part-time jobs and off-farm income. For the 62 families with income per capita above CNY2,000 (around USD300), the main income source was remittances from family members doing off-farm work.

In Africa, smallholders rely heavily on agricultural income and have limited property income or remittance income (this varies between African countries), and seldom hold part-time jobs because the industrial sector and other urban-based sectors have limited capacity to absorb surplus labour. Taking Village A as an example, a typical farming community had 12 households in 1959 and 65 households in 2009. The average household income is USD449.45, of which 66.76 per cent came from agriculture (USD300.07) and 33.24 per cent from non-agricultural activities. The average cultivated land per household is 3.64 ha, of which more than 70 per cent is used for crop planting (producing around 430kg of maize per hectare). Total maize production was barely enough for the villagers, and it was found that only one household in the village was able to sell agricultural products in local markets. The village is located not far from the capital Lusaka, but many young adults stay at home during the dry season from June to November instead of finding jobs in the towns and cities. It is very difficult for young adult labour force to shift to non-agricultural production sectors as there are simply insufficient opportunities in these areas. During the off-season, there are very few households selling charcoal for cash income. Part-time jobs such as charcoal selling and mutual assistance using hired labour are the main sources of income. This type of livelihood structure, lack of asset accumulation and lack of diverse income sources mean that smallholder families are particularly vulnerable to natural disasters such as flood, drought, plant disease and pests.

Furthermore, the structure of agricultural production income is different between China and Africa. In the main grain producing areas in the temperate part of China, farmer income is largely derived from grain production, with an additional proportion from raising livestock. In tropical areas, farmer income structure is increasingly diversified, with cash crop cultivation as the main income source. For example, in Fulong Village in Hainan province, household income derives mostly from cassava, followed by sugarcane and rubber (rubber is the primary income source for many farmers). For the three African villages visited for this research, crop farming is clearly the dominant activity. In Village B, villagers raise hardly any animals, not even chickens for daily meals. When asked about this, villagers claimed that they lacked experience and that eagles would prey on chickens. In some heavily forested countries in Africa, livestock pests have held back development of the livestock sector (Nkamleu et al., 2008).[5]

Thus, although China and African countries share similarities in agricultural production at the household level, China's smallholders have greater access to markets and as a result can mobilize resources to develop diversified income sources. Part-time jobs and diversified income sources enable small farmers to survive and recover from sudden shocks and the vulnerabilities of agricultural production.[6]

Application of Productive Technology at Household Level in China and Africa

In agricultural production in China, human labour and multi-functional animals are being increasingly replaced by machinery at the household level. Taking maize production as an example, by the end of 2007 more than 60 per cent of the areas sown used mechanical technologies (*China Agricultural Yearbook*, 2008). Moreover, the application and extension of new technologies can be seen in the adoption of new varieties, pesticides, fertilizer, herbicides, irrigation technologies and technologies for all the processes from sowing to harvesting. Meanwhile, the extension of mechanical technology in recent years has facilitated labour migration. African smallholders rely on traditional skills and machinery is rarely used, even on medium-sized farms.

Comparison of Rice Planting at the Household Level in China and Africa

Chinese smallholders not only fully exploit the potential of natural resources and the climatic conditions that they face, but they also attach great importance to detailed skills and techniques that maximize land productivity. Intensive rice planting is divided into eight main steps:

1 soil preparation
2 seed production
3 transplanting
4 weeding and pest management
5 fertilizer application
6 irrigation
7 harvesting, and
8 crop drying.

For all these steps, care must be taken to maximize productivity. Before sowing, farmers turn over the soil to make it soft and follow three steps: crude ploughing, fine ploughing and levelling. Then they select an area for seedling production, which is crucial for a high survival rate. In cases of manual planting, a small device is put on the left thumb to help farmers separate seedlings and transplant them into the field. Now modern transplanters are widely used, but manual planting is still applied in most areas, particularly for uneven or poor-quality farmland. Agrochemicals are used to control pests and weeds, and fertilizer is applied at carefully identified times. There are slight differences in irrigation and drainage practices between early rice and double-cropping rice: they both require abundant irrigation during young panicle formation and heading and flowering periods. In the past, people used sickles for harvesting and threshers for separating the rice from spikes; now they use harvesters to separate rice from the spikes directly. After this, the harvested rice is dried for storage.[7] All these practices have been carefully developed over time.

In Liberia, rice planting is not as complex as it is in China. Subsistence agriculture is still extensive and simple, with 'slash and burn' techniques widely practised. To be specific, smallholders divide the land into several portions of different sizes and plant different crops based on plot conditions. They burn the bush and level the land in April, then sow in May using hoes and mattocks without any draft power or machinery. They dig the soil with hoes and sow using dibble seeding. After that, they weed twice, but no further field management occurs. There are no seedling beds or irrigation facilities for rice planting. Compared with China, the biggest difference lies in the lack of seedling technology and procedures (in Liberia, direct sowing), irrigation facilities (in Liberia, rain-fed), seedling beds and field ridge (in Liberia, sowing casually without field management). No drainage or irrigation facilities are evident in most fields, and even in fields alongside rivers there are no artificial channels at all. In addition, most smallholders in China use herbicides in the weeding process, while the ones in Liberia do not. Due to lack of access and lower purchasing capacity, most of the interviewed farmers do not apply any chemical fertilizers, herbicides or pesticides or use machinery.

The considerable differences in rice planting between China and Liberia result in different input–output ratios at the household level (Table 7.2). In China's rice planting areas, the average cultivated land per household is 0.35 hectares, of which 0.29 hectares (82.86 per cent) are for grain. China's per-capita arable land is small, thus the only way to increase productivity is through more labour, applying fertilizer and using pesticide inputs. In Village C in Liberia, per-capita arable land is up to 13.2 hectares, of which 4.69 hectares (32.04 per cent) are dedicated to grain production: less than one-third of the total area.

Fertilizer, pesticides and improved seed inputs are used significantly less by smallholders in Liberia than farmers in China. In terms of fertilizer expenditure, Chinese farmers spend USD290.68 per hectare, while Liberian farmers spend USD4.26, only 1.47 per cent of China's figure. For pesticides, Chinese farmers spend USD83.25 per hectare, while Liberian farmers spend USD9.41, only one-tenth of Chinese usage. For improved seeds, Chinese farmers generally widely apply improved rice varieties to advance productivity. In 2007, China's high-quality rice application rate amounted to 72.3 per cent (*China Agricultural Statistical Yearbook*, 2008). Yet in Village C, only one household buys rice seeds and the other farmers reserve seeds for sowing the following year. When it comes to irrigation costs, animal power and mechanical cultivation, financial inputs in China are much more significant while almost no expense is made in Village C. In China, irrigation, animal power and mechanical cultivation costs on arable land per hectare are on average USD46.71, USD31.29 and USD119.73 respectively, while the figure is near zero in Village C.

The difference in hired labour costs between China (USD45.02) and Liberia (USD46.26) is relatively small. As shown in Figure 7.1, China's total capital input of rice planting per hectare is much higher than Liberia (the total input in China is USD671.74, it is only USD79.259 in Liberia). The rice output per hectare is 7,023kg in China and only 1176.25kg in Liberia. This gives a gross income per hectare of USD2285.59 (rice price per kg: USD0.325) in China and USD635.12 (rice price per kg: USD0.54) in Liberia; and a net income per hectare of USD1613.85 in China and USD555.86 in Liberia. As noted, possible explanations for this are intensive farming skills and a higher capital input (such as fertilizers, pesticides and irrigation) in China.

It can be concluded that the input–output ratios for rice planting are quite different between Liberia and China. Smallholders in China take more advantage of modern agricultural techniques for rice planting, such as using improved rice

TABLE 7.2 Comparison of Input–Output Ratios for Rice Planting in China and Liberia

	China	Liberia
Average arable land (ha/household)	0.35	13.2
Average rice planting area (ha/household)	0.29	4.69
Fertilizer expenditure (USD/ha)	290.68	4.26
Pesticide expenditure (USD/ha)	83.25	9.41
Seed expenditure (USD/ha)	54.42	0.00
Irrigation cost (USD/ha)	46.71	0.00
Animal power fee (USD/ha)	31.29	0.00
Machinery charges (USD/ha)	119.73	0.00
Hired labour costs (USD/ha)	45.02	46.26
Total input (USD):	671.74	79.259
Output (kg/ha)	7023.00	1176.15
Output (USD/ha)	1910.84	635.121
Subsidies (USD/ha)	246.5	0
Labour productivity	–	–
Land productivity [a]	7023.00	1176.15

Source: China: Rural Economic Research Centre, Ministry of Agriculture; Liberia: authors' field survey

a Land productivity = Crop yield/total acreage of crops (or harvested area)

Note: However, negative externalities of agricultural, e.g. environmental cost, is not calculated here

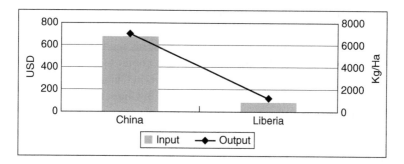

Figure 7.1 Comparison of Input–Output Ratios for Rice Planting in China and Liberia (Unit: USD; kg/ha)

seeds, fertilizer, pesticides and machinery. In Liberia, by contrast, rice planting is carried out mainly using traditional farming skills and saved seed, with limited fertilizer, pesticides and machinery inputs or utilization of irrigation facilities.

Comparison of Maize Planting at the Household Level in China and Africa

Nowadays, smallholders in China mobilize labour, animal power and machinery together for maize cultivation (including processes of land preparation, irrigation, weeding and harvesting). By the end of 2007, mechanized production for maize cultivation had risen to 60.47 per cent of the total production area (*China Agriculture Yearbook*, 2008). In addition, chemical herbicides and pesticides are rapidly replacing intensive labour inputs. In China, maize planting begins around 10 April. Soil preparation incorporates fine ploughing and ridge building to loosen the soil and preserve soil moisture. Following this, plastic film is applied and sowing takes place. Two fertilizer applications are made, including one top-dressing; pesticides and herbicides are applied three times in total and irrigation is carried out twice, once before seeding and again in the flowering period when maize is most sensitive to water shortage. Finally, harvesting relies on a certain amount of mechanical input.

In Africa, as mentioned previously, seasons are bimodal and smallholders plant maize and other crops in the rainy season. In Tanzania smallholders begin planting from March; in Zambia during the rainy season (November to December) and in Liberia from April. In the three countries, smallholders also sow seeds with careful spacing and thinning. Smallholders plant local varieties without any irrigation, fertilizer application or pesticide spraying. In Zambia, corn is planted without any machinery or animal draft power, and land preparation is basically done using manual tools. Rather than building ridges, farmers sow without irrigation, fertilizer application or use of pesticides, and when farmers harvest, the maize is left in the fields. In Liberia, staff from extension stations make specific recommendations on spacing, but most smallholders do not practise this as recommended and plant several seeds in one hole, and again they do not generally irrigate or use agrochemicals. There may be reasons for such rejection, as explained by many scholars such as Pretty *et al.* (2011), who mention that farmers need to see for themselves that added complexity and increased effort can result in substantial net benefits to productivity, but they also need to be assured that increasing production actually leads to increases in income. Too many successful efforts in raising production yields have ended in failure when farmers were unable to market increased output. Pretty *et al.* (2011) also argue that understanding how to access rural credit, or how to develop warehouse receipt systems and especially how to sell any increased output, becomes as important as learning how to maximize input efficiencies or build fertile soils. With reference to previous chapters in this book, we have noted that there are necessary packaged pre-conditions for farmers taking up innovated technologies in China, but these are not available in African countries.

Except for a few farmers who use machinery, most households in Africa rely on manual labour for planting. As shown in Figure 7.2, the proportion of smallholders adopting traditional tools is very high: above 80 per cent in all the three villages. In Liberia, the poorest country in West Africa, the proportion reaches 100 per cent. In the busy farming season, mutual aid and hired labourers are the primary mode for intensive labour input. The percentage of households with hired labour in the busy season is high: 60 per cent in Tanzania, 53.3 per cent in Zambia and 86.7 per cent (the highest) in Liberia.

Maize cultivation practices between China and Africa are clearly very different in relation to use of seeds, fertilizers, pesticides, machinery and hired labour, as well as management of land resources.

Zambian farmers, for example (Table 7.3), use on average 1.3 hectares of land for maize planting, accounting for 37.5 per cent of the 3.64 hectare average household land. Tanzanian households use 0.98 hectares, 82.4 per cent of the 1.19 hectare average household land area; but households in Village D in China use

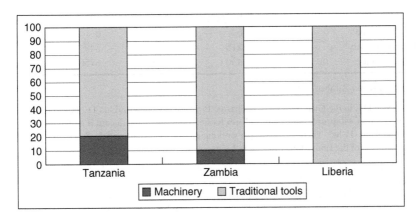

Figure 7.2 Use of Machinery at Three Village Sites

0.1 hectares planting maize, accounting for 25 per cent of the 0.4 hectare average household land area. In terms of inputs, smallholders in China make greater use of chemical fertilizer, pesticides, improved seeds, herbicides, irrigation facilities and machinery than their counterparts in Zambia and Tanzania. The input per-hectare totals are USD847.6 in China and USD14.59 and USD25.04 respectively in Zambia and Tanzania (Figure 7.4). For all inputs, fertilizer accounts for the largest proportion of expenditure in China. It is only USD1.776 per hectare in Zambia; none of the 30 Tanzanian farmers interviewed for this research used any chemical fertilizer at all. According to Research on Poverty Alleviation (Table 7.4), in Tanzania, 86 per cent of households have never used fertilizer, with 98 per cent from the poorest category of household; 72 per cent of households have never used herbicides, with 84 per cent from the poorest category; 77 per cent of households have never used improved seed varieties, of which 89 per cent are from the poorest category. Holmén (2005) and Larsson (2005) also point out that almost all smallholders in Africa are unable to afford suitable amounts of fertilizer.

TABLE 7.3 Comparison of Input–Output Ratios for Maize Planting in China, Tanzania and Zambia

	Zambia	*Tanzania*	*China[a]*
Average arable land (ha/household)	3.64	1.19	0.4
Average maize area (ha/household)	1.365	0.98	0.1
Fertilizer expenditure (USD/ha)	1.776	0	266.3
Pesticide costs (USD/ha)	0.66	0.27	110.9
Seed costs (USD/ha)	10.53	5.90	55.5
Hiring costs (USD/ha)	1.62	18.87	11.1
Machinery costs (USD/ha)	0	0	177.5
Herbicide costs (USD/ha)	0	0	26.6
Irrigation costs (USD/ha)	0	0	199.7
Total input(USD)	*14.59*	*25.04*	*847.6*
Output (kg/ha)	430	580	6750
Output (USD/ha)	86 (0.2)	133.4 (0.23)	1250 (0.186)
Subsides (USD/ha)	0	0	0
Labour productivity[b]	215	290	349
Land productivity[c]	430	580	6750

Source: Tanzania and Zambia: Village survey

a China: Village D is in the Guanzhong area of Shaanxi Province in China, and has 110 households with a population of 440 people. The total land area is of 660 acres (44 ha) and corn is grown on 25 per cent of the land (11 ha). There are 40 people working outside on off-farm work all year around; 213 main members of the labour force, including 136 women.

b Calculation refers to one labour unit producing maize within a year. Therefore the maize production for 30 households in Zambia within a year/the total number of labour force. Tanzania uses the same calculation. The data for China is based on the average of farmers in Village D and takes the maize production for one year for the whole village/the total number in the labour force.

c Calculated according to maize production (kg/ha).

In terms of productivity, China's figure is 6,750 kg/ha, while those of Zambia and Tanzania are 430kg/ha and 580kg/ha respectively (Figure 7.3). Based on maize prices in the three countries in 2008 (Figure 7.4), income from maize in China is USD1,250/ha and USD86/ha and USD133.4/ha in Zambia and Tanzania respectively. In terms of land productivity, China's output per hectare of corn reached 6,750kg, while in Zambia and Tanzania, 430kg and 580kg respectively. In addition, when examining labour productivity in the African countries (Figure 7.5), the difference among them is not significant. One farm labourer could produce 349kg of maize each year in China, but would only produce 215kg and 290kg in Zambia and Tanzania (Table 7.3). Recently, mechanization, coupled with chemical fertilizer and pesticides, has largely improved agricultural production in China and advanced land productivity, resulting in higher labour productivity than in Zambia and Tanzania.

In China, changes in macroeconomic policies have created many off-farm employment opportunities. At the same time, agricultural production technologies have improved and increased labour productivity substantially, adding to the surplus rural labour force. Hence, rural households have had incentives to adjust resource allocation and labour distribution: agricultural production is no longer the only or top choice in terms of productive activities. With subsistence needs satisfied, smallholders appear to be behaving as so-called 'rational peasants' (Liu *et al.*, 2006).

Taking the double-crop rice system of Ligong Village, Dongtang Town in the Xiangyin County of Hunan Province in 2008 as an example, rice output was 12,000kg/ha and the price was CNY1.82 per kilogram (USD0.26 per kg). Deducting the direct costs of CNY9,350 (USD1,334) per hectare (for seeds, seedlings, ploughing, chemical fertilizer, pesticides, water and electricity and harvesting), net sales income was CNY12,490 (USD1,770) per hectare. Adding to this food subsidies of CNY1,666.5 (USD238) per hectare (labour costs are not taken into consideration), net income was CNY14,156.5 (USD2,022.2) per hectare

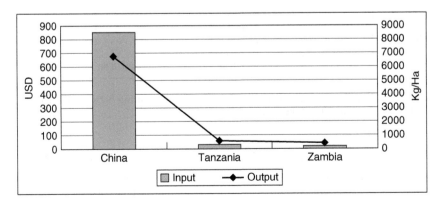

Figure 7.3 Comparison of Input–Output Ratio for Maize Planting between China, Tanzania and Zambia (Unit: USD; kg/ha)

TABLE 7.4 Proportion of Tanzanian Households Never Using Fertilizers and Other Inputs

	Poorest	*Middle*	*Least Poor*	*Total*
Chemical fertilizers	98	90	69	86
Agricultural chemical products (pesticides, herbicides, etc.)	84	72	60	72
Natural fertilizer	70	56	52	60
Improved seeds	89	76	66	77

Source: Research on Poverty Alleviation (2007)

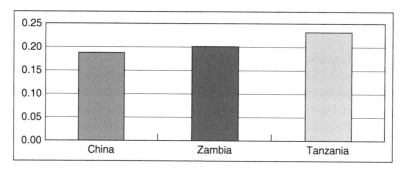

Figure 7.4 Maize Price Comparison between China, Zambia and Tanzania, 2008 (Unit: USD/kg)

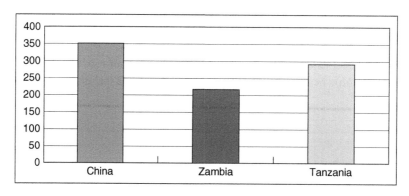

Figure 7.5 Comparison of Labour Productivity for Maize Planting between China, Zambia and Tanzania (Unit: kg/unit of labour)

(Yang, 2009). An able-bodied farm labourer or farmer could make around CNY80 (USD12) a day as a migrant worker. If they stay in the village planting double-cropped rice, this income should be regarded as an opportunity cost. In the market economy, because of low comparative benefits from agricultural production, rural labour will go to cities to seek opportunities as soon as these exist. Meanwhile, the extension of labour-saving technology, such as mechanization and potentially labour-intensive and land-intensive technologies such as agricultural biotechnology, have accelerated further a simplification of agricultural production systems (although possibly at some cost to biodiversity and farming system sustainability and resilience). As a result, labour force outflow does not impact significantly on agricultural output. Thus, when attracted by the opportunities offered in the industrial sector and urban areas, the farmers of China are capable of making decisions freely and reasonably. In addition, it can be argued that small farmers in China are experiencing a transition from subsistence-orientation to a more business-like mode of existence, whereas small farmers in Africa in many settings are focused more on subsistence, as they probably have a smaller range of livelihood options open to them. Although not discussed here, it cannot be ignored that there are some high-cost externalities to the high chemical, migrant labour/remittance farming system in China (i.e. high environmental and social cost).

Relationships between Smallholders and Agricultural Policies in China and Africa

Agricultural subsidies are the most important and most common policy measure in national agricultural support and protection frameworks, and are of great significance for agricultural development. Since 2004, farmers in China have benefited a great deal from two policies known as the 'Four Reductions and Remissions' and the 'Four Subsidies': the direct grain subsidy, the comprehensive direct subsidy, expanded grain area subsidy and farm machinery purchase subsidy. These subsidies indicated a shift in approach from indirect to demand-side subsidies, direct to supply-side and from the macro (national) level to the micro (farmer) level. Input subsidies have become an effective method for boosting the application of improved technologies, raising the return rate of new technology and lowering market risks and reducing the costs of farmer access to knowledge (cf. Johnson, 2005).

An example from Xiangyin County in Hunan Province illustrates the grain subsidy in operation. In 2009, the county's subsidized area was 31,930 hectares; the grain direct subsidy was CNY202.5 (USD29) per hectare; the comprehensive agricultural subsidy was CNY1,209 (USD173) per hectare; the improved seed subsidy was CNY150 (USD22) per hectare for early rice, CNY225 (USD32) per hectare for mid-season rice and CNY105 (USD15) per hectare for late rice. The agricultural machinery subsidy targets medium and large farming machinery, but not small farm machinery. (It should be noted that large farming machinery is not practical in southern upland areas, hence this subsidy is not discussed here.) Surveys of this county's food production and farmer income conducted by Yang (2009) suggest that since the direct grain subsidy policy was put into practice and indirect subsidies were switched to direct subsidies, food subsidy funds were distributed directly to small farmers, which has been a beneficial policy. Data show (Table 7.5) that from 2004 to 2008 for the grain-planting area, grain output and farmer income

TABLE 7.5 Xiangyin County Grain Production and Farmer Income

Year	Grain Growing Area (10,000 ha)	Grain Total Output (10,000 t)	Farmer Net Income Per Capita (USD)
2004	8.88	52.5	430
2005	9.01	54.0	471
2006	9.33	55.7	534
2007	9.34	57.5	591
2008	9.87	60.4	753

had all improved significantly in Xiangyin County. From the projections, a Chinese smallholder cultivating 1 hectare of double-crop rice would receive direct grain subsidies, comprehensive subsidies for farm materials and fine seed subsidies of USD246.5 per hectare, totalling 36.69 per cent of the overall input per hectare (Table 7.2). It is evident that food subsidies stimulate farmers' enthusiasm for grain production, and that a positive interaction between national policies and farmers has been actively realized.

By contrast, in most African countries few interventions have taken place that support farmer production: most policies are laissez-faire. In terms of agricultural development strategies, there are seldom supportive or favourable frameworks for agricultural development; at the micro level, there are limited opportunities for farmers to get subsidies or agricultural technologies. In Liberia, Zambia and Tanzania, there is no agricultural taxation or levy system, which contrasts with China's Royal Grain Tax, which lasted 2,600 years, neither are there any government agricultural subsidies. In Tanzania, only four out of the 30 investigated farmers had received 2kg of maize seed from the government. In Zambia, the government extends a few policies to support large-scale farms, but has very limited agricultural support policies for smallholders. A farmer on the Makombiro farm interviewed for this research claimed that he had not been granted any government support for agricultural production, not even the widely publicized fertilizer subsidies or agricultural credit. However, he did not have to pay any taxes except the annual land use fee (280 hectares, ZMK85,000, equivalent to USD20).

In facing the problems of food security and recovery from civil war, the Liberian government encouraged farmers who had fled to return home and cultivate abandoned land by launching a number of contingency plans, including tool and seed subsidies. In 2008, the Liberian government, funded by the United Nations Food and Agriculture Organization (FAO), spent USD25,000 to take the lead in buying rice from local farmers and distributing it to the poor; but only 15,000 rural households (3.6 per cent of the total) benefited from this programme, and only six households out of 30 interviewed for this research had obtained seed subsidies from non-governmental organizations (NGOs).

This can be argued to be an example of the tendency in Africa for 'strong societies and weak states' (Migdal, 1988). There are two aspects to this. Society is highly autonomous and organized around tribes, clans and other longstanding social structures. The state has limited financial resources to fund rural infrastructure. Communication between weak states and autonomous societies lacks depth and legitimacy, and under this particular configuration of state–society relations, agriculture can be seen as a social activity. The state has neither the fiscal capacity nor the technological competence to engage with it. The good governance tendency of a more accountable and transparent government and more participation in civil society would be of great help for agricultural development. Concerning governance in general, the African experience of the past two decades demonstrates that improvements cannot be accomplished only from the top, but call for concrete efforts at strengthening civil society, voice, citizen feedback and participation. Also, constructive external pressure through judicious conditioning of aid and improved aid effectiveness is important (McFerson, 2010).

Smallholder Access to Technology and Information in China and Africa

In China, there is a complete top-down research and extension system underpinning strategic national food security objectives and playing a role in agricultural production at the household level. As shown in Figure 7.6, although communication among farmers is the main technology extension channel, ways to access technology are varied and result in farmers having many choices. The state emphasis on food crops is articulated by different departments in the administrative system, with the

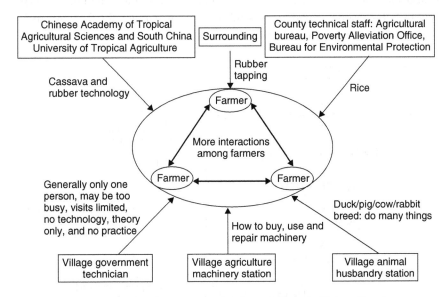

Figure 7.6 Access to Technology Services in Three Villages in Hainan Province
Source: Kuang (2007)

Agricultural Bureau, for example, dealing with rice planting technologies. There is also a support system that prompts farmers to look for more opportunities and more sources of income after their basic subsistence needs are met. Research in villages in Hainan Province, a tropical island in the South China Sea, shows the importance of rubber and cassava research and extension from the Tropical Crops Institute, as well as service provision in cultivation and harvesting techniques from rubber enterprises.

Research in several African countries shows that sources of ideas for new technology are often limited. Villagers in Village B in Zambia learn from each other; they also mention technical training by regional extension staff from organizations affiliated to the Ministry of Agriculture and Cooperatives. These sources are useful for learning skills such as preserving soil moisture, etc, but do not occur frequently, perhaps only once per year. In addition, villagers can learn about fertilizer and seeds from commercial enterprises (agribusiness). Thanks to a Japanese aid project, villagers also have some access to information through international institutions.

In Liberia, according to the administrative structure of the Ministry of Agriculture (Figure 7.7), the Agricultural Bureau is located at state level; one professional technician is assigned to each part of the state and responsible for technical extension in around eight to nine villages. The area technology extentionist in Bond stated that 'there is no technology for extension. I go to the villages to guide some international NGO research groups'. Some international institutions such as the FAO have turned out to be key information sources for villagers. These institutions give some agricultural production training in the project villages, covering pest management and field management, for example. In addition, a number of large private farms nearby provide new kinds of seeds to farmers for free, but such opportunities are very rare. Overall, farmers have very limited access to external

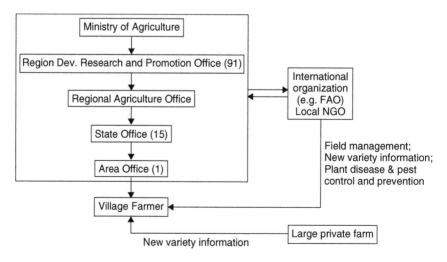

Figure 7.7 Access to Information by Smallholders in Liberia

information: this is one of the reasons why most farmers still use traditional varieties and farming methods.

Credit and Market Access for Smallholders in China and Africa

Small farmers in China generally have inconvenient access to agricultural credit, while demand for non-production-related credit is relatively high. The China Rural Finance Union and Beijing Normal University investigated 12 provinces and cities from January to March 2008. Among the 3,028 surveyed households, 920 had made loan applications and the rate was 30.4 per cent, 429 received loans and this coverage was 14.2 per cent, but the loan demand satisfaction rate was only 46 per cent. In terms of income level, the low-income households had the highest demand for loans. Chinese small farmers, either middle-income or low-income, do not seek loans to cover agricultural production inputs. As Huang (2000a) pointed out, 'small farmers borrow loans, either from relatives, neighbours or loan sharks, pawn shops, or land buyers, mostly in response to emergencies which are unrelated to farm production'. As discovered in the research into 1,273 Tianjin farmers, until 2006 the main financial burdens faced by farmers were house building, children's marriage and children's education. In fact, the credit demands of subsistence farmers were relatively low; only 17.6 per cent of them wanted commercial credit (Yang and Li, 2009). Many families do not invest all their savings in agricultural production, as savings are not intended for planting or breeding, but rather for house construction (Feng, 1994; Department of Rural Social Economic Investigation, 2006), pensions (Sun, 2002; Tian, 2005), children's education and marriage (Cui, 1999; Shi and Zhuo, 2007). From the beginning of the reform period, China's formal rural financial institutions have never targeted the non-agricultural credit demands of small farmers, concentrating instead on agricultural production where demand for loans is quite limited.

African smallholders also have inconvenient access to capital for both production and consumption for two reasons. First, the type of farming that African smallholders are engaged in does not rely on modern agricultural production inputs. Second, formal African rural finance organizations do not meet farmers' credit needs and manage only an extremely small number of loans; therefore, access to capital from formal financial institutions is limited. In the three villages in Africa, state credit to small farmers is tiny and it is difficult to obtain financial capital from formal channels. Of the 90 surveyed households, only one Tanzanian farm household had accessed a few loans (TZS58,000, equivalent to USD42) from a small bank to purchase agricultural production materials. In the absence of their own capital accumulation and external resource subsidies, small farmers are badly in need of loans. In Village B in Zambia, all rural households need credit because without access to finance they cannot afford fertilizer: this is critical, because in the rainy season a single fertilizer application can increase maize output by nearly one-third.

As a result, the general lack of financial capital in rural areas has had knock-on effects on investment in modern farming inputs and technologies. In Liberia in 2008, the average yields of upland and lowland rice were 736kg per hectare and 815kg per hectare, respectively. The average rice yield was about 3,900kg per hectare globally, and about 1,500kg per hectare in Sub-Saharan Africa – twice as much as in Liberia. This low productivity means that it is difficult to meet subsistence needs or generate a surplus. When natural disasters occur, small farmers are likely to suffer serious food shortages.

In terms of agricultural product markets, in most African countries less than one-third of the food produced by farmers is for sale (Sasakawa Africa Association, 2004). There are two main reasons for this. First, agricultural production is limited, and there is not much left after family consumption. Second, countryside road conditions are poor in Africa, and farmers cannot afford high transport costs. In sharp contrast, nearly 90 per cent of China's agricultural production is destined for local markets. From 1980 to 1992, rural markets increased from 37,890 to 64,678, up by 71 per cent; and the trade volume amounted to CNY6.68 billion (USD1 billion) – double the level in the early reform period.

Making Markets Work Efficiently

Transforming from a planned economy to a market economy is not easy for countries such as China and Tanzania. China did not adopt a completely free market system for agriculture during the reform era. Rapid agricultural growth during the 1980s was not derived from free markets, but from price increases. The government began to relax controls first on vegetables, fruit and livestock in the mid-1980s, but still controlled the grain crop and cotton markets. Efforts to relax food crop prices went back and forth during the 1980s and 1990s and in 1988, the government began to experiment with market reforms aimed at relaxing controls on grain crop prices. Based on several trials, all parts of the country released food crop prices in 1993. The government basically withdrew its controls on most agricultural products at the end of the 1990s and by 2004 the food crop market had been completely liberalized.

Before 2004, China made a huge investment in transport and markets that greatly enhanced agro-food marketing capacity. This investment made China's transport costs for maize, for example, much cheaper than those in the USA (Park et al., 2002). During the 1980s and even the 1990s, trade barriers across regions and different kinds of market charges significantly prohibited development of the agricultural market. The government gradually banned all of these barriers and charges to reduce marketing costs. The Food Reserve System is another measure that China developed after 1991 to stabilize food markets, by setting up the Food Risk Fund at the central and local levels. The Agriculture Development Bank was established to finance state purchase and operation of food reserves and later to begin financing the development of agro-business. Currently, agricultural markets are fully integrated into the market system and operate in an efficient way. For example, in 2008 the transport costs to market of 1 tonne of maize from production in Jilin Province to the wholesale market in Guangdong Province, more than 2,000km away, was only USD44.8. The market cost–farm gate ratio is relatively low.

TABLE 7.6 Transporting One Tonne of Maize from Production in Jilin Province to Wholesale Markets in Guangdong Province (USD/tonne)

Parameter	Farm Gate	Transport	Storage	Loading and Unloading	Market Price	Trader Cost
Expenditure (USD/tonne)	206	44.8	17.8	4.85	280	6.55
Share (%)	73.6	16	6.35	1.73	100	2.34

Source: Authors' calculations from case study by the Agriculture Policy Research Centre in China, 2008

Tanzania liberalized its agricultural markets in the 1980s, but this was not accompanied by significant improvements in infrastructure or state improvements to stimulate markets. Transportation costs are still the major constraint to improving market efficiency in Tanzania: these are estimated at 84 per cent of marketing costs, whereas they are only 60 per cent in China. Labour for loading and unloading is 11.7 per cent of total market cost in Tanzania, but only 6.6 per cent in China.

Transportation costs in China are low because rural roads have been the major focus of the country's transport development strategy. More than 90 per cent of villages have good-quality roads and can access main roads. In rural areas of China, to transport agricultural produce within 100km works out at less than USD0.04 per tonne per kilometre. The Chinese government has focused on infrastructure and spent more than 35 per cent of public expenditure in the agricultural sector on roads and other infrastructure. Lower costs for long distances are tied to the different modes of transport in China. For long distances, more than 70 per cent of grain is moved by rail and 20 per cent by water, with only 10 per cent by road.

In Tanzania, agricultural produce moves mainly by road: the increasing cost of fuel and high operational costs for trucks make transportation and storage costs high, which in turn largely explains the high cost of marketing in Tanzania. It costs USD23 per tonne to store maize for one month in Mbeya. Transportation costs USD0.3 per tonne per kilometre in Tanzania, while it only costs USD0.061 in China. Reducing transportation cost needs a well-developed network of rural roads, which requires persistent government investment.

It took 25 years for China to develop its agricultural markets. This market learning process suggests that market mechanisms only work when the marketplace and infrastructure (road and storage) are developed by a central agency as public investments, and to put those conditions in place requires full awareness of the importance of the state in making strategic public investments. Road development has been the largest investment sector for the Chinese government over the last 30 years: 'If you want to be rich, first build a road' has long been a development campaign slogan at all levels. Reducing the cost of transportation is a general path toward competitive agriculture.

TABLE 7.7 Market cost of Maize in China and Tanzania (USD/tonne)

Country	Farm Gate	Market Price	Derived Margin	Market Cost	Ratio of Margin	Share of Margin in Farm Gate Price (%)
Tanzania	180.4	286.0	105.6	90.5	0.86	50.2
China	206.0	280.0	74.0	67.45	0.91	32.5

Source: Tanzania: data from World Bank, 2009a

TABLE 7.8 Different Transport Costs in China (USD/tonne/km)

Means	Cost	Current Use for Grain Transport (%)
Railway	0.2795	70
Road	0.2925	10
Water	0.2275	20

Source: Yang Weilu, 2005

Conclusion

In China and Africa, smallholders dominate agricultural production and the family is the basic unit of agricultural production. Land, water, climate and human factors play a very important role, but huge differences in agricultural productivity between China and Africa manifest principally in the effective use and proper distribution of domestic and external resources. The differences are evident in land resource utilization, labour distribution, the gender division of labour, input–output ratios, technical information, agricultural policy incentives and access to credit. In terms of land use, Chinese farmers from different regions make use of land resources to their fullest extent according to local climate, seasons and other natural resources. In terms of labour distribution and the gender division of labour, after meeting their own food consumption needs, Chinese farmers take into account the low efficiency of agriculture and make rational choices in labour resource allocation. Most of the male labour force work outside the farm, and women are left behind to engage in agricultural production. This indicates to some degree that China's small farmers have shifted from a subsistence ethic and inward livelihood strategy to an outward-focused livelihood strategy, and are breaking away progressively from what has been labelled an agricultural 'involution'. More importantly, current national policy support for agriculture mobilizes farmers' enthusiasm and national agricultural policies create positive incentives for them. At the same time, agricultural production information channels have been diversified, comprising scientific research institutions, government departments and farmer-to-farmer exchanges, with two-way interaction very prevalent. The Chinese government has created the legal and institutional framework to help smallholders and to promote the development of farmer organizations in order to ensure farmers' economic interests. For example, on 1 July 2007, the government passed the Farmer Cooperatives Law, which promotes the rapid development of farmer cooperative organizations. While small farmers ensure their own food security, they also provide a guarantee for national food security. Due to the small land area farmed, China's smallholders have weak access to credit for agricultural production, but this does not completely prevent the high-input trend spreading in agricultural production. Chinese agriculture is now dominated by small families, but is very different from the historical low input–low output peasant economy. Now, while inheriting traditional farming knowledge and experience, China's smallholders actively absorb modern agricultural techniques and integrate them into their operations: hence the use of fertilizer, pesticides and improved varieties and plastic film technology, mechanical sowing, harvesting and mechanical irrigation technology are widely in evidence in the Chinese countryside.

By contrast, African smallholders' agricultural production systems are still very extensive and reliant on the use of traditional technologies. In general, African smallholders do not appear to utilize the land as intensively as their counterparts in China. In some places, large areas of land appear to be underused or not used at all. Moreover, irrigation facilities are absent in most areas, and basic farming techniques such as seedling production are ignored in agricultural production. In addition, African farmers lack the capital to invest in production technologies and techniques, which means limited use of fertilizer, improved seeds and agricultural machinery. The result is low land productivity and a low input–low output trap for the majority of smallholders.

In relation to allocating family labour resources, African smallholders are organized around a slack season, rather than the type of labour allocation seen in China. Family livelihood security is based predominantly on agriculture and farming production activities. Even when positioning African small farmers with a subsistence ethic and at a 'safety first' development stage, it remains difficult to achieve a sustainable balance with limited resources. Meanwhile, many African states are either not committed to engaging with agricultural development at the local level, or do not have the capacity to engage in agricultural development at all. Many African governments do not sufficiently prioritize agriculture or dedicate enough resources to agricultural research and extension; the absence of agricultural subsidy policies does not help farmers to break free of resource constraints. Agricultural policies in many African countries are not supporting the improvement of smallholder farming practices and many countries fail to facilitate, support and provide the right kind of incentives. In general, limited farmer resources and external resources mean that production is stuck at a low-level equilibrium. National agricultural strategies in many states emphasize market production of commercial crops based on theories of comparative advantage, downplaying smallholder production of food crops that meet their own food security needs (World Bank Independent Evaluation Group, 2006). This creates national food security problems (as discussed elsewhere in this book).

It is increasingly evident to many researchers that agricultural development and food self-sufficiency are inseparable (Djurfeldt *et al.*, 2005; Lipton, 2005; Timmer, 2005). This has profound implications for policies towards smallholder farmers and national agricultural strategies. The ways in which China has prioritized smallholder production as a building block of the national development strategy, as well as this approach, could offer inspiration for African agricultural development and the appropriate role of the small farmer.

8

LEARNING AND EXTERNAL SUPPORT FOR AGRICULTURAL DEVELOPMENT IN CHINA AND AFRICA

Earlier chapters of this book have discussed how different approaches to agricultural development in China and Africa can be traced back to historical, economic, social and technological factors. However, there is another important factor, namely communication with and learning from the rest of the world, and the role of external support in the history of agricultural development.

A Historical Review of Learning and External Support for Agricultural Development in China and Africa

Population and land crises have occurred repeatedly in Chinese history. Dating back to feudal times, agricultural development in China has been characterized by land expansion and increasing labour inputs. Yet this extensive agricultural development was unable to solve the population explosion crisis, and this led to the development of a sophisticated land system (including a land-based taxation system) and the household registration system built on land allocation and taxation. Whenever crises appeared across dynasties, there were two common measures taken by the governments. One was to increase land availability through cultivation (including frontier land settled and development of land by military units). From the Warring States Period (c. 475–221 BC), China's agricultural centre has been around the Yellow River; since then the agricultural area has expanded along with land reclamation. Examples of this process of land transformation include the development of agriculture in Fujian during the Tang (618–907) and Song Dynasties (960–1279); the spread of new forms of cultivation and settlement in Guangdong, Guangxi, Yunnan and Guizhou in the Song, Yuan (1271–1368) and Ming Dynasties (1368–1644); and the development of north-east China, Taiwan, Mongolia and Xinjiang in the Qing Dynasty (1644–1911). The other strategy has been to increase labour force inputs through birth and family planning policies. Labour migration for the purposes of land reclamation has been an effective way of providing more land for increasing populations. Large-scale and long-term migration from the Yellow River to the Yangtze River region has been the stimulus for economic development and prosperity in southern China since the Song Dynasty.

Similar tensions between population and land have occurred in the history of Africa, and migration also has been a common solution. The migration of the Cushitic people, now living in the central Ethiopian Highlands, turned the East African Rift Valley into a passageway for agricultural expansion and dissemination of agricultural techniques. The development of agriculture south of the Equator has been closely related to the great migrations of the Bantu people. As populations have grown, pressure on existing land grew, along with demand for new and better farmland and pastures. Bantu emigration started in the first century and ended in the nineteenth century (Lu, 2000). However, Africa has never witnessed a population explosion equivalent to that which occurred in China. The African population was just over 70 million by the end of the fifteenth century, while China's population had reached about 65 million (Ho, 1959) in 1400. Before colonization, there was never a single unified state in Africa or a formal population system as existed in China, and thus land shortage could be solved through the free movement of people, and so pressure to intensify farming systems was not so evident.

Since the Ming and Qing Dynasties, China's population growth was even more rapid than before, exceeding 100 million in the Ming Era (1600) and outrunning 300 million in the late Qianlong Era (at the end of the seventeenth century). Massive population growth and migration posed immense pressure, even in the 'untamed wilderness' area (that is, the areas that absorbed migrants, such as Qinling-Dabashan), demonstrating that traditional agricultural techniques were already inadequate for solving pressure for land. China recorded two developments in traditional agricultural techniques: the first was the practice of northern dryland agricultural techniques with a focus on drought resistance and soil moisture conservation, which made possible the development of arid and semi-arid land in the Yellow River Basin in the West and East Han period (206 BC to AD 220). The second was the formation of complex paddy field systems in southern China, with a focus on drought prevention and flood drainage in the low-lying Yangtze River Basin wetlands in the Tang and Song Eras. It can be seen that agricultural techniques mainly developed and utilized the Yellow River and Yangtze River land areas prior to the Qing Dynasty, enlarging the cultivated area to develop production. As available arable land had been largely exhausted by the time of the Qing Dynasty, people tried every means to increase yield per unit area to promote production. Multi-cropping intensive agriculture innovations also followed. This period marked the development of new agricultural techniques in China (Min, 2005), and a shift from expansion to intensification as a way of increasing agricultural output. It is also in this period that China found that traditional agricultural technologies could no longer assure the population's basic food security. Aspirations to study and learn from experiences beyond China began in a major way at this time.

Meanwhile, the political environment at that time was experiencing foreign learning. From the Qing Dynasty, especially in its final years, 'since the first Opium War, Western industrial civilization, or the "advanced" civilization as a whole . . . announced an end to the dominance and of Eastern farming civilization' (Feng, 1991: 19). Hearing this wake-up call, Chinese intellectuals set out to get in touch with the world and proposed and launched a series of political and economic reforms. At the same time, China's economy came under increasing strain, and western agricultural science and technology were introduced to China. China began to learn from the West and urgently needed to improve land productivity, which was exactly what western agricultural technology could offer. This is an example of cultural exchange stimulating a useful learning process.

BOX 8.1 LEARNING AND EXTERNAL SUPPORT IN CHINA'S AGRICULTURAL DEVELOPMENT SINCE THE OPIUM WAR

Introduction and Translation of Agricultural Works

Around the time of the First Opium War, China welcomed a massive influx of western learning. In 1837, the American missionary Ira Tracy compiled *What Can Chinese Farmers Learn from Agriculture in Singapore?* (Li and Kouzhan, 1996: 190), and in 1897 the *Journal of Agriculture* began to publish and translate writings on the latest foreign modern agricultural science and technology achievements in the fields of agriculture, forestry, animal husbandry, fisheries, water conservancy, agricultural machinery, sericulture, horticulture, pest control, soil fertility management, tea production and agricultural processing. The agricultural works introduced during this period were chiefly about western agricultural theory and farming techniques, such as chicken breeding, sericulture and fertility management (Li, 2009).

Introduction and Promotion of External Agricultural Varieties and Technology

In the late Qing Dynasty, China continued to adopt traditional seed selection methods, preserving superior and eliminating inferior seeds and establishing seed fields (referred to as 'selecting good ears among seeds and good grains among the picked ears'). These techniques worked well with the existing seed stock, but were unable to match the achievements of modern breeding techniques. At the end of the nineteenth century, modern scientific breeding methods from Europe and the USA began to flow into China. Jinling was the first Chinese research institution to carry out plant breeding experiments according to modern scientific methods. It has accomplished significant achievements in cotton, wheat and rice production since the 1820s (Shen, 2004).

Introduction of Agricultural Machinery

In 1908, Cheng Dequan, Governor of Heilongjiang, purchased two tractors from Tsarist Russia at a cost of 2.25 million silver taels. This was the start of government-run mechanized planting. In 1904, Russia mowing machines were used on the North China plains west of Xing'anling (Bai *et al.*, 1996).

Introduction of the Western Agricultural Education System

In 1894, Sun Zhongshan presented his vision of Chinese agricultural modernization in his *Petition to Li Hongzhang*. This entailed the introduction of western agricultural techniques and agricultural machinery presided over by feudal officials. In 1899, Dowager Empress Cixi released an imperial edict to 'encourage agriculture and foreign study' and sent students to Japan, Europe and the USA to study agriculture. According to incomplete historical statistics, by the time of the 1911 revolution, 112 students had been sent overseas to study agriculture in Japan, 12 in European countries and 51 in America (Cao, 2004). In addition, from 1901, Chinese and western blending of ideas spread to local agricultural bureaus, experimental farms and agro-forestry schools, which began to make significant progress (Yi and Lu, 2000) in the fields of agricultural technology, education and extension, and this process was not interrupted by the 1911 revolution. In 1929, the Nanjing Nationalist Government passed the University Organization Act and successively constituted colleges of agriculture affiliated to universities, independent colleges of agriculture and specialist agricultural schools. According to Ministry of Education 1946 statistics, there were 30 higher learning agricultural universities and colleges, including colleges of agriculture affiliated to universities, independent colleges of agriculture, provincial agriculture colleges and specialist agricultural schools, as well as a college of veterinary medicine (Zhuang, 1988). Most of the agricultural school systems were copied from the US land grant model, integrating teaching, research and extension.

Adaptive Alteration of Western Agricultural Technology

China generally absorbed and transformed western agricultural techniques in order to adapt them for domestic agricultural production. For example, in the southern part of north-east China, the introduction of western modern agricultural technology emphasized the validation and amendment of traditional agriculture with experimental methods, scientific selection and breeding of seeds, and the use of fertilizer and pesticides for intensive cultivation and increases in yield per unit of area. The northern part of north-east China gave priority to the introduction and application of agricultural machinery appropriate to the extensive agricultural operations in that area, and also to enhancing labour productivity (Bai *et al.*, 1996). In addition, farm machinery was often modified. For example, Zhang Hongjun, a native of Shuangliao in Liaoning, restructured agricultural machinery from machinery-towed to animal-towed after returning from Michigan State Agricultural University in the 1920s, which made it more suitable for China's practical agricultural development and easier to disseminate. In addition, fine foreign seed breeding technology was localized: for example, the pure breeding methods developed by the Cornell University crop breeder H.H. Love, which better fitted China's situation as the breeding cycle shortened from seven to nine years to four to five years, which complied with China's rice transplanting techniques and characteristics (Yi and Liu, 2000). After the 1911 revolution, the Republic of China transformed the administration of agriculture, agricultural educational institutions and agricultural university textbooks to better suit Chinese situations (Yi and Liu, 2000).

During the Ming and Qing dynasties (1368–1911), Africa was experiencing the beginning of its colonial era. In order to enforce the planting of export cash crops, the colonial powers adopted a series of administrative, economic and coercive measures which led to the creation of many cash crop production areas and the development of capitalist commodity agriculture and animal husbandry alongside a traditional peasant economy. These measures advanced the introduction and spread of new crops, drove the development of agro-industry and agricultural mechanization, and gave birth to Africa's dualistic structure of agricultural production, which is still in place today. In this period, substantial migration led to the opening up of agricultural land; however, population growth was slow and lagged behind the world average – land was not the major factor that hindered agriculture development. Meanwhile, the majority of small farmers clung to traditional farming methods and were unable to participate in the 'modern' farm economy promoted by colonialists. Africa was an isolated and 'forgotten continent' prior to colonial times. Unlike China, its modern agricultural technology was transferred directly from the West with little adaptation, and its agricultural trade basically tied in closely with the external world. However, technology and management have failed to effectively meld with African small-farm systems, and have not led to a transformation of African agriculture.

By contrasting external learning and support in the agricultural development histories of China and Africa, it can be seen that when China faced facing internal pressures, it sought out external learning, communication and collaboration, while

Africa remained relatively closed for a long period. In addition, China's intensive farming tradition implies high productivity. Taking Chinese and western breeding techniques as an example, China focused on developing the potential of existing varieties, while the West focused on selecting and breeding new varieties; in time, the two traditions naturally converged and created synergies. By contrast, most African small farmers have had limited access to the new technologies introduced by colonial authorities.

Comparison of Learning and External Support for Agricultural Development in China and Africa since the Mid-Twentieth Century

The 1950s–1970s Period

China experienced a relatively closed period after the founding of the People's Republic of China (PRC) in 1949. After two destructive wars, China quickly restored and reconstructed its original agricultural industry base and laid a good foundation for the development of agricultural means of production. The fertilizer industry was an outstanding example: Manchukuo Chemical Industry Co. Ltd was a legacy of the Japanese Occupation, and renamed as the Dalian Chemical Factory, recovering production within just a year and a half. Facing a blockade and embargoes against China by western powers, agricultural communications and cooperation were mainly conducted with the Soviet Union, Mongolia, North Korea and other Eastern European socialist countries. In particular, guided by 'lopsided' foreign policy, China accepted the assistance of the former Soviet Union in the 1950s: this was the most important assistance in the twentieth century and covered issues from economic structure to technology, management to theory and government mechanisms to education systems. As a result, China's economy, heavy industrial base and government institutions took shape.

BOX 8.2 THE SOVIET UNION'S AGRICULTURAL ASSISTANCE TO CHINA

The Soviet Union helped develop human resources in China. In August 1951, China formally sent 375 students to the Soviet Union, including graduate students. Before the Soviet Union withdrew its experts in 1960, China had dispatched more than 10,000 students to the USSR for higher education.

The Soviet Union helped establish large state farms. For example, in 1954 the Soviet people donated machinery and equipment, including crawler tractors, farming machines, combine harvesters, machine-powered ploughs, machine-powered grain planters and mowers to China. All these were required

---

to organize a 20,000-hectare state grain farm. They sent a group of experts, consisting of a state farm manager, state grain farm chief agronomist, mechanical engineer, repair shop director, chief accountant and many agronomists and mechanical engineers for diverse departments:

> This state-owned grain farm played an important demonstration role in promoting the socialist transformation of China's agriculture and helped China train skilled human resources for agricultural production. China also learned from the Soviet Union's valuable experience in wasteland and abandoned land reclamation. (Mao, 1954: 17)

Soviet experts helped develop the plan for solving flooding problems on the Yellow River and for developing water conservancy. At the beginning of 1954, Soviet experts proposed a vision and first-phase scheme for overall utilization of the Yellow River, which would irrigate more than 1 million hectares of adjacent land.

The Soviet experience was also a stimulus for China's agricultural cooperative movement. In his 1955 'Issues about Agricultural Cooperation' speech, Mao Zedong pointed out that in order to resolve the contradiction between annually increasing demands for commodity grains and industrial raw materials and the low output of key crops, China should adopt the Soviet Union's 'leading and developing agricultural cooperation through planning' approach. He remarked that accumulating agriculture was necessary to provide capital in order to complete national industrialization and agricultural technological transformation, pointing to direct agricultural tax and promotion of light industry to satisfy farmer needs for basic daily materials, which in turn would be exchanged with farmers for commodity grains and raw materials for light industry (Mao, 1955). This speech immediately spurred China's agricultural cooperation.

China learned a painful lesson from the uncritical adoption of Soviet models. In the 1950s, China used administrative means to forcibly promote the Michurin doctrine and deny Mendel-Morgan theory,[1] completely banning teaching and research on classical genetics and gene and chromosome theory. Scholars advocating forbidden ideas were persecuted and labelled 'rightists' and 'reactionary academic authorities'.

In the fertilizer industry, production equipment and advanced technology (Gong, 2003) were imported from the Netherlands, Italy and elsewhere. Technology was imported for compact wheat planting, ley farming, mechanical farming and cultivation and other techniques (Tang, 1999). Plastic-coated breeding of rice seedlings and plastic greenhouse cultivation techniques learned from Japan in the 1950s contributed greatly to China's agricultural science and technology. It is clear, then, that China's modern agricultural development relied heavily on learning from others.

Compared with China, African countries received an avalanche of assistance from the international community after attaining independence. During the 1950s and 1960s, aid focused on modernization and industrialization, and agricultural assistance concentrated on promoting the nationalization of research institutions. At that time, agriculture was not viewed as a key sector for economic growth in Africa, and the mainstream thinking was nationalizing regional research stations and training institutions established in the colonial era, and framing nationally-oriented industrialization plans. The vision was that within a generation a traditional agricultural society would be turned into a modern industrialized nation (Eicher, 2003). This thinking determined that African countries would put their hope in substantial investment in industrialization from donor countries, and expected that aid would lead to an increase in trade opportunities and promote economic growth. They were hungry for quick success. Following donor country assessments of appropriate development strategies, they concentrated on capital and technology transfer and neglected to protect and develop small farmer competencies.

BOX 8.3 AGRICULTURAL ASSISTANCE DEMAND OF AFRICAN COUNTRIES IN THE EARLY INDEPENDENCE PERIOD

The development economist W. A. Lewis was invited to Ghana in 1950 to write reports on rapid industrialization after Ghanaian independence. In 1953 he wrote the *Report on Industrialization and the Gold Coast* (cited in Bretton, 1958), which made him unpopular with the nationalist leadership for indicating that the 'number one priority' for that country was a 'concerted attack on the system of growing food, so as to get in motion an ever increasing (agricultural) productivity' (Lewis, 1953: 22). However, after Ghana attained its sovereignty in 1957, it did not follow his advice. Instead, it abolished the existing national extension system that served small farmers, adopted the Soviet state farm model, and sought to industrialize through national control over the market. However, technical and managerial skills were lacking, and incentive structures for running large-scale state farms, parastatals and trading companies were not in place. Kwame Nkrumah, the independence leader, was ultimately overthrown in 1966, following a prolonged economic crisis caused by agrarian socialist and industrialization policies.

On becoming independent, African countries set out to build up national economic capacity; however, they were unable to resolve structural problems of agricultural production. On the one hand, the newly independent countries were devoid of strong social mobilization mechanisms and could not rely on campaign-style labour inputs to compensate for shortage of capital and other key assets. Their great desire for economic growth shaped their heavy attachment to foreign aid. On the other hand, extraction of value from the agricultural sector for industrialization and modernization meant that they had to retain colonial-era large estates and farms, with established technologies and exporting to overseas market.[2] This intensified the polarization within the agricultural sector. As a consequence, African governments were unable to extend sufficient inputs to small farmers, as capital was allocated to sectors with potential for rapid economic growth. Moreover, heavy reliance on foreign aid induced continued economic and political dependence.

In the 1970s, following oil price surges and food crisis outbreaks, donors reinforced assistance to African agriculture, shifting the focus of aid to basic needs. In this period comprehensive rural development projects were the most common choice for delivering development aid. There were two reasons for this change in aid delivery: first, seeing the successful Green Revolution in Asia, donors aspired to apply this experience to Africa; second, doubts about the trickle-down effect stimulated donors to adjust assistance priorities, prioritizing household food security, health, sanitation and education and supporting agricultural production by small farmers through integrated rural development projects. However, despite injecting billions of dollars into integrated rural development and agricultural development projects, the desired results were not achieved. First, these harsh macroeconomic policies ignored profitable economic activities in the course of community development, which meant that social and agricultural services were not sustainable without foreign aid. Second, integrated development projects required the co-ordination of different sectors, which proved to be particularly difficult to achieve. Third, successful projects built on large sums of money were not replicable without concentrations of expensive technical support and material support such as cars. For example, as mentioned in Cohen's (1987) report, Sweden devoted USD41 million to the Chilalo Agricultural Development Unit rural development project in Arsi Province, Ethiopia over 26 years from 1967 to 1993; Holtsberg (1986) indicated that this project was too expensive for wider replication or scale-out.

A few basic conclusions can be drawn from this illustration of contrasts in agricultural learning processes and the role of external support in both China and Africa. First, China has always insisted on independence and self-reliance when receiving external support and refused to alter its ideology to win foreign aid, even following the Sino-Soviet split when the USSR recalled its foreign experts. African countries followed the development path of donor countries in pursuit of external foreign aid: this path was based on lessons from donor countries, and did not promote an African path to development. Agricultural foreign aid was remarkably consistent in this respect, with the economic framework for development directed or even mandated through conditionality agreements by donor countries.

Second, China developed its own agricultural industry, particularly an agricultural machinery base, by adopting external technology during this period and rapidly strengthening its agricultural machinery research, development and production capacity. For example, in the 1950s, a large number of new animal-towed farm tools and agricultural machines were copied from the Warsaw Pact countries, and agricultural mechanization research institutes and agricultural machinery testing and identification stations were founded. Conversely, African countries neither solved small farmer problems, nor made full use of the available research and development (R&D) technology systems and limited agro-industrial infrastructure left from the colonial period. Even now, Africa still relies heavily on external support for agricultural technologies and agro-industrial development; of course, there are many local smallholder innovations, but these are limited in specific areas and crops (see note 2).

Third, China continued to screen external support and adapt introduced varieties, technology and equipment, spreading benefits to small farmers quickly via an effective extension system, while Africa did not successfully shift away from the old production structure because aid was accepted indiscriminately and technologies such as new plant varieties were targeted on towards large farms.

Fourth, China and Africa experienced the effects of (semi-)colonial heritage to different degrees. In the 1950s, in a relatively closed state, large numbers of overseas returnees made great contributions to China's agricultural development. Meanwhile, the large factories, businesses and farms left by foreign actors all came into play, becoming a cradle of technological innovation and quickly benefiting small farmers. However, Africa's large farm and small farmer economies were completely separate and the cultivated varieties were different, thus they were less able to exchange technologies efficiently between the two sectors.

Comparison of Learning Processes and External Support for Agricultural Development in China and Africa since the 1980s

Since the beginning of the reform and opening-up period in China, the government has focused on economic construction, encouraging foreign assistance through multilateral diplomacy, expanding economic and trade exchange and integration into the international community. In the agricultural sector, China principally accepted external support through food aid, technical assistance and financial assistance. At the same time, the international community's agricultural assistance to Africa focused on economic growth via market liberalization, and donors deemed the state the key obstacle to economic growth in Africa (Lancaster, 1999). The World Bank *Berg Report* (1981) reported that paradoxically, the main cause of Africa's economic crisis was African governments themselves. However, the African Development Bank, Economic Commission for Africa and other institutions on the continent countered that export agriculture promotion and reliance on market forces had not delivered successful results, and should not be expected to lead to economic reconstruction in Africa (United Nations and Economic Commission for Africa, 1982). Since the 1980s, agricultural aid to Africa has centred on reforming agricultural research and extension systems, with flows of aid to agriculture also greatly reduced (Eicher, 2003). This trend is now changing, with donors seeing the need to invest in agriculture again.

Food Aid to China and Africa

In 1979, China began to accept food aid from the World Food Programme (WFP) and gradually accepted multilateral, bilateral and non-governmental assistance and donations. According to incomplete statistics, from 1979 to 2006 China absorbed more than USD1.4 billion in food aid (calculated in kind) from the WFP, European Union, Japan and Germany. During the 26-year period from 1979 to 2005, the WFP supported 70 grant-based food aid projects worth USD1 billion. Its aid fell into two categories: emergency assistance and development-oriented construction assistance. The main way that aid was provided domestically was through 'food for work': that is, providing food aid for labour engaged in agricultural development projects. The aid volume was huge for each project (Qin *et al.,* 2002). Through direct food assistance, food-for-work aid improves labour productivity. Foreign food aid to China helped those with food insecurity and more importantly, also led to new project management approaches and the introduction of ideas such as participatory development and the importance of focusing on gender. Since 1998, the Chinese government has put more than CNY50 billion (about USD5 billion then) of large-scale rural infrastructure construction into rural areas through food-for-work programmes, including basic farmland, irrigation and water conservation facility construction, rural roads (including bridge and culvert), human drinking water and animal drinking water and comprehensive treatment of small drainage areas. Most of this activity has been highly effective.

In contrast with China, the international community's food aid to Africa focuses on grain provision. This heavy dependence on 'grain aid' is highly problematic. The 1985 Ethiopian famine left 1 million dead and attracted close attention to the long-term food crisis in African countries (Eicher, 2003). More than 50 per cent of the WFP's total food aid has been allocated to the Sub-Saharan Africa region since 2003.

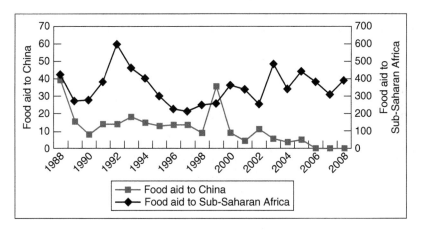

Figure 8.1 WFP's Food Aid to China and Sub-Saharan Africa (Unit: 10,000 tons). The peak figure, USD53.88 million, reflects emergency aid to China after the 1998 floods. This was the largest WFP project in China

Figure 8.1 shows the WFP's total food aid volume to China and Africa since 1988. It can be seen that food aid to Africa has stayed at a high level, while China stopped receiving assistance in 2006. African countries' dependence on food aid is significant: even in Zambia, a country which places much emphasis on agriculture, food aid climbed as high as 6.9 per cent of total food consumption from 2003 to 2005. In unstable Eritrea, this percentage amounted to 48.4 per cent.

China's course of agricultural development has changed from tackling food security to integrated rural development. International funders have shifted their support from agriculture to material and technical support for integrated development in rural areas, especially in poor and minority ethnic areas. China has become a donor to the WFP. Figure 8.2 shows the flows of food aid from China to Sub-Saharan African countries.

Comparison of Foreign Investment Utilization and Official Foreign Aid in the Chinese and African Agricultural Sectors

International development assistance to the agricultural sector has dropped from 19 per cent to 4 per cent as a percentage of overall aid flows since the 1980s (World Bank, 2009b). As the world's key target for development aid, Africa has claimed about one-third of international development aid. Poverty, agricultural production and food security problems came back onto donor agendas when countries made their Millennium Development Goals at the beginning of the new millennium. Donors became more aware of the need to enhance investment in agriculture. At the 2009 Group of Eight (G8) summit, USD20 billion was committed to food security and agricultural development, with a significant amount to flow to Sub-Saharan African countries (FAO, 2009b). Officially promised development aid for agriculture development assistance peaked in 2007 (at USD2.8 billion); however, this was still USD100 million less than was promised in the 1980s.

For Sub-Saharan African countries, international development assistance funds account for a high proportion of agricultural budgets. For 24 Sub-Saharan African

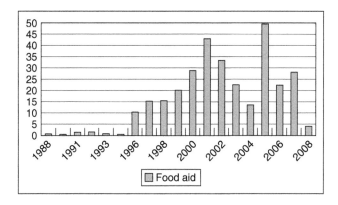

Figure 8.2 China's Food Aid to Sub-Saharan Africa through WFP (Unit: 10,000 tons)

countries, development aid takes up 28 per cent of total agriculture expenditure on average (World Bank, 2008). Ethiopia's foreign aid accounts for 22 per cent of national income; for Sierra Leone, this figure has reached 47 per cent (de Renzio, 2005). International Monetary Fund (IMF) statistics show that in 2005, Tanzania received a total of USD54 million of agricultural official development assistance (ODA), and distributed USD30 million in total as agricultural expenditure, far below the agricultural ODA value.

Generally, ODA invested in Sub-Saharan African countries has generally been more than USD1 billion (Figure 8.3), far higher than the figure for China. Germany, the UK and some other countries continue discussions about whether to eliminate aid to China. In 2012, China's agricultural support is dominated by technology exchange and cooperation. Take Japan's ODA as example: from 1985 to 2000, Japan supported 32 food production enhancement projects in China at a total value of CNY26.78 billion, equal to 18.4 per cent of Japan's total grant aid (as of 2004) to China. These projects were suspended in 2000.[3]

As shown in Figure 8.4, from 1979 to 2004, agricultural assistance per capita to China was much lower than that to Africa. In 2003, for example, agricultural assistance per capita was USD0.62 to China, and USD3.30 to Africa. In the same period, the annual growth of agricultural value added increased by 197 per cent in China and by only 89 per cent in Africa.

Foreign Direct Investment (FDI) is also important for agricultural development. Since the 1980s, along with agricultural development in China, the proportion of agricultural FDI in total agricultural investment has been decreasing. Figure 8.5 shows that the number of projects supported by foreign agricultural investment has increased substantially since the 1990s, but the proportion of agricultural FDI in the national total FDI has been decreasing.

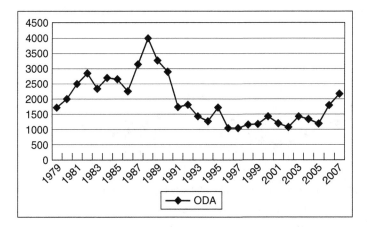

Figure 8.3 Annual Fluctuation of Official Development Assistance (ODA) to Sub-Saharan African countries (Unit: USD1 million)

Source: OECD Creditor Reporting System (CRS) database

As shown by the trend chart of contractual foreign capital and financial support for agriculture (Figure 8.6), the contractual foreign capital figure has increased, but takes up a very tiny portion compared with the latter.

Agricultural FDI has gradually taken a growing percentage of overall foreign capital in China. Prior to the Seventh Five-Year Plan period (1986–1990), foreign capital in agriculture was mainly in the form of foreign loans and aid from international organizations, amounting to more than 70 per cent. The proportion of FDI has expanded since the Eighth Five Year Plan (1991–1995) and was more than 95 per cent in the Ninth Five-Year Plan period (1995–2000), approaching 100 per cent in the Tenth Five-Year Plan period (2001–2005) (*China Statistical Yearbook*, 1978–2008).

FDI to Africa is also decreasing: it accounted for 25 per cent of FDI to all developing countries in the 1970s, with the proportion falling to 5.2 per cent in

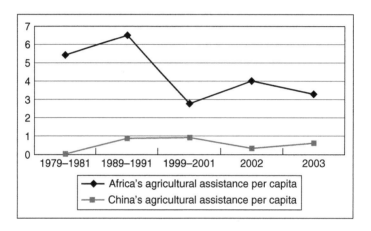

Figure 8.4 Comparison of Agricultural Assistance Per Capita to China and Africa (Unit: USD)

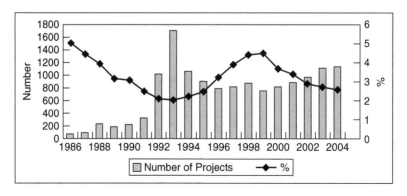

Figure 8.5 Structural Change of Foreign Capital in Agriculture in China, 1986–2004

Source: Ministry of Commerce

1992 and 3.8 per cent by 2000. Between 1982 and 1999, FDI flowed mainly to South Asia, East Asia, South-East Asia and Latin America. FDI to Africa decreased from 0.9 per cent to 0.3 per cent of FDI to all developing countries during the same period.

According to the World Investment Report (United Nations Conference on Trade and Development (UNCTAD), 2001), FDI to Africa decreased from USD10.5 billion in 1999 to USD9.1 billion in 2000. The proportion of FDI to Africa decreased to 1 per cent of FDI to all developing countries. FDI to Angola, Morocco and South Africa accounted for one-half of FDI to Africa. FDI to Sub-Saharan Africa decreased from USD8 billion in 1999 to USD6.5 billion in 2000. It increased by 80 per cent during the 2005–2007 period from USD29 billion to USD53 billion (see Table 8.1). A large part of total FDI to Africa is concentrated in oil-rich states, namely Nigeria, Sudan and Equatorial Guinea.

Of this large amount of FDI, only a small proportion flowed into the agricultural sector. For example, Tanzania received USD475 million of FDI annually during 2002–2005. The total FDI amounted to USD6.029 billion until 2005, accounting for 49.6 per cent of its GDP. About 57.2 per cent of FDI came from the OECD and 24.5 per cent came from the Southern African Development Community (SADC). FDI was used in the brewing, tobacco, electricity facility, transport, infrastructure and cement industries. FDI from China was invested in textile enterprises. FDI to the agricultural sector was very limited. Of the 2,288 FDI projects between 1990 and 2003, 163 were related to agriculture, and another 121 projects were related to natural resources. Research shows that FDI helps increase agricultural productivity, but is limited to tea and sugar. FDI contributes to alleviating poverty for smallholder farmers whose industries relate more to cash crops (Msuya, 2007).

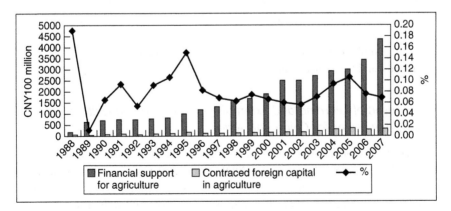

Figure 8.6 Financial Support for Agriculture and Contracted Foreign Capital in Agriculture in China

Source: Ministry of Finance

TABLE 8.1 FDI to Africa in 2007

FDI flow (USD billion)	Destination Country
>3	Nigeria, Egypt, South Africa
2–2.9	Morocco, Libya, Sudan
1–1.9	Equatorial Guinea, Algeria, Tunisia
0.5–0.9	Madagasgar, Zambia, Ghana, Kenya, Democratic Republic of the Congo, Namibia, Tanzania, Chad, Burkina Faso
0.2–0.4	Botswana, Mozambique, Côte d'Ivoire, Uganda, Mali, Congo, Mauritius, Cameroon, Gabon, Ethiopia, the Seychelles
<0.2	Djibouti, Cape Verde Islands, Mauritania, Somali, Guinea, Lesotho, Sierra Leone, Senegal, Togo, Zimbabwe, Rwanda, Gambia, Malawi, Benin, Liberia, Swaziland, Central African Republic, Niger, Guinea Bissau, Comoros, Burundi, Eritrea, Angola

In Ethiopia, 32 per cent of FDI flowed to the agricultural sector, increasing from USD135 million in 2000 to USD3.5 billion in 2008. It was mainly used in horticulture, meat production and biofuel and grain production, and its main sources were the European Union, India, Israel, Saudi Arabia and the USA. Table 8.2 shows that agricultural FDI is mainly used in cash crops and export-oriented crops rather than grain crops. Again, this illustrates the point made elsewhere in this book that African grain production is dangerously reliant on support from foreign aid.

There are big differences in patterns of utilization of foreign aid and investment between China and Africa. China uses increasingly less foreign aid for agricultural development and appears to have more of an autonomous discourse over how to use aid. China focuses on technological cooperation and stresses the introduction of external technologies and ideas: this approach has contributed to its achievements in agricultural development. Africa depends heavily on foreign aid, especially on food aid, and it is difficult for Africa to innovate with foreign aid. FDI inflow promotes employment and poverty alleviation, but does little to promote grain production and help smallholder farmers.

Comparison of Learning and External Support in the Agricultural Technology Sector for China and Africa

Multilateral technical assistance to Chinese agriculture mainly comes from the United Nations Development Programme (UNDP), United Nations Food and Agriculture Organization (FAO) and the European Community. From 1979 to 2006, China absorbed more than USD1.5 billion of technical assistance from the FAO, UNDP, World Bank, Asian Development Bank and Canada and other countries.

The aid methods and fields of operation of these organizations are diverse. UNDP's grant-based technical aid is used primarily for technical cooperation and

TABLE 8.2 Agricultural FDI in Ethiopia – Subsectors in Application

	2000–2005 Subsector	*2006–2008 Subsector*
European Union	Flowers 67.72%	Meat production 38.75% Biofuel 31.39% Flowers 15.47%
India	Flowers 91.21%	Sugar 80.45%
Israel	Flowers 82.44%	Flowers 44.98% Biofuel 24.77% Vegetable 15.06%
Saudi Arabia	Meat production 45.19% Flowers 31.65%	Meat 41.75% Biofuel 19.16%
USA	Grain 28.35% Biofuel 28.05% Flowers 14.93%	Flowers 30.48% Meat 22.41%

Source: Ethiopian Federal Investment Bureau, 2009

pre-investment activities. According to its technical cooperation programme, FAO provides technical assistance in three areas:

1 sending experts and advisers for guidance for a maximum period of one year;
2 short-term and practice-oriented training activities, mainly carried out at grass roots level and on site;
3 offering the necessary equipment and supplies for project activities with an outlay of generally not more than 50 per cent of the project budget, except for emergency projects.

The European Community's agricultural technical assistance to China is divided into two kinds: economic and technical. In the beginning, economic assistance was handled by the former Foreign Economic Relations and Trade Department (International Liaison Bureau), and technology assistance by the former State Science and Technology Commission (International Cooperation Agency).

BOX 8.4 LEARNING AND EXTERNAL SUPPORT FOR CHINA IN THE AGRICULTURAL TECHNOLOGY SECTOR

Germplasm

Between 1978 and 2008, more than 100,000 items of crop germplasm were introduced from overseas and contributed to the updating of Chinese varieties.

According to statistics from the Institute of Crop Germplasm Resources at the Chinese Academy of Agricultural Sciences, from 1978 to 2007 China exchanged plant germplasm resources with approximately 100 countries and regions, and bred a number of new varieties using only rice, wheat and maize germplasm resources. This led to the extension of 150 varieties for large-scale production.

Technology

More advanced technologies were brought in after 1979. For example, mulch planting, plastic greenhouses, dry rice cultivation, mechanization of rice cultivation, efficient and low-toxicity pesticides, compound fertilizers and drip-irrigation water-saving technologies were all widely applied in agricultural production to good effect. In order to improve agricultural science and technology, China launched the advanced Agricultural Science and Technology Plan in August 1994, referred to as the '948 Plan'. It is estimated that the technology projects introduced shortened China's agricultural science and technology R&D time by 10 to 15 years on average, and saved 30 to 50 per cent of R&D spending.

Equipment

By means of loans and grants, China absorbed various advanced forms of agricultural machinery and equipment, as well as feed processing equipment from the USA, Japan, Europe and other countries and regions. These contributed to greater labour productivity, land productivity and to reduce resource utilization challenges. The agricultural research and education sector took advantage of World Bank loans and aid projects to introduce a batch of advanced equipment that enriched the scientific world of key laboratories.

Talent

From 1979 onwards, China began to attach importance to agricultural knowledge-sharing and access to overseas expertise. More than 13,000 overseas agricultural experts and scholars from 57 countries and regions have been to China to lecture and provide technical guidance. Moreover, China availed itself of cooperation and exchanges to stimulate collaboration and share experience.

In the early 1980s, the World Bank launched a series of short-term structural adjustment and agricultural projects to implement market reforms, which included expanding farming systems research in eastern and southern Africa. Since the first loan issued to Sudan to strengthen agricultural research institutions in 1978, 26 Training and Visit extension systems have been established, and inputs into agricultural research and extension systems have increased (Collinson, 2000). In 1979, the International Service for Agricultural Research (ISNAR) was set up, followed by the Special Programme for National Agricultural Research in Africa (SPAAR) in 1985. These were created to enhance the national research systems in developing countries (Mrema, 1997). However, the World Bank's projects were not satisfactory in some key respects. Sector analysis did not place coherent and agriculture-oriented strategies into long-term growth targets or prioritize human, institutional and technical capacity-building as the basis for long-term growth. In addition, the goals of reforms imposed by the funders were not fully achieved: some reforms had to be stopped without external support. For example, Kenya did not implement food trade liberalization, Tanzania did not keep the exchange rate unchanged, Malawi put limits on land ownership and Senegal and Nigeria eventually abolished fertilizer subsidies (Lele, 1991).

From the 1990s, the focus of agricultural assistance to Africa has shifted to diverse agricultural research and extension models and returned to supporting regional agricultural research institutions. During this period, general agricultural aid and its impact on rural development, its sustainability and costs and benefits were evaluated, and the results were far from satisfactory: for example, The costly Training and Visit agricultural extension systems programme was negatively evaluated. The above factors reduced development agencies' and recipient governments' enthusiasm for investment in agricultural development (FAO, 2002; World Bank, 2002). As a consequence, a number of donors increased support for agricultural research and extension, and reduced back-up for agricultural higher education and postgraduate training programmes. Only 2 per cent (Willett, 1998) of the World Bank's USD4.8 billion expenditure for global agricultural research and extension and higher education between 1987 and 1997 went to higher education, and only three agriculture education projects in Africa were funded. Moreover, donors cut funding for the Consultative Group on International Agricultural Research (CGIAR) system. Many countries discovered that without external support they could not fund agricultural extension programmes (including staff time, fuel and other expenses).

During this period, external agricultural support to China demonstrated the following contributions to agricultural science and technology:

- enriching germplasm resource banks;
- increasing agricultural research capacity; and
- helping improve the agricultural management system.

External support backed and supplemented China's existing research and innovation system. As for Africa, agricultural aid is less about cooperation and exchange, and more about relating with funding – and external funding is often sufficient to dominate a country's agricultural research system. However, the African continent's unique site conditions and cultural traditions hold back those donors' good expectations. Take the FAO's farmer field schools as an example. By 2003, Kenya had 1,000 active farmer field school groups with nearly 30,000 farmers taking part (Sones *et al.*, 2003). However, Africa's farming system is more complex than Asia's rice production system, and the farmer field schools approach costs more than in Asia. From Training and Visit to farmer field schools and promotion of value-chain development and private sector engagement, each time the funders adjusted the aid model, they failed to learn from previous lessons and added to the burdens faced by local institutions and economic organizations.

BOX 8.5 AGRICULTURAL ASSISTANCE TO POSTWAR LIBERIA

The agricultural sector, including fishing and forestry, is the backbone of Liberia's national economy. The sector accounted for more than 75 per cent of GDP in 1998, and 50 per cent before the 2003 war that devastated the country. The agricultural sector also provides 75 per cent of employment opportunities in Liberia and hence needs more attention, resources and policy guidance.

Between 1991 and 1997, international donors, including the European Union, United States Agency for International Development (USAID), UNDP, FAO, Sweden and international non-governmental organizations (NGOs) provided support to the agricultural sector, including inputs such as seeds and tools as well as training and emergency interventions, and these benefited farmers nationwide. According to FAO statistics, 1995 rice production was only 25 per cent of the prewar level, and subsequently increased to 30 per cent, 50 per cent and 70 per cent in 1996, 1997 and 1998, respectively. The output of cassava, the second most important staple food, recovered to 50 per cent in 1995 and to 96 per cent in 1998.

China's Agricultural Assistance to Africa

Cooperation and assistance to African agriculture has played a fundamental role in the mutual exchange between China and African countries since the 1960s. As a result, governments and individual farmers in Africa can have direct access to Chinese experience with agricultural policies and technologies through various cooperation and aid projects, which contributes greatly to the study on experience-sharing in this arena as well as to the development of African agriculture in reality.

China's agricultural assistance to Africa began with the offer of food aid to the Government of Guinea Bissau in 1959. China–Africa agricultural cooperation has gone through three stages during the subsequent 50 years. The first stage can be characterized as running from 1959 to the 1970s and was dominated by development assistance. Generally the Chinese government offered grant aid to African countries and helped with the construction of farms, agricultural experiment stations and extension services, water conservation projects and technical expertise. The second stage, from the late 1970s to the end of the 1990s, saw a shift in China's agricultural development assistance strategy. The government gave up its dominant position and encouraged state enterprises to play a bigger role. An investment contract system was adopted for some assistance projects. In addition to non-reimbursable assistance, concessional loans gradually became a major part of agricultural assistance to Africa. Furthermore, China began to participate in multilateral aid activities on the African continent. The third stage, from 2000 onwards, involved a further deepening of Sino-African agricultural cooperation. The Forum on China–Africa Cooperation,[4] and the signing of a number of multilateral and bilateral agricultural cooperation documents, indicated that Sino-African agricultural cooperation is progressively turning from a project-based mode to a more strategic and sustainable form of institutional development. Sino-African agricultural cooperation now displays a range of mechanisms for cooperation, broad content and wide coverage. In addition to bilateral aid and economic cooperation, China is actively applying the United Nations system's Framework on South–South cooperation mechanism and other multilateral mechanisms to extend agricultural assistance to Africa. China and Africa's agricultural cooperation involves crop cultivation, fisheries management, technical cooperation, agricultural processing projects, agriculture infrastructure construction and personnel training, and has spread across 44 countries on the African continent. Agricultural cooperation has become an important part of China–Africa relations. For the period 1960–2006, China's agricultural assistance projects in Africa accounted for one-fifth of China's total aid projects in Africa (Bräutigam and Tang, 2009).

Agricultural assistance has been an important ingredient in China's commitment to Africa and has taken many forms, from stand-alone agricultural aid projects to the FAO Food Security Action Plan under the Framework on South–South Cooperation and other multilateral aid mechanisms. By 2005, China had established 145 agricultural aid projects in Africa, including demonstration farms, farmland water conservation repair, agriculture technical services, farm machinery processing and livestock and poultry breeding.[5] The major modes for aid are farm construction and the establishment of agricultural technology demonstration centres, and provision of agricultural experts, training and direct food aid. In the early days, China's agricultural assistance to Africa was provided on an *ad hoc* basis through projects, and less attention was paid to sustainability and institutional aspects. Now, China's agricultural assistance to Africa is moving towards a more institutional focus and the use of more coherent policy and planning mechanisms. The Chinese government began its South–South cooperation with FAO and Ethiopia in 1996. Since then, the Chinese Ministry of Agriculture has signed tripartite cooperation agreements with Sierra Leone, Gabon, Ghana, Mali, Mauritania and Nigeria. In addition to multilateral mechanisms, China has established bilateral cooperation mechanisms through the Forum on China–Africa Cooperation with many African countries. By the end of 2008, China had signed agricultural, pastoralist and fisheries cooperation agreements with 10 African countries including Egypt, South Africa, Ethiopia and Sudan, and formed bilateral agricultural cooperation teams with Egypt and South Africa.

Farm Construction Assistance

Farm construction assistance is a long-established form for Chinese agricultural assistance to Africa. After the Second World War, the prevailing view in international development discourse favoured government-led large-scale agricultural operations, with an emphasis on mechanization and seeking to achieve high productivity. This became the dominant approach to solving agricultural problems (Yun, 2000b) for many developing countries. A good many countries in Africa, including Ghana, Senegal, Tanzania, Guinea Bissau, Botswana, Mozambique, Democratic Republic of the Congo, Congo-Brazzaville, Madagascar, Benin, Togo and Ethiopia, implemented forms of collective agriculture in a similar way to China. This affected China's approach to Africa's agricultural assistance. In the 1960s and 1970s China helped build a large number of farms in Africa, including the Mbarali farm and Tuvu farms in Tanzania, the Fano farm in Somalia, the Chipemba farm in Uganda, the Coba sugarcane farm in Guinea, two sugarcane farms in Mali, the Beam Mpoli rice farm in Mauritania, the sugarcane farm in Sierra Leone, four reclamation areas in Niger, sugarcane plantations in Togo and a sugarcane farm in the Democratic Republic of the Congon, among others (Wang, 2000; People's Daily, 2000). This type of agricultural aid to Africa utilizing a farm model resulted from prevailing ideology in international development aid and the needs of African countries after independence. Farm-based assistance to Africa took into account the agricultural development path of African countries at that time, reflecting important lessons from China's own agricultural development. Special farms in border areas run by the military, known as *bingtuan*, have been an important force in China's agricultural development. This approach relied on tackling inadequate agricultural investment by pooling human resources. Such a work pattern demanded extremely powerful government management and mobilization capacity, which resulted in very high management costs. After African countries achieved independence, governments lacked the management capacity to mobilize societies largely organized along tribal lines. Thus in Africa, farms with Chinese experts and financial assistance often ran soundly and saw significant crop yield increases until they were transferred to recipient governments, when farms were likely to run into operational and management challenges that were not easy to surmount. For example, the Government of Ghana was unable to pay salaries for ten members of staff and maintenance costs, and ultimately assigned the land of a planned farm to 700 farmers, meaning that the mechanized production that Chinese aid had supported could not be used (Yun, 2000b). By the late 1980s, many farms were facing serious sustainability problems and ended up going into receivership. Farm construction projects relying entirely on government forces had not achieved the desired result.

It is interesting to note that government-managed, state-owned farms in Africa encountered similar management problems to the People's Communes in China, which also relied on high levels of mobilization. As the communes were falling apart, the government began to reform the state-owned farm system by introducing market mechanisms. This was good for farm development, and the approach influenced China's assistance in farm construction to Africa. As the Chinese foreign aid system was gradually reformed, the Chinese government encouraged and allowed some enterprises, especially state-owned enterprises, to join in foreign aid work. China's State Farm Group and provincial State Farm Groups contributed to the restructuring and reform of farms in Africa. The farm model changed from an entirely government-run model to one where government set policy and financial incentives, but where the enterprise is run on a commercial basis. There are now two models for farm assistance. One is the Sino-African joint venture, such as the Sukala Sugar Farm in Mali, which has developed into a large enterprise integrating sugarcane growing and sugar production. The other is where the farm is purely a Chinese enterprise: examples of this are the Sino-Zambia Friendship Farm, Xiyangyang Farm and the Sunshine Farm run by the Jiangsu State Farm Corporation, all in Zambia. In this model, farm management personnel are Chinese, and they hire local farmers as workers to produce the agricultural products needed locally and sell them in local markets. Since the additional investment came from business, these farms gradually became overseas ventures for Chinese firms and demonstrated the characteristics of agricultural economic cooperation. This reform also stimulated some of China's private capital to flow to African agriculture. A typical example is Liu Changming's private farm on the outskirts of Lusaka, Zambia.

These types of joint ventures or directly-owned enterprises are a kind of new approach to agricultural aid in Africa from the Chinese viewpoint. International development aid agencies have not paid sufficient attention to this approach, even though it is much more sustainable and the enterprises are still functional and disseminating technologies as for-profit firms. Many small and medium-sized enterprises in the environs of the Sukala Sugar Farm in Mali and the Sino-Zambian farms are adopting many technologies based on the experience of Chinese farms.

Experimental Stations and Agricultural Technology Demonstration Centres

In the 1950s, China began to set up a complete agricultural technology popularization system in order to rapidly disseminate agricultural technologies and transform them for agricultural production. Sharing practical agricultural production technology with Africa is also a key part of China's agricultural development assistance. The early experience with experimental stations focused on infrastructure building: for example, China helped build an agricultural technology experimental extension station at Kindia in Guinea Bissau in 1979, and handed it to the Government of Guinea for management once it was completed in 1982. However, project-oriented aid faced challenges around sustainable management, which was not handled well by local people with limited skills and management capacity. China's agricultural technology experiment stations are based on China's agricultural technology extension system, but experimental stations need strong financial and administrative support with experienced technicians linked to end–user farm households. Most African countries have not had effective and systematic agricultural technology extension systems, and lack dissemination mechanisms for practical technologies from agricultural technology demonstration stations.

The recipient governments were short of experience in operating extension stations and found it difficult to keep running them. The Kindia Agricultural Experiment Station went through a hard time, and the Chinese government provided funding and sent out experts again from 1989 to 1999. After 1999, when investment and specialist assistance ceased, the test station closed once more. This process was labelled 'Build – Transfer – Suspend – Reinvest – Re-transfer – Re-Suspend' in China, and was not specific to Kindia extension station but occurred with the majority of agricultural technology extension stations that China supported in Africa. However, experience in some countries shows that with continuing investment, extension stations could play an important role in extending practical agricultural technologies to farmers.

BOX 8.6 SIERRA LEONE'S RICE TECHNOLOGY EXTENSION STATION

In 1971, the Chinese government set-up 13 rice technology extension stations and reclaimed 1,100 hectares of new farmland, promoting agricultural technology across 2,390 hectares of land through economic aid projects in Sierra Leone, and raising yields per unit area three times higher than local yields. However, with the withdrawal of Chinese agricultural technicians, extension sites came to a total standstill. In 1988, the Chinese government sent more agricultural staff and provided loans for three agricultural technology extension stations – Macari, Lang Bei Yama and Langley – established in the 1970s. Since 1991, when China began this new phase of agricultural technical cooperation, the stations have been running smoothly and adapted hybrid rice varieties such as Shanyou 63 to good effect.

Source: Ministry of Agriculture

After 2006, the Chinese government began to establish agricultural technology demonstration centres in Africa and planned 20 projects, of which 14 are already under construction. These centres also provide practical agricultural technologies for African countries through building infrastructure, creating field-testing and breeding programmes and providing training services. They provide a wide range of technology demonstrations (as shown in Table 8.3) and are also suited to the agroecological and socioeconomic characteristics of different countries, which means that the focus differs, from aquaculture in Uganda and South Africa to rice in Liberia, Cameroon, Rwanda and Tanzania, maize and wheat in Sudan, vegetables in Benin, cassava and vegetables in Congo-Brazzaville and cash crops in Ethiopia.

Given the poor sustainability of previous extension and experimentation stations and the success of market-oriented reforms in the large-farm sector, the model for these centres has been to encourage universities, research institutes and enterprises to take responsibility for the running of these centres. Construction of the centres relied on government aid, but maintenance comes from enterprise management by companies established to continue it after grant funding ends. So far, the key agricultural enterprises involved in the construction of centres are the China National Agricultural Development Group Corporation, Sichuan Phoenix, Shaanxi State Farm Group, Yuan Long Ping High-Tech, Chongqing State Farm, Guangxi Bagui and Shandong Foreign Economic and Technical Cooperation Group.

Market-oriented enterprise development is also a key feature of China's agricultural extension and diffusion experience in recent years. China's current agricultural technology research and marketing network is diversified, and enterprises are granted strong fiscal and policy support from government to participate in agricultural extension and provide technology services which can be thought of as public goods. Moreover, the process of agricultural development has led to some differentiation. Farmers or agricultural practitioners with purchasing power are large-scale. Agricultural enterprises adopt diverse business models to sell agricultural means of production such as fertilizer, pesticides and improved seeds, and support the supply of agricultural technology services. Agricultural companies can be the backbone of agricultural technology service provision.

For most African countries, it is primarily only large-scale farms that can afford agricultural technology, and this is mainly imported technology and management from the West; at the same time the majority of farmers are not able to pay for such services or technologies – African governments and farmers both have a serious shortage of purchasing power and without Chinese capital, these commercial enterprises would still find it challenging to operate technology demonstration centres. Although joint ventures or enterprise-type farms are successful, managing agricultural technology demonstration requires a more novel approach than that of marketing agricultural products. Agricultural demonstration centres managed purely as enterprises will face many problems; in addition, there is no definite mechanism to guide these enterprises to cooperate with local agricultural research institutes, or with non-profit research institutions set up by international bodies. Moreover, it is no small challenge for these technology demonstration centres to constitute an effective agricultural extension network that coordinates with international and local efforts in Africa. At the same time, it should be noted that once these centres are completed, they will shift to a business-oriented model that will contrast with non-profit public welfare research institutions supported by donors. This could lead to criticism of China. However, in order to get past the aid dependency trap, it is a new attempt to explore sustainable development aid projects through a market orientation. In any case, at present all the centres are at the construction stage, and so operation, management and substantive activities cannot be assessed.

The farms, experimental stations and today's agricultural technology demonstration centres reflect similar assistance mechanisms and embody the valuable experience of China's agricultural development at different stages. They represent an agricultural development strategy of substituting scarce land, the core resource of agricultural production, with financial and technological resources which can stimulate agricultural development through a strong developmental state with policy and financial management capacity. Even so, China's public farms are unlikely to be converted into market-oriented enterprises, and most extension stations rely on scientific research institutions or enterprises to run smoothly. Now, when copying this model to Africa, it is clear that these institutions cannot survive through reliance on local government administrative capacity: these centres, managed by Chinese universities, agricultural academies and enterprises, will have to be managed as enterprises. The centres draw on previous lessons, but it is very uncertain if these enterprises will be able to continue to operate them when funding ends, given the current policy, market and institutional environments in Africa. How to integrate the non-profit and profit making functions of the centres remains a challenge without a completely satisfactory answer as yet.

Agricultural Technology Expert Programme

China first sent agricultural experts to Africa in the 1960s. These experts were mainly appointed in response to invitations and requests from African partners. In 1961 and early 1962, the Government of Mali requested an expert team for tea and sugarcane trials; in 1976, at the request of Government of Uganda, water conservancy and rice experts were dispatched to help develop rice production in the marshland in the Dohe area. This process of exchange support has been an important way of assisting African agricultural development and is increasingly being institutionalized into a continuous operational mode. It is applied in both bilateral and multilateral mechanisms.

In 1996, China began to participate in the FAO Special Programme for Food Security and began sending agricultural experts and technicians to Africa, Asia and the South Pacific. In May 2006, the Chinese government signed a Letter of intent between the itself and the FAO on South–South Cooperation Strategic Alliance Establishment and, in so doing, became the first 'South–South Cooperation' strategic alliance partner. Through the FAO, China has signed tripartite cooperation agreements with several aid recipient countries and contributed to South–South projects, in the process playing an important role in promoting world food security and solving poverty issues. China chiefly concentrates on Africa and is active in Nigeria, Sierra Leone, Gabon, Mauritania and Ghana. Taking the tripartite cooperation with Nigeria as an example, as of March 2007, a total of 15 groups of technical personnel (496 people) had been sent to work across 36 states in Africa, focusing on water resource management, agriculture, animal husbandry and

TABLE 8.3 China's Agricultural Technology Demonstration Centres in Africa

African Country	Chinese Responsible Agencies	Date of Construction	Focus Areas	Contents of Construction
South Africa	China National Agricultural Development Group Corporation	Oct. 2009	Experimental study of freshwater aquaculture species, technology demonstration promotion and personnel training	Training centre buildings, laboratories, fish breeding centre and feed mill
Tanzania	Chongqing Zhongyi Seed Industry Company and Chongqing State Farm Holding Group	Oct. 2009	Rice	12-hectare experimental display area, 50-hectare production demonstration area
Zambia	Jilin Agricultural University	Nov. 2009	To be confirmed	–
Mozambique	Hubei State Farm Group	7 Jul. 2009	Breeding improved varieties of crop and livestock and poultry, agro-processing	Management training and technical R&D centre, logistical centre and storage centres
Uganda	Sichuan Huaqiao Fenghuang Group	Sep. 2009	China's freshwater aquaculture technology	
Zimbabwe	Zhongji Meinuozz Tech Company		Agricultural machinery and irrigation	Construction of offices, training, living and production housing
Sudan	Shandong Foreign Economic and Technical Cooperation Group and Shandong Academy of Agricultural Sciences	Apr. 2009	Farming, agricultural seed engineering, fertilizer application production technology, mechanical engineering, crop disease/insect/pest monitoring and forecasting system	Construction of offices, training, living and production housing; construction of irrigation facilities and farm roads, providing equipments and agricultural machinery

TABLE 8.3 Continued

African Country	Chinese Responsible Agencies	Date of Construction	Focus Areas	Contents of Construction
Liberia	Hunan Province Yuan Long Ping Agriculture High–Tech Service Company	Apr. 2009	Promotion of hybrid rice	—
Congo	Chinese Academy of Tropical Agricultural Sciences	Sep. 2009	Cassava	—
Benin	China National Agricultural Development Group Corporation China National Agricultural Development Group Corporation	Apr. 2009	Corn, chicken and vegetable production	—
Togo	Jiangxi Province Huachang Infrastructure Company	Oct. 2009	Rice	Laboratory, demonstration site and rice production base
Rwanda	Fujian Agriculture and Forestry University	Apr. 2009	Rice cultivation, sericulture, bacteria grass techniques and soil and water conservation	—
Cameroon	Shaanxi State Farm Group	Jul. 2009	Experimental study on crop variety and seed selection	—
Ethiopia	Guangxi Bagui Agricultural Technology Company	Oct. 2009	Modern agriculture, new technologies and new varieties	—

Source: Ministry of Foreign Affairs, Ministry of Commerce and Xinhua websites

aquaculture technology. Four hundred and fifty people have returned to China already after reaching the end of their respective tours of duty. In the case of multilateral mechanisms, China has adopted a series of actions and measures to ensure the effectiveness of the experts provided. China's Ministry of Agriculture is responsible for overall coordination and management, assigning expert tasks to provincial departments and linking provinces to African countries with similar agricultural development characteristics, climate and agro-ecologies. Under this partnering arrangement, Sichuan Province partners with Ethiopia, while Hubei Province partners with Sierra Leone, for example.

BOX 8.7 CHINESE AGRICULTURAL EXPERTS IN SIERRA LEONE

China–Sierra Leone 'South–South Cooperation' under the FAO Special Programme on Food Security was officially launched in 2007. China sent 18 agricultural experts and technicians to Sierra Leone's four project districts: Moyamba, Makali, Kabala and Kono for technical assistance work.

Chinese experts and technicians overcame many difficulties and launched a series of productive activities during their two years in Sierra Leone: first, by taking agricultural technical guidance to the grass roots level. Chinese experts and technicians conducted on-site and in-depth research to learn about local agricultural resources, climate, soil land current agricultural production practices. They carried out more than 800 training sessions with local farmers and taught 58 practical skills.

Second, broad financial and active demonstration and teaching of China's agricultural production technology was brought to Sierra Leone. In order to fully demonstrate and teach advanced agricultural production technologies for two years, Chinese experts and technicians raised SLL198 million (USD50,000), built 32 small-scale agriculture demonstration sites and shared around 20 practical agricultural production technologies for rice cultivation, fish breeding, vegetable cultivation, farm machinery use and maintenance, small-scale livestock farming, beekeeping and plant protection.

Third, extensive agriculture technical training has been based on local conditions. Chinese experts and technicians extended 57 pertinent technical guides, taught 38 practical skills and trained 1,200 people. Fourth, the project showed clearly how to fully develop local agricultural resources. Agricultural experts and technicians in the Moyamba area developed 10 acres of fertile farmland, and in Falaba a 2.5 acre intensive fishing pond on an original swamp. These demonstrated how to plant the hybrid rice bred in China and obtain yields of 431kg per mu, three times higher than the local rice yield, while also harvesting 500,000 high-quality tilapia fry every year in fish ponds. Fifth, the scheme has dealt with promoting local technological innovation. The Makali project area included a new rice variety breeding project covering 30 acres, reaping 12,000kg of rice seeds; the Kono project area demonstrated planting of 1 acre of watermelons, producing 8,200kg of watermelon; Kabala undertook GX-9 rice variety breeding and extension, beekeeping technology transformation and hay storage technology demonstration projects, which were highly appreciated by both the government and FAO.

Source: Ministry of Agriculture

Bilateral cooperation has moved forward following the third Forum on China–Africa Cooperation in 2006. China has dispatched nearly 100 agricultural experts from higher education colleges, agricultural research institutes and professional agricultural institutions such as seed stations, environmental protection stations and agricultural technology extension departments in successive African countries. These experts offer services in the farming and processing of agricultural products, covering vegetable cultivation, horticulture, use of agricultural machinery, irrigation, livestock management and agricultural development policy planning. The experts were selected through various channels including online publications and local recommendations, and have been designated to more than 30 countries in Africa so far. These experts generally work in the assigned country for more than one year, with costs covered by the Chinese arm. Most of these Chinese experts work in the frontline of domestic agricultural technology research and extension, and do not work independently or join in agricultural assistance projects initiated by China in Africa. Generally, they assist the agricultural sectors and relevant agencies, and work together with the recipient's agricultural technology research and extension staff so as to ensure that African experts will be able to continue spreading new technologies after they depart.

Chinese experts have made many achievements in Africa and won high praise from their African counterparts as well as the international community. Experts are screened according to the recipient countries' requests and needs and provide agricultural technology services on demand. Sometimes, the majority of these experts come from China's grass roots level and are familiar with harsh conditions, and thus are able to adapt quickly to difficult environments in Africa. Most of them not only bring their expertise into play, but also furnish other agricultural production technologies needed in the workplace. From a review of the CVs of 24 agricultural experts in Nigeria at the time of writing, it is clear that the agricultural technical services offered by Chinese agricultural experts are both practical and diverse (Table 8.4).

BOX 8.8 CHINESE AGRICULTURAL EXPERT PROVISION OF COMPREHENSIVE SERVICES IN NIGERIA

Since 2006, Chinese agricultural experts have done the following:

- conducted 320 small-scale water conservancy projects, including earth dam construction, insertion of tube wells, rainwater harvesting and drip irrigation, hand-pump wells and concrete water-saving irrigation ditches in five technology assistance fields;
- demonstrated how to implant and promote rice, maize, cassava, soybeans and millet crops;
- introduced organic fertilizer composting techniques, tissue cultivation, mushroom production, bacteria-based breeding and other practical technologies;
- helped design and manufacture multi-function wood-fire drying rooms, agricultural product drying platform devices, threshers, winnowing machines, simple planters, fruit pickers and other farm machinery;
- taught food processing technologies, including soy product-making and vegetable and grain storage technologies;
- improved beekeeping and bee propagation techniques and invented Lang's beehives and honey extraction machines;
- built hundreds of biogas digesters and energy-saving stoves;
- promoted livestock and poultry breeding, fertilization, disease control techniques, improved chick hatching rates to 90 per cent and solved chick supply shortage problems; and
- enhanced aquaculture, hatching, aquatic product processing and other production technologies.

Source: Ministry of Agriculture

In addition to long-term agricultural experts assigned through bilateral and multilateral mechanisms, the Chinese government, including provincial and other local governments or research institutions, often appoints short-term agricultural experts to Africa for agricultural technical service work. As they come from different institutions and there is a lack of systematic statistics, the quantity and scale of these short-term agricultural expert visits are hard to estimate. However, along with long-term experts, these experts have all contributed to practical agricultural technology popularization in various parts of Africa. Although they have played a positive role in technology diffusion in the farms and areas where they work, there are limits to how far technologies are able to spread due to a lack of capacity to scale up or make use of supporting industrial production, for example, of equipment.

TABLE 8.4 Some Technical Services Provided by Chinese Agricultural Experts in Nigeria

Name	Technology Services	Name	Technology Services
QFG	Vegetable cultivation, use of biogas digesters, beekeeping techniques	LG	Large-scale production of maize and vegetable standardization
LJB	Fruit tree grafting, high-yielding maize demonstration and Chinese millet demonstration	SHR	Millet demonstration
HXS	Vegetable cultivation and training in use of biogas digesters	THM	Beekeeping
CZY	Poultry hatching and rubber cultivation	TYB TYB	Hybrid maize breeding
GHZ	Vegetables and beekeeping	WWX	Cassava cultivation
GZXGZX	Agricultural electromechanical equipment and farm machinery repair	WWZPZP	Irrigation, fruit tree and vegetable cultivation
JFLJFL	Rice and vegetable cultivation, animal husbandry and water conservancy	XYFXYF	Agriculture, beekeeping, biogas, agricultural processing and agricultural machinery technology
JLY JLY	Plant disease and insect pest cure and prevention	YBKYBK	Biogas digester construction
LBYLBY	Fruit and vegetable technology demonstration	YQXYQX	Beekeeping
LTLLTL	Rice, maize and agricultural machinery	ZJYZJY	Use of biogas digesters and cattle fattening
ZLYZLY	Seed processing machinery, promotion of artificial agricultural tools	ZZWZZW	Mushroom cultivation and seed production
ZXXZXX	Rice, maize cultivation demonstration, construction of biogas digesters	ZABZAB	Agricultural fertilizer and edible fungi

Source: Summary of key areas of work of Chinese agricultural experts in Nigeria

Nevertheless, compared with aid-supported farms, experimental stations and agricultural technology demonstration centres, sending agricultural experts has shown some clear advantages. First, these exchanges are low-cost and do not encourage aid dependence. Farms, experimental stations and agricultural technology demonstration centres all require the recipient countries to build infrastructure facilities and require significant investment. For example, the total cost for the agricultural technology demonstration centre programme is approximately CNY40 million (USD6 million). Lessons from the operation of large-scale farms and experimental stations in the past suggest that these large-scale investment programmes will not meet people's expectations without effective and continuous follow-up capital investment: there is a danger that aid funds will be wasted. However, constant investment also risks creating a form of aid dependency, which Chinese assistance seeks to avoid. Appointment of African agricultural experts could reduce aid dependency somewhat and achieve impact by bringing technicians from China and the recipient countries to work together as partners on demonstration farms and in agricultural research and extension departments.

Training

China provides agricultural training for Africa in two main ways. One is by sending agricultural experts to train agricultural technical personnel and small farmers in agricultural demonstration projects in African countries. These training activities lack systematic statistics and the size and number of participants are difficult to determine. According to interviews with some agricultural experts in Nigeria, each of them has trained hundreds of people. From 1985 to the end of 1999, China had trained 905 technical staff in 46 African countries in the areas of rice and vegetable cultivation, integrated fish farming, meat processing, agricultural machinery, solar energy, weather forecasting and so forth. Since 2000, China has placed great emphasis on training technical personnel in Africa, setting up an African human resource development fund and holding a variety of training courses for African personnel (to date, nearly 7,000) in China. Agricultural training hosts include higher education agricultural colleges and universities and other research and training institutions. China Agricultural University, for example, held 17 professional training courses for 386 people from Algeria, Benin, Côte d'Ivoire, Egypt, Ethiopia, Ghana, Guinea Bissau and other African countries between 2001 and 2008, covering many areas from agricultural product processing, water-saving irrigation technology and management to modern agricultural education, training in rural development for local government, rural energy, agricultural machinery and livestock and poultry breeding (Table 8.5). In 2008, training was scaled up rapidly and the number trained increased from 38 in 2007 to 127 in 2008. Training typically mixes classroom instruction with farm visits and inspections; however, given the short time for each training period, trainees usually cannot truly master the agricultural technologies being demonstrated.

For training courses held in China, training schedules and arrangements are mostly developed by the training institutions, while the Chinese embassies in the African countries are responsible for trainee recruitment. Training courses are devised and recruitment is conducted in tandem. The course is designed primarily according to the capacity and knowledge structure of the training institutions and the expressed needs of African trainees. No systematic and scientific training needs assessment is carried out, and training courses are often out of touch with agricultural

TABLE 8.5 China Agricultural University Training List for Africa, 2001–2008

Time	Project
2001	Processing of agricultural products in Africa
2004	Water-saving irrigation technology and management, modern agricultural education, official capacity building of African rural education
2005	Modern agricultural education, water-saving irrigation technology and management and biotechnology for Africa
2006	Rural energy and agricultural machinery, modern agricultural equipment, water-saving irrigation technology and management, Ethiopian farm management
2007	Ethiopia's agriculture cultivation management, modern agricultural education
2008	Modern agriculture irrigation management, livestock breeding management, biomass energy comprehensive utilization technology, rural energy and agricultural machinery

Note: No available data for 2002 and 2003.

Source: China Agricultural University

development needs in Africa. Although the training classes are divided into French and English classes, taking into account the different official languages of the African countries, African countries speaking the same language have obvious distinctions in agricultural development and technology needs, and this is overlooked in most courses. Completion of training is not followed by systematic follow-up and evaluation: some courses extend immediate assessment, but this relates more to the training organization, teaching methods and other technical issues. Trainee feedback is generally satisfying, mainly because they are curious about China and are content with the logistical services arranged by the host organizations. The effectiveness and applicability of this training is assessed, but a true and accurate judgement is hardly reflected by real-time assessment. Training Chinese style, considering language, time and other barriers, has meant that impacts are not always as great as originally hoped. The Chinese government is planning to change this training approach and hopes to establish special agricultural aid institutions through a trust fund promised to the FAO (within the framework of the FAO Food Security Action Plan). For example, the Chinese Hybrid Rice Technology Training Centre, opened by the Longping High-tech Rice Company, is supposed to organize pertinent training activities using foreign aid.

Student exchange is of one of the oldest forms of China–Africa agricultural cooperation. In the 1950s, China accepted 24 African students and further education personnel; in 1955, China sent seven students to study in Egypt. In the 1960s, at the request of several African countries, China provided scholarships to study in China not only to African countries that had obtained national independence, but also to political parties and mass organizations in areas not yet independent. In the 1990s, China increased educational exchange and cooperation with African countries and welcomed students from more than 50 African countries. For a decade, there have been 5,569 African student visits to China. In 2001, a total of 1,224 students in Africa enjoyed Chinese government scholarships, accounting for 24.73 per cent of Chinese government foreign scholarships (4,950 people in all). As of 2002, Egypt, Kenya, Morocco, South Africa, Nigeria, Senegal, Tanzania and Tunisia and other countries had received around 270 Chinese students. At present, China's Ministry of Education provides scholarships for more than 1,000 people to African countries each year. African students studying in China concentrate on agriculture, animal and plant science, information technology and economics (Compilation Group of Education Cooperation, 2005). The China Agricultural University, China's largest agricultural university, has enrolled 35 African students in recent years, including 11 doctoral students, 14 master's students and 10 undergraduates. These students major principally in plant pathology, agricultural mechanization engineering, food science and engineering, rural development and management.[6] However However, taken overall, the number of students from African countries studying agriculture in China is still relative small, hardly engendering a significant impact on the development of African countries and their agricultural systems.

Provision of Food Aid and Material Assistance

China also provides direct material assistance and food aid to Africa. Material aid originates from China's construction projects in Africa and African countries' needs, and mainly consists of agricultural machinery, chemical fertilizer and other agricultural production materials. In 2006, in response to Sierra Leone's request, China offered a batch of farm machinery and tools, including 16 tractors, eight combine harvesters, six sets of rice threshers and matching trailers, disc ploughs, disc harrows and other equipment. In addition to material aid, China affords food aid to African countries through the WFP. As per the WFP (2007) report, in 2005 China became the world's third largest food aid donor after the USA and the European Union.

China is constantly modulating the content, methods and means of its aid to Africa. In terms of aid content, coverage is increasingly wide, incorporating all aspects of agricultural production including, for example, irrigation, planting, aquaculture and horticulture. In terms of aid methods, the traditional bilateral cooperation mechanism has been replaced by bilateral and multilateral combined mechanisms. China is participating in an increasing number international multilateral donor arrangements to assist Africa. Aside from paying membership funds and making donations to international agencies, China is building a tripartite Food Security Action Plan and providing assistance for food security problems in Africa through the South–South cooperation framework. Bilateral aid has gradually changed from a project approach to signature of bilateral cooperation agreements with African countries. To be specific, assistance has altered from financial to economic and technical aid. In the past, using a grant model, China mainly assisted African countries to build infrastructure facilities, farms and experimental stations, and usually transferred projects to the African countries for self-management and operation, but poor African management capacity resulted in unsustainable projects.

Now China is making greater use of technical assistance: sending agricultural experts and organization of trainings claims a growing proportion of assistance. Even for economic assistance, the traditional government-led approach has been substituted with an emphasis on encouraging China's enterprises, especially state-owned enterprises, to participate. Grant aid is now for early construction stages; corporate planning and business management is introduced at the operational phase to ensure the sustainability of projects.

As mentioned previously, China has gradually shifted from direct material assistance to Africa to a focus on spreading key agricultural technologies, and the ways and methods shared have all proved effective and practical in China. China developed its Building a Prosperous Agriculture through Science and Education strategy in the 1980s and made use of agricultural experiment stations, agricultural experts, demonstration projects and other useful measures and ways to encourage agricultural science and technology promotion. However, the effectiveness of these measures is based on sound and systematic financial and administrative support systems, while many African countries lack this kind of capacity – therefore, the likelihood of solving deep-seated agricultural development problems by relying solely on foreign experts and demonstration centres, while institutional development and financial capacity-building problems are unresolved, is of limited potential. This is why Chinese experts and agricultural projects can play a good role in the service area, but cannot necessarily be institutionalized effectively. Whether China's agricultural assistance to Africa has truly stimulated agricultural development in Africa is difficult to judge without systematic assessment. Yet it is definite that China's assistance strategy for African agriculture derives from its own experience, especially the aforementioned Building a Prosperous Agriculture strategy. China hopes to provide technical assistance accompanied by necessary economic assistance measures to enhance Africa's agricultural production technology. However, China's agricultural science and technology strategy does not work without a set of relatively sound financial and administrative policies. These measures and capabilities are weaker in Africa, therefore China's agricultural technology meets system-level bottlenecks, and 'agricultural project results fall short of the expectations of both sides' (Yun, 2000a).

It should be pointed out that in the process of providing agricultural assistance to African countries, China has learned a great number of agricultural techniques too. China has sent expert technology groups to study citrus cultivation techniques in Morocco; brought in sisal technologies from Zambia, which have been extended in suitable areas in southern China with good results (Liu, 2000); learned cotton cultivation techniques from Egypt and Togo; brought in coffee varieties from Cameroon; and invited Zimbabwean experts to resolve ostrich breeding problems.

Sino-African Economic Cooperation in the Agricultural Sector

Economic partnerships between China and Africa in the agricultural sector have become increasingly close, as revealed by the swift growth in agricultural trade volumes and the scale of Chinese investment in agriculture in Africa. China and Africa's economic cooperation in the field of agriculture has become an important part of wider Sino-African relations.

Sino-African Trade Cooperation

Before the 1960s, total trade and agricultural trade between China and Africa were both very small, as the majority of African countries were not independent and were deprived of trade autonomy. Over the next decade or so, Sino-African trade slowly grew, reaching a temporary peak in 1965. Then the trade volume declined, reflecting the political environment of the time, until China's reform and opening up. Sino-African trade decreased in the mid-1980s, then began to rapidly rise after China adjusted its foreign policies. Since the 1990s, Sino-African trade volumes have soared.

From Table 8.6 it can be seen that Sino-African agricultural product trade accounts for a small proportion of China's agricultural trade, but that the share is growing rapidly. Import trade increased from USD189 million in 2000 to USD1.224 billion in 2006, with an annual growth rate of 2.45 per cent. After 2006, the total trade volume of agricultural product imports began to decline. The trade status of Sino-African agricultural products has oscillated: from 2000 to 2003, China posted a decreasing surplus. Between 2004 and 2006, China posted a deficit in farm product trade of USD360 million, USD407 million and then USD333 million. Since 2007, China has reverted to a surplus and posted a trade gap of USD201 million and USD618 million. In 2008, China's agricultural trade surplus with Africa reached a peak.

Among China's agricultural exports to Africa, grain (principally rice) ranks first. In 2000, for example, China exported 1.175 million tons of rice to Africa at a value of USD187 million (39 per cent of total exports). Following rice are green tea, dried beans, peanuts and chicken. China's agricultural imports from Africa are mainly cotton, tobacco and oilseeds. The Sino-African agricultural trade structure is not significantly different from either China or Africa's respective international agricultural trade structures: Africa still needs to import large quantities of grain from China, which creates an opportunity for China to promote agricultural development in Africa. China is not optimistic about its food security situation; Guangdong and Zhejiang provinces have become major rice importing provinces, and thus it is an enormous challenge to continue to increase food exports to Africa. African countries have to use a large share of limited financial capacity to pay for food, which is obviously not conducive to resolving its food security problem. Therefore, how to improve Africa's own food production capacity is crucial for its countries' food security. At the same time, China has been a net grain exporter every year since 1999 except for 2004; its net cereal exports reached 8.354 million tons in 2007. However, China faces shrinking arable land resources, water shortages, frequent disasters, deteriorating arable land quality and other agricultural production challenges including climate change, as well as the hollowing out of rural areas, a trend

TABLE 8.6 China–Africa Agricultural Trade within China's Total Agricultural Trade (unit: USD100 million, %)

		2000	2001	2002	2003	2004	2005	2006	2007	2008
China import	Global	112.57	118.37	124.46	189.36	279.94	287.05	320.8	362.83	560.02
	Africa	1.89	1.87	2.78	5.11	9.22	10.73	12.24	9.35	9.30
	Proportion	1.68	1.58	2.23	2.70	3.29	3.74	3.82	2.58	1.66
	Growth rate	—	0.1	0.65	0.47	0.59	0.45	0.08	−1.24	−0.92
China export	Global	156.94	160.89	178.55	210.7	230.02	272.78	314.15	370.28	508.4
	Africa	4.58	4.27	4.47	6.53	5.62	6.66	8.91	11.36	15.48
	Proportion	2.92	2.64	2.50	3.08	2.44	2.44	2.84	3.07	3.04
	Growth rate	—	−0.28	−0.14	0.58	−0.64	0	0.4	0.23	−0.03

Source: Sun *et al.* (2007); Ministry of Commerce website statistics

for agricultural work to become part-time, ageing and feminization of the rural labour force and other worsening social conditions for agricultural production caused by intensive industrialization and urbanization. Even with increased agricultural science and technology and policy inputs, it is still a severe challenge to ensure the current production level of 500 million kilograms of grain per annum. Coupled with population increase, adjustment of food consumption patterns as well as ever-increasing feed grain and industrial food consumption, overall food demands are growing. Experts predicted that China's grain demand in 2010 would total 525 million tons at least (Yin, 2009) and reach 593 million tons by 2020. Therefore, it is unknown whether China can sustain a net grain export agricultural trade structure and export grain to Africa. If China's grain production cannot maintain the current 95 per cent self-sufficiency rate, it will need to resort to international trade in agricultural products to safeguard its own food security. Therefore, improving agricultural productivity in Africa to spur food self-sufficiency and reduce dependence on international agricultural markets is meaningful as a way of easing China's grain security pressures (Freeman *et al.*, 2008). This is also one of the reasons for China's growing assistance to Africa in recent years.

China's Agricultural Investment in Africa

China's aggregate agricultural investment in Africa is quite low, but adjustment of its Africa aid programme will encourage more enterprises to participate in government-led aid projects such as farm reconstruction and agricultural technology demonstration centre construction and management. First, agricultural investment in Africa makes sense for many Chinese enterprises, given domestic constraints including the current land tenure system and production conditions. Agricultural production in China is costly, whereas Africa has good conditions for agricultural production. Most countries boast rich land resources with cheap lease and purchase prices and long lease periods. In Zambia, for example, land can be leased for 99 years and the rent is quite low (Table 8.7).

TABLE 8.7 Annual Rent of Agricultural Land in Zambia since February 1997 (Unit: ZMK5,000 = USD1)

Land Prices< 20 km in Lusaka, Ndola and Jitewei		Land Prices > 20 km in Lusaka, Ndola and Jitewei	
Area	*Annual Rent (ZMK)*	*Area*	*Annual Rent (ZMK)*
Below 1	30,000	Below 1	20,000
1–50	30,000 + 5,000/ha	1–100	20,000 + 250/ha
50–100	275,000 + 4,000/ha	100–250	44,750 + 500/ha
100–250	475,000 + 2,000/ha	Above 250	119,750 + 1,000/ha
Above 250	775,000 + 1,500/ha		

Source: Z. Huang (2008)

Second, Africa has a huge appetite for agricultural products, and the prices are higher than China. Furthermore, labour costs are very low. The daily wage of a farm worker in Zambia averages only USD 1 to USD2. Although agricultural production inputs such as fertilizer and pesticides are expensive, the profit margin is higher than in China (Table 8.8). The China State Farms Agribusiness Corporation has built up Sino-Zambian Friendship Farms and Sino-Zambian Farms in Zambia. Since 1990, the Corporation has established 10 agricultural and husbandry production and processing projects in Zambia, Guinea Bissau, Tanzania, Gabon, Ghana, Mali, Togo, Mauritania and other African countries. At of the end of the dry season in 2002, it generated a total of 2,120,000 tons of wheat, 1,180,000 tons of corn, 6,000 tons of soybeans, 2 million litres of milk, 2,000 pigs for slaughter and reported an accumulated profit of USD2 million. The Sino Cotton Corporation ran a cotton and textile project in Malawi in 2009 with a total investment of USD19 million, aiming to improve the cotton processing level in Malawi through improving seed quality, ginning, oil pressing and spinning techniques. This is the largest agricultural project that China has ever conducted in Africa to date.[7] The China National Fisheries Corporation has launched 23 fishery projects in 13 African countries, owning more than 450 fishing boats and employing nearly 10,000 labourers, generating more than 400,000 tons of aquatic products annually and reporting high profits.

However, China still lags behind developed countries and even some developing country counterparts in terms of aiding farms or making direct investments. Of 3,000 modern farms run as a business in Zambia, one-third are investments from Europe and the USA, one-third are from South Africa and approximately one-third are from India and Pakistan. Only 18 farms are Chinese investments: these include six state-owned and 12 privately-run farms.

TABLE 8.8 Net Proceeds of Crops in Africa and China (Unit: USD/ha)

	Wheat	Green corn	Soybean
Africa	1000	1500	300
China	260	355	122

Source: Africa: field research; China: Yin (2009).

BOX 8.9 INPUT AND INCOME OF CHINESE-FUNDED FARMS IN ZAMBIA

China-Jiangsu Prospect Company

- land area: 40 hectares
- land price: USD60,000

- development investment: USD300,000
- annual working capital input: USD180,000
- gross profit: USD300,000
- net income: USD 120,000.

Sunlight Limited Company

- land area: 80 hectares
- land price: USD120,000
- development investment: USD700,000
- annual net income: USD150,000.

China–Zambia Friendship Farm

- 400 hectares of reclaimed land, extensive operation
- annual net income: USD400,000.

Source: field investigation

Chinese farms in Zambia have been very successful despite the limited scale of investment. They are not significantly different to farms set up by other investors, and are clearly focused on meeting local market demand. In Zambia, most Chinese farms are either livestock-based (breeding chickens and cows), crop farms (planting maize, wheat and other field crops) and vegetable farms. There are three Chinese vegetable farms selling at Lusaka's Tuesday Market for the poor. Over ten years the China–Zambia Friendship Farm has supplied 2,900,000 trays of eggs, 2,810,000 chickens and retired layers, 2,730,000 litres of fresh milk, more than 1,200 beef cattle and more than 10,000 live pigs to the sideline food markets in Lusaka, and generated a total of 13,227 tons of grain and soybeans. At present, it holds nearly a 20 per cent share of the agricultural and sideline products market in Lusaka, creating jobs for 7,000 people, of whom most are temporary workers in the busy season, and contributing to the food security of 14,000 people.[8] Many foreign investors, particularly those from Europe and the USA, focus on the planting of wheat, roses, tobacco and other cash crops. Some farms also grow vegetables, but target the local high-end market and international markets. Chinese farms are very similar to local small and medium-sized farms in terms of their structure and business model. With low levels of mechanization, they are seen as rivals by local farms, but play a significant role in balancing the prices of agricultural products and increasing overall supply. A woman from the suburbs of Lusaka said thanks to the Chinese farms, as they could buy cheap and good cabbage the whole year round. Moreover, the Chinese farms play an important role in terms of disseminating technologies. A large number of farm workers and surrounding small farmers noted that they have learned a lot of advanced and practical production technologies from their Chinese farm experience.

BOX 8.10 JC'S EXPERIENCE ON CHINESE FARMS

We interviewed workers at China-Jiangsu Prospect Farm and Sunlight Farm (about 10km outside Lusaka City) and neighbouring farmers. JC, having worked with Sunlight Co. Ltd for three years, said that she is allowed to return home to Monze (200km from the farm), in the district of Mwaza in September and October each year. She loves to work on the farm because she can learn some techniques and take maize and soybean varieties and some fertilizer back home, bringing back sweet potatoes to share with her fellow workers as well as the farm managers. She gets along well with the farm managers and understands their difficulties. Knowing that they are hardworking, she tries to help them by working even harder. It is easy to hoe the soybean brought from the farm. Manure is utilized in her local area, but on the farm fertilizer is preferred. They only fertilize maize when it reaches one foot in her hometown, but fertilize it as soon as sowing has taken place on the farm. She welcomes the Chinese farms and hopes more Chinese will come to Africa, as the farm has created work opportunities. She hopes to go to China and learn more agricultural techniques.

Source: Interview at Sunlight Farm, 29 June 2009

Notwithstanding these promising cases, China faces many difficulties when it comes to making investments in Africa due to political instability and weak policy environments, and price fluctuation in agricultural products in the international market. In Zambia, many Chinese farm managers worry that their assets might be confiscated by the government as part of a nationalization policy. They hope that the Chinese and African governments will be able to establish bilateral trade and investment protection mechanisms. However, this is difficult as there are still many privately-run businesses that are not registered locally or with the Chinese Embassy, and therefore lack official status. Moreover, global agricultural product prices fluctuate wildly, and many producers are granted subsidies or protection by the government. Chinese farms in Africa do not have access to these subsidies and are responsible for their own profit and losses, which make them quite vulnerable to price fluctuation in the global market. In Zambia, the highest price for wheat was USD600 per tonne in 2008, but as low as USD350 per tonne in June 2009. Limited and poor-quality infrastructure and storage facilities in Africa also affect Chinese small-to-medium enterprise investment decisions, meaning that most agricultural investment is concentrated in the suburbs near to the cities.

A mature management mechanism for private investment in Africa has yet to be established. Many investors lack in-depth knowledge of African laws, regulations, policies, religions and traditions. These factors as well as language barriers mean that There are some Chinese farms using alternatives to save production costs: for example, by hiring large numbers of part-time workers to avoid making social insurance payments. Although these behaviours follow local laws, they show a kind of opportunism which could mean negative ramifications for China's image in Africa. It is also the case that wages and hours of labour are usually specified in legislation that is based on western models. Many Chinese farms often require substantial overtime work, which can lead to disputes. Salaries and wages can be the lowest locally, despite high work intensity and long hours. Sometimes the number of part-time workers is substantially higher than the number of full-time workers. Therefore, the Chinese government should standardize investment and especially private investment modes, while also encouraging businesses to invest and set up in Africa. It is necessary to strengthen the study of agricultural production conditions, policies, laws and regulations, cultures and traditions in Africa, and to share the results with African partners in order to maximize the benefit of Chinese aid to Africa and enhance strategic economic cooperation.

Most Chinese farms in Africa still follow an extensive management pattern, with production structures similar to local farms and based on primary agricultural products. On the one hand this satisfies local market demand, but on the other, it puts pressure on local competitors and causes problems among local market actors. Therefore, it is important to specify clearly the areas for investment and the appropriate role of Chinese farms in Africa. Making sure that there is adequate space for African countries to develop their own agriculture is critically important when it comes to tackling food security, which is also very important for China's own development.

Conclusion

It is clear that in agriculture, China has been very effective at learning from other countries and actively making use of external support. Introduced technologies have been adapted and promoted through national mobilization. Another factor is, as mentioned previously in this book, that China views agriculture as the foundation of the state and development ('*yinongliguo*'). The intensive nature of production has required technological breakthroughs at different stages in order to maintain the agricultural base and its role in national development. During the Ming and Qing dynasties, rapid population growth forced the Chinese government to constantly open doors to the outside world and make 'foreign things serve China'. Historically, Africa has been rich in natural resources but relatively closed to change. Sufficient land resources have enabled African tribes and social groups to meet their own food needs and intensive agriculture was not necessary, given that migration and extension of the agricultural frontier were effective means to address production constraints. Africa did not need to learn from abroad in the same way as China.

African tribal structures limited technology transfer and dissemination, while the dual structure of agricultural production left behind by colonial powers inhibited the application of modern technologies in the traditional food crop sector of the economy.

China began its communication with the outside world about agricultural development in the nineteenth century. As development based on extensive agriculture came to an end, traditional intensive cultivation could no longer increase the productivity of the land, given the rapid increase of the Chinese population. These factors gave rise to internal demand for improvements in land productivity. It was in such circumstances that western agricultural science and technology, with its industrial features and capacity to promote land and labour productivity, was introduced into China. Therefore, learning from western agricultural education, research and extension systems became essential not only to safeguard food security in China, but also to achieve national prosperity. Conversely, Africa began its exchange with the West much earlier than China; however, western agricultural production systems and technologies were transplanted to Africa without any modification, and could be seen as an extension of western economic systems. Mostly, these technologies were not well integrated into the small farmer production system in Africa; furthermore, the tension between population growth and limited land in Africa has not been a stimulating factor in the way it was in China. The pressing need to improve land productivity found in China has not been so evident in Africa on the whole, although of course there are exceptions. Therefore, it is not surprising that western agricultural technologies have not led to a transformation of traditional African agriculture.

The twentieth century saw notable agricultural development in China, which should be attributed to processes of learning from, and exchange with, the outside world. China built production, research and technology extension systems in the 1950s based on key aspects of the Soviet model, such as its integrated agricultural research and education system. From the 1980s onwards China began to turn to western societies for agricultural development lessons. This led to a reinvention of advanced education, scientific research and extension systems. A solid foundation was built to meet international criteria. It should be noted that a modern agricultural system with Chinese traits has been established through processes of learning from the outside, but by adapting and transforming ideas to fit Chinese circumstances. African countries have received international development assistance since the 1950s and have learned from both the former Soviet Union and western countries. In addition, they have built relatively viable agricultural research and extension systems; however, these systems are not independent and controlled solely by African states, rather they are often dependent on external support. Therefore, a successful agricultural development process cannot be guaranteed because assistance is subject to geopolitical influences and often abrupt changes of priority and strategy by different donors. Consequently, the effectiveness of learning from the outside world is limited.

Both the international community and African countries are paying increasing attention to China's agricultural development experiences. At the same time, China is promoting Sino-African cooperation and development assistance. The development assistance provided by China to Africa has changed from entirely grant-based development assistance to comprehensive economic and technological cooperation, shifting from assistance to investment. A first phase of agricultural assistance focused on the creation of large demonstration farms, which failed to completely achieve their objectives – nevertheless, they provided useful lessons as to how China could support agricultural development in Africa. Field stations and technical experts have helped share development experiences with Africa and this has been an important approach, although this is facing new challenges in terms of how it could be better applied.

The new focus of Chinese aid since 2006 has been the creation of agricultural technology demonstration centres. These aim to share lessons from China's agricultural development experience, such as substituting labour resources for scarce financial and technological resources. China's non-profit farms in Africa have gradually transformed into enterprises. Demonstration centres are being managed by universities and research institutions, or by state enterprises. Aid-recipient countries in Africa should adjust their agricultural, technological and fiscal policies to realize long-term benefits from the operation of the demonstration centres. China's agriculture is evolving from being labour intensive to being both labour and modern input and technology-intensive. This requires that aid-recipient countries strengthen support for research and extension to accommodate Chinese technologies.

Sino-African economic cooperation is growing and attracting interest from the international community. A critical issue for cooperation is how to solve the problem of unbalanced imports and exports through investment in Africa, because China has a favourable trade balance for agricultural produce at present. Another key strategic issue is how to attract Chinese capital into agriculture in Africa, because domestic capital in China, both state and private, is significant. and because the marginal returns to agriculture in China are already minimal while Africa has vast untapped lands and great potential to develop through extensive agriculture. Existing investments from China in African agriculture remain limited, although they have played a vital role in introducing Chinese agricultural technologies and relieving the problem of food shortages in Africa. However, institutional and social challenges remain for Chinese actors operating in Africa and unless these are addressed, investment flows and the impacts of investment will remain sub-optimal.

CONCLUSION

General Results

This study is based on a comparison of agricultural development performance in China and Africa since the 1950s, especially since the late 1970s, as well as comparative analysis of factors affecting agricultural development such as history, policy, investment, science and technology, natural conditions, learning and external support. As mentioned in the Introduction, this study is a normative comparison and not positivist research offering universal conclusions based on quantitative data. Although there are very diverse situations in both China and Africa, this study has not attempted to analyse so much the specific conditions in different agro-ecological and economic zones; rather, it has taken an overall Chinese perspective as a lens to look at a range of agricultural and related issues in African countries, and to identify similarities and differences among issues. The research summarizes evidence from the available literature and field sites.

As we know, despite negative effects such as rural/urban dualism, wealth gaps, land tenure security, environment pollution and resource degradation, it is safe to say that, leveraging market forces and farmers' engagement in different historical periods, the Chinese government has adopted a consistent series of strategies, policies and measures to advance agricultural development. In Africa, despite the existence of some high-yielding and export-oriented modern agricultural enterprises, the continent has never fully succeeded in feeding its booming population. The agriculture sector in Africa also has largely failed to stimulate growth in industrial sectors, although some value chains are now beginning to emerge. Conversely, there has been less pressure on the environment and natural resource base in Africa than in China. The research presented in this volume seeks to provide an explanation of this difference between agricultural performance in China and Africa from historical, social and economic perspectives, taking into account internal and external factors, and allowing for the fact that performance varies greatly within China and African countries; also, that there can be several different farming 'worlds' within the same locality, in both China and Africa.[1]

The agricultural development gap between China and Africa is mainly manifested in a great disparity in land productivity

Chinese agriculture has maintained steady growth over the past 30 years, and this has made an important contribution to its economic development and poverty reduction. Meanwhile, African agriculture has failed to make commensurate progress, and this has been a major impediment to economic growth and poverty reduction. However, we have noted that Chinese agriculture is facing great challenges of sustainable development, while Africa has new opportunities for sustainable development alongside the challenge of food security.

- China has displayed a strong tendency for rapid agricultural development over the past 30 years and the growth rate of agricultural GDP and per-capita GDP has been impressive, but most African countries have experienced stagnation in the agricultural sector.
- Agricultural development makes contributions to the national economy in different ways in China and Africa. China's agricultural policy makes grain security a top priority, and thus agricultural development has been encouraged to the point where a high grain self-sufficiency target has been met. This means that the food supply for China's large population is now basically guaranteed, although there are challenges for the future (as described in this research, see p. 27). Most African countries deem agriculture to be a key source of foreign exchange earnings, and therefore agricultural development in many African states concentrates on the production of export-oriented cash crops, leaving grain self-sufficiency at a very low level, which in turn leads to urgent food security issues and a widening gap between grain demand and supply in the context of rising grain consumption by urban populations. Africa has to import grain from the international market or receive foreign food aid (consisting largely of grain) to meet grain demand.
- Significant agricultural development in China has resulted from increasing productivity based on a mix of traditional agricultural practice and modern technology. This has not happened in Africa on anything like the same scale; in addition, a fast-growing population in Africa compromises the benefit from productivity improvement.
- China's rapid agricultural development, along with accelerated urbanization and industrialization, has resulted in damage to natural resources and the environment, leading to an increasingly difficult situation for further agricultural development.

Distinctive historical legacies in China and Africa have contributed to the current situation and prospects for future agricultural development

From a historical perspective, it can be seen that very different farming heritages contribute part of the explanation for the difference in agricultural achievement between China and Africa.

- China has enjoyed a long history of agricultural development without any major interruptions to agricultural civilization; however, in Africa local agricultural production systems were subject to western colonial interventions in the fifteenth century. These fundamental historical events introduced major discontinuities into Africa's agricultural history.
- Inherited agricultural 'assets' are very different between China and Africa. There is a grain-oriented planting structure in most parts of China; this has fitted well with the requirements for a 'Green Revolution'. However, because of the nature of local crops and cropping systems, Africa has been unable to benefit from wheat or rice-based Green Revolutions, which have not focused on crop priorities for Africa.
- Modern agriculture in China and Africa has emerged from different historical experiences. The continuity in China's traditional agricultural civilization has given rise to a highly adaptable agricultural production system, production structure and set of cultivation methods. The pattern of China's agricultural development has been to increase land productivity by substituting capital inputs with land improvement inputs (including communal labour time) and technology inputs. This intensive cultivation remains suited to the fundamental realities of modern China and is also the foundation of the prevailing small peasant economy within Chinese agriculture. The pioneering style of land development caused by China's long-term population pressure has resulted in enormous challenges for modern agriculture. Meanwhile, Africa's traditional agricultural civilization was interrupted by invasion by European states, which meant that the agricultural production structure and patterns had to change to meet the demands of colonial economic systems. This created a dilemma whereby traditional small peasant economies focused on planting food crops on the African continent could no longer meet food security requirements, while capital-intensive plantation operations focused on the production of cash crops could not effectively create employment opportunities. This situation has exerted strong influence on the development of African agriculture, and these patterns of development have resulted in underutilization of land in some areas, leaving considerable opportunities to expand the agricultural frontier.

The focus of state intervention on ensuring food production may be the main difference between Chinese and African agricultural development strategies and policies

Both the Chinese government and governments in many African countries have seen the future in terms of industrialization and urbanization, while agriculture has been the foundation of the national economy and responsible for providing a surplus for industrialization and urbanization processes. What differs between China and African countries is that China has made food security a basic priority, while ensuring adequate primitive accumulation in the agriculture sector to underpin industrialization and urbanization, which remains central to Chinese agricultural development policies. Specifically, China has set up a package of policy systems and relevant measures to ensure food production-oriented agricultural development including land tenure policies, pricing policies, investment in science and technology, agricultural subsidies and construction of agricultural infrastructure. In contrast, many African countries have treated agriculture as source of export income and financial revenue for central government, giving priority to export-oriented economic crop production and paying less attention to food production and national food security. The absence of endogenous agricultural development strategies has led to a heavy reliance on external support and a weak capacity for developing and implementing agricultural policies. Sadly, agricultural growth in Africa has been stagnating for decades, and only now are domestic and international priorities being reset to address this critical problem.

- In order to ensure primitive accumulation from agriculture to industry and other sectors, the Chinese government has encouraged the prevalence of 'price scissors' and depreciated the price of agricultural produce. To keep production costs low, it organized an agricultural cooperative movement so that a low-cost labour force could substitute for other high-cost production factors. The planned economy also enabled agricultural surplus to be invested directly into industrial production, bypassing the market. China has been gradually adjusting this orientation so that rural areas, farmers and the agricultural system can benefit from industrial and urban development. China is now in a phase of integrated urban–rural development, subsidizing agriculture with industrial profits. The high degree of centralization of state power guarantees policy consistency and continuity during this shift. In comparison with China, in practice African countries have sought to generate capital accumulation for industrialization and urbanization mainly through development of the commodity export sector, both minerals and agricultural raw materials, with minimal value-added, reflecting static comparative advantage. However, this strategy has not resulted in food security and accumulation for industrialization. Instead, economic downturns and unstable societies in Africa have been accompanied by a number of other factors: for example, inadequate foreign exchange and domestic savings to meet balance of payments requirements (with continuing reliance on foreign aid); an elbowing out of small farmer and food crop production; an inability to plan and control the value produced by export-oriented agricultural production; limited support to industry; missing institutions, whether private or public, for mobilizing populations and organizing the labour force needed to generate local economic development; a failure to effectively imitate either western or Chinese approaches; and inconsistency and interruption of development strategies in response to pressure from both international donors and local demands.

- China has a well-developed agricultural administrative system that enables effective implementation of agricultural development strategies and policies. This system allows for easy information and mobilization at the village level and at different levels of government. Meanwhile, the agriculture education, research and extension system coordinated by different agencies has played an important role in the cycle of policy development, experiments, implementation, feedback loops and adjustments in agricultural strategies and policies in China. This system helps to improve responsiveness to the demands of agricultural and rural populations. By contrast, many African countries have never had a hierarchical residential registration system or land tenure system, and national governments have limited sway over society with a limited capacity to mobilize their people. A relatively disadvantaged sector, food production has not held a fundamental place within government organizational systems. Agricultural policies have barely reached dispersed small farmers producing food crops. Capacity to reform and determine strategy, then adjust agricultural policies through critical feedback loops, have been missing for the most part.

- Different policy effects can be identified in China and Africa, where similar agricultural strategies have been implemented through different policies and specific measures. Agriculture in China has contributed a lot to the provision of basic needs as well as the establishment of an industrial base within a short period of time. In this day and age, agriculture in China is a buffer during economic crisis and other emergency incidents by ensuring basic food security. Although in many African countries government functions and basic policies have been reformed more than once, food security has never been realized, and consequently social problems occur repeatedly. Furthermore, as African countries are frequently constrained by internal political structures and incentives and unreliable external conditions, all too often they are incapable of providing sufficient support to agriculture or guaranteeing the implementation and supervision of policies. Quite a few policies, particularly supportive ones, have been merely nominal and difficult to maintain. The adoption of the Comprehensive African Agricultural Development Programme (CAADP) in 2003, and its progressive implementation by more than 30 African states through country compacts, was motivated by African leaders' recognition that these fundamental weaknesses had to be addressed.

- Undoubtedly, agricultural development strategies and policies in China and Africa are instructive in different ways. China has prioritized the development of industry and urban areas for decades, and this can be identified as one of the main causes of numerous social problems in its transition, especially the greater income disparity between urban and rural residents. As mentioned previously, China has emphasized food security and promoted land productivity through a land tenure system which separates ownership and use rights, and a residential registration system which creates a dualistic rural–urban system. However, it has failed to cater to the actual benefits of the rural farming population, which has resulted in problems of surplus and an underemployed labour force when productivity has reached a certain level. Additionally, a high level of investment in agricultural production has given rise to severe ecological problems and degrading natural resources. Offsetting the negative impacts caused by past policies generates huge economic and social costs. As with China, many African governments have sought to extract economic surplus from agriculture to support urbanization and industrialization. Problems such as underemployment, uncontrolled migration, internal colonization and wasted resources also occurred. However, African countries have not been effective at solving these problems. Neither the market nor external economic forces have been able to fundamentally address these issues. It is notable that Africa is endowed with natural resources and great agricultural potential. It may achieve a truly sustainable agriculture through effective policies to manage and develop resources and mobilize society, and the CAADP now constitutes an established framework for such a breakthrough in African agricultural development. The experience of agricultural development in China provides some illuminating lessons deriving from both the similarities and differences in a range of conditions, problems and opportunities.

The high intensity of land utilization in China explains the great disparity in agricultural productivity between the two areas

The extension-type approaches used in China's agricultural development are already experiencing diminishing returns. Meanwhile, in Africa there remains substantial scope for agricultural extension to make a significant contribution to development. China has already formed an agricultural technology and management system that is characterized by intensive cultivation, a strong capacity for disaster reduction and full utilization of natural resources. African states not only often lack adequate technical systems for making full use of natural resources, they also lack comprehensive capacity for effectively controlling disaster events, and so agricultural systems in Africa are relatively fragile.

- China has developed an agricultural production structure that makes full use of land, light and temperature through intensive cultivation, soil conservation, intercropping and other techniques; in many parts of Africa agricultural operations are still extensive, excluding plantations.
- Compared with China, the Sub-Saharan African region has an obvious advantage in the total cultivated area and per-capita cultivated area. The growth

of agriculture in Africa has come mainly from the expansion of cultivated area. Although the total cultivated area in the Sub-Saharan African region has continued to grow since the 1980s, due to rapid population growth the per-capita area of cultivated farmlands in Africa has been on the decline since the 1980s; meanwhile, per-capita agricultural output has been declining.

- Land use for farming in China follows a 'land conservation by land utilization' approach. This helps maintain the balance of water and nutrients on cultivated land, and farmers master associated techniques. In African countries, due to extensive production models and the pressure of population growth on per-capita cultivated area, soil quality has been in decline, which further constrains the enhancement of agricultural production. By contrast, China's modern soil maintenance technologies and traditional experience enables the country to basically maintain and enhance its land fertility. This is potentially highly relevant to African settings.

- Without adequate irrigation as a basic condition for production, fluctuating climate and rainfall have direct impacts on agricultural production volumes. This is the major reason why the African region has relatively low levels of agricultural production. Despite the uneven distribution of climate and rainfall in China, as well as the relatively higher impact of agricultural disasters such as drought, floods and locusts, China has a strong capacity to control these factors, so the losses in agricultural production caused by these natural factors are far less than the average level for the Sub-Saharan Africa region.

- The process of earlier extension development coupled with intensive land use has caused enormous problems in sustainable agricultural development in China. To date, Africa has not suffered from the problems of intensive agriculture that currently trouble China. This is a useful basis for the sustainable development of African agriculture in the future.

China has established a high-investment and high-yield agricultural production system, while Africa remains trapped in a low-investment and low-yield cycle

During the process of Chinese agricultural development, the government's support for the adoption of marketization mechanisms has boosted agricultural production. In Africa, insufficient support from the government and radical market liberalization has left farmers with insufficient access to key resources such as agricultural inputs.

- The big discrepancy in fiscal inputs into agriculture in Africa compared to China leads to differences in investment in agricultural infrastructure, agricultural technology and subsidies, the coverage rate of irrigation facilities, irrigation acreage, production factor inputs and market procurement. Because of land scarcity pressure, China has made efforts in technology substitution for land resources, so input of fertilizer and irrigation have become important factors in agricultural development.

- The main characteristic of China's agricultural input system is to make full use of state-controlled resource mobilization systems to turn labour surplus into capital, substituting for the inadequacy of financial capital. African countries do not have a similar system, so on the one hand, there is an agricultural labour surplus, while on the other hand, overall mobilization of labour resources is ineffective.
- China's progressive marketization provides some guidance for Africa in the deepening of market reforms. Agricultural policy reform, the construction of agricultural product market infrastructure and promotion of agricultural industries are indispensable in the progress of agricultural marketization. Giving priority to agricultural production to foster farmers' purchasing capability and developing markets has been key. In Africa, poor agricultural infrastructure and weaknesses in related industries continue to be bottlenecks for scale effects and access to markets.
- It should be noted that in China, under the guidance of food security-centred agricultural strategies and policies, it is possible to increase the availability of modern material inputs despite relatively limited arable land resources. However, this has made China's agriculture economically expensive and carbon-intensive. To reverse this trend huge additional investment will be needed, but it will be necessary to reduce production, which will result in pressure on international grain markets at a time when significant pressure on these markets is already widely forecast.

Swift agricultural growth in China has been boosted by continual technology innovation and application, while agricultural growth in Africa has been largely confined by relatively low technological capacities

There are obvious differences in agricultural technology adoption and development between China and the African continent. With the impetus of the Green Revolution, China has made significant progress in the use of high-tech, high-yielding and improved varieties and in modern agricultural technology with fertilizer, pesticides and plastic film as core methods. In contrast, the African continent has largely failed to capture the benefits from the Green Revolution due to the failure of research to concentrate on African priorities without considering the complexity of cropping systems or the dominance of minor crops. In recent years, many African countries have improved the varieties and yields of major crops such as rice and cassava with the support of international organizations, but the adoption of improved varieties and modern agricultural production technology remains at a low level. The Forum for Agricultural Research in Africa (FARA), established in 2003, now provides a focal point for the development of integrated national, sub-regional and continental research systems in Africa. Working with CAADP, FARA is filling a critical institutional role that has been missing in African agricultural development so far, as the historical problems identified below so graphically illustrate.

- The Chinese government has made 'developing agriculture relying on technology' a basic strategy for national development, formulated related plans, and given top priority to agricultural technology development. A system involving development objectives, projects, measures, capital and human resource supplies has been established. Africa has formulated agricultural technology development strategies as well, but no specific implementation plans. In addition, many agricultural technology strategies cannot be implemented without significant increases in public expenditure for agriculture. CAADP and FARA are now addressing these problems, as noted previously.

- China and Africa have built up mature agricultural research systems, with public research institutions and universities as major bodies. Thus government-led agricultural research institutions and universities have been the main drivers for agricultural scientific research institutions for both Africa and China. The number of personnel in China's agricultural research institutions is large, and agricultural researchers are concentrated in national and provincial research institutes and agricultural universities. Overall, a cohesive agricultural research and development system exists. By contrast, most African agricultural research institutions are small-scale, with low research capability. A recent report indicates that while this situation is being addressed in a few countries, there are very few centres of excellence, and most African countries have research systems that are not only completely inadequate but in crisis. The World Bank's Consultative Group on International Agricultural Research (CGIAR) system has assisted with strategic research tasks, and World Bank loans for agricultural research, having faltered in the 1990s, are now being expanded via a West Africa agricultural productivity programme and an East Africa agricultural productivity programme for generating and disseminating improved agricultural technologies. In addition, private philanthropic financing and organization is now playing a key role: for example, the Alliance for a Green Revolution in Africa (AGRA) (Beintema and Stads, 2011).

- China's investment in agricultural research mainly comes from national fiscal funds, which increase rapidly year-on-year. With improvement in research institutions' capability for self-help, self-raised funds have been expanding gradually. Africa's agricultural research investment is inadequate, and different countries' funds differ greatly. In a considerable number of states, a large proportion of funds are provided by foreign countries which have made important contributions. However, instability and insecurity in agricultural research funding has been a significant associated problem (Beintema and Stads, 2011).

- Both China and the African continent research crop planting related to food security. The difference is that China not only emphasizes new varieties for cultivation but also production-related technologies such as soil improvement, irrigation, pest and disease control and new field management techniques, so that the entire farming system has improved. Africa has put most of its capital into variety breeding rather than other aspects related to production, which lowers the adaptability of new varieties and slows down the promotion of improved varieties. With a large population and limited land reserves, China has developed a technology system focusing on land productivity improvement. In this way, labour force advantages can be made utmost use of; meanwhile, Africa is unable to form such a system due to basic problems of capital and labour mobilization, and in spite of a land resource advantage.

- China has built a complete agricultural technology extension system, linking government agricultural technology extension agencies, non-governmental organizations (NGOs) and the private sector, as well as multi-oriented and multi-level extension systems. Coupled with effective and stable funding from state and modern agricultural technology transmission facilities, China's agricultural technology promotion abilities constitute a farmer-centred agricultural innovation system with interactions among a wide range of actors in society, which forms a system of mutually reinforcing learning activities at both national and local levels.[2]

- Only a few African countries have national agricultural technology extension systems. As noted previously, most African countries' agricultural extension depends on international assistance and is constrained by economic capacities and infrastructure conditions, which have greatly affected the availability and coverage of agriculture technology promotion. However, there is some recent experience with cluster approaches involving an innovation systems approach, and the Chinese experience is highly relevant to the expansion of this approach in Africa, which will be critical to the modernization of African agriculture as a key to sustainable growth and reducing poverty (see China–DAC Study Group, 2011).

- China's agricultural technology system is not only labour-intensive and technology-intensive, but is also high-input and carbon-intensive, which poses challenges for sustainable development. African agricultural technology systems are linked with low-input, low-carbon agriculture, which is a relatively favourable basis for future sustainable development.

The small farmer production system in China is gradually shaking off the plight of involution, while small farmers in Africa remain trapped in low-investment and low-yield extensive farming systems

Between China and Africa, smallholder family operations dominate the agricultural sector, and the family is the basic unit for allocating agricultural production factors. Differences in agricultural performance between China and Africa are represented by differences in resource allocation, production technology and smallholder market integration.

- In terms of land use, Chinese farmers from different regions make use of land resources to the fullest according to the local climate, seasons, rainfall and other natural resources. In terms of labour distribution and the gender division of labour, after being satisfied with their own food, Chinese farming families take into account the low efficiency of agriculture and make rational choices in labour resource allocation during the organization of family production. Most of the male labour force work off-farm and many women are left at home to engage in agricultural production. This indicates to some degree that China's small farmers are gradually moving from a 'survival ethic', inward-oriented livelihood strategy, to a 'survival rationality' outward-oriented livelihood strategy, and are progressively breaking away from agricultural 'involution'. More importantly, current national policy support for agriculture is reinforced and mobilizes farmers' enthusiasm, hence a benign interaction between small farmers and national agricultural policy comes into being. At the same time, agricultural production information channels have been diversified, including relations between scientific research institutions, government departments, private companies and farmers (in the systems approach described previously). While small farmers are ensuring their own food security, they are also providing a guarantee for national food security. Due to their small landholdings, China's small farmers have weak access to credit for agricultural production, but this does not prevent the high-input trend spreading in agricultural production. China's agriculture is still dominated by small family operations but has moved away from the historical 'low input–low output' peasant economy model. While inheriting traditional farming knowledge and experience, China's small farmers have been actively absorbing the essence of modern agricultural techniques and integrating them by welcoming fertilizer, pesticides and improved varieties, and by employing plastic film technology, mechanical sowing, harvesting and mechanical irrigation technology.

- In contrast, the production of African small farmers is still very extensive and traditional tools predominate. They utilize land resources only partially, leaving the majority of land idle. Moreover, irrigation facilities are absent in most areas and some farming techniques in evidence in China (such as the use of rice seedlings) are not used in agricultural production. Moreover, with little access to production capital, Africa's small farmers suffer a shortage of agricultural production factor inputs (for example, fertilizer, pesticides and weeding technologies), remaining stuck with low land productivity and trapped in a 'low input–low output' vicious cycle. Maintaining family livelihood security relies only on agriculture and farming production activities. Even positioning African small farmers at a 'survival ethic' and 'safety first' development stage, it remains difficult to achieve a sustainable balance with limited resources. Besides, African countries' general under-prioritization of agricultural development has led to the undersupply of agricultural research and technical support, compounding the absence of agricultural subsidy policies to encourage small farmers to break resource constraints. With a large proportion of households still engaged in subsistence agriculture, national food security problems stand out when small-scale food production cannot fulfil household food needs. In the context of small farmer and family farm production, agricultural development and food self-sufficiency are inseparable. China's incorporation of small-scale household production as an important part of the national development strategy should offer inspiration for Africa's agricultural development strategy in relation to the position of small farmers.

Agricultural development in China and Africa have exhibited diverse learning patterns

Another important factor causing the great disparity between China and Africa in agricultural development lies in the differential effects of external communication and utilization of outside support. The ever-growing population and limited land resources have generated strong internal pressure in China to promote agricultural productivity, which happens to be exactly what western modern agricultural technologies can do: therefore, the inner impetus to learn from European and US experiences is generated. Western agricultural technological know-how has been successfully adapted and integrated into the agricultural production system in China via the innovation systems approach. However, no comparable approach has emerged on a widespread basis in Africa. This widespread failure to integrate western agricultural technological knowledge into African local agriculture has made it impossible for the former to exert positive influences on the latter. At the end of the 1980s, when it was apparent that African agriculture was in crisis and in need of modern inputs, the international effort faltered and declined just when China began to draw increasingly on western agricultural knowledge and apply it at the small farmer level in tandem with the marketization process. More recently there have been some important initiatives on new seed varieties that show how new agricultural technologies can transform the situation of small farmers in Africa, but more comprehensive agricultural transformation approaches remain relatively rare.

- China began its communication with the outside world in agricultural devel-opment in the nineteenth century. Development based on extensive agriculture came to an end as traditional cultivation could no longer generate sufficient production per unit of land, with the population in China rising in huge numbers. These factors gave birth to internal demand to improve land produc-tivity further. It was in such circumstances that western agricultural science and technology, supportive of industrialization and able to promote great land and labour productivity, was introduced into China. Therefore, learning from western agricultural education, research and extension has become essential not only to safeguard food security in China, but also to achieve national prosperity. Conversely, Africa had begun communication with western societies in agri-cultural development much earlier than China. However, western agricultural production systems and technologies were transplanted into Africa on a colonial basis, and served as an extension of the western economic system. These production systems failed to integrate small farmer production systems in Africa. Furthermore, the imperative to dramatically increase land productivity seen in

China has not been evident in Africa. Thus it is not surprising that western agricultural technologies have not been able to transform traditional African agriculture.

• The coming of the twentieth century ushered in a period of notable agricultural development in China, which should be attributed to learning from and communication with the outside world. China constructed its production, research and technological extension system in the 1950s, modelled on the system in the former Soviet Union, particularly its integrated agricultural research and education institutions. China has turned to experience from western societies as a source of inspiration for agricultural development since the 1980s. Since then advanced education and scientific research and extension systems in agriculture have been reinvented, and a solid foundation has been built in accordance with international criteria. It should be noted that such a modern agricultural system with Chinese traits has been established through introducing and learning from and adapting lessons from external sources. While African countries have received international development assistance since the 1950s and learned from both the former Soviet Union and western countries, few viable agricultural research and extension systems have been created, and these agricultural research, management and extension systems have not been highly reliant on external support mechanisms. A continuous agricultural development process has not been generated, and inevitably the assistance agenda has been impacted over time by geopolitical structures and tensions, both international and domestic. The key underlying constraints have been the product of unstable objectives for agricultural development and their contribution to the development process overall. Consequently, effective collaboration and learning from the outside world have been restricted to well below the scale needed for transforming African subsistence agriculture. This creates a huge imperative for a major new effort of modernization through innovation. The African Union and international donors are now working to build a new dynamic through the CAADP framework; China's initiatives within the Forum on China–Africa Cooperation (FOCAC) process are also a response to this imperative.

• The international community and African countries are giving growing attention to Chinese agricultural development experiences. At the same time, China is promoting Sino-African cooperation and development assistance. In general, the development assistance provided by China to Africa has moved from grant-based development assistance to comprehensive economic and technological cooperation, ranging from assistance to investment. The large farm pattern approach in the earliest phase failed to achieve its original development goals. Nevertheless, this first attempt by China provided valuable experience as to how it could best support agricultural development in Africa. Field stations and dispatched experts have helped to share development experiences with Africa and remain an important approach for China to assist with agricultural development. This approach is facing new challenges in terms of how it can be better applied, notably by drawing on China's innovation systems approach.

•   Sino-African economic cooperation is growing and generating interest from the international community. A critical issue in cooperation is how to solve the problem of unbalanced imports and exports through stimulating more investment in African agriculture. China has a favourable balance of trade in agricultural produce at present. A key strategic issue here is how to attract Chinese capital into agriculture in Africa: domestic capital in China, national or individual alike, is considerable, and marginal returns to agriculture in China are already falling to minimal levels, while Africa has vast untapped lands and great potential to develop intensive cultivation systems. The existing investment from China to African agriculture remains limited: it has played a vital role in introducing Chinese agricultural technologies and helped to relieve problems of food shortage in Africa, but what should be kept in mind is that investments in Africa have faced a number of challenges from local laws as well as social culture.

Conclusions and Recommendations

In general, the success of Chinese agriculture over the past three decades can be attributed to the long-term national development strategy based on agriculture, the choice of agricultural policies, the application of technological innovations and continual investment in the sector. These experiences and processes are relevant to African agricultural development. The core lesson from China is the importance of the functional integration of government, market and rural households in an interactive and dynamic system, and the role of government is critical: it is very important to have responsible government. Admittedly, the success of Chinese agriculture has been accompanied by various negative consequences, including an imbalance between urban and rural development, income disparity between urban and rural residents, encroachment on farmers' land rights and degrading natural resources. These can be regarded as lessons that Africa should not repeat. Chinese agricultural prospects have been affected by limited land resources, the large population, a changing food structure and growing demands for agricultural produce due to economic growth and deteriorating water resources and natural environment. In comparison with China, African agriculture is endowed with rich natural conditions., but food security is at stake on the continent. Africa has tremendous potential to develop if its states could successfully absorb the lessons gained from western agriculture and other experiences around the world, including recent Latin American and Asian farming innovations, emulating the Chinese innovation systems approach and adopting sustainable development strategies and policies, while shunning the relevant negative aspects of the Chinese experience. The research conclusions and recommendations that follow are based on Chinese experiences and reflect a Chinese perspective on the challenges of African agricultural development.

Africa should make food production its top priority for agricultural development and national development strategies

Agriculture in Africa has great potential, as the continent has a huge deposit of arable land. Utilized lands in most African countries account for fewer than 50 per cent of the total arable land area (although it should be noted that the land that appears unutilized in fact may form part of a range of different types of agricultural or pastoralist systems). Food shortages could be greatly reduced through an increase in land utilization, even if production per unit remains the same. Conversely, production per unit could improve significantly, as land productivity in Africa is surprisingly low at present. With a low level of inputs in agriculture, the marginal return to productive factors is high and on the rise, therefore the comparative benefits are also quite high in regard to the additional inputs to the land. An increase in land productivity alone cannot solve the food shortage problem, but it can save and earn foreign exchange and contribute directly to the deepening of African economies and their capacity to generate employment and value-added. Within the new initiatives for African agricultural development, there should be an important effort to promote grain production. The demand from a growing urban population for grain and grain-based foods is creating a fast growing domestic market in Africa, which at present is being served by imported grains. This represents a major growth opportunity for African farmers. It is highly recommended that China provide necessary technical support to African countries in this regard, because China has rich experience in developing and implementing food-production-oriented agricultural development strategies and policies. China should provide more of this knowledge and experience in more comprehensive assistance packages, with impact at the local level at the core of an expanded effort to promote African grain production in China's portfolio of development aid to Africa, and economic cooperation with Africa.[3]

The dual structure of African agriculture should be adjusted and rebuilt, developing specialized agricultural production zones

In most African countries, a dualistic agricultural production structure exists that is composed of a small farmer food production system that remains for the most part relatively underdeveloped and barely self-sufficient at the household level, although with some emerging examples of commercialization and an economic crop production system that are relatively more modern, and with some emerging success stories. However, many areas still face productivity and organizational challenges. Modern management and techniques have not been successfully integrated into the small farmer production system, although there are several exceptional cases in cotton and coffee production and cut flowers. African countries can make the best use of the strategic coordination mechanisms in the African Union – which is working together with regional economic commissions supported by the African Development Bank and the United Nations Economic Commission for Africa – to conduct regional agro-eco zoning and agricultural development planning, into which African countries would be incorporated according to their climate and natural endowments. A scaled-up agricultural system based on such zoning, including different crop belts, can then be supported through various regional development mechanisms, so that Africa can take the full advantage of local land conditions, rainfall patterns and climatic resources for agriculture, just like China. Grain production would be a key element of this strategy, which could set in motion an induced adjustment of African agricultural structure in conjunction with the agricultural innovation systems approach outlined above. With the African Union and its partner organizations already conducting technical work along these lines, it is recommended that international development agencies and the Chinese government work to support this planning process.

Enhancing local capacity to develop and implement agricultural development strategies is the key to promoting the development of African agriculture

As with China, Africa has developed different agricultural development strategies and policies during different periods. These have reflected the interests of both African governments and international organizations. However, donor agendas and local strategies have not been well integrated, and local strategies could not be put into practice due to insufficient funds and weak implementation capabilities. This explains why a consistent strategic policy system could not be established when the general framework was heavily dependent on fragmented and unreliable external development assistance. Although there is no evidence for showing what would have happened without donor assistance, the historical data show that external support could not be internalized as a domestic development agency in many African countries. The Chinese experience demonstrates that a strategic policy system will not work unless it fits with the basic situation in the country, and can be implemented with national resources and evolving national capacity. This experience also shows that the key to promoting agricultural development lies in implementing strategies and polices for the agricultural sector and coherence in overall macro-economic and structural policies. International development organizations along with China should not only help Africa to constitute various strategies and policies, but also focus on how to promote local capacity to implement policies. This involves capacity for policy development and implementation within government as well as think tank-type organizations. International development agencies and China could jointly sponsor capacity-building for agricultural policymaking and implementation; of course, this will only be effective if there is sufficient buy-in from African countries.

Current agricultural production systems in Africa underuse natural resources. An important way to improve food production is to enhance land and other resource utilization through promoting appropriate multiple cropping

Africa possesses outstanding physical and natural foundations for agricultural development: these include fertile land, desirable sunshine and temperature, which make it possible to develop annual multiple-cropping systems. The production per unit of land could be markedly improved if Africans could learn from Chinese experiences with multiple-cropping, and achieve an increase in the cropping index and land productivity. However, achieving these goals is hindered by insufficient labour incentives, inadequate agricultural investment and low mechanization levels. Another approach is to develop the way in which the available labour can be transformed into capital under present conditions. An important aspect of the Chinese experience has been the effective utilization of human resources for agricultural development over long periods of time, compensating for shortages in monetary capital. Africa can share with China how the multiple-cropping system can be developed within existing Sino-Africa development cooperation, especially within the programme of Sino-African agricultural technology demonstration centres and technical assistance.

The main factor constraining the development of African agriculture is insufficient investment: one possible solution involves overcoming the dilemma of labour surplus and investment insufficiency

Inadequate investment in African agriculture can be attributed to a lack of inputs and structural problems. Most African countries have long been unable to mobilize domestic finance for development, and have had to rely on foreign assistance and investment for agricultural inputs. The problem is that additional foreign investment cannot be attracted for agricultural development in Africa if unstable political situations and constant uncertainty in the flow and direction of international development financing prevail. Therefore, it is fundamental to establish a stable African system for financing agricultural development, as the CAADP is attempting to do via targets for public expenditure on agriculture. Meanwhile, the international community has pledged a large amount of assistance, but disbursement arrangements remain highly uncertain. The African Development Bank could have a vital role to play: in terms of agricultural investment, priority could be given to agricultural infrastructure, especially irrigation systems, capital construction on farmland, agricultural storage systems and market development. In addition, agro-industry in Africa is extremely weak, and the high price of chemical fertilizer is an important factor constraining the development of African agriculture. Therefore, it is highly advisable for African countries to put agricultural infrastructure and agro-industry at the top of the list for agricultural investment, with development of irrigation systems and the fertilizer industry as priorities. China's experience in the mass construction of mini-irrigation systems in rural communities, drainage basins and water collection innovations at the household level can be used as a reference for African countries. The ongoing Sino-African agricultural technology demonstration centres can develop joint research agendas to adapt and redevelop technology in order to make the technology more suitable for Africa. Furthermore, in African countries labour is still far from full employment, although the labour supply is limited by various factors including malnutrition, ill-health and hunger. 'Food for work' programmes in China could be studied by African policymakers in order to compensate for insufficient agricultural investment, as intensive agriculture promotes employment. Given the dilemma of labour surplus and investment insufficiency in African agriculture, Africa should raise expectations about income and employment opportunities in the agricultural sector in order to attract labour into rural investment and enterprises, similar to China's 'food for work' programme and its other rural development incentive schemes.

An essential approach for the development of African agriculture is to strengthen local research and development capacity in agriculture

Unlike China, most African countries have never developed full capabilities in systematic research and development in agriculture. Agricultural research and development has to depend on external support because of this weak research and development (R&D) foundation and a failure to attract and keep sufficient numbers of talented or qualified individuals. Hence it has become essential for African countries to coordinate external assistance organizations to support African agricultural R&D. The key to integrating external resources rests on how to integrate numerous assistance projects into local research and innovation systems. With a few notable exceptions, the capacity of African research agencies and staff is weak. Often, independent project management offices have been set up with foreign aid programmes to promote operational efficiency, and although research projects and institutes have been set up by various assistance organizations, contributing greatly to African agricultural research and development, they have failed to establish close relationships with local development agenda in African countries. Inappropriate aid is one of the main reasons for dependence on aid. Independent organizations have even weakened local capacities in R&D as their relatively high salaries encourage many of the most talented individuals to move outside the state system. Low salaries in local research institutions are now being increased in order to retain and recruit more researchers (Beintema and Stads, 2011).

With new activity and prospects in agricultural research and technology in Africa now visible, including important external actors, African countries could consider developing relevant policies and statutes to ensure that a dynamic, locally driven African agricultural innovation system emerges, linked closely to small farmers' needs and commercializing their activities. This could involve setting up priority lists for national R&D, stipulating that external support coordinates with local research institutes in principle, and that external assistance accords with clearly set-out national priorities and contributes to an agricultural innovation systems approach. China's agricultural technology demonstration centres, which are being expanded in Africa, face the same challenge and should not repeat past errors. Agro-industry enterprises' research and technology dissemination efforts, including foreign enterprises, also can be harnessed and encouraged in an agricultural innovation systems approach, as they have been in China.

The foundation for developing African agriculture is the transformation of small farmer production systems

Just like China, African agriculture is dominated by small farmer production systems. According to past experiences in China, agricultural policies, investments as well as the extension and application of agricultural science and technology should be geared towards the ever-increasing productivity of small-holder systems and their incorporation into growing agricultural markets, locally, nationally, continentally and globally. This means that Africa needs a plan to reconstruct small farmer production systems: this requires dissemination of agricultural policy, investment and technology at the household level. The reality in Africa is that despite small farmers being the backbone of African agriculture, they find it difficult to obtain direct benefits from favourable agricultural policies, inputs, technological extension and external support. African countries can share their experiences with China regarding technology transfer, training, information services and technological extension at village or even household level. All these measures have been used to invigorate small farmer production systems in China, and this agricultural innovation systems approach through extension could become an important part of Sino-African cooperation.

Africa needs to develop an agricultural technology approach appropriate to the continent

Political, economic, social and cultural conditions in Africa differ greatly from western societies and China, therefore agricultural development in Africa cannot imitate either of them indiscriminately. The agricultural technology pattern in western societies is based on a high-investment and high-output model featuring substitution of labour with intensive capital, while China has a labour-intensive agricultural sector where labour substitutes for capital and land. However, Africa is deficient in both capital and labour relative to its vast arable land area. It needs to develop technologies to substitute labour as well as capital, particularly the latter. One main option might be to improve production through irrigation systems and greater application of fertilizer, alongside expansion into underused lands. A number of capital-substitutive technologies in China might be adapted and adjusted to fit with the situation in Africa.

The pivotal issue for effective support to African agriculture lies in how to gradually transplant external support for local production systems and develop an effective learning process

To date, management ideas and technology introduced through exchanges between Africa, the West and China have not had the transformational impacts for which many have hoped: how to transfer external support into internal innovation is critical. In order to do this, African countries need to develop effective learning mechanisms. Faced with severe problems in food security and poverty, African farmers, leaders and society as a whole have a strong desire to learn from others' experiences, which emanates from an internal motivation to change an impoverished situation. As with China, Africans will definitely need to set up a system to absorb management and technologies in ways that cohere with local culture and social dynamics. This will require realistic strategies based on good governance as well as international support. For Africa as well as China, direct technology transfer from external sources requires prudence: to be more specific, agricultural technologies have been bred in social, economic and cultural conditions in China and may not always be directly useful in Africa without modification. China should assist Africans to adapt and localize these technologies.

As part of developing the agricultural innovation systems approach, Sino-African agricultural technology demonstration centres can be a base for adapting and reconstructing Chinese agricultural techniques in Africa. The centres should focus on research, application and extension of suitable agricultural technologies. Three districts should be set up around the centres: i.e. an innovation district, a demonstration district and a dissemination district. The centres should work together with African countries, local governments and rural communities to define respective responsibilities for the districts, and must coordinate with local African research institutes and international actors such as CGIAR. It is recommended that a systematic mechanism be established for the collaboration of research institutes in Africa and China after these centres begin to operate. This mechanism could include a cooperation advisory committee and cooperative working groups in different areas in the countries where China has centres. The centres should draw on lessons learned by international organizations in their agricultural aid operations in Africa, as CGIAR centres have a wealth of experience on the continent. Close cooperation with these centres will be important for this new form of Chinese agricultural aid in Africa.

Lessons learned by China from its agricultural aid to Africa can be instructive for international development agencies and western agricultural aid to Africa

China has a long history of agricultural aid to Africa. Aid policies have been adjusted to accommodate changing circumstances and avoid dependence on aid. First, at the beginning of agricultural aid to Africa in the 1960s, China provided a package of agricultural technology and equipment and tried to copy its system of agricultural research and extension in Africa, but with limited success. Based on these lessons and further domestic experience following economic reforms, China turned the technological and knowledge dissemination packages into an enterprise-based system with favourable impacts. Joint ventures with aid-recipient countries promote African agricultural development in a sustainable manner. Second, Chinese experts familiar with practical farm technologies and field situations should be selected to work in Africa. Ideally they should be familiar with the type of resources and agro-ecosystems in the partner African country: with such a background, Chinese experts can quickly make progress in their cooperation with African counterparts. These experts are less costly and have been working in rural China, especially in poor rural areas similar to Africa, so it is relatively easy for them to transfer to this environment. Crucially, they have acquired experience of working in the systems approach to agricultural innovation, building linkages between a whole range of actors and local and international institutions. Therefore, it is recommended that international development agencies work with China to experiment with a trilateral cooperation model, in which international development agencies provide funds and China provides experts within the African country agricultural compacts, and innovation strategies and African-level planning for agricultural development across borders. This will be a win-win approach for foreign aid to Africa.

APPENDIX: NOTES ON SOME FURTHER KEY POLICY ISSUES

Incentive Structures, Land Rights and Sustainability

African countries must formulate supporting policies to balance the agricultural prices system structure

As developing countries, China and African nations have not been able to sidestep the phase where agriculture provides massive primitive accumulation for the whole economy. For a long time, a strategy which has given precedence to urban and industrial development has been one of the causes of various social tensions and distress in the transition period in China, in particular the income gap between urban and rural areas and between different regions. 'Price scissors' between industrial and agricultural products is a policy-driven problem that has existed in the Chinese industrial and agricultural price system for a long time. It is estimated that the Chinese government probably obtained USD303 billion[1] (CNY510 billion) through price scissors between industrial and agricultural products from 1950 to 1978, and USD58 billion (CNY97.8 billion) of agricultural tax revenue and USD94 billion (CNY157.7 billion) of financial support for agriculture over the same period. At the same time, the Chinese government has extracted USD267 billion (CNY450 billion) of net agricultural surplus through the collection system. Before the reform, the average net capital outflow from the agricultural sector is estimated to have been USD9 billion (CNY15.5 billion) each year (Guo, 2005). At that time, the price scissors strategy, which kept down agricultural product prices to ensure the low cost of industrial inputs in China sacrificed peasants' economic interests in order to promote advancement of the whole national economy. Of course, when agricultural production and macroeconomic aggregates increased to a certain extent, many agricultural and rural issues became exposed gradually, and the gap between urban and rural enlarged very visibly. Faced with this crisis, the Chinese government abolished the grain tax, which had lasted thousands of years. With economic reform and tangible efforts in family farm and food crop production, the agricultural development strategy began to lean towards peasants' interests. In addition, the government has issued many policies that provide more agricultural support and allowances, so that peasants have had more incentives and initiative. Similarly, for Africa after independence, the development of industrialization was commonly seen as requiring support from agriculture, and so African governments have imposed explicit and implicit taxes on agriculture in different periods, especially on the export of agricultural commodities. More recently, in order to attract investments in agriculture, especially for the diversification of agricultural exports and development of commercial agriculture, there has been a trend towards providing a large number of preferential measures. However, the incentive structure gives no consideration to the interests of a large number of small farmers and peasants who are engaged in subsistence farming; indeed, these populations seem to be estranged from national agricultural policy. Therefore, African countries need to pay attention to promote the interests and potential of subsistence farmers and small farm enterprises in formulating agricultural development policy and strategy, otherwise the gap between urban and rural areas will become increasingly serious, and the sustainability of rural and agricultural development severely compromised. The impact of new incentives has been apparent recently in Africa in the case of Malawi, which introduced input subsidies for seeds and fertilizer, and in a different form in Ethiopia, where a new commodities exchange has spread price information throughout the country and provided rapid cash settlement services for small farmers.

African countries need to secure smallholders' legal rights and interests in land policies

Within the context of a sparse population, abundant land resources and complex land systems, the urbanization process in Africa highlights the problem of smallholders' land property rights. In China, the relationship between human and land resources have always been strained throughout a long history; moreover, this conflict became more and more serious with the urbanization process. While separation between ownership and the use rights of land, and between urban and rural areas, continuously promoted land productivity to some extent, it has failed to secure equitable development in both urban and rural areas. During the last 50 years, the provisions governing land ownership have experienced several changes. Land reform in the early 1950s gave peasants land ownership, but before long this property right dissipated with the implementation of advanced social and People's Communes. Then a subsequent, irrational process of land collectivization was promulgated in the mid-1950s. About 25 years later, with the sudden advent of the Household Responsibility System, householders in Chinese rural areas established the right to contract and use land once again, although this system was largely informal and ownership remained with the collectives. In the 1990s, the large-scale urbanization process mainly promoted by local governments led to an increasing number of households losing their land rights.

In the era of reform and opening up, a large amount of cultivated land was occupied for urban use. In order to protect farmland and promote well-balanced land use in urban and rural areas, the Chinese government strengthened the land tenure system. The 1998 amendments to the Land Management Law formalized the land use control system. This gave the government an important institutional tool to implement land-use planning and land-transfer controls, combining the Land Acquisition and Land Use Regulation systems. According to the law, apart from land for township enterprises, public welfare undertakings in rural areas or farmers' homesteads, all other farmland usage must receive permission from the state, whether for public purposes such as infrastructure construction, or for private purposes, such as real estate development. With the population growth mode changing and large numbers of rural people moving into urban areas through these years, the rural population fell into a declining trend after reaching a peak (859 million) in 1995. By 2001, this number fell to 796 million people, and the growth rate of rural households slowed down. All of these trends provide conditions for stabilizing rural land ownership. While we can count on these trends and the promulgation of relevant laws (such as the Law on Rural Land Contract of 2003) to eventually solve the contradiction between human and land resources, land reallocations within rural communities cannot be eliminated within a short time. In addition, the land transfer supply stimulated by labour mobility cannot meet present demand. In this situation, collective economic organizations will be driven by particular interests, and it is attractive for them to require householders to 'transfer' their land, even where this violates householders' land property rights. In brief, the main reason for the insecurity of peasants' rights in this regard is the lack of actual ownership on the ground, which has resulted in the unclear legal status of rural land and instability of land rights. The collective does not effectively protect peasants' rights of utilization, alienation and benefit from land. This situation provides some lessons for managing agricultural development and urbanization of Africa, so that hopefully the problem of land ownership in China will not be repeated in Africa. African countries need to secure the lawful rights and interests of small householders in land policies in order to ensure effective agricultural development and equitable societies.

African countries need to attach importance to protecting resources and realizing sustainable agricultural development

In China, long-term tensions between population dynamics and land use have accelerated the tradition of intensive farming. On the one hand, this intensification mode can greatly increase land productivity, while on the other, it can lead to over-cultivation of forests, grasslands and wetlands and a series of environmental problems. Agricultural production in China has moved to a high-input and high-output mode with the development of modern agrarian technology. As a result, enormous inputs of chemical fertilizer and pesticides have caused serious environmental pollution. Among the 40 million hectares (0.54 billion mu) of natural grassland in Qinghai Province, 90 per cent has been moderately degraded. For the rural households that live in Jilin Xianghai National Nature Reserve at Kerqing Sandy Land, the underground water level has lowered by nearly 20 metres in the last ten years. By the end of 2006, China had cumulatively invested more than USD16.67 billion (CNY130 billion) into the project of restoring reclaimed land into forest, and another USD28.3 billion (CNY206.6 billion) was added in 2007 when the project period was prolonged. At the same time, investment in protecting natural forest resources has added up to USD12.96 billion (CNY94.58 billion) since the initiation of this project in 1998. The cumulative investment in the project of sandstorm source control and grassland restoration in Beijing and Tianjin, which was initiated in 2000, has reached USD89.3 million (CNY6.52 billion). There is a high price to pay in managing this order of environmental damage from excesses in land-use, which should be recognized by African countries.

Without question, China has to reverse the negative impacts of previous agrarian development strategies and policies at considerable economic and social cost. Compared with China, most African countries have abundant land resource stocks and huge potential for agricultural production. They can proceed with resource allocation and social mobilization in a more effective way, and better realize sustainable agricultural development through learning lessons from China's experience.

NOTES

Introduction

1. Source: PovcalNet, World Bank.
2. There are now 54 states since the Republic of South Sudan gained independence on 9 July 2011.

1 Agricultural Development in China and Africa: An Overview

1. The *World Development Report 2008: Agriculture for Development* (World Bank, 2008) divided all countries in the world into three categories: traditional agricultural countries, transforming countries and urbanized countries.
2. The FAO recommends three measurements for grain security: (1) the state's grain self-sufficiency ratio must reach more than 95 per cent; (2) per-capita grain production should reach more than 400kg; and (3) the grain reserve should reach 18 per cent of grain consumption for the current year, with 14 per cent denoting a red line, suggesting serious vulnerability.

2 Agricultural Development in China and Africa in Historical Perspective

1. Source: Interview with Economic and Commercial Counsellor's Office, Embassy of the People's Republic of China in Zambia, June 2009.

3 Comparison of Strategies and Policies for the Development of Agriculture in China and Africa

1. A key policy document published annually often focusing on rural areas.
2. The dominant assumption underlying the mainstream focus on the African policy environment is simple: Africa's economic crisis was, in origin, primarily the product of accumulated policy distortions built up since independence in the 1960s (World Bank, 1981; Bates, 1981). Overcoming the crisis required wholesale revisiting of the policy

environment to eliminate the distortions that hampered economic growth and discouraged private initiative. This perception of the root of the African economic crisis, first popularized by the Berg Report (World Bank, 1981), was soon to be codified into the ubiquitous structural adjustment programmes that the IMF and the World Bank encouraged African countries to adopt throughout the 1980s and 1990s. Indeed, under the banner of 'getting prices right', structural adjustment became the main overarching framework within which different efforts have been made to improve the African policy environment.

3. The first leap was the Household Responsibility System – except in terms of buying, selling and titled ownership – given from agriculture labour organizations to individual families. In effect, the pre-revolutionary system was restored, with the state holding claim to part of the crop instead of the landlord. The second leap was 'agricultural scale benefit', whose main goal was to transform traditional agriculture into modern agriculture.

4. In 2008, the total area of fallow land in the world was 57.808 million hectares, of which 11.281 million hectares existed in Africa (source: FAOSTAT).

5. See, for Zimbabwe, Gumbo et al. (2001), for Kenya, Sinha (1984) and Kenyan Social Watch Coalition (2004). For Côte d'Ivoire and Burundi, landless returnees are the most vulnerable groups, according to the observations of many international organizations, such as the United Nations. For Namibia, see Karuuombe (2003).

6. Egypt, Ethiopia, Kenya, Sudan, Tanzania, Uganda, Madagascar, Mozambique, South Africa, Zambia, Zimbabwe, Cameroon, Côte d'Ivoire, Ghana, Nigeria, Senegal, Benin, Burkina Faso, Chad, Mali and Togo.

7. Source: Alliance for a Green Revolution in Africa, http://www.agra-alliance.org (accessed 23 January 2012).

8. Jiao Jinpu's speech in the Asia Regional and Rural Financial Forum, 4 December 2006: http://bank.stockstar.com/SS2006120430502181.shtml.

4 Comparison of Agricultural Production Conditions in China and Africa

1. According to the regulations specified in the Land Administration Law and the Land Classification issued by the Ministry of Land and Resources, 'agricultural land' means the land used for agricultural production, including farmland, gardens, forests and for other agricultural use. 'Arable area' means land that can be used for cultivation, including current farmland and wasteland, but not land required to be returned to forest and pasture due to their sloping nature and severe soil loss. 'Farmland' means land for crops, including cultivated lands, newly developed reclaimed lands, fallow lands, rotating retirement lands, grass farm rotation land, the lands mainly planted with crops with some fruit trees, mulberry or other trees inbetween, and developed lowlands and shallows capable of harvesting one season in every year. Farmland also consists of ditches, roads and ridges with a length of <1.0m in the south, and <2.0m in the north, including irrigated rice paddies, fields on hilltops, irrigable land, dryland and vegetable fields.

2. According to the World Bank's definition, there are 48 countries in Sub-Saharan Africa. In this study, we primarily focus on 46 of them (excluding South Africa and Nigeria).

3. Source: http://www.cpirc.org.cn/news/rkxw_gn_detail.asp?id=10595.

4. Source: www.forestry.gov.cn.

5. Estimations made based on 1km² of cultivated land indicate that each hectare of cultivated land contains approximately 660kg of nitrogen, 75kg of phosphorus and 450kg of potassium. By comparison, each hectare of arable land in North America during the same period includes 2,000kg of nitrogen, 700kg of phosphorus and 1,000kg of potassium (Source: UNU–INRA/World Bank, 1999).

6. Source: FAO, 2006; AQUASTAT database: http://www.fao.org/ag/aquastat (AQUASTAT is the FAO's Information System on Water and Agriculture).

7. We take Tengxian County, Guangxi Province as the comparison object, because the precipitation situation in the region of Wuzhou, Guangxi is similar to that in Chongwe

District, with the average precipitation reaching 254mm in June and 32mm in December, the month with the lowest precipitation (mean values of the data from 1 January 1951 to 31 December 2008 from: http://php.weather.sina.com.cn/search.php?c=1&city= 梧州&dpc=1).

8. Source: http://www.fao.org/nr/water/aquastat/investment/index.stm.
9. We selected the projects, year of project and irrigation technology by considering the available and comparable data.

5 Comparison of Agricultural Production Inputs in China and Africa

1. According to our investigations in Liberia, Tanzania and Zambia in June–September 2009, small farmers are more interested in fertilizer than other factors such as seeds and pesticides which are easier to procure than fertilizer. In light of the urgent need to lift grain output, increasing appropriate fertilizer use is critical.

6 Comparison of Agricultural Technology Development in China and Africa

1. Source: http://www.naro.go.ug.
2. Source: Agricultural Scientific Research Investment Status of Developing Countries.
3. FECC Investigation Report on Agriculture of Sierra Leone: http://www.fecc.agri. gov.cn/.
4. Source: Annual Report of the Bank of Sierra Leone.
5. Source: NFIS website: http://www.nafis.go.ke/.

7 Comparison of Agricultural Production at the Household Level in China and Africa

1. Chinese experts told the authors that from 2005 onwards, the Chinese government has cooperated with the University of Liberia and sent five agricultural experts to teach at the Department of Agronomy on Chinese farming techniques and hybrid rice cultivation techniques. The climate of southern China (especially Hainan Island) is very similar to Liberia's, thus China's hybrid rice has strong adaptability in Liberia and can be grown for three-quarters of the year. However, Liberian farmers usually plant for only one-quarter (May–October), which shortens the production season. If Liberian farmers could grow rice for three-quarters of the year (using spacing typically 20cm x 20cm), output would increase substantially even without the use of chemical fertilizer.
2. The above data concerning Baisha County come from the *Hainan Yearbook* 1996–2005; Fulong village statistics are from a Fulong Government statistics report, 1 March 2006.
3. In 2007, China's rural migrant labour force reached 126 million, and the township enterprise employees 150 million. With the overlapping part deducted, rural migrant workers amounted to 225 million in 2007 (source: former Minister of Agriculture, Sun Zhengcai).
4. However, because of cultural diversity and regional differences in China, women dominate the migrant force in some areas. For example, in some villages in Lincang in Yunnan, women find jobs more easily in domestic service and other industries, while men are accustomed to making decisions rather than engaging in labouring activities, and could not bear the hardship of taking outside work. Therefore, young women constitute the majority of the migrant workforce.
5. Here, the heavily forested countries in Africa are distributed between 10° latitude north and south of the Equator. The temperature is high and is rainy all year round in such

countries (the monthly average temperature is between 25° and 28°, with annual precipitation up to 2,000–5,000mm).
6. 'Vulnerability' here means individuals or families that encounter certain risks to their livelihood more easily, and as a consequence can suffer loss of wealth and a decline in quality of life (see Han, 2001).
7. See: http://www.baidu.com.

8 Learning and External Support for Agricultural Development in China and Africa

1. Michurin made a major contribution to the development of genetics, especially in the field of pomology. Michurin studied aspects of heredity in connection with the natural course of ontogenesis and external influence, creating a whole new concept of predominance. He proved that predominance depends on heredity, ontogenesis and phylogenesis of the initial cell structure and on individual features of hybrids and conditions of cultivation. In his works, he assumed the possibility of changing genotype under external influence. Michurin was one of the founding fathers of scientific agricultural selection: he worked on hybridization of plants of similar and different origins, cultivating methods in connection with the natural course of ontogenesis, directing the process of predominance, evaluation and selection of seedlings, and accelerating the process of selection with the help of physical and chemical factors.
2. From the African Smallholder Farmers Group Report, 2010: see http://www.practical action.org.
3. Source: Embassy of Japan in China website: http://www.cn.emb-japan.go.jp/oda.htm.
4. An official forum between the PRC and African states. There have been four summits held to date, with the most recent meeting on 8–9 November 2009 in Sharm el-Sheikh, Egypt. Previous summits were held in October 2000 in Beijing, December 2003 in Addis Ababa and November 2006 in Beijing.
5. Source: West Africa Division, Ministry of Commerce, 2006.
6. Source: China Agricultural University.
7. Sino-Africa Development Fund website, 'Memorabilia': http://www.cadfund.com/cn/Column.asp?ColumnId=12
8. Source: interviews with staff from the farm.

Conclusion

1. OECD/DAC POVNET 2005 publication on agriculture regarding the various farming worlds – from commercial exporters of niche products such as cut flowers, high-grade coffee, etc. to traditional crop growers and plantations, to small farmers supplying local markets, to subsistence farmers to landless peasants.
2. For the concept of an agricultural innovation system, see Juma (2011). See Chapter 3 in Juma (2011) for a description of China's agricultural innovation system in action in the Shouguang Vegetable Cluster in Shandong Province as it has evolved through the last three decades.
3. The exchange rate of USD to CNY used for 1978, 2006 and 2007 is 1.684, 7.8 and 7.3, respectively.

Appendix: Notes on Some Further Key Policy Issues

1. The exchange rate of USD/CNY used for 1978, 2006 and 2007 respectively is 1.684, 7.8, and 7.3.

BIBLIOGRAPHY

Abugre, C (nd) 'Partners, Collaborators or Patron-Clients: Defining Relationships in the Aid Industry', mimeo.

Africa Investment Website, 'Agricultural Policy in Zimbabwe', http://www.invest.net.cn/club/nongye/chyzhc/jbbwchyzhc.htm/ (accessed 20 July 2009).

African Development Bank (2007) 'Framework for the Establishment of the Africa Fertilizer Financing Mechanism', http://www.afdb.org/fileadmin/uploads/afdb/Documents/Policy-Documents/10000033-en-framework-for-the-establishment-of-the-africa-fertilizer-financing-mechanism.pdf (accessed 20 July 2009).

Ai, Z. and Lu, T. (1995) 'Preface', in He F. and Ning S. (eds) *General History of Africa*, East China Normal University Press, Shanghai, pp. 1–2.

Ai, Z., Lu, T. and Ning S. (1995) *General History of Africa*, Huadong Normal University Press, Shanghai.

Ajao, O.A. (2008) 'Empirical Analysis of Agricultural Productivity Growth in Sub-Sahara Africa: 1961–2003', http://www.afdb.org/fileadmin/uploads/afdb/Documents/Knowledge/30753777-EN-2.2.3-AJAO.PDF (accessed 15 October 2010).

Alene, A. and Coulibaly, O. (2009) 'The Impact of Agricultural Research on Productivity and Poverty in Sub-Saharan Africa', *Food Policy* 34(2): 198–209.

Alston, J. M., Chan-Kang, C., Marra, M. C., Pardey, P. G and Tj, W. (2000) 'A Meta-analysis of Rates of Return to Agricultural R&D: Ex Pede Herculem?', International Food Policy Research Institute (IFPRI) Research Report 113, IFPRI, Washington, DC.

Alston, J. M., Pardey, P. G. and Smith, V. H. (eds) (1999) *Paying For Agricultural Productivity*, Johns Hopkins University Press, Baltimore, MD.

Anderson, K. and Masters W. A. (2008) 'Distortions to Agricultural Incentives in Africa', in Anderson, K. and W.A. Masters (eds) *Distortions to Agricultural Incentives in Africa*, World Bank, Washington DC, pp. 3–67.

Anríquez, G. (2007) 'Long-Term Rural Demographic Trends', ESA Working Paper No. 07–19, May, http://www.fao.org/es/esa (accessed 15 November 2009).

Anríquez, G. and Stloukal, L. (2008) 'Rural Population Change in Developing Countries: Lessons for Policymaking', ESA Working Paper No. 08–09, November, http://www.fao.org/es/esa (accessed 15 November 2009).

Asiema, J. (1994) 'Africa's Green Revolution', *Biotechnology and Development Monitor* 19: 17–18.

Australian Agency for International Development (AusAID) (2008) *Food Security in Africa: Toward a Support Strategy for Australia*, Government of Australia, Canberra.

Bai H., Du, F. and Min, Z. (eds) (1996) *Agricultural Science and Technology History in Modern China*, China Agricultural Science and Technology Press, Beijing.

Barrios, S. (2008) 'The Impact of Climatic Change on Agricultural Production: Is it Different for Africa?', *Food Policy* 33(4): 287–98.

Bates, H. and Lofchie, M. F. (1980) *Agricultural Development in Africa: Issues of Public Policy*, ABC-CLIO, New York.

Bates, R. (1981) *Markets and States in Tropical Africa*, University of California Press, Berkeley, CA.

Baum, W. C. and Lejeune M. L. (1986) *Partners Against Hunger: The Consultative Group on International Agricultural Research*, World Bank: Washington, DC.

Beck, T., Fuchs, M. and Uy, M. (2009) 'Finance in Africa: Achievements and Challenges', *Policy Research Working Paper* 5020, World Bank, Washington, DC.

Beintema, N. M. and Stads, G. (2004) 'Investing in Sub-Saharan African Agricultural Research: Recent Trends', *2020 African Conference Brief 8*, International Food Policy and Research Institute, Washington, DC.

Beintema, N. M. and Stads, G. (2006) *Agricultural R&D in Sub-Saharan Africa: An Era of Stagnation*, International Food Policy Research Institute, Washington, DC.

Beintema, N. and Stads, G.-J. (2011) *African Agricultural R&D in the New Millennium: Progress for Some, Challenges for Many*. International Food Policy Research Institute, Washington, DC.

Beintema, N. M., Ngahulira, T. M. and Kirway, T. N. (2003) 'Agricultural Science and Technology Indicators: Tanzania', ASTI Country Brief No. 18, International Food Policy and Research Institute, Washington, DC.

Beintema, N. M., Castelo-Magalhaes, E., Elliott, H. and Mwala, M. (2004) 'Agricultural Science and Technology Indicators: Zambia', ASTI Country Brief No. 18, International Food Policy and Research Institute, Washington, DC.

Bezemer, D. and Headey, D. (2008) 'Agriculture, Development and Urban Bias', *World Development* 36(8): 1342–64.

Binswanger-Mkhize, H. P. (2009) 'Challenges and Opportunities for African Agriculture and Food Security: High Food Prices, Climate Change, Population Growth, and HIV and AIDs', paper presented at the Expert Meeting on How to feed the World in 2050, United Nations Food and Agriculture Organization, Economic and Social Development Department, 24–26 June.

Bloom, D. and Sachs, J. (1998) 'Geography, Demography and Economic Growth in Africa', Brookings Papers on Economic Activity 2, Brookings Institution, Washington, DC.

Borlaug, N. E. (1979) *Civilization Will Depend More upon Flourishing Crops than on Flowery Rhetoric*, Kansas State University, Manhattan, KS.

Bräutigam, D. and Tang X. (2009) 'China's Engagement in African Agriculture: "Down to the Countryside"', *The China Quarterly (London)* 199: 686–706.

Bruce, J., Migot-Adholla, S. and Atherton, J. (1994) 'Institutional Adaptation or Replacement', in Bruce, J. and Migot-Adholla S. E. (eds) *Searching for Land Tenure Security in Africa*, Kendall/Hunt Publishers, Dubuque, IO, pp. 251–266.

Burghardt DuBois, W. E. (1896) *The Suppression of the African Slave-Trade to the United States of America 1638–1870*, Longmans, Green & Company, New York.

Cai, F., Wang, D. and Du, Y. (2008) *China's Rural Reforms and Transition: The Evolution and Experiences of the Past Three Decades*, Shanghai People's Press, Shanghai.

Calzadilla, A., Zhu, T., Rehdanz, K., Tol, R. S. J. and Ringler, C. (2009) 'Economy-Wide Impacts of Climate Change on Agriculture in Sub-Saharan Africa', Working Paper FNU-170, Hamburg University and Centre for Marine and Atmospheric Science, Hamburg.

Camara, O. and Heinemann, E. (2006) 'Overview of the Fertilizer Situation in Africa', paper presented to the African Fertilizer Summit, Abuja, 9–13 June.

Cao, X. (2004) 'From Introduction to Localization: Agricultural Science and Technology of the Republic of China', *Ancient and Modern Agriculture* 1: 45–53.

Centre for Research on the Epidemiology of Disasters (2007) 'Annual Disaster Statistical Review: Numbers and Trends 2006', May, http://www.cred.be/sites/default/files/ADSR_2006.pdf (accessed 25 January 2012).

Chen, S. and Ravallion, M. (2007) *Absolute Poverty Measures for the Developing World, 1984–2004*. World Bank, Washington, DC.

Chen, Y. and Qiao, J. (2005) 'Current Status, Problem and Countermeasures about China's Agricultural Utilization of Foreign Capital', *World Agriculture* 2: 8 –11.

China Cotton Research Institute (2008) 'National Cotton Variety Monitoring Report for 2008', http://www.agri.gov.cn/fxycpd/mh/t20081120_1175997.htm (accessed 20 July 2009).

China–DAC Study Group (2011) *Economic Transformation and Poverty Reduction: How it Happens in China, Helping it Happen in Africa*, China Fiscal and Economic Press, Beijing.

China International Economic Cooperation Society (1997) *International Economic Cooperation in the 21st Century*, Foreign Trade and Economic Publishing House, Beijing.

China Irrigation and Drainage Development Centre (2008) *2007 China Irrigation and Drainage Development Report*, http://www.zgggzx.com/frontpages/view.php?aid=3514 (accessed 20 October 2009).

China Land Society (2008) 'Report on Land Management Surveys to South Africa, Kenya and Egypt', http://www.zgtdxh.org.cn/information/info/querying/gettingInfoRecord.asp?infoIdx=5022 (accessed 20 July 2009).

Chinese Rice Research Institute (1989) *Regional Planning on Rice Planting in China*, Zhejiang Science and Technology Press, Hangzhou.

Chongwe District Council (2005) *Chongwe District Development Plan 2006–2011*, Chongwe District Council, Zambia.

Cleaver, K.M. and Schreiber, G.A. (1994) *Reversing the Spiral: The Population, Agriculture and Environment Nexus in Sub-Saharan Africa*, World Bank, Washington, DC.

Cohen, J. M. (1987) *Integrated Rural Development: The Ethiopian Experiences and the Debate*, Scandinavian Institute of African Studies, Uppsala.

Collinson, M. P. (ed.) (2000) *A History of Farming Systems Research*. CABI Publishing, Wallingford.

Commercial Counselor's Office of the Chinese Embassy in the Republic of Mozambique (2006) 'Brief Introduction of Agricultural Resources, Agricultural Polices and Preferential Policies for Foreign Investment', http://mz.mofcom.gov.cn/aarticle/ztdy/200603/20060301771650.html (accessed 18 July 2009).

Compilation Group of Education Cooperation and Exchange between China and African Countries (2005) *Education Cooperation and Exchange between China and African Countries*, Beijing University Press, Beijing.

Cornia, G. A., and Helleiner G. K. (eds) (1994) *From Adjustment to Development in Africa: Conflict, Controversy, Convergence, Consensus?* St Martin's Press, London.

Crees, J. (2000) 'Changing Agricultural Policy in Tanzania', in Starkey P. and Simalenga T. (eds) *Animal Power for Weed Control. A Resource Book of the Animal Traction Network for East and Southern Africa (ATNESA)* CTA, Wageningen, p. 172.

Cui, X. (1988) 'State Monopoly of Purchase and Marketing and Industrial Accumulations', *China Economic History Research* 4: 120–35.

Cui, Y. (1999) 'Six Motivations of Habitants' Saving Behaviour', *Economic Forum* 5: 5.

Davies, M., Edinger, H., Tay, N. and Naidu, S. (2008) *How China Delivers Development Assistance to Africa*, Centre for Chinese Studies, University of Stellenbosch, Stellenbosch.

Davis K. E. (2009) 'Extension in Sub-Saharan Africa', *Rural Development News* 1: 48–53.

De Jager, A., Nandwa, S. M. and Okothb, P. F. (1998) 'Monitoring Nutrient Flows and Economic Performance in African Farming Systems (NUTMON): I. Concepts and Methodologies', *Agriculture, Ecosystems and Environment* 71: 37–48.

De Renzio, P. (2005) 'Can More Aid Be Spent in Africa?' http://www.odi.org.uk/resources/download/489.pdf (accessed 20 July 2009).

Delgado, C. L. (1995) 'Africa's Changing Agricultural Development Strategies: Past and Present Paradigms as a Guide to the Future', Food, Agriculture, and the Environment Discussion Paper 3, International Food Policy Research Institute, Washington, DC.

Deng, X. (1982) 'Be Prepared for the Second Ten Years during the First Ten Years', in *Selected Works of Deng Xiaoping, Vol. 3,* People's Publishing House, Beijing.

Department of Economics and Commerce, Embassy of the People's Republic of China in Mozambique (2007) 'High Bank Interest Impedes Agricultural Developments in Mozambique', http://www.all-africa.net/Get/feizhoushanglv/152555898.htm (accessed 20 July 2009).

Department of Planning, Ministry of Agriculture (ed.) (1949–1986) *Complete Statistics of China's Rural Economy,* China Agriculture Press, Beijing, pp. 112–17.

Department of Rural Social and Economic Survey, National Bureau of Statistics (2007) *Rural Statistical Yearbook of China,* China Statistics Press, Beijing.

Department of Rural Social and Economic Survey, National Bureau of Statistics (2008) *Rural Statistical Yearbook of China,* China Statistics Press, Beijing.

Department of Rural Social Economic Investigation, National Bureau of Statistics (2006) *Compilation of China Agricultural Statistics of 1949–2004,* China Statistics Press, Beijing.

Diouf, J. (1989) 'The Challenge of Agriculture Development in Africa', http://www.world bank.org/html/cgiar/publications/crawford/craw5.pdf (accessed 20 July 2009).

Djurfeldt, G., Holmén, H., Jirström, M. and Larsson, R. (eds) (2005) *The African Food Crisis: Lessons from the Asian Green Revolution,* CABI Publishing: Wallingford.

Du, Z. (2008) 'Input in Agricultural Infrastructure and Achievements', http://www.zgxcfx.com/Article_Show.asp?ArticleID=11380 (accessed 20 July 2009)

Economic Commission for Africa (2004) *Land Tenure Systems and Their Impacts on Food Security and Sustainable Development in Africa,* Economic Commission for Africa, Addis Ababa.

Economic Commission for Africa (2005) *African Governance Report 2005,* Economic Commission for Africa, Addis Ababa.

Economic Commission for Africa (2008) *Sustainable Development Report on Africa: Five-Year Review of the Implementation of the World Summit on Sustainable Development Outcomes in Africa (WSSD+5),* Economic Commission for Africa, Addis Ababa.

Economic and Commercial Counselor's Office, Embassy of the People's Republic of China in the Republic of Guinea (2006) 'The Growing Impoverishment of African Land', http://gn.mofcom.gov.cn/aarticle/ztdy/200606/20060602518311.html (accessed 20 July 2009).

Editorial Department (2007) 'Main Features of Agricultural Production in Africa', *China Agricultural Information* 4: 18.

Eicher, C. K. (2003) 'Flashback: Fifty Years of Donor Aid To African Agriculture', paper presented to the Conference on Successes in African Agriculture: Building for the Future', Pretoria, 1–3 December.

Eilitta, M. (2006) 'Achieving an African Green Revolution: A Vision for Sustainable Agricultural Growth in Africa', paper presented to the African Fertilizer Summit, Abuja, 9–13 June.

Eswaran, H., Almaraz, R., Reich, P. and Zdruli, P. (1997) 'Soil Quality and Soil Productivity in Africa', *Journal of Sustainable Agriculture* 10(4): 75–94.

Evenson, R. E. (2003) 'Production Impacts of Crop Genetic Improvement', in Evenson, R. E. and Gollin, D. (eds) (2003) *Crop Variety Improvement and its Effect on Productivity. The Impact of International Agricultural Research,* CABI Publishing, Wallingford, pp. 447–72.

Fan, S. (1991) 'Effects of Technological Change and Institutional Reform on Production Growth in Chinese Agriculture', *American Journal of Agricultural Economics* 73(2): 266–75.

Fan, S. (1997) 'Production and Productivity Growth in Chinese Agriculture: New Measurement and Evidence', *Food Policy* 22(3): 213–28.

Fan, S., Johnson, M., Saurkar, A. and Makombe, T. (2008) 'Investing in African Agriculture to Halve Poverty by 2015', IFPRI Discussion Paper 00751, International Food Policy Research Institute, Washington, DC.

Fan, S., Qian K. and Zhang X. (2006) 'China: An Unfinished Reform Agenda', in Pardey, P. G., Alston, J. M. and Piggott, R. R. (eds) *Agricultural R&D in the Development World: Too Little, Too Late?*, International Food Policy Research Institute, Washington, DC, pp. 29–64.

Farmer Daily (2009) 'China Is Gradually Losing its Rural Financial Policies', 20 February, http://finance.aweb.com.cn/2009/2/20/22520090220103412360.html (accessed 15 July 2009).

Faurès, J. M. and Santini, G. (eds) (2008) *Water and the Rural Poor: Interventions for Improving Livelihoods in Sub-Saharan Africa*, FAO, Rome.

Fei, X. (1938) *Peasant Life in China*, PhD thesis, London School of Economics.

Fei, X. (2006[1945]) 'Farmland in Lu Village', in Fei X. and Zhang Z., *Three Villages in Yunnan*, Social Science Academic Press, Beijing, pp. 1–202.

Feng T. (1991) '"Open Your Eyes to See the World": Statecraft School in the Daoguang and Xianfeng Years', *Modern History Research* 2: 18–30.

Feng, H. (1994) 'Saving Motivation of Farmers in China: Characters and Trend', *Survey World* 3(30): 13–16.

Food and Agriculture Organization of the UN (FAO) (1995) *Irrigation Development Costs*, FAO, Rome.

FAO (1998) *FAO Production Yearbook*, FAO, Rome.

FAO (2002) *The State of Food and Agriculture: Agriculture and Global Public Goods: Ten Years after the Earth Summit*, FAO, Rome.

FAO (2004) *The State of Food and Agriculture: Agricultural Biotechnology: Meeting the Needs of the Poor?*, FAO, Rome.

FAO (2006) 'Report on Food Deprivation towards the MDG on Hunger Reduction', http://www.fao.org/fileadmin/templates/ess/documents/food_security_statistics/workin g_paper_series/WP008e.pdf (accessed 29 July 2009).

FAO (2007a) *The State of Food and Agriculture: Paying Farmers for Environmental Services*, FAO, Rome.

FAO (2007b) 'Addressing the Challenges Facing the Agricultural Mechanization Input Supply and Farm Product Processing', in Sims, B. G., Kienzle, J., Cuevas, R. and Wall, G. (eds) *Proceedings of an FAO Workshop Held at the CIGR World Congress on Agricultural Engineering. Bonn, Germany, 5–6 September 2006*, FAO, Rome.

FAO (2008a) *Report on FAO Activities in the Region 2006–2007 with a Focus on the Achievement of the Millennium Development Goals, Twenty-Fifth Regional Conference for Africa, Nairobi, Kenya, 16–20 June*, FAO, Rome.

FAO (2008b) *The State of Food Insecurity in the World 2008: High Food Prices and Food Security – Threats and Opportunities*, FAO, Rome.

FAO (2009a) *The State of Food Insecurity in the World: Economic Crises – Impacts and Lessons Learned*, FAO, Rome.

FAO (2009b) 'Rapid Assessment of Aid Flows for Agricultural Development in Sub-Saharan Africa', Investment Centre Division Discussion Paper, September, http://www.fao.org/docrep/012/al144e/al144e.pdf (accessed 25 August 2010).

FAO (2010) 'The State of Food Insecurity: Addressing Food Insecurity in Protracted Crises', http://www.fao.org/docrep/013/i1683e/i1683e.pdf (accessed 10 September 2011).

FAO (2012) 'Globally Important Agricultural Heritage Systems (GIAHS): Hani Rice Terraces System (China)', http://www.fao.org/nr/giahs/pilot-systems/pilot/hani-rice/maasai-agropastoral-summary0/zh/ (accessed 25 January 2012).

FAO Media Centre (2009) 'Red Locust Disaster in Eastern Africa Prevented: Biopesticides Being Used on a Large Scale', http://www.fao.org/news/story/en/item/21084/icode/ (accessed 20 July 2009).

FAO, International Fund for Agricultural Development (IFAD) and World Food Programme (WFP) (2002) 'Reducing Poverty and Hunger: the Critical Role of Financing for Food, Agriculture and Rural Development', paper presented to the Conference Financing for Development, Monterey, 18–22 March.

FAO (2011) 'The State of Food and Agriculture 2010–11: Women in Agriculture – Closing the Gender Gap for Development', http://www.fao.org/docrep/013/i2050e/i2050e.pdf (accessed 23 January 2012).

FAO/Global Information and Early Warning System on Food and Agriculture (GIEWS) (2005) *Foodcrops and Shortages*, FAO, Rome.

Forum for Agricultural Research in Africa (FARA) (2006) 'Framework for African Agricultural Productivity', paper presented to the Conference on Forum for Agricultural Research in Africa, Accra, June 2006.

FARA (2008) 'FARA 2007–2016 Strategic Plan: Enhancing African Agricultural Innovation Capacity', paper presented to the Conference on Forum for Agricultural Research in Africa, Accra, 15 September 2006.

Freeman, D., Holslag, J. and Weil, S. (2008) 'China's Foreign Farming Policy: Can Land Provide Security? Brussels Institute of Contemporary Chinese Studies Asia Paper 3(9): 3–27.

Gabre-Madhin, E. Z and Haggblade, S. (2004) 'Successes in African Agriculture: Results of an Expert Survey', *World Development* 32(5): 745–66.

Gakuru, M., Winters, K. and Stepman, F. (2009) 'Innovative Farmer Advisory Services using ICTs', in Cunningham, P. and Cunningham, M. (eds) *IST-Africa 2009 Conference Proceedings*, http://ist-africa.org/Conference2009/outbox/ISTAfrica_Paper_ref_85_doc_2692.pdf (accessed 23 January 2012).

Gao, X. (1994) 'Rural Labor Transfer and Feminization of Agriculture in Contemporary China', *Sociological Studies* 2: 83–90.

Gautam, M. (2003) *Debt Relief for the Poorest: An OED Review of the HIPC Initiative*, World Bank, Washington, DC.

Gepts, P. (2001) 'Origins of Plant Agriculture and Major Crop Plants', in Tolba M. K. (ed.) *Our Fragile World: Challenges and Opportunities for Sustainable Development*, EOLSS Publishers, Ramsey, Isle of Man, pp. 629–37.

Gillson, I. (2005) 'Trade: How Cotton Subsidies Harm Africa', *Overseas Development Institute: Opinions*, September. http://www.odi.org.uk/resources/download/465.pdf (accessed 25 September 2012).

Gong, Q. (2003) 'China's Chemical Fertilizer Industry Status and Development Trend', *Chemical Fertilizer Industry* 31(1): 3–17.

Gu, Z. (1999) *Rising Africa*, China Youth Press, Beijing.

Gumbo, P. et al. (2001) 'Landlessness and Farm Invasions in Zimbabwe: Lessons for Social Workers Practising Community Work', *Regional Development Studies* 7: 79–86.

Guo, H. (2005) 'Negative Impact of Scissors on Agricultural Development', *Cooperative Economy and Science* 12(24): 23–4.

Guyer J. I. and Peters P. E. (1987) 'Introduction', *Development and Change* 18(2): 197–214.

Haggblade, S., Hazell, P., Kirsten, I. and Mkandawire, R. (2004) 'Building on Successes in African Agriculture: Past Performance, Future Imperatives', http://www.ifpri.org/sites/default/files/publications/focus12_01.pdf (accessed 20 July 2009).

Hall, D. O. (1996) 'Reversing the Spiral: The Population, Agriculture, and Environment Nexus in Sub-Saharan Africa', *Population Studies* 50(1): 136–7.

Han, Z. (2001) 'Application of Vulnerability Analysis and Mapping System in China's Poverty Alleviation Project', *China's Agricultural Resource and Zoning* 1: 23(1): 20–5.

Havnevik, K., Bryceson, D., Birgegård, L., Matondi, P. and Beyene, A. (2007) *African Agriculture and the World Bank: Development or Impoverishment?* Elanders Sverige AB, Stockholm.

Hearn, J. (2001) 'The "Uses and Abuses" of Civil Society in Africa', *Review of African Political Economy* 28(87): 43–53.

Henao, J. and Baanante, C. A. (1999) 'Estimating Rates of Nutrient Depletion in Soils of Agricultural Lands of Africa (Technical Bulletin, International Fertilizer Development Center T-48.)', International Fertilizer Development Center, Muscle Shoals, AL.

Hine, J. and Rutter, J. (2000) 'Roads, Personal Mobility and Poverty: the Challenge', paper presented at the Transport and Poverty Alleviation Workshop, World Bank, Washington, DC, June.

Ho, P. (1959) *Studies on the Chinese Population, 1368–1953.* Harvard University Press, Cambridge, MA.

Holmén, H. (2005) 'The State and Agricultural Intensification in Sub-Sahara Africa', in Djurfeldt, D., Holmén, H., Jirstrom, M. and Larsson, R. (eds) *The African Food Crisis: Lessons from Asian Green Revolution*, CABI Publishing, Wallingford, pp. 87–112.

Holmén, H. (2006) 'Myths about Agriculture, Obstacles to Solving the African Food Crisis', *European Journal of Development Research* 18(3): 453–80.

Holtsberg, C. (1986) 'The Development of Rural Development: Swedish Strategies for the Countryside', in Fruhling, P. (eds) *Swedish Aid in Perspective: Policies, Problems and Results*, Almquist and Wiksell, Stockholm, pp. 157–64.

Hope, K. R. (2002) 'From Crisis to Renewal: Towards a Successful Implementation of the New Partnership for Africa's Development', *African Affairs* 101(404): 387–402.

Household Survey Office, National Bureau of Statistics of China (2011) Quantity, Structure and Character of New Generation of Farmer-Workers', http://www.stats.gov.cn/was40/gjtjj_detail.jsp?searchword=%D0%C2%C9%FA%B4%FA%C5%A9%C3%F1%B9%A4&channelid=6697&record=5 (accessed 25 January 2012).

Hu, L., Li, Q. and Liu, C. (2000) 'Discussion on the Grain Price Protection System in China', *Agricultural Economy Issues* 6: 32–4.

Hu, Y. (ed.) (2004) *Progress of China's Agricultural Science in 20th Century*, Shandong Education Press, Jinan.

Hu, Y. (2006) 'The Lost choice: Village Women Still Cling to Farmland', *China Book Reviews* 10: 5–6.

Huang, J. (2003) 'Development and Prospects of China's Agriculture', *Management Review* 115(1): 17–20.

Huang, J. (2004) 'The Past and the Future of China's Agriculture', *Management World*, 3: 95–104.

Huang, J. (2008) *Institutional Changes and Sustainable Development: China Agriculture and Rural Areas in the Past Thirty Years*, Gezhi Publishing and Shanghai People's Publishing House, Shanghai.

Huang, J. and Bouis, H. (1996) 'Structural Changes in Demand for Food in Asia', IFPRI Food, Agriculture, and the Environment 2020 Paper Series 11, International Food Policy Research Institute, Washington, DC.

Huang, J. and Rozelle, S. (1996) 'Technological Change: Rediscovering the Engine of Productivity Growth in China's Rural Economy', *Journal of Development Economics* 49(2): 337–69.

Huang, J. and Rozelle, S. (1998) 'Market Development and Food Consumption in Rural China', *China Economic Review* 9: 25–45.

Huang, J., Xu, Z. and Hu, R. (2002) 'Input and Application of Agricultural R&D Fund', Report of Sub-project of Study on the Reform of Management System on Chinese Government Supporting Agriculture Fund, March.

Huang, J., Liu, Y., Martin, W., Rozelle, S. and Yang, J. (2008a) 'Viewing the Integration of China Agricultural Products Market and Global Market from the Perspective of Agricultural Policy Intervention', *Journal of World Economy* 4: 3–10.

Huang, J., Otsuka, K. and Rozelle, S. (2008b) 'Agriculture in China's Development: Past Disappointments, Recent Successes and Future Challenges', in Brandt, L. and Rawski, T. G. (eds) *China's Greatest Economic Transformation*, Cambridge University Press, Cambridge, pp. 467–504.

Huang, Y. and Sun, W. (2006) '20 years Soil Organic Carbon Dynamics in Cropping Land in Mainland China', *Chinese Science Bulletin* 51: 750–63.

Huang, Z. (2000a) *The Peasant Economy and Social Change in North China*, Zhonghua Book Company, Beijing.

Huang, Z. (2000b) *The Peasant Family and Rural Development in the Yangtze River Delta*, Zhonghua Book Company, Beijing.

Huang, Z. (2006) 'The Institutionalized "Half Work Half Farm" Involuted Agriculture', *Dushu* 3: 30–37.

Huang, Z. (2008) *Guideline for Zambia: Tourism, Trade and Investment*, China Commercial Press, Beijing.

Humanitarian News and Analysis (2008) 'Malawi: Subsidising Agriculture Is Not Enough', 5 February, http://www.irinnews.org/report.aspx?reportid=76591 (accessed 25 September 2010).

Ibhawoh, B. and Dibua, J. I. (2003) 'Deconstructing Ujamaa: The Legacy of Julius Nyerere in the Quest for Social and Economic Development in Africa', *African Association of Political Science* 8(1): 59–83.

Ijioma, S. I. (1996) 'Agricultural Credit in Africa: Retrospection and Prospect' (in Chinese), *Agriculture Development and Finance* 5: 36–7.

Independent Evaluation Group (2007) *World Bank Assistance to Agriculture in Sub-Saharan Africa: An IEG Review*, World Bank, Washington, DC.

Inocencio, A., Kikuchi, M., Tonosaki, M., Maruyama, A., Merrey, D., Hilmy, S. and de Jong, I. (2007) *Costs and Performance of Irrigation Projects: A Comparison of Sub-Saharan Africa and Other Developing Regions*, International Water Management Institute, Colombo.

Institute for Market Ecology and Klaus Dürbeck Consulting (2005) *Guidance Manual for Organic Collection of Wild Plants*, Swiss Import Promotion Programme, Switzerland.

Inter Academy Council (2004) 'Realizing the Promise and Potential of African Agriculture', Report of the Ad-Hoc Follow-up Committee, InterAcademy Council, Amsterdam.

Intergovernmental Panel on Climate Change (IPCC) (2007) *Climate Change 2001: Impacts, Adaptation and Vulnerability*, Intergovernmental Panel on Climate Change, Geneva.

International Food Policy Research Institute (IFPRI) (2010) *What Is the Irrigation Potential for Africa?* IFPRI Discussion Paper 00993, June, International Food Policy and Research Institute, Washington, DC.

Ishii, H. (1992) *Earth Environment Report* (in Chinese), China Environment Science Publishing House, Beijing.

James, C. (2009) 'Global Status of Commercialized biotech/GM Crops, 2009', International Service for the Acquisition of Agri-Biotech Application (ISAAA) Brief 41, ISAAA, Metro Manila.

Jayne, T. S., Govereh, J., Mwanaumo, A., Nyoro, J. K. and Chapoto, A. (2002) 'False Promise or False Premise? The Experience of Food and Input Market Reform in Eastern and Southern Africa', *World Development* 30(11): 1967–85.

Jiang, H. and Sun, Y. (2001) 'Crop Breeding in China: Status and Strategy', *Management of Agriculture Science and Technology* 6: 12–18.

Jiang, Z. (2008) 'Opportunities and Challenges on Agricultural Cooperation in China and Africa: On the "Granaries of Africa" Strategy', speech to the 25th Anniversary Celebration of International Economic Cooperation Society of China and China–Africa Agricultural Cooperation Forum, Beijing, 23 October.

Johnson, D. G. (2005) *Agricultural, Rural and Peasant Issues in Economic Development* (trans. Lin, Y. and Zhao, Y.), Commercial Press, Beijing.

Jones, M. (2011) 'Enhance the Investment to Agricultural R&D in Africa', speech to the China–Africa High-level Experience-sharing Programme on Agriculture and Rural Development, Beijing, 4–10 September.

Juma, C. (2011) *The New Harvest: Agricultural Innovation in Africa*. Oxford University Press, New York.

Karuuombe, B. (2003) 'The Land Question in Namibia: Still Unresolved', paper presented at the Land and Livelihoods in Eastern and Southern Africa Seminar, South Africa, 27–31 January 2003.

Keeley, J. and Scoones, I. (2003) *Understanding Environmental Policy Processes: Cases from Africa*, Earthscan, London.

Kenyan Social Watch Coalition (2004) '"Hot peace" and Landlessness', http://www.socwatch.org/node/10915 (accessed 18 September 2010).

Killick, T. (2003) 'Macro-Level Evaluations and the Choice of Aid Modalities', paper presented to the OED Conference on Evaluating Development Effectiveness, World Bank, Washington, DC, 15–16 July.

Kong, L. (1986) 'Issues in the Origin of Agricultural Cultivation', *Agricultural Archaeology* 1: 28–37.

Kuang, Z. (2007) 'Study on Recognition and Behaviour of Farmers in Development Dissemination', PhD thesis, China Agricultural University, Beijing.

Kuang, Z., Li, H. and Zuo, T. (2008) 'Agricultural Knowledge and Information Systems: Cases from Tiantang Village and Xin Village, Fulong Town, Hainan Province', *Journal of China Agricultural University (Social Sciences Edition)* 25(4): 127127–36.

Lancaster, C. (1999) *Aid to Africa: So Much to Do, So Little Done*, University of Chicago Press, Chicago, IL.

Larsson, R. (2005) 'Crisis and Potential in Smallholder Food Production: Evidence from Micro Level', in Djurfeldt, G., Holmén, H., Jirström, M. and Larsson, R. (eds) *The African Food Crisis: Lessons from the Asian Green Revolution*, CABI Publishing, Wallingford, pp. 113–38.

Lele, U. (eds) (1991) *Aid to African Agriculture: Lessons from two Decades of Donors' Experience*, Johns Hopkins University Press, Baltimore, MD.

Lewis, W. A. (1953) *Report on Industrialization and the Gold Coast*, Government Printer, Accra.

Li, G. (1993) 'Multi-Interaction Points of China's Agricultural History Development', *Journal of China Economic History* 1: 1–20.

Li, G. (2010) *Agriculture in Ancient China*, China International Radio Press, Beijing.

Li, G. and Dong, L. (2006) 'The Meteorologic Disasters Affecting Agricultural Production in China', *Geological Education* 1: 33.

Li, H. (2009) 'Translation and Introduction and Promotion of Western Modern Agricultural Science and Technology in the Late Qing Dynasty', *Agricultural Archaeology* 3: 46–8.

Li, J. (1991) 'Origin and Contribution of African Agriculture', *Agricultural Archaeology* 1: 67–74.

Li, S. (2001) 'Rural Women's Employment and Income: Empirical Analysis of Several Sample Villages in Shanxi Province', *Social Sciences in China* 3: 56–69.

Li, S. (2006) 'Thinking on Constructing China's Private Farm System's Several Problems', *Special Zone Economy* 1: 74–6.

Li, S. and Shi, Ji. (2008) 'Food Crisis and Agricultural Development in Africa', *World Agriculture* 10: 1–2.

Li, T. and Kouzhan, Ch. (eds) (1996) *Series Book of Cultural Communication between China and Japan – Technology Volumn*, Zhejiang Renmin Press, Hangzhou.

Li. Z. (1998) 'Analysis on Constraints of Africa's Modernization', *West Asia and Africa* 1998 (1): 36-9.

Liao, X. (2006) 'Land Conflict: New Problems on Farmers after the Cancellation of Agricultural Tax', *China Rural Findings* 1: 81–6.

Liao, Y. (2009) 'Analysis on the Impacts of Reform of Irrigation Water Price on Irrigated Water, Grain Production and Farmers Income', *China Rural Economy* 1: 39–48.

Lin, C. (1988) 'A Forecast on the Inevitable Trend of Future Agricultural Technology Revolution from Past Changes in Per Hectare Yield of Farmland', *Agricultural Archaeology* 1: 26–37.

Lin, Y. (1992) *Rural Reforms and Agricultural Growth in China*, Shanghai Joint Publishing Company and Shanghai People's Press, Shanghai.

Lin, Y., Cai, F. and Li, Z. (2008) *The China Miracle: Development Strategy and Economic Reform*, Gezhi Publishing, Shanghai Sanlian Bookstore and Shanghai People's Publishing, Shanghai.

Lipton, M. (2001) 'Reviving Global Poverty Reduction: What Role for Genetically Modified Plants?' *Journal of International Development*, 13: 823–46.

Lipton, M. (2005) 'The Family Farm in a Globalizing World: The Role of Crop Science in Alleviating Poverty', 2020 Discussion Paper 40, International Food Policy Research Institute, Washington, DC.

Liu, B. and Qi, G. (2010) 'Research on Farmers' Land Circulation in Modern Agricultural Demonstration Project Areas', *Journal of Anhui Agricultural Science* 38(21): 1587–90.

Liu, C. (1989) 'Agricultural Strategy and Policy of Côte d'Ivoire', *West Asia and Africa* 4: 37–40.

Liu, H., Li, C. and Wen, T. (2006) 'Opportunity Cost in "Forced leisure" and its Effect on Food Production', *Journal of Renmin University of China* 6: 21–30.

Liu, J. (2000) 'Longstanding China–Africa Agricultural Cooperation', *World Agriculture* 10: 3–4.

Liu, L. and Xie, C. (2006) *The History of Education on Anti-illiteracy in New China*. Anhui Education Press, Anhui.

Liu, S. (2001) 'The Meanings of Historical Facts Connected with Agricultural Development in Ancient China towards the Exploitation of Modern Agriculture', *Journal of Subject Education* 11: 17–19.

Lu, J. (2005) 'Analysis of the Relationship of Rural Surplus Labour: Transforming Rural Labour Quality', *Journal of Huazhong Agricultural University (Social Sciences Edition)* 4: 28–30.

Lu, L. (2007) 'Staged Changes to Agricultural Subsidy Policies in China and Result Evaluation since 1978', *Reformation & Strategy* 11: 70–3.

Lu, T. (2000) *A Brief History of African Agricultural Development*, China Financial and Economic Publishing, Beijing.

Lu, X. (2006) 'Design and Building Requirements of Plant Germplasm Database', *Chinese Bulletin of Botany* 23(1): 119–25.

Lu, Y., Wang, S. and Guo, H. (2007) 'Relationship between Huang-Huai Rivers' Land-making and Flood in North Jiangsu in the Ming and Qing Dynasties', *Journal of the Nanjing Agricultural University (Social Sciences Edition)* 7(2): 78–88.

Lu, J. (2005) 'Analysis and Countermeasures on China's Financial Mechanism for Agricultural Scientific and Technological Investment', *Journal of Huazhong Agricultural University (Social Science Edition)* 5–6: 4–7.

McFerson, H. (2010) 'Developments in African Governance since the Cold War: Beyond Cassandra and Pollyanna',. *African Studies Review* 53(2): 49–76.

McMillan, J., Whalley, J. and Zhu, L. (1989) 'The Impacts of China's Economic Reforms on Agriculture Productivity Growth', *Journal of Political Economy* 97(4): 781–807.

Maddison, A. (2007) *Chinese Economic Performance in the Long Run,* Organisation for Economic Co-operation and Development (OECD), Paris.

Mao, Z. (1934) 'Our Economy Policies', in Editorial Committee of the CPC Central Committee (ed.) *Selected Readings of Mao Zedong,* People's Publishing House, Beijing, pp. 121–4.

Mao, Z. (1954) 'Thankyou Letter to the Soviet Government Delegation', *PRC State Council Bulletin,* Beijing.

Mao, Z. (1955) *Agricultural Cooperation Issues.* People's Publishing House, Beijing.

Mao, Z. (1957) 'A Speech on the Conference of Party Committees of Provinces, Cities and Autonomous Regions', in Editorial Committee of the CPC Central Committee (ed.) *Selected Readings of Mao Zedong,* People's Publishing House, Beijing, pp. 330–62.

Mao, Z. (1958) 'A Speech on the Enlarged Conference of Political Bureau of the Central Committee', in Editorial Committee of the CPC Central Committee (ed.) *Selected Readings of Mao Zedong,* People's Publishing House, Beijing, May 1996, pp. 121–4.

Mao, Z. (1959) 'A Letter to Comrades in Provinces, Cities, Counties, Communes and Production Groups', in Editorial Committee of the CPC Central Committee (ed.) *Selected Readings of Mao Zedong,* People's Publishing House, Beijing, Vol. 8, p. 49.

Maputo Declaration on Agriculture and Food Security in Africa (2003) http://www.africa-union.org/root/au/Documents/Decisions/hog/12HoGAssembly2003.pdf (accessed 10 September 2011).

Martin, G. (1985) 'The Historical, Economic, and Political Bases of France's African Policy', *Journal of Modern African Studies* 23(2): 189–208.

Mataya, C. (nd) 'Country State of LED Draft Report: Malawi', http://www.uncdf.org/english/local_development/LED/reports/UNCDF-LED_Malawi.pdf (accessed 20 July 2009).

Migdal, J. S. (1988) *Strong Societies and Weak States: State–Society Relations and State Capabilities in the Third World,* Stanford University Press, Stanford, CA.

Min, Z. (2005) 'Agricultural Achievement of the Qing Dynasty', *Agricultural History of China* 1: 60–6.

Minde, I., Jayne, T. S., Crawford, E., Ariga, J. and Govereh, J. (2008) 'Promoting Fertilizer Use in Africa: Current Issues and Empirical Evidence from Malawi, Zambia, and Kenya', Regional Strategic Analysis and Knowledge Support System (ReSAKSS) Working Paper No. 13, ReSAKSS, Pretoria.

Ministry of Agriculture (2009) 'Agricultural Achievements of the People's Republic of China in the Last 60 Years since 1949', http://www.moa.gov.cn/zwllm/zwdt/200909/t20090922_1355033.htm (accessed 18 December 2009)

Ministry of Agriculture and Co-operatives (Zambia) (2004) *National Agricultural Policy 2004–1015,* Ministry of Agriculture and Co-operatives, Lusaka.

Ministry of Agriculture Food Security and Cooperatives (Tanzania) (2008) *Annual Report 2007 to 2008,* Ministry of Agriculture Food Security and Cooperatives, Dodoma.

Ministry of Agriculture of the People's Republic of China (2008) *China Agriculture Yearbook,* China Agriculture Press, Beijing.

Ministry of Agriculture Rural Economy Research Center (2009a) *Studies on Rural China,* China Financial and Economic Publishing House, Beijing.

Ministry of Agriculture Rural Economy Research Center (2009b) *Rural China Research Report 2008,* China Financial and Economic Publishing House, Beijing.

Ministry of Finance (2001) *Notice Regarding Distribution of the Fund Management Method for Agricultural Disaster Prevention and Relief Decree*, Ministry of Finance, Beijing.

Ministry of Finance (2007) 'Intensify Implementation Efforts to Agricultural Subsidy Policy', http://www.gov.cn/ztzl/czsy/content_646790.htm (accessed 20 July 2009).

Ministry of Finance (2008a) 'Investment on Rural Taxation Reforms and Comprehensive Rural Reforms from 2000 to 2007', http://zgb.mof.gov.cn/zhengwuxinxi/tourudongtai/200806/t20080616_45475.html (accessed 20 July 2009).

Ministry of Finance (2008b) 'Report on the Implementation of Central and Local Budget of 2007 and Draft of Budget in Central and Local Government in 2008', Report to the Conference on the 1st Session of 11th NPC, Beijing, 5 March 2008.

Ministry of Finance (2009) 'Report on the Implementation of Central and Local Budget of 2008 and Draft of Budget in Central and Local Government in 2009', Report to the Conference on the 2nd Session of 11th NPC, Beijing, 15 March.

Moussa, S. Z. (2002) 'Technology Transfer for Agricultural Growth in Africa', Economic Research Papers No. 72, African Development Bank, Tunis.

Mrema, G. C. (1997) 'Agricultural Research Systems in the ECA Sub-Region', in G. C. Mrema (ed.) *Development of a Long Term Strategic Plan for Agricultural Research in the Eastern and Central African Region*, Kampala, Uganda: ASARECA.

Msuya, E. (2007) 'The Impact of Foreign Direct Investment on Agricultural Productivity and Poverty Reduction in Tanzania', MPRA Paper No. 3671, Kyoto University.

Munthali, J. and Mulenga, K. (2009) 'Zambia Removes Tax on Agricultural Equipment', http://www.africanagricultureblog.com/2009/02/zambia-removes-tax-on-agricultural.html (accessed 20 July 2009).

Murdock, G. (1959) *Africa: Its Peoples and Their Culture History*, McGraw-Hill, New York.

Naiman, R. and Watkins, N. (1999) 'A Survey of the Impacts of IMF Structural Adjustment in Africa: Growth, Social Spending, and Debt Relief', http://www.cepr.net/index.php/a-survey-of-the-impacts-of-imf-structural-adjustment-inafrica/#zim (accessed 16 December 2009).

National Bureau of Statistics (2008a) 'Main Data of the 2nd National Agricultural Census for 2006 (No. 2)', http://www.stats.gov.cn/tjgb/nypcgb/qgnypcgb/t20080222_402463937.htm (accessed 20 July 2009).

National Bureau of Statistics (2008b) 'Main Data of the 2nd National Agricultural Census for 2006 (No. 5)', http://www.stats.gov.cn/tjgb/nypcgb/qgnypcgb/t20080227_402464718.htm (accessed 20 July 2009).

National Research Council (1996) *Lost Crops of Africa*, National Academy Press, Washington, DC.

Naughton, B. (2007) *The Chinese Economy: Transition and Growth*, MIT Press, Cambridge, MA.

New Partnership for Africa's Development (NEPAD) (2003) *Comprehensive Africa Agricultural Development Programme*, NEPAD, Johannesburg.

NEPAD (2004) 'Implementing the Comprehensive Africa Agricultural Development Programme and Restoring Food Security in Africa', NEPAD, Johannesburg.

NEPAD (2006) 'Towards a Prioritized Outcome-based Approach to Implementing Africa's Food Security Commitments', paper presented to the Preparatory Meeting of Officials Attending the Food Security Summit, Abuja, 4–7 December.

Niemeijer, D. (1996) 'The Dynamics of African Agricultural History: Is it Time for a New Development Paradigm?' *Development and Change* 27(1): 87–110.

Niu, D. (2009) 'Thirty Years Development of Agricultural Products Trade in China', *Farmer Daily*, 16 January, http://www.farmer.com.cn/news/jjsn/200901/t20090116_420862.htm (accessed 15 October 2010).

Nkamleu, G. B., Sylla, K. and Zonon, A. (2008) 'What Accounts for Growth in African Agriculture', *American Journal of Agricultural and Biological Science* 3(1): 379–88.

Nkonya, E. and Kaizzi, C. K. (2003) 'Poverty–Natural Resource Management Linkages: Empirical Evidence from Uganda', paper presented at the Planning Workshop for Research on Poverty–NRM linkage in Uganda, Hotel Africana, Kampala, 23–24 January.

Nyerere, J. K. (1967) *The Arusha Declaration*. Written for the Tanganyika African National Union, 5 February 1967, http://www.marxists.org/subject/africa/nyerere/1967/arusha-declaration.htm (accessed 30 January 2012).

Oldeman, L. R., Hakkeling, R. T. A. and Sombroek, W. G. (1991) *World Map of the Status of Human-Induced Degradation: An Explanatory Note*, International Soil Reference and Information Centre, Wageningen.

Organisation for Economic Co-operation and Development (OECD) (2005) *Review and Evaluation of Chinese Agricultural Policy (in Chinese)*, China Economics Publishing House, Beijing.

Organization of African Unity (1980) *Lagos Plan of Action for the Economic Development of Africa 1980–2000*, Organization of African Unity, Addis Ababa.

Pan, Y. (1998) *China's Overseas Investment Development Strategy*, Economic Science Press, Beijing.

Pardey, P.G., Alston, J. M. and Piggott, R. R. (eds) (2006) *Agricultural R&D in the Development World: Too Little, Too Late?*, International Food Policy Research Institute, Washington, DC.

Park, A., Jin H., Rozelle, S. and Huang, J. (2002) 'Market Emergence and Transition: Arbitrage, Transaction Costs, and Autarky in China's Grain Markets', *American Journal of Agricultural Economics* 84(1): 67–82.

Peacock, T., Ward, C. and Gambarelli, G. (2007) *Investment in Agricultural Water for Poverty Reduction and Economic Growth in Sub-Saharan Africa Synthesis Report*, Collaborative program of ADB, FAO, IFAD, IWMI and World Bank.

People's Daily (2000) 'Agriculture Cooperation: Everlasting Contribution and Benefit', 13 September, http://www.ahnw.gov.cn/2006nwkx/html/200009/{40CDE7BC-F1BF-4DD9-920F-DB7EAD0C6EFD}.shtml (accessed 9 January 2012).

Perkins, D. H. (1969) *Agricultural Development in China 1368–1968*, Aldine Publishers, Chicago, IL.

Poulton, C., Kydd, J., Wiggins, S. and Dorward, A. (2006) 'State Intervention for Food Price Stabilisation in Africa: Can it Work?', *Food Policy* 31: 342–56.

Pretty, J. N., Morison, J. I. L. and Hine, R.E. (2003) 'Reducing Food Poverty by Increasing Agricultural Sustainability in Developing Countries', *Agriculture, Ecosystems and Environment* 95(1): 217–34.

Pretty, J., Toulmin, C. and Williams, S. (2011) 'Sustainable Intensification in African Agriculture', *International Journal of Agricultural Sustainability* 9(1): 5–24.

Putterman, L. (2006) 'Agricultural Transition Year: Country Data Set', Brown University, Providence, RI.

Qian, Y. (2002) 'How Reform Worked in China', in Rodrik, D. (ed.) *In Search of Prosperity: Analytic Narratives on Economic Growth*, Princeton University Press, Princeton, NJ, pp. 297–333.

Qin, F., Li, Y., Zhang, J., Wu, S. and Zhang, Y. (2002) 'Research on China's Foreign Capital Utilization in Agriculture', *Economic Problems of Agriculture* 1: 42–7.

Rauschning, D., Wiesbrock, K. and Lailach, M. (1997) *Key Resolutions of the United Nations General Assembly, 1946–1996*, Cambridge University Press, Cambridge.

Reij, C., Scoones, I. and Toulmin, C. (1996) *Sustaining the Soil: Indigenous Soil and Water Conservation in Africa*, Earthscan, London.

Research on Poverty Alleviation (2007) *Views of the People*, Research on Poverty Alleviation, Dar es Salaam.

Riddell, P. J., Westlake, M. and Burke, J. (2006) 'Demand for Irrigated Products in Sub-Saharan Africa', Water Report No. 31, FAO, Rome.

Rondinelli, D. A., McCullough, J. S. and Johnson, R. W. (1989) 'Analysing Decentralization Policies in Developing Countries: A Political–Economy Framework', *Development and Change* 20(1): 57–87.

Roseboom, J. and Pardey, P. G. (1995) 'Statistical Brief on the National Agricultural Research System of Zambia', ISNAR Indicator Series Project: Phase II, International Food Policy Research Institute, Washington, DC.

Rosegrant, M. and Perez, N. (1997) 'Water Resources Development in Africa: A Review and Synthesis of Issues, Potentials, and Strategies for the Future', Environment and Production Technology Division Discussion Paper No. 28, International Food Policy Research Institute, Washington DC.

Rosegrant, M., Cai, X., Cline, S. and Nakagawa, N. (2002) 'The Role of Rainfed Agriculture in the Future of Global Food Production', Environment and Production Technology Division Discussion Paper No. 90, International Food Policy Research Institute, Washington, DC.

Rosegrant, M. W., Cline, S. A., Li, W., Sulser, T. B. and Valmonte-Santos, R. A. (2005) 'Looking Ahead: Long-term Prospects for Africa's Agricultural Development and Food Security', 2020 Discussion Paper 41, International Food Policy Research Institute, Washington, DC.

Rural Social-Economic Survey Team, National Bureau of Statistics (2006) *Collection of China's Agricultural Statistics 1949–2004*, China Statistics Press, Beijing.

Sahn, D. E., Dorosh, P. A. and Younger, S. D. (1997) *Structural Adjustment Reconsidered: Economic Policy and Poverty in Africa*, Cambridge University Press, Cambridge.

Sandrey, R. and Edinger, H. (2009) *The Relevance of Chinese Agricultural Technologies for African Smallholder Farmers: Agricultural Technology Research in China*, Centre for Chinese Studies, University of Stellenbosch, Stellenbosch.

Sasakawa Africa Association (2004) *Annual Report 2003–2004*, Sasakawa Africa Association, Geneva, http://www.saa-safe.org/e-libraries/pdf/annualreport/annualreport_2003–2004.pdf (accessed 5 September 2009).

Scoones, I. (eds) (2001) *Dynamics and Diversity: Soil Fertility and Farming Livelihoods in Africa: Case Studies from Ethiopia, Mali, and Zimbabwe*, Earthscan, London.

Scoones, I., Devereux, S. and Haddad, L. (2005) 'Introduction: New Directions for African Agriculture', *IDS Bulletin* 36(2): 1–12.

Scoones, S. (2008) *Organic Agriculture in China: Current Situation and Challenges. EU–China Trade Project*, May.

Secular, T. (1992) 'China's Agricultural Policy during the Reform Period', in *China's Economic Dilemmas in the 1990s: The Problems of Reform, Modernization, and Interdependence*, Government Printing Office, Washington, DC, pp. 340–64.

Shao, K. and Bu, F. (2007) 'Introduction and Promotion of Food Crops in Ming and Qing Dynasty Based on a Sweet Potato Study', *Journal of Anhui Agricultural Science* 35(22): 7002–3.

Shen, Z. (2004) 'Introduction and Utilization of U.S. Crop Variety Improvement Technology in Modern China: Taking the University of Nanking Agricultural College and Central University College of Agriculture as Examples', *Agricultural History of China* 4: 24 24–31.

Shi, Q. and Zhuo, J. (2007) 'Behaviour of Savings and Borrowing of Rural Households in China: Survey from 5 Provinces in 3 Years', *Learning and Practice* 6: 40–55.

Shu, Y. (2005) 'Reflections on a Number of Objective Restraining Factors in the Development Process of African Countries', *Journal of Shanghai Normal University (Philosophy & Social Sciences Edition)* 34(5): 113–18.

Sinha, R. (1984) *Landlessness: A Growing Problem*, FAO, Rome.

Smaling E. M. A., Nandwa S. M. and Janssen B. H. (1997) 'Soil Fertility in Africa Is at Stake', in *Replenishing Soil Fertility in Africa*, SSSA Special Publication No. 51, Soil Science Society of America, Madison, WI, pp. 47–62.

Sones, K.R., Duveskog, D. and Minjauw, B. (2003) 'Farmer Field Schools: The Kenyan Experience', conference report of the Farmer Field School Stakeholders' Forum, Nairobi, 27 March.

Stavrianos, L. S. (1999) *A Global History: From Prehistory to the 21st Century*, Prentice-Hall, Upper Saddle River, N.J.

Stoorvogel, J. and Smaling, E. M. A. (1990) *Assessment of Soil Nutrient Depletion in Sub-Saharan Africa*, Winand Staring Centre, Wageningen.

Sun, D., Liu, H. and Zhou, A. (2007) 'Structure and Characters of Agricultural Products Trade between China and Africa', *China Rural Economy* 11: 15–25.

Sun, F. (2002) 'Analysis on Uncertainty of Household Consuming Behaviour in China', *Nankai Economic Studies* 2: 58–63.

Tan, J. and Chen, J. (2005) 'Rural Land System and Transition of Policies on Land Circulation', *China Economy Weekly* 33: 21.

Tan, R. and Chen, X. (2008) 'China's Investment in Developing Countries as Reflected by Sino-Africa Cooperation', *Economic Research Guide* 6: 143–4.

Tang, L. (2009) 'The Livelihoods and Assets of The Poor: Characteristics, Access and Utilization: Observation of Shuicun Village, Dingxi City, Gansu Province', PhD thesis, China Agricultural University, Beijing.

Tang, Z. (1999) 'China's Agricultural Foreign Exchange and Cooperation for 50 Years', *World Agriculture* 10: 21–3.

Tang, Z. (2002) 'Broad Outlook for Sino-Africa Agricultural Cooperation', *West Asia and Africa* 6: 13–17.

Tefft, J. (2005) 'Agricultural Policy and Food Security in Liberia', ESA Working Paper No. 05–11, Agricultural and Development Economics Division, Rome.

Thirtle, C., Lin, L. and Piess, J. (2003) 'The Impact of Research-Led Agricultural Productivity Growth on Poverty Reduction in Africa, Asia and Latin America', *World Development* 31(12): 1959–75.

Tian, G. (2005) 'Empirical Study on the Uncertainty and Constrains of Financing and Rural High Saving Situation in China', *Economic Sciences* 1: 5–17.

Tiffen, M. (2003) 'Transition in Sub-Saharan Africa: Agriculture, Urbanization and Income Growth', *World Development* 31(8): 1343–66.

Timmer, C. P. (2005) 'Agriculture and Pro-poor Growth: An Asian Perspective', Working Paper No. 63, Center for Global Development, Washington, DC.

Tong, P. (2001) 'China's Maize Germplasm Resource File and Achievements', *China Seed Industry* 3: 7–8.

Tong, X. and Long, Y. (2002) 'Reflection and Reconstruction: Review of Research on Gender Labor Division in China', *Zhejiang Academic Journal* 4: 211–16.

Tostau, E. and Brorsen, W. (2005) 'Spatial Price Efficiency in Mozambique's Post-reform Maize Markets', *Agricultural Economics* 33(2): 205–14.

United Nations (2006) *Investment Policy Review of Zambia*, United Nations, New York.

United Nations Capital Development Fund (UNCDF) (2008) LDC Fund to Develop Savings-led Market Leaders for Inclusive Finance (2008–2013), http://www.uncdf.org/

english/microfinance/uploads/project/2008–10–27_21%20October_08_Savings_Led_
Market_Leaders_LDC_FIF.pdf (accessed 25 January 2012).

United Nations Conference on Trade and Development (UNCTAD) (2001) *World Investment
Report 2001: Promoting Linkages*, United Nations, New York.

United Nations Conference on Trade and Development (UNCTAD) and United Nations
Environment Programme (UNEP) (2008) 'Organic Agriculture and Food Security in
Africa', http://www.unctad.org/en/docs/ditcted200715_en.pdf (accessed 20 July 2009).

United Nations University, Institute for Natural Resources in Africa and World Bank (1999)
'Africa Can Feed Just 40% of Its Population in 2025', press release for World Food Day,
Legon, Ghana and Washington, DC.

Van den Boscha, H., Gitarib, J. N., Ogaroc, V. N., Maobed, S. and Vlaminga, J. (1998)
'Monitoring Nutrient Flows and Economic Performance in African Farming Systems
(NUTMON) III: Monitoring Nutrient Flows and Balances in Three Districts in Kenya',
Agriculture, Ecosystems and Environment 71: 63–80.

Van der Veen, R. (1998) *What Happened to Africa: Understanding to the Rich and Poor Continent*
(in Chinese), Guangdong People's Publishing House, Guangzhou.

Vitousek, P. M., Naylor, R., Crews, T., David, M. B., Drinkwater, L. E., Holland, E.,
Johnes, P. J., Katzenberger, J. Martinelli, L. A., Matson, P. A., Nziguheba, G., Ojima, D.
Palm, C. A., Robertson, G. P. Sanchez, P. A., Townsend, A. R. and Zhang, F. S. (2009)
'Nutrient Imbalances in Agricultural Development', *Science* 324(5934) 1519–20.

Voortman, R., Sonneveld, B. G. J. S. and Keyzer, M. A. (2003) 'African Land Ecology:
Opportunities and Constraints for Agricultural Development', *Journal of the Human
Environment* 32(5): 367–73.

Wade, A. (2008) *Fate of Africa* (in Chinese), Xinhua Publishing House, Beijing.

Wang, B. (2004) 'Reorganization of Agricultural Production in China', *Lingnan Science Journal*
6: 77–9.

Wang, C. (2000) 'Agricultural Cooperation: Success in the Present and Benefits in the
Future', 13 September, http://www.ahnw.gov.cn/2006nwkx/html/200009/{40CDE
7BC-F1BF-4DD9–920F-DB7EAD0C6EFD}.shtm (accessed 25 January 2012).

Wang, C., Lou, X. and Wang, J. (2007) 'Influence of Climate Disaster on the Output of
Agricultural Products in China', *Journal of Natural Disasters* 16(5): 37–43.

Wang, D. (1988) 'Agricultural Development Policies and Measures in Malawi', *West Asia
and Africa* 5: 46–48.

Wang, D. (2008a) 'Agricultural Subsidy is No Better than Opening Grain Price', *People Forum*
10: 46.

Wang, D. (2008b) 'Research and Comment on State Monopoly of Purchase and Marketing',
Contemporary Chinese History Research 1: 50–61.

Wang, P. and Yang, W. (2002) 'Agricultural R&D Investment Status of Developing
Countries', *Journal of Agricultural Science and Technology* 4(5): 74–9.

Wang, S. (2008) 'Thirty Years' Reforms on Rural Credit Cooperatives', http://www.dz
www.com/xinwen/xinwenzhuanti/2008/ggkf30zn/ssncj/xnc/200805/t20080509_3538
088.htm (accessed 20 July 2009).

Wang, Z. and Chen, Q. (1995) 'Another Discussion on the Origin and Dissemination of
Chinese Agriculture', *Agricultural Archaeology* 3: 30–42.

Wen, J. (2009) 'Building the New Type of China–Africa Strategic Partnership', http://www.
pambazuka.org/en/category/africa_china/60183 (accessed 5 January 2010).

Wiggins, S. (2000) 'Interpreting Changes from the 1970s to the 1990s in African Agriculture
through Village Studies', *World Development* 28(4): 631–62.

Willett, A. (1998) *Agricultural Education Review: Support for Agricultural Education in the World Bank and by Other Donors,* World Bank, Washington, DC.

Wopereis, M. C. S., Tamélokpo, A., Ezui, K., Gnakpénou, D., Fofana, B. and Breman, H. (2006) 'Mineral Fertilizer Management of Maize on Farmer Fields Differing in Organic Inputs in the West African Savanna', *Field Crops Research* 96(2–3): 355–62.

World Bank (1981) *Accelerated Development in Sub-Saharan Africa: An Agenda for Action (The Berg Report),* World Bank, Washington, DC.

World Bank (1989) *Sub-Sahara Africa: From Crisis to Sustainable Growth,* International Bank for Reconstruction and Development/World Bank, Washington, DC.

World Bank (1994) *World Development Report 1994: Infrastructure for Development,* Oxford University Press, New York.

World Bank (2000) *World Development Report 1999–2000: Entering the 21st Century,* World Bank, Washington, DC.

World Bank (2002) *The Role and Effectiveness of Development Assistance: Lessons from World Bank Experience,* World Bank, Washington, DC.

World Bank (2004) *World Development Report 2004: Making Services Work for Poor People,* World Bank, Washington, DC.

World Bank (2007) *Africa Development Indicators 2007,* World Bank, Washington, DC.

World Bank (2008) *World Development Report 2008: Agriculture for Development,* World Bank, Washington, DC.

World Bank (2009a) *Eastern Africa: A Study of the Regional Maize Market and Marketing Costs,* Report No.49831-AFR, 31 December.

World Bank (2009b) *2008 Development Cooperation Forum Report: Trends and Progress of International Development Cooperation,* World Bank, Washington, DC.

World Bank Independent Evaluation Group (2006) *World Bank Assistance to Agriculture in Sub-Saharan Africa,* World Bank, Washington DC.

World Bank Independent Evaluation Group (2011) 'Tanzania: Agriculture and the World Bank: An OED Review', http://lnweb90.worldbank.org/oed/oeddoclib.nsf/DocUNID ViewForJavaSearch/B941425F2E8BC85D852567F5005D6F62?opendocument (accessed 10 September 2010).

World Food Programme (WPF) (2007) *World Food Programme 2007,* Division of Communications and Public Policy Strategy, World Food Programme, Rome.

World Food Programme (WFP) (2007) *World Hunger Series 2007: Hunger and Health,* Earthscan, London.

World Health Organization (WHO) (2009) *World Health Statistics 2009,* WHO, Paris.

Wortmanna, C.S. and Kaizzi, C.K. (1998) 'Nutrient Balances and Expected Effects of Alternative Practices in Farming Systems of Uganda', *Agriculture, Ecosystems and Environment* 71: 115–129.

Wu, H. (1988) 'The Issues of Calculation on Unit Production of Food in Qing Dynasty', *Agricultural Archaeology* 1: 57–64.

Wu, H. (2001) 'The Current Situation and Prospects of China's Cropping Structure Adjustments', http://www.hljnw.com/lanmu/zjzx/zxdetail (accessed 20 July 2009).

Wu, H. (2008) 'Study on Left-behind Women in Rural China with Actor-oriented Perspectives', PhD thesis, China Agricultural University, Beijing.

Wu, L. (2001) 'Discussions on Balance of "Price Scissors" in China from 1949 to 1978', *China Economy History Research* 4: 3–12.

Wu, Y. and Wang, D. (2002) 'Status Analysis and Mid–Long-term Forecasting of Per Hectare Yield of Major Crops in China', *Chinese Journal of Agricultural Resources and Regional Planning* 23(1): 20–5.

Xiang, F. (1987) 'Agricultural Reforms in Senegal', *West Asia and Africa* 1: 44–6.

Xu, H. (2009) Remember the Giant Contribution of Farmer-Workers to Urbanization in China, http://www.snzg.cn/article/2009/1201/article_16446.html (accessed 25 January 2012).

Xu, X. (2004) *Science and Technology Policies for the Poor*, PhD thesis, China Agricultural University, Beijing.

Yamano, T. and Jayne, T. S. (2004) 'Measuring the Impact of Working-age Adult Mortality on Small Scale Farm Households in Kenya', *World Development* 32(1): 91–119.

Yang, D. and Li, S. (2009) 'The Originality Credit and Evolution of the Farmer Credit: Views of Long-term', *China Rural Survey* 3: 11–18.

Yang, L. (2009) 'Analysis of Hunan Grain Subsidy Policy Performance and its Policy Recommendations: The Example of Xiangyin County', *Research on Agricultural Modernization* 30(5): 584–86.

Yang, Weilu (2005) 'Discussion on China's Food Crop Transport', *China Food Economics* 12: 36–40.

Yao, G. (2002) 'Origin of Agricultural Crisis in Africa', *West Asia and Africa* 3: 22–5.

Yao, Y. (2008) *Economy Reforms during System Innovation Process*, Gezhi Publishing and Shanghai People Publishing, Shanghai.

Yi, B. and Liu, J. (2000) 'Orient and West Blend and Traditional Agriculture Evolution in Modern China', *China Agricultural History* 19(2): 65–72.

Yin, C. (2009) 'Serious Situation of World Supply and Demand of Grain', *Rural Working Newsletter* 12: 30–31.

Yin, F. and Xu, S. (2004) *A History of Chinese Ancient Culture*, Peking University Press, Beijing.

Yun, W. (2000a) 'Agricultural Cooperation of China and Africa in the 21st Century', *West Asia and Africa* 5: 38–42.

Yun, W. (2000b) 'China's Assistance to African Agriculture from the Perspective of International Assistance Development', *West Asia and Africa* 2: 17–23.

Zeng, Z. (1984) *African Agricultural Geography*, Commercial Press, Beijing.

Zeng, Z. (1988) 'Discussing Agricultural Development Strategies of Africa', *West Asia and Africa* 3: 23–30.

Zhang, B. (2005) *Ten Planting Patterns with High Efficiency and Multiple Cropping in Grain Production Area in China*, China Agricultural Press, Beijing.

Zhang F., Cui, Z, Wang, J., Li, C. and Chen, X. (2007) 'Current Status of Soil and Plant Nutrient Management in China and Improvement Strategies', Chinese Bulletin of Botany 24(6): 687–94.

Zhang, J. (2006) '50 Million Women Left-behind: Investigation', *China Economic Weekly* 40: 15–19.

Zhang, J. and Qu, Y. (2008) 'Discussions on the Drought Disasters Evolution Rule of China in the Last 30 years and Measures for Resisting Drought Disasters', *Flood and Drought Prevention in China* 8: 47–52.

Zhang, Y. (2009) 'Farmer Household Allocation of Labor Resources and the Impact on Agricultural Development – Investigation and Analysis of 8 Sample Villages in China's Western Region', *Agricultural Technology and Economy* 2: 4–16.

Zhang, Z. and Ma, F. (2003) *Development Sociology*, China Social Science Publishing, Beijing.

Zheng, F., Cui, H. and Lang, X. (2009) 'Reflections on Agricultural Irrigation Construction in China: Problems, Challenges and Solutions', http://www.snzg.cn, (accessed 25 January 2012).

Zhong, F. (2006) 'Agricultural Growth and Rural Development: Smallholder Economy's Future', in Guo, P., Xin, X. and Wang, X. (eds) *Globalization and China's Agriculture*, China Agriculture Press, Beijing, pp. 308–15.

Zhou, R. (2001) 'Comprehensive Review and Re-estimation on Arable Land Area in Early Qing Dynasty', *Jianghan Tribune* 9: 57–61.

Zhu, X. and Zhao, J. (2011) 'Strong Pushing Strengths of Accelerating China's Agricultural Mechanization', *Peasants' Daily*, 1 April, p. 1.

Zhuang, M. (1988) 'History of Higher Agricultural Education in China', *China Agricultural History* 2: 106–24.

Zhuang, R. (1982) 'Position and Characteristics of African Agriculture', *World Agriculture* 3: 7–10.

INDEX

agricultural technology 166*f*, 227, 233, 235*t*; Chinese investment 248; collective agriculture 230; crops 25, 120, 120*f*, 150, 151*t*; exports 24*t*; field studies 5; fiscal inputs 95–6; food security 95; foreign aid 221; Foreign Direct Investment 223; implementation agencies 98; industrialization strategy 22; locusts 125; maize planting 194, 195, 196, 196*t*, 197, 197*f*, 198*f*, 198*t*; markets 205, 206*t*; purchasing and selling policy 81, 82–3; researchers 173; smallholders 185, 186–7, 189, 194; strategies since 2000 70; structural adjustment 64; taxation policy 77, 78, 80; trade policy 89; *Ujamaa* movement 22, 48, 64, 135

tassas 140–1

tea 25, 26*t*, 41, 50*t*

Togo: agricultural GDP 21*t*; agricultural technology 166*f*, 169, 236*t*; Chinese investment 248; collective agriculture 230; crop output 120*f*; exports 24*t*; food security 96; independence 45*t*

Town and Village Enterprises (China) 135

Tracy, I. 211

trade: agricultural trade policies 87–90; Sino-African cooperation 245–7, 246*t*; *see also* imports and exports

transport linkages in rural areas 145–6

Two Labour system (China) 134

Two Leaps (China) 67, 282n3.3

Two Transfers (China) 67

Uganda: agricultural extension 180, 182*t*; agricultural GDP 21*t*; agricultural technology 163, 166*f*, 170, 171*t*, 233, 234, 235*t*; collective agriculture 230; crop output 120, 120*f*; exports 24*t*; independence 45*t*; land systems 76; National Agricultural Research Act 159, 160, 162; rural credit policy 93; strategies since 2000 71; taxation policy 77, 78

Union Economique et Monétaire Ouest-Africaine 95

United Nations Central Emergency Response Fund 125

United Nations Conference on Trade and Development (UNCTAD) 140, 223

United Nations Development Programme (UNDP) 224

United Nations Environment Programme (UNEP) 111, 140

Wang, Z. 35

water conservancy 118, 120, 121–2, 134, 140–1, 143–5, 144*f*, 175, 215

Watkins, N. 64

Wen, J. 4

wheat 37, 37*t*, 41, 150, 151*t*

World Bank 2, 12, 29, 63, 64, 67, 73, 78, 109, 173, 227, 281–2n3.2

World Food Programme (WFP) 219, 219*f*, 243

World Health Organization (WHO) 137

World Trade Organization (WTO) 83, 88, 90

Xiang, F. 65

Xianghai National Natural Reserve 110

Yang, L. 199

Yao, Y. 72

Yuan, L. 159

Zambia: agricultural credit 203; agricultural extension 181, 182*t*, 183*t*, 202; agricultural GDP 14, 21*t*; agricultural subsidies 200; agricultural technology 166*f*, 170, 172*t*, 235*t*; agro-ecological regions 126–7; Chinese-funded farms 231, 248–50; Chinese investment 248; climate 119, 119*f*; collective agriculture 231; crop output and rainfall 120, 120*f*, 121, 121*f*; crop variety improvement 150, 151*t*; exports 24*t*; fertilizer 85, 85*f*, 86–7, 139; field studies 5; fiscal inputs 132*f*; food aid 220; GM crops 178*t*; independence 45*t*; land cultivation 108, 112; land prices 247, 247*t*; land reforms 74–5; land use 41–2; maize planting 194–5, 196, 196*t*, 197, 197*f*, 198*f*; National Agriculture Policy 160–1, 162; regional development strategy 102–3, 103*t*; research domains 174; researchers 173; rural finance policy 93; smallholders 185, 186–7, 188, 189, 190, 194–5; strategies since 2000 70–1; taxation policy 77, 78, 79

Zhang, Y. 188

Zimbabwe: agricultural GDP 21*t*; agricultural technology demonstration centre 235*t*; crops 120, 120*f*, 150; exports 24*t*; fiscal inputs 130, 132, 132*f*; land reforms 74; land systems 76; liberalization reform 83; rural credit policy 93; taxation policy 77, 79

For Product Safety Concerns and Information please contact our EU representative GPSR@taylorandfrancis.com Taylor & Francis Verlag GmbH, Kaufingerstraße 24, 80331 München, Germany